P9-CDG-992

OLD DELHI
Pages 88–97

DELHI FURTHER AFIELD
Pages 98–115

DELHI CITY CENTRE

Dehra Dun

NORTH OF DELHI

DELHI

U T T A R
P R A D E S H

Ganges

Yamuna

Mathura

AGRA

Chambal

Gwalior

AGRA AND AROUND

Jhansi

Betwa

Red Fort

OLD DELHI

Connaught Place

NEW DELHI

NIZAM-UDDIN TO PURANA QILA

Yamuna

NEW DELHI
Pages 66–79

NIZAMUDDIN TO PURANA QILA
Pages 80–87

M A D H Y A P R A D E S H

EYEWITNESS *TRAVEL GUIDES*

DELHI
AGRA & JAIPUR

DK EYEWITNESS *TRAVEL GUIDES*

DELHI
AGRA & JAIPUR

Main Contributors: ANURADHA CHATURVEDI
DHARMENDAR KANWAR & RANJANA SENGUPTA

DK PUBLISHING

LONDON, NEW YORK,
MELBOURNE, MUNICH AND DELHI
www.dk.com

PROJECT EDITOR Aruna Ghose
ART EDITOR Alpana Khare
EDITORS Ira Pande, Madhulita Mohapatra, Razia Grover
DESIGNERS Anand Naorem, Benu Joshi, Mugdha Sethi
CARTOGRAPHY Uma Bhattacharya
PICTURE EDITOR Radhika Singh

MAIN CONTRIBUTORS
Anuradha Chaturvedi, Dharmendar Kanwar, Partho Datta,
Premola Ghose, Ranjana Sengupta, Subhadra Sengupta

PHOTOGRAPHERS
Aditya Patankar, Amit Pashricha, Dinesh Khanna,
Fredrick & Laurence Arvidsson, Ram Rahman

ILLUSTRATORS
Ajay Sethi, Ampersand, Ashok Sukumaran, Avinash,
Dipankar Bhattacharya, Gautam Trivedi, Mark Warner

Reproduced by Colourscan, Singapore
Text film output by Express Colour Scan, Delhi
Printed and bound by South China Printing Co. Ltd., China

First American Edition, 2000

Reprinted with revisions 2001, 2003

03 04 05 10 9 8 7 6 5 4 3 2

Published in the United States by
DK Publishing, Inc., 375 Hudson Street,
New York, New York 10014

ISSN 1542-1554
ISBN 0-7894-9717-4

THROUGHOUT THIS BOOK, FLOORS ARE REFFERED TO IN
ACCORDANCE WITH EUROPEAN USAGE, I.E. "FIRST FLOOR" IS ONE FLIGHT UP.

The information in this
Eyewitness Travel Guide is checked regularly.
Every effort has been made to ensure that this book is as up-to-date
as possible at the time of going to press. Some details, however,
such as telephone numbers, opening hours, prices, gallery hanging
arrangements and travel information are liable to change. The
publishers cannot accept responsibility for any consequences arising
from the use of this book, nor for any material on third party
websites, and cannot guarantee that any website address in this
book will be a suitable source of travel information. We value the
views and suggestions of our readers very highly. Please write to:
Publisher, DK Eyewitness Travel Guides,
Dorling Kindersley, 80 Strand, London WC2R 0RL, Great Britain.
The external boundaries of India as shown on the maps are
neither correct nor authentic.

◁ **A view of Taj Mahal from the river**

A bullock-cart and mustard fields

CONTENTS

HOW TO USE THIS GUIDE 6

Kishangarh miniature

INTRODUCING DELHI, AGRA & JAIPUR

A sandstone *jaali*

A traditional *thali*

Image of the young Krishna

Humayun's Tomb

HOW TO USE THIS GUIDE

THIS GUIDE helps you to get the most from your visit to the region. It provides both detailed practical information and expert recommendations. *Introducing Delhi, Agra and Jaipur* maps the region and sets it in its historical and cultural context. The three regional sections, plus *Delhi,* describe important sights, using maps, photographs and illustrations. Features cover topics from music and dance to food and festivals. Restaurant and hotel recommendations can be found in *Travellers' Needs.* The *Survival Guide* has tips on everything from transport to using the telephone, and the *Glossary* explains Indian terms and words.

DELHI

The city is divided into areas, each with its own chapter. A last chapter, *Further Afield,* covers peripheral sights. All sights are numbered and plotted on the chapter's area map. Information on each sight is easy to locate as it follows the numerical order on the map.

Sights at a Glance lists the chapter's sights by category: Mosques and Tombs, Museums and Galleries, Streets and Gardens, Historic Sites, Monuments and Markets.

Stars indicate the sights that no visitor should miss.

All pages relating to Delhi have red thumb tabs.

A locator map shows where you are in relation to other areas of the city centre.

1 Area Map
For easy reference, sights are numbered and located on a map. City centre sights are also marked on the Delhi Street Finder map (pages 122–31).

2 Street-by-Street Map
This gives a bird's-eye view of the key areas in each chapter.

A suggested route for a walk is shown in red.

3 Detailed information
The sights in Delhi are described individually. Useful addresses, telephone numbers, opening hours and other practical information are also provided. The key to the symbols used is on the back flap of the book.

1 Introduction
The landscape, history and character of each region is outlined here, showing how the area has developed over the centuries and what it has to offer to the visitor today.

BEYOND DELHI AREA BY AREA
Apart from Delhi, the region has been divided into three areas, each of which has a separate chapter. The most interesting cities, towns and villages, and other places to visit are numbered on a *Pictorial Map.*

2 Pictorial Map
This shows the road network and gives an illustrated overview of the whole region. All interesting places to visit are numbered and there are also useful tips on getting to, and around, the region by car and public transport.

Each area can be quickly identified by its colour coding, shown on the inside front cover.

3 Detailed information
All the important towns and other places to visit are described individually. They are listed in order, following the numbering on the Pictorial Map. *Within each town or city, there is detailed information on important buildings and other sights.*

For all top sights, a Visitors' Checklist provides the practical information you will need to plan your visit.

Story boxes explore related topics.

4 The region's top sights
These are given two or more full pages. Historic buildings are dissected to reveal their interiors. The most interesting towns or city centres are shown in a bird's-eye view, with sights picked out and described.

INTRODUCING
DELHI
AGRA & JAIPUR

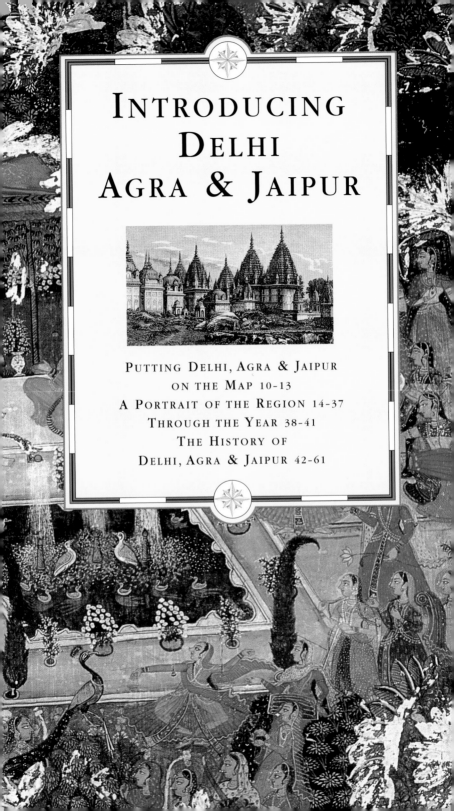

Putting Delhi, Agra & Jaipur on the Map

THE DELHI, AGRA AND JAIPUR region lies in the heart of North India. It covers an area of about 114,000 sq km (44,000 sq miles) and has a population of over 23 million. Delhi is the capital of India, while Jaipur is the capital of Rajasthan. Agra is a major district headquarters in Uttar Pradesh. Delhi has an international airport. Agra and Jaipur are serviced by domestic flights. The region also has good road and railway connections, with Agra about three hours and Jaipur about four by train from Delhi.

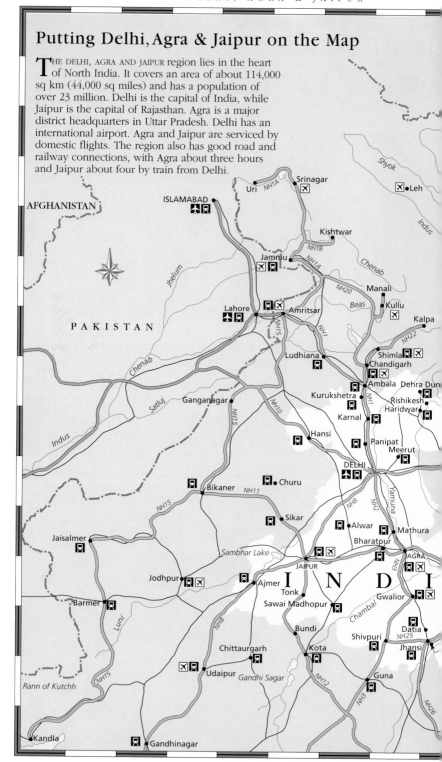

AFGHANISTAN

ISLAMABAD

PAKISTAN

Uri   NH1A   Srinagar   Leh
Shyok
Indus
Kishtwar
NH1B
Jammu   NH1A
Chenab
NH20   Manali
Lahore   Amritsar   Beas   Kullu
Kalpa
NH15   NH1   NH22
Ludhiana   Shimla
Chandigarh
Ganganagar   Ambala   Dehra Dun
NH15   NH110   Kurukshetra   Rishikesh
Satluj   Karnal   Haridwar
Indus   Hansi   Panipat
Meerut
DELHI
Bikaner   NH11   Churu
NH8   Yamuna
NH15   Sikar   NH2
Jaisalmer   Alwar   Mathura
Sambhar Lake   Bharatpur   AGRA
Jodhpur   Ajmer   JAIPUR   I N D I
Tonk
Barmer   Sawai Madhopur   Gwalior
Luni   NH8   Bundi   Chambal   Datia
Shivpuri   NH25
Chittaurgarh   Kota   Jhansi
Udaipur   Gandhi Sagar
NH15   Guna
Rann of Kutchh   NH12   NH3   NH26
Kandla
Gandhinagar

◁ **Miniature painting of a Rajput prince, surrounded by female attendants in a garden pavilion**

The external boundaries of India as shown on this map are neither correct nor authentic.

Putting India on the Map

KAZAKHSTAN

MONGOLIA

UZBEKISTAN

TURKMENISTAN

CHINA

AFGHANISTAN

IRAN

PAKISTAN   Delhi

Jaipur • Agra   NEPAL

INDIA   BANGLA-
DESH

BURMA

LAOS

THAILAND

VIETNAM

CAMBODIA

SRI
LANKA

MALAYSIA

SINGAPORE

I N D O N E S I A

C H I N A

T I B E T

Kathgodam

Rampur

N E P A L

Shahjahanpur

KATHMANDU

Lucknow

A   Kanpur

Gorakhpur

NH28

NH2

NH29

Ganges

NH24

NH2

NH25

Orchha

Allahabad

Ghazipur

Varanasi

NH7

NH7

KEY

Delhi, Agra and Jaipur region

International airport

Domestic airport

Railway station

— Railway line

= National highway

= Major road

-•- International border

0 kilometres   100

0 miles   50

Delhi City Centre and Greater Delhi

SOME OF DELHI'S MOST IMPRESSIVE buildings can be seen in this area. The sights described in this book are grouped within three areas, each of which can be explored on foot. Vijay Chowk is the vantage point for the grand sweep of Raj buildings grouped on Raisina Hill. To the north, the magnificent Jami Masjid with its busy hive of lanes, was once the heart of the Mughal empire and is still the focus of Old Delhi. The past and present mingle here and yet preserve their own space and identity. To the east, the medieval quarter around the *dargah* of the Sufi Nizamuddin Auliya leads along Mathura Road to the ruined Purana Qila. This ancient site has interesting origins, going back to a distant mythological past.

Vijay Chowk *(see p70)*, at the base of Raisina Hill, surrounded by government offices

Buddha Jayanti Park *(see p104)*, created on the Ridge in northwest Delhi

GREATER DELHI

NH1
NH10
NH24
Delhi
New Delhi
Nizamuddin
NH8
NH2
Yamuna
Jaipur
Agra

0 kilometres   8
0 miles   8

Greater Delhi

North Delhi houses the university and historic sites associated with the Old City. South Delhi, around the Qutb Minar and Mehrauli, has grown into a busy commercial and residential area.

Jami Masjid *(see p92)* the city's main mosque near Chandni Chowk

Purana Qila *(see p84)*, Delhi's oldest historical site, now an integral part of the city

KEY

⬜	Major sight
⬛	Built-up area
⬜	Greater Delhi
✈	International airport
⊠	Domestic airport
🚉	Railway station
Ⓜ	Metro station
🚌	Bus station
ℹ	Tourist information
🚓	Police station
🛕	Temple
Gurudwara	*Gurudwara*
✝	Church
C	Mosque
🪦	Tomb
⊠	Post office
—	Railway line
=	National highway
=	Major road
=	Minor road

**Map labels:**

SAD MUKHERJI MARG
RING ROAD
LAJPAT RAI MARKET
CHANDNI CHOWK
NAI SARAK
H C SEN RD
Red Fort
MAHATMA GANDHI ROAD
NETAJI SUBHASH MARG
VIJAY GHAT
CHAWRI BAZAAR
CHURI WALI GALI
JAMI MASJID
SITARAM BAZAAR ROAD
BAZAAR CHITLI QABAR
SHANTI VANA MARG
ANSARI ROAD
ZINAT-UL-MASJID
SHANTI VANA
SHAKTI STHAL
AF ALI ROAD
TURKMAN GATE
AGORE ROAD
JAWAHARLAL NEHRU MARG
RAJGHAT
RING ROAD
MIRDARD MARG
BAHADUR SHAH ZAFAR MARG
FEROZE SHAH KOTLA
MAHARAJA RANJEET SINGH MG
TURKMAN ROAD
KOTLA MARG
INDIRA GANDHI INDOOR STADIUM
MAHARAJA LAJPAT DAYAL UPADHYAYA MARG
JANSEN MARG
INDRAPRASTHA MG
AKHAMBA ROAD
ASEN'S OLI
MANDI HOUSE
SIKANDRA ROAD
COPERNICUS MARG
BHAGWAN DAS ROAD
TILAK MARG
MATHURA MARG
PRAGATI MAIDAN
RING ROAD
Crafts Museum
BHAIRON MARG
INDIA GATE
SHERMAN ROAD
NATIONAL GALLERY OF MODERN ART
PURANA QILA
KHAIR-UL-MANAZIL
JHANJHAHAN ROAD
PANDARA ROAD
DR ZAKIR HUSSAIN MARG
MATHURA ROAD
NATIONAL ZOOLOGICAL PARK
KHAN MARKET
ARCHBISHOP MAKARIOS MARG
BRAMANICAL BHARTI MARG
MAHARISHI RAMAN MARG
DELHI GOLF COURSE
MATHURA ROAD
Humayun's Tomb
DI ROAD
ARAB KI SARAI RD
RAHIM KHAN ROAD
MATHURA GANDHI MARG
MARKHA ROAD
Nizamuddin
ISBT Sarai Kale Khan

0 metres   800

0 yards   800

A PORTRAIT OF
DELHI, AGRA & JAIPUR

THE DELHI, AGRA AND JAIPUR REGION *lies at the geographical heart of North India. Its strategic location along the north-south and east-west routes has given it a focal position in Indian history and many great empires have been ruled from here. What we see today is a dynamic blend of the old and the new, a proudly traditional social structure within a modern liberalized economy.*

This landlocked region is enclosed by mountains to the north, the desert and the forested Aravallis to the west. To the east are the agriculturally rich riverine plains, with vast fields of sugarcane, wheat, mustard and lentils. Southwards, these flat plains dramatically metamorphose into the earth pillars of the Chambal ravines, a rugged landscape once inhabited by fierce bandits. Invaders, entering the subcontinent from the mountain passes of the northwestern frontiers, conquered this region centuries earlier and made it their home.

Ganesha mask

THE LEGACY OF THE PAST
The earliest civilization in this region was the Harappan culture in the second millennium BC. However, it was the Aryan settlements in the next millennium that provided the region with its philosophical moorings, epic literature, such as the *Ramayana* and *Mahabharata,* and its early Hindu kingdoms. In the first and second centuries, the area was the centre of a Buddhist empire when the Kushana emperors who ruled from Taxila (now in Pakistan) made Mathura their second capital. After the decline of the great Hindu and

Men in colourful turbans at the village square

◁ A young Rajasthani girl at work in a mustard field

Cenotaphs of the Bharatpur kings at Kusum Sarovar near Brindavan

Buddhist empires, powerful Rajput rulers seized control of parts of North India. Many of the magnificent forts from which their feudal kingdoms were ruled can still be seen today.

Religion has always been the cultural link between the epochs, and by the 13th century, Hinduism had been influenced by the Bhakti Movement which stressed the need for a personal god. This resulted in the Krishna cult, centred around Mathura and Brindavan – places associated with the youth of this popular god. Even as the Bhakti Movement flourished, invaders from Afghanistan and Central Asia conquered the north. Delhi, and later Agra, became the capitals of the Muslim sultans. The cross-fertilization of indigenous and Islamic cultures bred a unique hybrid that influenced art, architecture, music and cuisine, reaching its zenith with the Mughals.

The 19th century saw the decline of the Mughal empire and the growing

An open-air village school near Neemrana

power of the British East India Company. In 1858, the East India Company's territories in India were transferred to the British Crown, and the country settled down to a 90-year span of Pax Britannica. The legacy of the British Raj lives on in modern India's administrative and educational systems, and English is today the common language of communication between India's different linguistic regions and states.

In 1947, British rule came to an end and India became an independent nation. Since then, the country has faced the challenge of building industries, and tackling the social problems of illiteracy, poverty and the caste system. As the population of India raced towards one billion, these problems became more pressing. So, in the 1990s, India adopted an open-market economy, adding yet another dimension of change to a land that is constantly on the move.

PEOPLE AND CULTURE

The capital of India, New Delhi, is known as a city of migrants. After the violent Partition of India and Pakistan in 1947, millions of people, mainly from West Punjab, flocked here in search of a new life. Since then, there has been a continuing influx of people from all over India. The majority of Delhi's 12 million citizens have settled here primarily for economic reasons – the average wage here is twice that of the country as a whole.

This mega-city nevertheless retains a small-town friendliness in its different neighbourhoods. Life still centres around the family, even though the joint family system is breaking down here, as is the case in all big Indian cities. Beyond the family is the larger world of the regional community which plays a significant role in the city's social and cultural life. Diaspora groups very often come together for auspicious occasions such as marriages or festivals, with which the Indian calendar is punctuated.

Its mixed population has made Delhi a resolutely cosmopolitan city where Hindus, Muslims, Christians and Sikhs live side by side. Yet, each community has retained its distinct cultural identity, and the city is less a melting pot than a

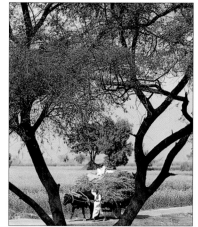

Bullock carts transporting rural goods

A fashion model

thali (plate) whose offerings may either be savoured singly or in interesting combinations.

Different levels of development are evident in Delhi, Agra and Jaipur. But in all three cities, with the liberalized economy bringing in a sudden flood of consumer goods, and cable television channels beaming foreign cultures into their homes, the lifestyles and expectations of the people are rapidly changing.

What makes the region so interesting is that contrasts often exist here in perfect harmony – a bullock cart plods placidly beside the latest luxury car; weather forecasts are made both by satellite imaging and astrological calculations; and jeans-clad youngsters eating pizza in fast food joints are just as much at ease in a sari or *dhoti*, sitting cross-legged on the floor at home, to participate in traditional ceremonies or rituals.

A religious procession in Jaipur moving along in traditional splendour

Landscape and Wildlife

THE DELHI, AGRA AND JAIPUR REGION lies at the heart of Northern India and covers a wide ecological zone, flanked by the Himalayas to the north and the ravines of the River Chambal to the south. To the west are the Aravalli mountain range and the Thar Desert, and to the east stretch the riverine plains watered by the Yamuna and the Chambal. Forests once covered much of this area but, with growing urbanization, have now been reduced to a few pockets around the national parks. These are the habitats of many prized species, like the endangered tiger.

INDIAN TREES
The region's rich variety of trees has local species as well as some of recent import. Some are sacred, others are valued for their healing qualities.

Banyan leaves

The peacock, India's national bird

SUB-HIMALAYAN REGION
The Indian pine *(chir)* and *sal (Shorea robusta)* once formed thick forests that covered this area, but few remain today. However, there are still areas with sufficient forest cover to support a varied wildlife.

DRY DECIDUOUS FORESTS
This ecological zone covers the arid and semi-arid tracts along the Aravallis. The mixed vegetation of scrub and deciduous trees, comprises acacias, cassia and *dhak (Butea monosperma)*, cacti and wild grasses.

Indian elephants *are smaller than the African species and are found on the lower Himalayan slopes. These gentle, intelligent animals are easy to train and domesticate.*

Sambar, *India's largest deer, is crowned with impressive antlers.*

Cheetal, *the graceful Indian spotted deer, is found in herds in the grassland areas.*

Tiger, *the national animal, is now a protected species. Loss of forest cover today has brought it to the brink of extinction.*

Monkeys *of two types, the rhesus and the langur, are found here.*

Crested serpent eagle, *with its underwing pattern of black and white bands, is a large raptor often seen in the Ranthambhore forests.*

Ashoka (Saraca indica), *one of India's five sacred trees, is extolled in Indian literature.*

Pipal (Ficus religiosa), *a hardy tree that grows anywhere, is also the sacred Bodhi tree under which the Buddha attained enlightenment in Bodh Gaya.*

Kadamba (Anthocephalus cadamba) *is a tall majestic tree associated with Krishna and Brindavan.*

Neem (Azadirachta indica). *This large, shade-giving tree has an extraordinary range of medicinal, antiseptic and disinfectant properties.*

WETLANDS

In the southwest are shallow, inland lakes, marshes and swamps that have been formed from subterranean artesian wells. This is the habitat of otters and a wide variety of resident and migratory birds who feed on fish and aquatic plants.

RIVERINE AREAS

These lie to the south and east along the Yamuna and Chambal rivers. The southern area is marked by desolate ravines, formed by erosion and covered with tufts of wiry grass, but to the east the rich alluvial plains form a thriving agricultural belt. The rivers support a rich aquatic wildlife.

Painted stork *with its black and pink plumage, keeps its long beak immersed in water, probing the sediment at the bottom for food.*

Gharial (Gavialis gangeticus) *is a species of crocodile found in the Ganges and its tributaries. It is named after the pitcher-like (ghara) hump on its long, lean snout.*

Darter or snake bird *is a bird with dark, glossy plumage. Large flocks can be found in marshy areas, spearing fish with their sharp beaks and then swallowing them.*

King cobra *is the world's largest venomous snake. This lethal reptile has a characteristic mark on its hood and is considered to be one of Shiva's sacred creatures.*

Religions

INDIA IS A MOSAIC of different religions, varying from the ancient animistic beliefs of the tribal communities to the rigid orthodoxies of the Hindu caste system. The majority of India's population are Hindus, while around 200 million (20 per cent) are Muslims. Several other religions, such as Sikhism, Buddhism, Jainism and Christianity, also flourish. Jawaharlal Nehru *(see p78)* saw a unity in this diversity, and the Constitution of India declares it to be a secular republic, where the state has no official religion and all faiths can be freely practised.

Hindu symbols of life and fertility

Sufi mystic at a *dargah*

HINDUISM

THE BEDROCK of Hinduism constitutes the four *Vedas* and the *Upanishads,* which are a holistic compilation of knowledge, philosophy and ethics. Yet, Hinduism is not a religion of the Book, but a way of life that has systematically evolved over the past 5,000 years.

In practice, Hindus worship a huge pantheon of gods and goddesses *(see pp22–3).* Socially, they can be divided into four castes – the upper caste Brahmins (priests), the Kshatriyas (warriors), the Vaishyas (merchants and traders), and the lowest caste, Sudras (workers). The caste system envisioned

The sacred feet of Vishnu

society as an organic whole with each part or caste performing a vital function.

The traditional family structure was that of a joint family presided over by its patriarch. This is now fast disappearing in urban areas. Yet, *sanskara,* traditional values, are still instilled into children, and complicated rites mark each stage of orthodox Hindu life. There is also an aspect of Hinduism which shuns idol-worship, and prefers to concentrate on larger philosophical issues. Sadhus, who wear saffron to indicate their retreat from the material world, are its most visible practitioners. They hold a most respected position in Hindu society.

ISLAM

ISLAM WAS INTRODUCED into Western India in the 8th century by Arab traders, but it gained prominence in the north only after the 12th century, when it was declared the state religion under the medieval Muslim rulers.

Today, Muslims are India's second largest religious community, despite a large exodus to Pakistan after the traumatic Partition of 1947 *(see pp58–9).* Muslims can be broadly divided into two sects, the Sunnis and the Shias. The latter believe that Prophet Mohammed's cousin Ali and his descendents are the true imams. Traditional Muslim education, based on the Koran, is still imparted by the clergy in *madrasas* near mosques, which are central to the entire community. In India, the Friday public prayers, led by the local imam, are only open to men, and nearly all Muslim places of worship follow strict rules of segregation.

Sufism is a less orthodox mystic Islamic order. Its teachings emphasize direct experience of god, and Sufis believe that mystical ecstasy can be attained even through music and dance. Sufi saints like Nizamuddin Auliya *(see p82)* attracted many converts from Hinduism, and the fusion of the two religious traditions led to a flowering of poetry, music and art.

Matted hair, saffron clothes and ash-smeared bodies mark sadhus

SIKHISM

SIKHISM IS a reformist religion founded by Guru Nanak in the 15th century. Eschewing idol worship, rituals and the caste system, it believes in a formless god. The Sikh, with his characteristic turban, is easy to identify. He is supposed to abide by the five "k"s': *kesh* (long hair), *kachha* (underpants), *kirpan* (small sword), *kangha* (comb) and *kara* (bracelet). The Sikhs follow the teachings of ten gurus that are contained in their holy book, the *Adi Granth*, kept in the Golden Temple at Amritsar (Punjab).

Religious persecution by the later Mughals led the tenth guru, Gobind Singh, to reorganize the community in 1699 as a military order called the Khalsa, based on the principles of *sangat* (congregation), *simran* (meditation), *kirtan* (hymn singing), *langar* and *pangat* (sharing and partaking of food in a common kitchen).

Sikh priest reciting verses from the *Adi Granth*

CHRISTIANITY

THE RISE OF CHRISTIANITY in this region dates to the late-15th century when Catholic missionaries travelled to India in the wake of Portuguese traders. About this time, Christian Armenian communities also settled in Mughal India, procuring a licence to trade. There is evidence that the

Church services are often conducted in local dialects

Mughal emperor Akbar *(see pp52–3)* invited Jesuit priests to religious discussions held in Fatehpur Sikri *(see pp170–71)*. With the coming of the East India Company, Protestant missionaries spread across the country, setting up educational institutions and hospitals in the 18th and 19th centuries. Many are still run by dedicated workers. They also involved themselves with reform movements and influenced the government to take measures against practices such as *sati (see p48)*. Marriages between Indians and the Europeans who came led to the birth of the Anglo-Indian community. During the Raj *(see pp56–7)*, the railways and many of the subordinate civil services were run by them.

Indian Christians believe that the apostle St Thomas brought the religion to South India in the 1st century AD. Today, church services have been Indianized to a large

extent by absorbing some dialects, practices and rituals to make it easier for local worshippers to follow them.

OTHER RELIGIONS

APART FROM THESE four major groups, India has other smaller though distinct religious communities. **Buddhists** are followers of Gautam Buddha who lived and preached the gospel of non-violence and peace. From India, Buddhism spread to other countries in Asia but, ironically, it has now nearly vanished in the land of its birth. The 14th Dalai Lama, the spiritual leader of the Tibetan Buddhists, now lives in India with his followers in exile and is a widely respected figure. **Jains**, the followers of Mahavira, are a pacific and non-violent community

A golden Buddha statue

who respect life in every form, and observe rigid fasts and self-denial. They are divided into the Svetambaras (dressed in white) and the Digambaras (who shun clothing). The **Parsis** are followers of Zoroaster and came from Persia in the 7th century. A small community, they have nevertheless played a significant role in Indian industry and are known for their philanthropy. The first **Jews** came to India in about 587 BC and now live mainly in Mumbai and Cochin.

Jain nuns cover their mouths to avoid swallowing insects

The Pantheon of Gods and Goddesses

THE GREAT PANTHEON of Hindu gods and goddesses is a bewildering array, ranging from anthropo-morphic symbols and shapes to exotic half-human, half-animal forms. Each god has a personal *vahana* (vehicle) and symbols of power. Although community worship takes place in temples, especially on festivals, for most Hindus, the home with its own shrine and personal deities is where the daily *puja* (prayer) is conducted.

Lakshmi, the goddess of wealth, is also the consort of Vishnu. Her vahana is an owl.

Shesh Nag is the hundred-headed leviathan on whose coils Vishnu reclines.

Narada, the sage, accompanies Vishnu.

Ganesha, remover of obstacles.

Saraswati, the goddess of learning and music, is the consort of Brahma and has a swan as her vahana. Seated on a lotus, with a garland of white flowers, she is seen as the embodiment of purity.

Hanuman, the monkey god, is a faithful attendant of Lord Rama.

Vishnu, the Preserver, floats on Kshirsagar (the sacred ocean), the source of all life.

RELIGIOUS SYMBOLS

Kamal ("lotus") is a Vaishnavite symbol for purity.

Chakra ("wheel") is a universal symbol of the wheel of life.

Om, a symbol of the primal sound, is recited to start all religious ceremonies.

Trishul ("trident") is a Shaivite symbol of ascetism.

Shankh ("conch shell") is a Vaishnavite symbol of the life-giving ocean.

Rama (right), *the epitome of virtue, was* Vishnu's seventh avatara *(incarnation), and* **Krishna** (left), *the embodiment of love, was the eighth. Vishnu is said to assume these avataras to save the world from destruction. The last avatara, Kalki, will fashion a new world when this one reaches the end of its time.*

Ganesha, *the elephant-headed son of Shiva, is invoked at the start of any auspicious task.*

Hanuman *the monkey god* (see p197), *is invoked by those in need of courage and fortitude.*

Brahma sits on a lotus attached to Vishnu's navel.

Shiva lives atop Mount Kailash. The River Ganges flows from his matted locks.

Nandi, the bull, is Shiva's vehicle and is always present at Shiva temples.

Garuda is Vishnu's vehicle on his travels through the cosmos.

Parvati *lives in the Himalayan hills with Shiva. This gentle daughter of the mountains is worshipped in many forms, which collectively represent the Devi (goddess) cult.*

Durga *rides a tiger with her deadly arsenal of weapons and destroys evil, in the form of the buffalo-demon Mahishasura. She is the fierce persona of the gentle Parvati.*

THE HOLY TRINITY

A popular calendar picture depicts the Holy Trinity that comprises Brahma the Creator, Vishnu the Preserver, and Shiva the Destroyer. Vishnu mediates between Brahma and Shiva to preserve life. The world was created when the ocean was churned by the gods and demons *(see p45)* to extract the divine nectar *(amrit)*. The present age (Kaliyuga) is only one stage of the unending cycle of life.

Kali, *wearing a garland of skulls, rampages through creation, annihilating evil. Along with Durga, she is the patron goddess of many Rajput clans who lived by the sword.*

Architecture: A Brief History

IN NORTH INDIA, monumental architecture followed historical and political change. The wide variety of styles that emerged were executed in a distinctly "Indian" way, influenced by climate and local building traditions. Sadly, few buildings before the 12th century survived the ravages of time, war and climate, but the region is rich in medieval remains, of which the Taj Mahal is the centrepiece. An interesting feature is the mingling of Hindu and Islamic styles, which blends the sensuous beauty of temple sculpture with the austere grandeur of Islamic architecture. Gardens, fountains, screened arches and shaded interiors are some features used for keeping buildings cool.

Carved niche at Agra Fort

EARLY INDIAN ARCHITECTURE (UP TO 12TH CENTURY)

The temple was the social and economic focus of a town. Early Hindu temples, built on a square base, follow sacred building rules. The deity lies within the sanctum, and the outer surface is profusely decorated.

Carved frieze on shikhara

The **shikhara** is a pointed arch that meets over the sanctum.

The **mandapa** is a hall in front of the sanctum.

Garbhagriha, the womb-like inner sanctum sanctorum.

The **entrance** is spanned by a square stone lintel, carved with sacred images.

Piled stone blocks raise the temple's height

Teli ka Mandir (9th century) at Gwalior (see p174) is a rare example of a North Indian temple of that time.

SULTANATE ARCHITECTURE (13TH TO 15TH CENTURIES)

A sandstone and marble panel

Techniques for constructing true arches and domes were learnt by Indian masons from the Muslims after the 12th century. Mortar, another significant technology transfer, made it possible to build high structures. Hindu carving skills added a new element to the Islamic architectural lexicon.

The **dome** is crowned with a finial.

Islamic arches are often trimmed with a Hindu lotus bud fringe.

Detail of a geometric panel

Geometric ornamentation is an Islamic feature.

Alai Darwaza (c.1311) in Delhi, with one of the oldest surviving domes, is one of the gems of early Islamic architecture (see p112).

MUGHAL ARCHITECTURE (16TH TO LATE 18TH CENTURIES)

Mughal buildings awe the viewer and assert the exalted status of their imperial patron. Whether built of red sandstone or marble, symmetry, grandeur and landscaping are some common features. Inlay work, decorative *jaalis* and cusped arches give these buildings an ethereal grace that offsets their massive size.

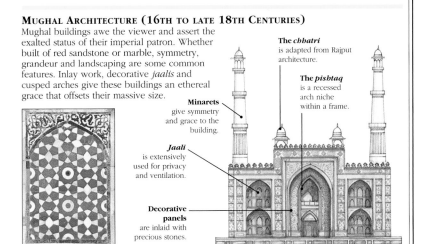

The *chhatri* is adapted from Rajput architecture.

The *pishtaq* is a recessed arch niche within a frame.

Minarets give symmetry and grace to the building.

Jaali is extensively used for privacy and ventilation.

Decorative panels are inlaid with precious stones.

Decorative panel on façade

Gateway of Akbar's tomb at Sikandra *(see p160)*

COLONIAL ARCHITECTURE (19TH TO EARLY 20TH CENTURIES)

The European classical style was introduced during the British Raj. A later development was the Indo-Saracenic style, a marriage of the Victorian Gothic with Indian decorative elements, visible in 19th-century universities, municipal offices and railway stations. New Delhi, built by Lutyens between 1912–31 *(see p68)*, marks the end of this phase.

Neo-Classical frontage of Hyderabad House, New Delhi *(see p71)*

Balustraded terraces

Colonnaded verandahs

Clock tower

Portico

Ajmer's Mayo College, built in the Indo-Saracenic style in 1875 *(see p219)*

BUNGALOWS

An architectural legacy of the Raj, originally designed to house Europeans living in remote outposts, bungalows have broad, covered verandahs, a front porch and a balustraded roof. The term

Government bungalow in New Delhi *(see p69)*

was a corruption of "Bangla", or Bengal, for its basic structure was derived from the indigenous, Bengali rural hut. Until 1947, few bungalows outside towns had running water or electricity but their high ceilings and shaded interiors kept them dark and cool in summer. However, when Herbert Baker *(see p68)* designed a bungalow for New Delhi's mandarins, its unhappy occupants christened his airless edifice "Baker's Oven".

Architectural Styles

Marble podium at Delhi's Jami Masjid

SOME OF THE COUNTRY's finest forts and palaces lie in this region. Forts often served both as defensive buildings and as self-sufficient walled cities, built along natural outcrops or near rivers. Palaces were either part of a fort complex, or individual royal residences with public and private spaces separated by gardens and courtyards. Later, during the Raj, fortified palaces gave way to stately mansions inspired by European models. The beautiful garden tombs, of which the Taj is the most famous example, were a Mughal innovation. In contrast to these are rural houses that blend into the landscape. These eco-friendly structures, based on indigenous building skills are well-insulated, and both cheap and easy to build.

FORTS

Most Mughal forts, built of red sandstone with marble trimmings, contained a city complex, with private and public areas and were seats of imperial power. Rajput forts, like Amber (*see pp200–201*) and Gwalior, on the other hand, follow a different plan and their solid bastions were built primarily for self-defence.

Ramparts have pierced holes for cannons.

The *burj* acted as a watchtower.

Foundation inscription from the Red Fort

Lahore Gate is named after the direction it faced.

Red Fort at Delhi (*see pp94–5*)

PALACES

Some of the region's most spectacular palaces date to the 19th century in a style that imitated English stately homes. The older, medieval palaces nestle within forts and had separate quarters for men (*mardana*) and women (zenana) with landscaped gardens and private mosques or temples.

The bangaldar roof is crowned with decorative spikes.

A grand flight of steps leads to the gorgeous interior.

The simple exterior conceals a rich interior.

Detail from a mirrored room

Samode Palace, *built in the 19th century and now a heritage hotel (see pp232–3), has fabulously gilded and mirrored rooms. It is built in the traditional design but has period furniture rather than the usual cushions and floor coverings used in older palaces.*

THE GARDEN TOMB

The charbagh (see p167) *is a terraced garden that surrounds the tomb to give its austere lines a soft focus. The Taj Mahal, set at the edge of one, is the most famous example of this style.*

The dome surmounts the central space.

Arched cloisters lead to the crypt.

Humayun's tomb (see p83) *is one of the earliest Mughal garden tombs, which were set on a raised plinth within a* charbagh. *Other features include a private mosque and crypts for other royal graves.*

TRADITIONAL HOUSES

Indian villagers usually live in simple houses made of local material, often mud and thatch. They have cool, shaded interiors and are brightly decorated on the outside. Building materials come from the land and are renewed annually at Diwali (see p37).

Thatched roofs keep the interiors cool and shaded.

Mud walls are reinforced with straw and cowdung.

Ritual paintings brighten mud walls.

A rural Indian house at Mandawa (see p213)

HAVELIS

The *haveli*, a multi-storeyed mansion for wealthy merchant families, was usually built around one or more courtyards which formed a focal point for the domestic activity of the joint family. Shekhawati's painted *havelis* (see pp212–13) are examples of this architectural style.

The terrace gave an airy overview of the surroundings.

Covered verandahs separated living areas into smaller private units.

Haveli **of the Bhartiya family, Shekhawati region**

GLOSSARY OF TERMS

Baoli Underground stepwell, such as Ugrasen's Baoli (see p76).

Burj Residential or fortificatory tower; also bastion.

Chajja Overhanging eaves or cornices to protect buildings from the sun and rain.

Chhatri Open square or octagonal pavilion, literally an umbrella.

Chhatri

Diwan-i-Aam Hall of Public Audience.

Diwan-i-Khas Hall of Private Audience.

Gumbad/gumbaz Dome, often crowned with a finial; the term is also used for a mausoleum.

Gumbad

Jharokha Overhanging oriel window supported on brackets; some were used for the official appearances of the ruler.

Masjid Mosque.

Mihrab Arched niche facing Mecca in a mosque.

Jharokha

Minar Free-standing tower such as the Qutb Minar (see p112).

Mohalla Quarter of town inhabited by members of one caste.

Namazgah Space near mosque for celebration of major Muslim festivals.

Qila Castle, fortress, citadel.

Sheesh Mahal Chamber profusely decorated with mirror mosaic; glass palace.

Minaret

Stambha Stately pillar, post or column.

Stupa Tumulus, burial or reliquary mound.

Stambha

Music, Dance and Theatre

Iᴺᴅɪᴀ'ꜱ ᴘᴇʀꜰᴏʀᴍɪɴɢ ᴀʀᴛꜱ are simultaneously modes of worship and a joyous celebration of life. Music and dance originated in the temples, gradually acquiring a secular, more sensuous character as royal patrons founded individual schools *(gharanas)*. Two prominent classical forms in this region are Kathak and Hindustani music. The artiste creates a mood *(rasa)* which invites the audience to participate in it so as to make the performance a mutually shared experience.

Sarangi and bow

Qawwalis and bhajans are devotional songs that go back to medieval Sufi and Bhakti cults. Sung intensely to arouse mystical ecstasy, they celebrate the power of divine love.

Raslila, a folk variation of Kathak, narrates the life of Lord Krishna. Traditionally, the Ramlila (below) and the Raslila featured young boys.

Hands are used in stylized *mudras*, symbolic movements that follow the *Natya Shastra*, a classic treatise on the performing arts.

Lebenga, a long skirt worn over tight pyjamas, accentuates the swirling movement of the dancer.

Ramlila enacts the story of the epic Ramayana in a cycle of ten episodic folk plays during the Dussehra festival (see p37).

HINDUSTANI MUSIC

The origins of Hindustani music date to about 3000 BC and the *Sama Veda (see p319)*. The *raga* (melodic mode) and *tala* (rhythmic cycle) are the foundation of Indian classical music, of which the Dhrupad and the Khayal are two major vocal styles. Indian classical music has no formal notational score, giving artistes a wide scope to elaborate the mood of a *raga*, each with its own set of notes. To preserve individuality, knowledge was passed down orally from teacher to pupil through schools called *gharanas*. The Gwalior *gharana (see p174)* is said to be the oldest one in the region.

Ravi Shankar, one of India's foremost sitar players, introduced classical music to the West.

Amjad Ali Khan belongs to a famous family of sarod players, who developed the rabab, a medieval lute from Central Asia, to its present form.

*Nine **rasas** (moods) are mentioned in the 4th-century treatise Natya Shastra. From the erotic, comic and pathetic to the odious, marvellous and quiescent, rasa covers every mood and expression, whether in music or painting. This 17th-century Ragamala painting (see pp30–31) depicts the mood of the morning Raga Todi.*

BAYADÈRE OF MEWAT.

Nautch Girl was the pejorative title given to dancing girls in the 19th century when Kathak became mere entertainment.

Rapid body movements keep time with the beat of the accompanying percussionist.

Ghungroos are brass bells that aid the rhythmic beat. Foot stamping controls and varies their sound.

Gorgeous jewellery and the colour red on the hands and feet make the intricacies of the dance easy to see.

KATHAK

This North Indian classical dance form, that received lavish patronage in the court of Jaipur, derives from the epic tales *(kathas)* narrated by balladeers. A typical Kathak performance is a blend of complex footwork and facial expressions *(abhinaya)* to enact an episode, often from Krishna's life.

Bismillah Khan plays the shehnai, a ceremonial reed pipe of the oboe family that is now also a concert instrument.

Zakir Hussain plays the tabla, a pair of drums that provide percussion to most music and dance performances.

Contemporary theatre draws on classical Sanskrit drama. Avant-garde street plays are popular with fringe and protest theatre groups. The National School of Drama Repertory (see p120) often produces Indian adaptations of classical plays, such as King Lear, seen above.

Painting

A bird by Mansur

Two distinct schools of painting, Rajput and Mughal, emerged in 16th-century North India. The meteoric growth and popularity of miniature painting was due to the introduction of paper as well as the lavish patronage of Muslim and Rajput rulers. The Mughals encouraged Persian miniature painters to settle in India where they came into contact with indigenous traditions. A fusion of the two styles under Akbar, Jahangir and Shah Jahan led to a burst of artistic activity when court painters, such as Mansur, produced folios of birds, flowers, royal portraits and illustrated manuscripts. As Mughal patronage declined in the 18th century, other regional centres of art developed in North India.

Jain palm leaf manuscripts, such as this piece (c.1439), use bright primary colours. Their large-eyed human figures and narrative depiction of themes influenced early Rajput art.

Early Mughal paintings were pictorial narratives of historical events and literary texts. This leaf from a 16th-century Babur Nama *shows Babur crossing the River Son. Mughal landscapes are rendered realistically, unlike the more romantic Rajput allegories.*

Monsters symbolize the threats to Krishna at birth.

Space is divided into units, each dealing with a separate episode of the story.

Rajput paintings are known for their bright colours and stylized figures. Classical texts and religious figures are recurrent subjects, such as this 18th-century page from the Rasikapriya *romance of the Bundi School.*

Ragamalas *are sets of paintings strung like a garland, that depict the mood of individual* ragas *(see p28). This 17th-century* Ragini Dev-Gandhari, *an early morning* raga, *has dainty figures, and the delicate floral border that was a hallmark of Mughal paintings.*

Pahari painting emerged from the hill (pahari) states of the western Himalayas, where many artists went in search of work after the decline of Mughal patronage. Raja Sansar Chand of Kangra, a patron of this style, can be seen in this late 18th-century Pahari painting.

The Company School flourished in the colonial period. This portrait of King Edward VII and Queen Alexandra, attired in Indian clothes and ornaments, was painted by a local artist as a specially commissioned work.

Nature is depicted in metaphorical terms, as in the snake-like ripples of lightning.

Narrative progression shows the growth of Krishna from infancy to boyhood.

Human faces are drawn in profile and space lacks perspective.

Colours and pigments were extracted from precious stones and plants.

RAJPUT MINIATURES

Rajput ateliers were named after their patron courts *(see p215)*, each with a distinctive style, such as this 18th-century Mewar miniature, *Krshna Revealing his Divinity as Visnu to his Parents*. Rajput paintings have a narrative theme – a court episode or a mythological tale. Unlike Mughal paintings, their treatment of space and the natural world is poetic rather than realisitic and evokes a musical mood or *rasa (see p29)*. *Baramasa* (cycle of seasons) and *Ragamala* (garland of *ragas*) paintings are famous examples of this romantic style.

CONTEMPORARY INDIAN ART

A nationalist poet, musician, philosopher and educationalist, Rabindranath Tagore (d.1943) pioneered the 19th-century Bengal Renaissance art movement, which was a step towards the modernist impulse in Indian art. He drew heavily on the rich mythic content of folk art. Later, Amrita Shergill (d.1940) brought a European style to Indian themes and scenes. Contemporary Indian art evolved from the work of these and other seminal artists. Yet it retained an Indian identity even when experimenting with fashionable European styles. Modern Indian artists have experimented with Tantric symbols, mythology and miniature paintings to produce a vibrant art style which has tried to retain the richness of its folk and classical art forms even as they work with different media and materials.

**Head Study,
Rabindranath Tagore**

Indian Design

INDIAN DESIGN HAS EVOLVED out of a very close bond between the artist and his craft, in which the skill of the hand is regarded as a sacred gift, passed down from father to son in an unbroken line. This has ensured a design tradition that is both a living art form as well as a means of fulfilling the everyday needs of the community, be they sacred or functional. Freely enriched by the traditions of other races and cultures, India's artistic heritage is renowned throughout the world for its vibrancy and creativity.

Mughal flower motif

Geometric designs form the base of traditional decoration.

Mud and thatch are regarded as sacred media, being the gift of Mother Earth.

The rounded shape of the pot has not changed since 2500 BC.

Pottery has a 5,000-year-old history (see pp44–5) making it one of the world's oldest skills. The potter's wheel produces cheap, eco-friendly objects of daily use.

The wheel or *chakra* is regarded as a symbol of the eternal circle of life and death.

Lime wash applied on the mud surface adds colour and repels pests.

The living space is embellished with surface decorations ranging from relief carvings to mirror-work. Whether a mud hut or palace, the Indian home is the origin of most forms of art.

COLOUR

The colours of Indian design are taken from nature, with names to match. The five shades of white are lyrically compared to the clouds when the rain is spent, the August moon, conch shell, jasmine flower and the surf of the sea. Indigo, madder and turmeric are valued for their dyes, and the crushed flowers of the flame of the forest (*Butea monosperma*) yield a soft yellow colour still used in rural India for playing Holi (*see p36*). Each colour has a ritual significance as well: red is associated with weddings and festivals, saffron is the colour of warriors and ascetics, yellow is worn during the spring festival of Vasant, and green in the monsoon. The Indian dyer (*right*) uses plants and roots for extracting colour.

A dyer at work

The **peacock** is a popular symbol of royalty.

The **lotus** is associated with grace and purity.

Animal and flower motifs *can be seen everywhere. The most elegant floral patterns were perfected in Mughal and Rajput painting (see pp30–31), while the popular lotus and peacock motifs are inherent to Buddhist and Hindu temple iconography. Worked in a variety of forms these motifs are most visible in textiles, carpets, painting, jewellery, ceramics and zardozi (see p153).*

Paisley motifs are stylized representations of the mango and cypress.

The poppy, the iris, narcissus and tulip are textile motifs inspired by Mughal art.

Marble inlay *can be traced to Mughal pietra dura (see pp156–7). Agra still has families of craftsmen whose ancestors worked at the Mughal court.*

Precious stones such as amethyst, lapis, carnelian and jade are inlaid by hand on marble.

Floral patterns, inspired by the Islamic paradise garden concept, are common.

HOME AND FAMILY

The earliest art objects were those needed for everyday life. Emerging from the home and its daily rituals, the shape and form of articles was based on religious symbols which ensured their survival down the ages. With time, sophisticated materials and techniques learnt from royal courts enhanced design consciousness, resulting in a more exclusive range of decorative art.

Wall paintings are often inspired by nature.

Flame of the forest

Spices

Saffron turban for warriors

A vermilion-daubed shrine

Form and function *are equally important in Indian design, endowing even everyday utility objects with beauty. As architectural skills developed over the centuries, basic forms and materials became more sophisticated. This graceful trellised stone window is an example of this change.*

Popular Culture

MTV logo

THE CONTACT between Indian traditions and a Western global culture has triggered off a spontaneous and vibrant response among both rural and urban societies. The new trends in lifestyle, fashion and entertainment are influenced to some extent by commercial cinema and television. Combining the traditional with the modern, they reflect a change in popular tastes.

Rangoli *patterns are a traditional form of renewable art, created daily at entrances to homes. Elaborate designs are seen on auspicious occasions.*

Statues *of leaders such as Ambedkar, a champion of the oppressed classes, are a common sight. These colourful but tawdry images made by local sculptors are often installed in public parks.*

The groom, accompanied by a young boy, wears a string of flowers (*sehra*), over his face.

Plastic products *are vastly popular throughout India and include toys and decorative items, as well as functional objects of everyday use.*

The wedding chariot is an extravagant gilt-plated carriage.

Signboards *scream their messages in lurid colours.*

Street dancers, *transvestites and eunuchs entertain audiences with bawdy dances.*

The photographer's tent *with its fanciful backdrop of exotic locations or film stars, is unique to village fairs.*

Advertisement on wheels ranges from slogans and romantic verse to paintings of film stars and landscapes. Trucks, taxis, even the bicycle of a street vendor selling home-made ice-cream, are gaily painted with tempting messages.

Bidis are local cigarettes. The different brands have highly whimsical names with lurid wrappings that promote a virile, macho image.

Rakhi, the simple thread tied on the wrist on the festival of Raksha Bandhan (see p39), is today made of imitation gold and silver.

Hindi films (often called Bollywood offerings) are India's response to Hollywood, especially the spaghetti western. The average formula film is a great mix of themes and emotions – love, violence, comedy, tragedy – generously peppered with song and dance sequences.

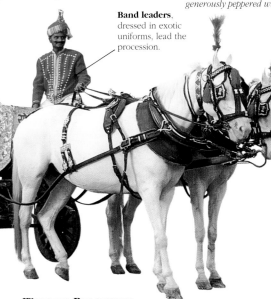

Band leaders, dressed in exotic uniforms, lead the procession.

Fashion designers, models and beauty queens like Aishwarya Rai, Miss World 1997, are cult figures in urban India today.

Popular music such as Indipop and Bhangra Rap, popularized by Daler Mehndi and others, is a con-temporary form of folk music. MTV and Channel V are its promoters.

WEDDING PROCESSION

Indian weddings are noisy, colourful affairs. The musical escort of the horse-riding bridegroom is a brass band dressed in music hall or Salvation Army style uniforms, complete with braids and epaulettes. Sometimes the groom comes riding a gaudy, gilt-plated chariot, accom-panied by an entourage of young relatives dancing to popular tunes from Hindi films. The whole spectacle is a modern day re-enactment of the pomp and pageantry associated with royal wedding processions in the past.

Festivals in India

INDIANS LOVE CELEBRATIONS. Festivals are both religious and social events, where ritual fasting and joyful feasting often go hand in hand. Hindu festivals usually follow the lunar calendar and both the full moon (*purnima*) and the new moon (*pradosh*) are considered auspicious. Some fairs and festivities are connected to the pantheon of gods and goddesses, others to ancient pastoral, fertility or martial rites. Muslim festivals, too, are determined by the new moon. This means that the dates of festivals vary from year to year.

Effigy of Ravana

SHISHIR (JAN–MAR)

THIS IS the most auspicious period in the Indian calendar. **Lohri** and **Makar Sankranti** follow one another in early January. The former is observed mainly by Punjabis as the height of winter, and the latter, confined to Jaipur, marks the movement of the sun from the equator to the Tropic of Capricorn. The wind usually changes direction on this day and colourful kites fill the sky. **Vasant Panchami**, towards the end of January, is

Child sports Holi colours

considered the first day of spring. In February, devotees of Shiva observe **Shivaratri**, or the night of his celestial wedding to Parvati. **Holi**, one of the most important Hindu festivals in this region, takes place on a full-moon night, and is celebrated as the end of winter. On the eve of Holi, bonfires are lit and an effigy of the demon Holika is burnt to signify the triumph of good over evil. The next day, people swarm the streets, sprinkling coloured water and powder (*gulal*) on each other. This festival was especially dear to Lord Krishna, and around Mathura (*see p161*) it is played with great abandon.

VASANT (MAR–MAY)

THE HINDU YEAR begins with Vasant (spring). Nine days of fasting (*navaratris*) precede the birth of the hero-god Rama (*see p23*) on **Ramnavami**. During this period, most households prepare special vegetarian foods, which are cooked in *ghee* (clarified butter) without garlic or onions.

In March, Shia Muslims observe **Muharram**, a ten-day period of mourning for the martyrdom of the Prophet's grandson, Hazrat Imam Hussain, at Karbala (Iraq). On the tenth and final day, impressive processions of *tazias* (replicas of his tomb) are taken out, followed by drummers and young boys and men dressed in black, who flagellate themselves in a frenzy of religious fervour.

The pastoral festival of **Baisakhi** on 13 April heralds the harvest season in North India, and is celebrated with singing and dancing. Later in in the month comes **Shitala Ashtami**, a Rajasthani folk festival to commemorate Shitala Devi, goddess of smallpox and a manifestation of Durga. A religious fair is held at the Chaksu temple (*see p222*) to appease the goddess, and is attended by hundreds of villagers.

Holi celebrations in the villages of Brajbhumi, near Mathura

GRISHMA (MAY–JUN)

As THE HEAT intensifies, the festival season comes to a halt. Muslims all over India celebrate **Milad-ul-Nabi**, the birthday of the Prophet. The devotees keep night-long vigils at mosques, praying or reading from the holy Koran.

VARSHA (JUL–SEP)

With THE MONSOON comes **Janmashtami**, the birth of Lord Krishna on a moonless night. Celebrations reach their peak at midnight, while the day is given to fasting. In Brindavan *(see p162)* and Mathura, pilgrims perform a circumambulation *(parikrama)* of sacred sites.

Dussehra images being prepared

SHARAD (SEP–OCT)

This SEASON OF festivals begins with **Dussehra**. For ten days, Ramlilas *(see p28)* are held and fairs organized to celebrate the legend of Rama. These dramatize episodes from the *Ramayana*: the exile of Rama, his brother Lakshman and wife Sita. Her abduction by the demon-king Ravana of Lanka and the epic battle for her rescue glorifies the monkey god, Hanuman, who helped Rama defeat Ravana and return in triumph to Ayodhya. Huge effigies of Ravana, his brother and son are stuffed with fireworks to be set alight on the last day,

Muslim pilgrims at the Urs at Ajmer

Vijaya Dashami. Dussehra is preceded by the *navaratri* fasts. Bengalis celebrate this period as **Durga Puja**, when grand marquees *(pandals)* are erected over images of the goddess Durga.

Diwali, or the festival of lights, marks Rama's joyous entry into Ayodhya when the town was lit with lamps to greet him. It also heralds the Hindu New Year when old accounts are closed. Hindus believe that Lakshmi, the goddess of wealth, visits her devotees on that night, so houses are painted, sweets exchanged, and a profusion of *melas* encourages wild spending on homes and clothes. **Bhai Duj**, two days later, is a family festival in honour of brothers, who give gifts to their sisters. **Govardhan Puja** or Annakut in both Rajasthan and Mathura commemorates the day Krishna lifted Mount Govardhan on his little finger

Diwali crackers on sale at pavement stalls

to protect the area from a deluge sent by an irate Indra, the god of rain. With the new moon of the season comes the **Urs** at Ajmer. This is the time for one of the biggest Muslim fairs in the subcontinent, held over 13 days at the *dargah* of the great Sufi saint Moinuddin Chishti *(see pp220–21)*.

HEMANT (NOV–JAN)

The ONSET OF WINTER ushers in a number of festivals such as Christmas that are now national celebrations. In Rajasthan, the **Pushkar Fair** *(see pp216–17)* attracts tourists as well as ordinary pilgrims and herdsmen. On the full moon after Diwali, Sikhs celebrate **Guru Purab**, the birthday of Guru Nanak, the founder of Sikhism. **Id-ul-Fitr** marks the end of Ramadan or Ramzan, the month of fasting **Paper kite** for Muslims, commemorating the period when the Prophet received the message of the Koran from Allah. The actual day of celebration varies according to the sighting of the new moon. A special *namaaz* is held at Delhi's Jami Masjid. This festival is also called Mithi (sweet) Id, as *sewian*, a delicacy made with sweetened vermicelli, is distributed at all homes.

DELHI, AGRA & JAIPUR
THROUGH THE YEAR

THREE DEFINITE seasons, the summer, monsoon and winter, with a brief but glorious spring and autumn, span the year in the region. The calendar is filled with festivals and fairs celebrated by each of the diverse religious

Bauhinia blossom

or local communities. Some follow the changing seasons and mark pastoral occasions, while others celebrate anniversaries and events of national importance such as the Republic Day *(see p71)*. Most cultural shows are held during the winter.

SUMMER (MAR–JUN)

FROM MID-MARCH until June the North Indian plains experience a hot and dry summer. The temperatures in March and April can be mild and variable, but by May and June the heat builds up to a crescendo with the mercury rising above 40° C (104° F). This is a signal for many residents to move to the Himalayan hill stations. Those who stay back remain indoors and only venture out after sunset. Most festivities, too, come to a halt during this period.

Holi *(Mar)*. This exuberant festival of colour marks the end of winter. In and around Brindavan *(see p162)* Holi celebrations last two weeks.

Elephant Festival *(Mar)*, Jaipur. Around Holi, 60 decorated elephants parade through the streets bearing revellers who throw colour at one another. Elephant polo matches are also held at Chaugan Stadium.

Nauchandi Mela *(Mar)*, Meerut. Held around the shrine of a Muslim saint and a

Procession of Buddhist lamas on Buddha Jayanti

temple, this fair has come to symbolize Hindu-Muslim unity. Its origins date to the late-17th century when local leaders decided to merge festivities held concurrently at both shrines. Today, this is more a fun-filled carnival than a religious event.

Jahan e Khusrau *(Mar)*, Delhi. The three-day international Sufi music festival is one of the city's most eagerly awaited events. Performances are held at Humayun's tomb.

ITC Sangeet Sammelan *(Mar)*, Delhi. This important Hindustani classical music event, sponsored by a major Indian industrial house, attracts all music-lovers in the capital.

Elephant Festival

Gangaur Festival *(Mar/Apr)*, Jaipur. For 18 days, new brides and young girls worship Gauri, one of the manifestations of Parvati, the

consort of Shiva. Bejewelled images of the goddess are carried through the city, escorted by bullock-drawn chariots, bands of musicians and women singing hymns.

Shankarlal Sangeet Sammelan *(Mar)*, Delhi. This is the capital's oldest classical vocal and instrumental music festival.

Baisakhi *(13 Apr)*. On this day Gobind Singh, the last Sikh guru, founded the Khalsa, the "Holy Army of the Pure". Gala processions, dancing and feasting mark the occasion. It also signals the onset of summer and the start of the harvest season.

Urs *(Apr)*, Delhi. For three days devotees of the Sufi saint Nizamuddin Auliya *(see p82)* celebrate his birth anniversary with night-long qawwalis and a funfair.

Buddha Jayanti *(May)*, Delhi. The Buddha was born, attained enlightenment and died on the full moon of the fourth lunar month. Prayer meetings are held at Delhi's Buddha Jayanti Park.

AVERAGE DAILY HOURS OF SUNSHINE

Hours

12
10
8
6
4
2
0

Jan Feb Mar Apr May Jun Jul Aug Sep Oct Nov Dec

Sunshine Chart
Ranging from balmy to fiercely hot, North India has sunshine through the year. To those unaccustomed to tropical weather, even the winter afternoons of this region may be uncomfortably warm. Sun hats, dark glasses, sunblock and several glasses a day of mineral water are highly recommended.

Summer Theatre Festival
(May/Jun), Delhi. A theatre festival is organized by the National School of Drama.

MONSOON (JUL–AUG)

JULY, AUGUST and most of September are hot and humid with intermittent showers. All newspapers eagerly report the progress of the southwest monsoon and though rainfall is scanty in the region, this season is celebrated for its magical transformation of the earth.

Mango Festival *(early Jul),* Delhi. Held at the peak of the mango season, over 1,000 varieties of delicious mangoes grown in North India are on view at the Talkatora Stadium.

National Film Festival *(Jul),* Delhi. During this two-week-long festival, regional films from India that have won awards and have been made by prominent directors, are screened at the large Siri Fort Auditorium.

Shehnai **player at Teej**

Teej *(Aug),* Jaipur. Young girls, dressed in green, sing songs and play on specially erected swings. This joyous event venerates Parvati, the goddess of marital harmony. It also heralds the advent of the much awaited monsoon.

Independence Day *(15 Aug).* This is a national

A dancing peacock announcing the coming of the monsoon

holiday, commemorating India's freedom from British rule in 1947. The Prime Minister addresses the nation from the ramparts of the historic Red Fort in Delhi.

Raksha Bandhan *(full moon in Aug).* Young girls tie sacred threads *(rakhis)* on their brothers' wrists as a token of love, and receive in exchange, gifts and a promise of everlasting protection.

Janmashtami *(Aug).* Krishna's birth is celebrated all over India. In Brindavan, Raslilas are performed, and in Delhi, there are shows of *Krishna Katha,* a dance-drama on the Krishna story.

NATIONAL HOLIDAYS

Republic Day (26 Jan)
Independence Day (15 Aug)
Gandhi Jayanti (2 Oct)

PUBLIC HOLIDAYS

Shivaratri (Feb)
Holi (Mar)
Id-ul-Zuha (Mar)
Good Friday (Apr)
Baisakhi (13 April)
Ramnavami (Apr)
Mahavir Jayanti (Apr/May)
Buddha Jayanti (May)
Milad-ul-Nabi (May/Jun)
Janmashtami (Aug)
Dussehra (Oct)
Diwali (Oct/Nov)
Guru Purab (Nov)
Christmas (25 Dec)

Independence Day celebration

AVERAGE MONTHLY RAINFALL

Rainfall Chart
Apart from local showers, this region receives its rain mostly during the southwest monsoon, which lasts from July to September. The landscape turns lush green but the humidity, sometimes as high as 90 per cent, makes this the wrong season for travelling in the plains of North India.

WINTER (OCT–FEB)

THIS IS THE MOST perfect season when the monsoon has cleared the dust haze and the days begin to grow cooler. The onset of winter also marks the sowing of winter crops such as mustard and wheat.

The winter chill is at its worst between mid-December and mid-January, and though temperatures often fall below 3° C (37° F), the days are sunny. Spring is the main season for weddings, parades, picnics, polo and cricket matches, flower shows and various cultural events.

Cricket, the national obsession

Gandhi Jayanti *(2 Oct)*. Mahatma Gandhi's birthday is widely celebrated as a national holiday.

Phoolwalon ki Sair *(early Oct)*, Delhi. A colourful procession of floral banners and fans from the Jogmaya Temple and the Sufi shrine of Qutbuddin Bakhtiyar Kaki culminates at Jahaz Mahal in Mehrauli *(see pp110–13)*. Music and poetry recitations *(mushairas)* are also held.

Qutb Festival *(Oct)*, Delhi. A feast of Indian classical music and dance, organized by Delhi Tourism, is held against the dramatic backdrop of the Qutb Minar.

Dussehra *(Oct)*. For nine days, episodes from the *Ramayana* depicting Rama's battle against Ravana are enacted all over the region. The tenth day, Vijaya Dashami, celebrates Rama's defeat of Ravana, and huge effigies of the demon-king, his brother and son are burnt with fireworks. In Delhi, the Shriram Bharatiya Kala Kendra's month-long dance-drama encapsulates the much-loved epic.

Urs *(Oct)*, Ajmer. The festival in memory of the Sufi saint Khwaja Moinuddin Chishti attracts thousands of Muslim and Hindu devotees from all over the country.

Diwali *(Oct/Nov)*. Oil lamps illuminate each home to commemorate Rama's return to Ayodhya after 14 years of exile. Firecrackers are lit and sweets exchanged. During this period every locality holds Diwali *melas*.

Pushkar Fair *(Nov)*, Pushkar. Asia's largest camel and cattle fair, takes place in this pilgrim town *(see pp216–17)*.

Kartik Cultural Festival *(15–21 Nov)*, Ballabhgarh. This festival is held at an 18th-century palace on the Delhi-Mathura Road.

International Trade Fair *(14–21 Nov)*, Delhi. Pragati Maidan hosts this major event for Indian industry, exhibiting goods manufactured in India and abroad. Cultural events are also held in the fair grounds.

Balloon Mela

Balloon Mela *(14 Nov)*, Delhi. This festival coincides with Nehru's birthday, celebrated as Children's Day.

Jhansi Festival *(Nov)*, Jhansi. A five-day arts and crafts extravaganza unfolds against the backdrop of the historic 18th-century fort.

Tansen Festival *(Nov)*, Gwalior. Classical singers pay homage to the most famous of Indian musicians, Tansen, Mughal emperor Akbar's favourite singer.

Chrysanthemum Show *(1st week Dec)*, Delhi. The YWCA organizes a display of magnificent blooms.

Kathak Utsav *(Dec)*, Delhi. Exponents of this North Indian dance form enthrall audiences with their artistry.

Car display at the Trade Fair

AVERAGE MONTHLY TEMPERATURE

Temperature Chart
This region is hot and dry throughout the year, barring October to February. The mercury begins to rise from March, and by May heat wave conditions prevail with hot and dusty gusts of the "loo" winds. By the end of June, however, dark clouds signal the onset of monsoon.

Bagpipers at the Beating Retreat ceremony

Christmas *(25 Dec)*. A public holiday, Christmas is celebrated all over and is an occasion for everyone to shop, feast and party.

New Year's Eve *(31 Dec)*. All hotels and clubs organize New Year's Eve balls.

Lohri *(13 Jan)*. Bonfires are lit amidst song and dance to mark the height of winter.

Makar Sankranti *(14 Jan)*, Jaipur. Kites are flown to celebrate the return of the sun from the equator to the Tropic of Capricorn.

Republic Day *(26 Jan)*. A national holiday. Pomp and pageantry mark India's birth as an independent republic. In Delhi, a colourful military parade is held at Rajpath.

Beating Retreat *(29 Jan)*, Delhi. A moving ceremony that recalls the end of the day's battle when armies retreated to their camps. There is a grand display of regimental bands performing against the spectacular backdrop of North and South Blocks. As the sun sets, a

bugle sounds the retreat, fireworks are lit and fairy-lights outline the buildings.

Surajkund Crafts Mela *(1–14 Feb)*, Surajkund. This handicrafts fair is held at an 11th-century historic site on the outskirts of the capital.

International Yoga Week *(2–7 Feb)*, Rishikesh. Scholars and students from all over the world participate in classes and seminars on the banks of the Ganges.

Vintage Car Rally *(Feb)*, Delhi. *The Statesman*

newspaper organizes this event when vintage cars, or the "grand old ladies", are flagged off from Rajpath to embark on a 20-km (12-mile) race. Their owners often dress up in period costumes.

Vasant Panchami *(Feb)*. A spring festival when crops ripen and nature is in full bloom. People wear yellow and worship Saraswati.

Flower Shows *(Feb)*. A number of flower and rose shows are held in Delhi and elsewhere. The Rashtrapati Bhavan's Mughal Gardens are also open to the public.

Taj Mahotsav *(18–27 Feb)*, Agra. A ten-day cultural fiesta of music and dance in the vicinity of the Taj Mahal.

Shivaratri *(Feb)*. Night-long celebrations mark the marriage of Shiva on the 14th day of a lunar fortnight.

Kathak Bindadin Mahotsav *(Feb)*, Delhi. A five-day dance festival orga-nized by the Kathak Kendra.

Dhrupad Festival *(Feb)*, Delhi. Leading exponents of this ancient musical tradition present a series of recitals.

Vintage cars testing their strength on an uphill road outside Delhi

THE HISTORY OF DELHI, AGRA & JAIPUR

NORTH INDIAN SOCIETY sprang from the wide plains of the Indus and Ganges rivers, sites of continuous human settlement since about 2500 BC, when a sophisticated urban culture flourished along the Indus Valley. After 600 BC, powerful empires such as the Mauryas, Kushanas and Guptas presided over the rise of Buddhism and Hinduism, two major religions that emerged from North India.

Overland trade with Central Asia and the Far East invited conquest and settlement as well. Interestingly, India is a derivative of "Indoi", a Greek word given to people who lived across the River Sindhu, or Indus. From 1500 BC on, North India was home to immigrants. These included the Aryans, Greeks and Parthians, Scythians, Huns and Mongols.

An important development took place in AD 1192 when Muhammad Ghori displaced the Rajputs from

Statue of the Holy Trinity, Gupta Age

Delhi to found the first major Islamic kingdom in the region. Later, with the coming of the Mughals in 1526, North India underwent a process of social and political change that lasted nearly 300 years, as a vibrant Indo-Islamic cultural fusion took place. Imperial centralization under the Mughals brought peace and prosperity in its wake, while art and architecture scaled new heights of excellence.

The rise of the British East India Company in the 18th century, after the decline of the Mughals, was the start of 200 years of British rule in India. The colonial period, which also marks the political unification of the subcontinent, ended in 1947 when India became independent. Today a mature democracy, India is trying to tackle poverty and illiteracy with economic and political reform in the new millennium.

A 16th-century map, which helped the Dutch and English locate trading bases in India

◁ Royal procession, a mid-19th-century mural in the Moti Mahal, Gwalior

Early Civilizations

INDIAN CIVILIZATION first flourished between 2500 and 1500 BC in the Harappan settlements along the River Indus. These sophisticated urban settlements, with an underground drainage system and well laid out streets, were spread over an area much larger than either ancient Egypt or Mesopotamia. The reasons for the decline of this early civilization are still unclear, but by 1500 BC, the Aryans, who had entered India through the passes of the Hindu Kush, had settled down in Northwest India. Sacred texts such as the *Rig Veda* record aspects of their culture. By 600 BC, with the gradual adoption of widespread crop cultivation, several new urban sites had emerged in the Ganges Valley. Many of these were capitals of independent kingdoms, and some cities of that age, such as Mathura, Patna and Varanasi, still exist.

Mother Goddess icon, Indus Valley

EARLY CIVILIZATIONS

— *Extent of Indus Valley Civilization*

☐ *Extent of Aryan settlements*

Copper Harpoon (*c.1500 BC*)
Copper and bronze implements for farming and hunting were used in the Indo-Gangetic valley.

Indus Seal (Tree)
Over 2,000 steatite seals have been found in the Indus Valley, each with an emblem and a script that has still not been fully deciphered.

Burial urn from a Harappan site.

Platter (*c.800 BC*)
A Painted Grey Ware platter from the Ganges Valley area. Austere and functional, such objects were made of baked clay.

TIMELINE

Early Stone Age relics		**1500 BC** Aryans migrate to Northwest India	**1000–600 BC** Later Vedic Age. Painted Grey Ware and iron used	
	6000–1000 BC Neolithic or New Stone Age			
8000 BC		**6000**	**1000**	**900**
8000–4000 BC Mesolithic or Intermediate Stone Age	**2500–1500 BC** Harappan culture flourishes along the Indus Valley		**1000 BC** Iron discovered	**950 BC** Mahabharata war supposed to have been fought
	1800–800 BC Regional farming communities emerge		**1600–1000 BC** Period of the *Rig Veda*	*Palm leaf manuscript extract from the Mahabharata*

Beliefs and Ideas
Sacred Rig Vedic hymns, composed by the Aryans in praise of Nature and various gods, were later absorbed into Hinduism. Several Hindu gods and rituals, even the caste system (see p20), *can be traced to Aryan beliefs.*

This **toy cart** indicates the use of the wheel.

Toy animals testify to the Harappan artisan's skill.

Baked clay was used by the Harappans to shape various objects such as this anteater.

Grain was stored in wide-mouthed jars.

HARAPPAN CULTURE
The Indus Valley (or Harappan) Civilization (2500–1500 BC) had an efficient system of government based on trade and a thriving agricultural economy. Worshippers of a mother goddess and trees, they used water for ritual practice. These Harappan artifacts are in the National Museum.

WHERE TO SEE HARAPPAN ARTIFACTS

Harappan dice at the National Museum

The finest collection of Indus Valley artifacts, arranged chronologically, is in New Delhi's National Museum (see pp 72–3). Some archaeological finds, especially Painted Grey Ware from the site of Indraprastha mentioned in the epic *Mahabharata*, are lodged in a small museum in Delhi's Purana Qila itself (see p84). The state museums at Kurukshetra (see p140) and Mathura (see p161) have a good collection of statues and archaeological finds excavated from this region.

The Origin of Life
An 18th-century painting depicting the popular Hindu myth that life was created when the divine nectar (amrit), hidden in the Ocean of Milk, was won by the gods from the demons (see p23).

600 BC Rise of cities such as Mathura and Varanasi in the Ganges Valley

486 BC Death of the Buddha

468 BC Mahavira, founder of Jainism, dies

327–325 BC Alexander the Great in India

315 BC Megasthenes, Greek ambassador to India, writes social treatise, *Indika*

600	500	400	300

493–461 BC Reign of Ajatshatru, King of Magadha

600 BC *Upanishads*, early philosophical texts

362–321 BC Nanda dynasty

321 BC Accession of Chandragupta, founder of the Mauryan dynasty

Indo-Greek coins

Ancient Empires

Ashokan capital

Uɴᴅᴇʀ ᴛʜᴇ ᴍᴀᴜʀʏᴀɴ ᴇᴍᴘᴇʀᴏʀ Ashoka, North India saw its first large-scale empire. Contact with Central Asia, which began around 200 BC, determined crucial political alliances after the Mauryas, and by the 1st century AD, the Kushanas from Central Asia had an empire that extended up to the Ganges Valley. This period also saw the rise and spread of Buddhism. In the 4th century, the Gupta kings presided over the flowering of classical Sanskrit at the hands of writers such as Kalidasa. The emergence of the Holy Trinity *(see pp22–3)* and temple worship also date from the Gupta Age.

EARLY EMPIRES

☐ *Mauryan Empire*

— *Kushana Empire*

— *Gupta Empire*

Buddhism

A peaceful, non-violent religion, its message of tolerance and social equality won Buddhism many followers, among them the Mauryan emperor Ashoka. Its rise had a profound impact on social, political and cultural life.

Speckled red sandstone was extensively used in Mathura art.

The human form, sensuously carved, has expressive lines. The gold ornaments and elaborate hair styles of the figures reflect the court fashions of the age.

Ashokan Edict

(3rd century BC) Considered valuable historical records, such rock edicts, installed throughout his kingdom, proclaim Ashoka's ethical code (dhamma) *as well as important events.*

TIMELINE

273–232 BC Ashoka's reign

260 BC Battle of Kalinga leads Ashoka to embrace Buddhism

180–165 BC Foundation of Indo-Greek empire by Demetrius

80 BC Maues, Shaka king in Northwest India

AD 78–110 Reign of Kushana king Kanishka; Fourth Buddhist Council held in Kashmir

2nd-century Buddhist begging bowl

200 BC	100 BC	AD 1	AD 100	200

185 BC Accession of Sungas in Magadha

165–145 BC Menander, Indo-Greek king, rules over the northwest

Mauryan sculpture

AD 20–46 Gondophernes, Indo-Parthian king in Taxila; St Thomas comes to South India

150 Rudradaman, the Shaka king in West India; first Sanskrit inscription on imperishable material dates from his reign

Kanishka *(AD 78–110)*
This famous Kushana king came from Central Asia (as the boots and cloak of his headless statue reveal) to control a large part of North India. Another great patron of Buddhism, his reign presided over its spread to China, Central Asia and Afghanistan, along the famous Silk Route.

Yakshas and **yakshis**, male and female nature spirits, as well as the foliage behind them, represent fertility and an abundance of life. Their presence highlights the mood of revelery and fecundity.

Greek features like curly hair and sharp noses distinguish Gandhara sculpture.

Vasantasena, a courtesan, slumped in a drunken state, is helped to her feet.

MATHURA SCHOOL OF ART
Between the 1st and 6th centuries AD, a renowned school of art flourished at Mathura *(see p161)*. Statues of Jain, Buddhist and Hindu divinities, with remarkably expressive faces, were produced along with secular art such as this dramatic 2nd-century Kushana panel, *The Drunken Courtesan.*

WHERE TO SEE ANCIENT ART

The Government Museum, Mathura *(see p161)* and the National Museum, New Delhi *(see pp72–3)* have fine collections of Mauryan, Kushana, Gupta and Sunga sculptures. The Northern Ridge *(see p103)* and Feroze Shah Kotla *(see p97)* have well-preserved Ashokan pillars.

Sunga pillar, National Museum

Gandhara Sculpture
After the 1st century AD, a distinct Hellenistic style first emerged in Gandhara in the northwest. The Buddha was now depicted in a sublime human form, rather than through symbols such as the lotus and chakra, with expressions that recall classical Greek sculpture.

Iron pillar

300–399 *Ramayana, Mahabharata* compiled. *Bhagavad Gita* written

375–415 Reign of Chandragupta II

399–414 Chinese traveller Fa Hsien in India

500–527 Hun control over North India

630–44 Hiuen Tsang, a Chinese Buddhist scholar, travels in India

300	400	500	600	700

335 Accession of Samudragupta

319–20 Accession of Chandragupta I, and establishment of the Gupta dynasty

476 Birth of Aryabhatta, the astronomer

606–47 Harsha's reign

712 Arab conquest of Sind

Gold coin of Samudragupta

18th-century painting of the 4th-century Gupta erotic treatise, Kamasutra

Rajput Dynasties

RAJPUT CLANS ROSE to prominence in North India from the late 7th century. Claiming a high caste warrior status *(kshatriya)*, they traced their lineage to the sun and moon to firmly establish their legitimacy, and ruled over North, West and Central India. After losing Delhi and Kannauj to the Muslims, they confined their activities to the western region, now Rajasthan, where rival clans fought for supremacy. Widely renowned for their loyalty and valour, most Rajput clans were welcomed as allies by Mughal rulers.

Rajput shield with sun emblem

LOCATOR MAP

☐ *Extent of Rajput Kingdoms*

Turbans indicate the home, region and status of a person.

Prithviraj Chauhan of Ajmer
The last Rajput ruler of Delhi, he was defeated in 1192 by Muhammad Ghori. The Qutb Minar and a mosque were built over his citadel, Rai Pithora.

Pageantry was a vital part of the Rajput concept of kingship.

Sacred Beliefs
Rajput kings were patrons of Hinduism and worshipped martial gods such as Hanuman (see p197) and Shakti. They were also prolific builders of beautiful temples.

Sati Sites
Hand imprints mark the sites where women immolated themselves by jumping into their husbands' funeral pyres. This cruel practice, called sati, *was made illegal in 1829.*

TIMELINE

736 Dhilika (Delhi) is founded by the Rajput Tomaras

760 The Palas rule over Bengal and Bihar

800–1036 The Gurjara-Pratiharas rule over Kannauj

750	775	800

11th-century copper plate inscriptions of a Rajput king, Raja Chachuka

800 Shankaracharya, the Hindu philosopher, challenges Buddhism and Jainism

A Rajput court dress

Rajput Art
Rajput rulers were great patrons of architecture and painting. This unusual 18th-century miniature from Jaipur shows Rajput women playing polo (see p195).

Man Singh I of Amber
This loyal Mughal ally, one of the "nine jewels" (navaratna) of Akbar's court, was among the first Rajputs to befriend the Mughals. Such alliances paved the way for peace in North India and a fusion of Hindu and Islamic cultures, especially in architecture.

Palanquins, such as this fanciful one, were carried by a retine of clansmen during ceremonial processions.

The ruler epitomizes the best of Rajput chivalry and valour.

Weapons are an essential part of a Rajput's attire.

WHERE TO SEE RAJPUT INDIA

Amber *(see pp200–201)* and the jungle fort at Ranthambhore *(see pp 224–5)* are some famous Rajput forts in this region. The museum inside the City Palace, Jaipur *(see pp188–91)* and Alwar *(see p206)* display private collections. The National Museum, New Delhi, also has a wide display of Rajput miniature paintings *(see pp30–31)*, sculpture and jewellery.

Amber Fort *(see pp200–201)*

A ROYAL PROCESSION

Rajput princes enjoyed a divine status in the eyes of their clan. Rajputana, literally the land of princes, once had some 21 kingdoms ruled by rival clans which included the Sisodias of Mewar, Kachhawahas of Amber and Jaipur, Rathors of Marwar and Bikaner, Haras of Kota and Bundi, Chauhans of Ajmer, and Bhattis of Jaisalmer.

883–1026 The Hindu Shahis rule over Kabul and the Punjab

973–1192 The Chahamanas of Sakambhari rule over Ajmer, Rajasthan

974–1238 The Solankis rule Anhilwad in Gujarat

875　900　925　950　975

916–1202 The Chandellas rule over Bundelkhand and build the Khajuraho temples in Central India

Phad, a Rajput folk painting

974–1233 The Paramars rule Dhar in Central India

10th-century Khajuraho temple

The Delhi Sultans

Astrolabe

THE FABULOUS WEALTH of India attracted Arab traders and raiders, such as Mahmud of Ghazni. A slave general of Muhammad Ghori, called Qutbuddin Aibak, established himself in North India and founded the Mamluk (Slave) Dynasty. Followed by the Khiljis, Tughlaqs, Sayyids and Lodis, these Muslim rulers, called the Sultans of Delhi, established an empire that survived into the early 16th century and changed the cultural and urban milieu of much of the subcontinent by introducing new technologies and customs.

COMING OF ISLAM

— *Empire of Mamluks (1236)*

☐ *Empire of Tughlaqs (1335)*

Illustrated Koran *(17th century)*
The noble Islamic art of calligraphy was introduced by Muslim rulers and used to embellish royal decrees, manuscripts and copies of the Koran, as well as buildings.

Ceramic Tiles
Jamali Kamali (see p111) has fine examples of this Islamic art.

Qutbuddin Aibak built the first storey of the Qutb Minar and a mosque to proclaim his victory over the Rajputs.

Quwwat-ul-Islam, which means "Might of Islam", was the first congregational mosque in Delhi.

***Madrasa* and tomb of Alauddin Khilji**

Persian Wheel
The water wheel came in the wake of Muslim rule. Its simple technology is still used in rural areas to draw underground water for irrigation.

TIMELINE

1000–1027 Mahmud of Ghazni makes 17 raids, carries back loot

1206–10 Reign of Qutbuddin Aibak, founder of the Mamluk Dynasty. Erects the Qutb Minar

1175–1206 Invasion of Muhammad Ghori

1221 Mongol invasion of Northwest India led by Chengiz Khan

1050	1100	1150	1200	1250

Sultanate weaponry

1192 Defeat of Prithviraj Chauhan in Second Battle of Tarain at the hands of Muhammad Ghori

1210–36 Reign of Iltutmish

1266–86 Reign of Balban

1236–40 Reign of Razia, first woman ruler of Delhi

Feroze Shah Tughlaq added the topmost storeys in 1368.

Iltutmish, Qutbuddin's successor, built the second and third storeys.

Alai Darwaza was built by Alauddin Khilji in 1311.

WHERE TO SEE THE DELHI SULTANATE

The Mehrauli area (see pp110–13), Hauz Khas (see p106), Tughlaqabad (see p114), Feroze Shah Kotla (see p97), Purana Qila (see p84) and Lodi Gardens (see p79) show the various architectural styles of the Sultanate. The National Museum (see pp72–3) has a fine collection of artifacts dating to this period.

Begampuri Masjid (see p109)

Nizamuddin Auliya
Mystic sages called Sufis were among the immigrants from Central Asia. This 17th-century miniature shows Nizamuddin Auliya (see p82) with the poet Amir Khusrau. Together, they raised metaphysical love, poetry and music to the level of divine worship.

Music
Amir Khusrau, poet and musician, is said to have introduced the multi-stringed sitar and the raga style to North Indian music.

THE QUTB MINAR
In 1193, Qutbuddin Aibak built the Qutb Minar (see p112) and a mosque to announce the advent of the Muslim sultans. This 19th-century lithograph shows a part of the Qutb complex that was built over the remains of an earlier Rajput citadel at Mehrauli (see pp110–11).

1288–93 Venetian traveller Marco Polo visits South India
1296–1316 Reign of Alauddin Khilji, great general, builder and administrator
Tughlaq coin
1414–51 Sayyids of Delhi

1300 | **1350** | **1400** | **1450**

1320–1414 Tughlaqs rule Delhi
1398 Timur the Lame's invasion of Delhi
1451–1526 Rule of Lodis, last of Delhi's Sultans
1302 New capital built at Siri
1290–1320 Khiljis rule Delhi

Bara Gumbad, a 15th-century Lodi tomb

The Great Mughals

Mughal cooking vessel

THE MUGHALS, like the Ottomans of Turkey, the Safavids of Iran and the Tudors of England, were one of the greatest medieval dynasties. For over 200 years they held firm political control over the subcontinent, establishing a stable administrative system and a rich pluralistic culture blending the best of Hindu and Islamic traditions. Great patrons of art and architecture, they also encouraged the translation of Sanskrit texts into Persian. Markets and cities flourished under them, making India famous.

MUGHAL EMPIRE

☐ *Mughal Empire at the end of the 17th century*

Hierarchy of nobles depended on the rank given by the emperor.

Buland Darwaza at Fatehpur Sikri
Erected to celebrate Akbar's victory over Gujarat in 1572–3, Buland Darwaza (see p173) is part of the great Mughal architectural legacy that still dominates the region.

Rajput princes were often loyal Mughal supporters. Shah Jahan's grandmother was a Rajput princess.

Mughal Art
A ruby-studded ceremonial gold spoon, Jahangir's jade wine cup, a gold enamelled glass hookah base and Mughal miniature paintings (see pp30–31) offer vivid glimpses of their extravagant patronage of art.

TIMELINE

1526 Babur defeats Ibrahim Lodi at Panipat

Babur, the first Mughal emperor

1539 Sher Shah Sur defeats Humayun at Chausa

1540–55 Sur Sultans rule in Delhi

1556 Death of Humayun. Accession of his son Akbar

Jahangir

1530 Death of Babur. His son Humayun succeeds him

Akbar the Great

1569 Humayun's Tomb built at Delhi

1571–85 Fatehpur Sikri built

1605 Death of Akbar. His son Jahangir succeeds him

1525 1550 1575 1600

Order and Symmetry
The "taming of the land" that took place under the Mughals, whether it was their landscaped gardens or their system of justice and revenue settlement, was founded on this dual principle.

Shah Jahan
with his son in the foreground receiving a gift from a noble.

Diwan-i-Khas
was used for special audience with the emperor and his advisors.

Court robes
and turbans indicated status and religion.

A railing
separated the imperial circle from lower state officials.

WHERE TO SEE MUGHAL INDIA

Fatehpur Sikri *(see pp170–73)* and the Taj Mahal *(see pp154–5)* are among the finest examples of Mughal architecture in this region. The area around Delhi's Red Fort *(see pp94–5)* also has several Mughal relics. Important collections of Mughal art, manuscripts, coins, jewellery, costumes and armoury are housed in both the National Museum, Delhi *(see pp72–3)* and the City Palace Museum, Jaipur *(see pp188–9).*

Mughal necklace

Military Organization
All senior administrators (mansabdars) *maintained an armed retinue* (sawars) *and rank* (zat) *determined salary.*

SHAH JAHAN'S COURT

The splendour of the Mughal court is illustrated in this 17th-century painting of Shah Jahan among his nobles, grouped in strict hierarchical order round the throne. Mughal emperors, seated in an elevated alcove, used glittering court rituals to display their supreme political position as they took stock of the state affairs from their officials.

1622 Tomb of Itimad-ud-Daulah built by Nur Jahan at Agra

1638–48 Shah Jahan builds new capital at Shahjahanabad, Delhi

1659 Aurangzeb crowned emperor

1707 Death of Aurangzeb, the last Great Mughal

| 1625 | 1650 | 1675 | 1700 | 1725 |

1652 Taj Mahal completed

Aurangzeb

1627 Accession of Shah Jahan

The Taj Mahal

European Traders, Colonizers and Mercenaries

THE INDIAN MUTINY OF 1857

☐ *Areas where British administration was disputed*

• *Site of major revolt in 1857*

CRIPPLED BY THE SACK of Delhi in 1739 by Nadir Shah of Persia, Mughal power declined rapidly. This was exploited by petty rulers, European mercenaries, and the British East India Company, set up in the 1690s to trade in spices and cotton.

Sahib and mahout   Its commercial success led to the rise of the Company as a political power, which ushered in some social reforms and new power equations. Yet, the social instability engendered by the Company's unpopular trade and political practices erupted in the Indian Mutiny or Great Revolt of 1857.

British officer killing a rebel leader at Fatehpur.

The Decline of the Mughals
Nadir Shah's plunder of Delhi (see p92) was the signal for the rise of the Jats and Marathas. Suraj Mal Jat (see p166) filled Bharatpur Fort, seen above, with looted Mughal treasures.

Sepoys mutinied against animal grease on bullets as it violated religious taboos.

Economic Exploitation
A 19th-century lithograph shows the impoverishment of cotton ginners as cheap English mill-made cloth flooded the Indian market.

Indian rebels led by disgruntled princes ultimately lost the war.

TIMELINE

1757 Clive's victory at the Battle of Plassey establishes political supremacy of the Company in Bengal

1761 Ahmad Shah Abdali defeats Marathas in the Third Battle of Panipat

Nadir Shah's battle axe

1750

1775

1739 Nadir Shah invades Delhi

1764 Battle of Buxar gives the Company the Diwani of Bengal and the right to collect revenue

1771 Marathas occupy Delhi

1770 Great Bengal Famine

A Maratha soldier

A Nabob and his Concubines
A corruption of nawab, this name described officials who made huge fortunes from the East India Company's cotton and spice trade in India. Many adopted the feudal lifestyles of the Indian princes as this 19th-century painting shows.

The plains of North India were the main battle areas.

Palanquins transported rebel princes and gentlefolk to the scene of battle.

Indian Sepoys
The Company's commercial interests were protected by its military establishment, which employed Indian foot soldiers called sepoys.

WHERE TO SEE EUROPEAN INDIA

Sardhana (see p142) has a cathedral built by Begum Samroo, the Indian wife of Walter Reinhardt, a European mercenary. Meerut's church, where the first shots of the sepoy mutiny were fired, survives in mint condition (see p142). The cantonments in Meerut and Agra, the Agra cemetery (see p152) and St James's Church in Delhi (see p101) are other sites that go back to the time of the Indian Mutiny.

Sardhana Cathedral (see p142)

SEPOYS REBELLING AT FATEHPOOR
This lithograph of a pitched battle during the Mutiny show sepoys and Indian leaders being tackled by the Company's troops. The Indian Mutiny or Great Revolt of 1857 was seen as India's first war of independence from colonial rule by some nationalists as it shook the foundation of the East India Company's rule in India.

1784 William Jones elected first president of the Asiatic Society of Bengal

1803 Delhi captured by the British

1829 *Sati* abolished

1835 Company strikes its own coins omitting Mughal emperor's name

Queen Victoria's head on a Company coin

1853 First railway from Bombay to Thana

1857–8 The Indian Mutiny

1856 Annexation of Oudh leads to wide public outrage against the Company

Oudh's Nawab Wajid Ali Shah

1800 | 1825 | 1850

Pax Britannica

The Victoria Cross

THE FOUNDATION OF BRITISH RULE, or the Raj, was laid only after the Indian Mutiny, which truly revealed the unpopularity of the East India Company. An Act of Parliament in 1858 brought its rule to a close and its Indian territories became part of Britain's empire. India was now ruled directly by the Crown through a viceroy. Though the Raj was unabashedly Victorian and conservative, and its *raison d'être* was economic profit and political control, its abiding legacy was the political unification of the subcontinent, and the introduction of modern Western education, a centralized civil administration and judicial system, along with a wide network of railways and postal services.

BRITISH INDIA

☐ *British territory, 1858*

Old Delhi
is relegated to the background.

Indian attendants
in viceregal livery re-enact a Mughal procession.

The Steel Frame
Some 2,000 British officers ruled over a subcontinent of 300 million people. The paternalistic civil service brought order and justice even to remote outposts.

Memsahib with her Tailor
Despite the climate, the English clung to their own dress. Children were sent "home" to study, and a large Indian staff enabled a leisurely lifestyle.

TIMELINE

Lord Canning, the first Viceroy

1859 Withdrawal of Doctrine of Lapse, a major cause of the 1857 revolt

1861 Indian Council Act

Lord Dalhousie, author of the notorious Doctrine of Lapse (see p319)

1875

1858 Victoria proclaims Lord Canning first Viceroy of India

1876 Victoria proclaims herself Empress of India

1865 Telegraphic communication is established with Europe

1877 Lytton's Delhi Durbar

A Sahib Travelling
A vast rail network was set up by the British to facilitate commerce and travel. This lithograph of first-class travel, a privilege of "whites only", is from the 19th century.

Raj Cuisine
While kababs, curry and rice became a part of British culinary preference, Westernized Indians took to drinking tea and nibbling biscuits. An early 20th-century biscuit tin label reflects this exchange of tastes.

Caparisoned elephants carry the new rulers.

Crowds line the streets to see the grand spectacle.

WHERE TO SEE BRITISH INDIA

Raisina Hill and the surrounding area *(see pp68–9)*, Agra's St John's College *(see p152)*, Mayo College *(see p219)* in Ajmer are examples of colonial architecture. Delhi's Coronation Park *(see p103)* and the University area *(see p103)* are other sites with a Raj connection.

Detail of India Gate *(see p71)*

THE DURBAR, 1903

This painting of Curzon's Delhi Durbar (1903), held to celebrate the coronation of Edward VII, shows a procession winding through the historic streets of Delhi. Held periodically, such assemblies announced both the grandeur and the political might of British rule in India.

1878
Vernacular Press Act

1885
Indian National Congress founded

1883–4 Illbert Bill controversy

1878–80 Second Anglo-Afghan War

Lord Curzon, Viceroy 1899–1905

1899
Curzon becomes Viceroy

1905
Partition of Bengal by Curzon causes national outrage

1900

1904 Ancient Monuments Preservation Act

The Freedom Movement

Gandhi's spinning wheel

THE FOUNDING of the Indian National Congress in 1885 gave Indians a platform from which to demand freedom from foreign rule. Their ideology was provided by Gandhi, whose message of non-violence and economic self-reliance gave them moral confidence, and united castes and communities under a common cause. At first the movement for freedom was ruthlessly suppressed, but by the 1930s it became too large for the British to handle. Finally, weakened by World War II and under growing international pressure, England granted India formal independence in 1947.

FREEDOM MOVEMENT

• *Major towns associated with the Freedom Movement*

Huge crowds turned out to register their support. Gandhi united castes and communities as never before.

Khadi, homespun cloth, was worn as a statement of patriotism.

Round Table Conference (1931)
The British tried to work out a settlement with Gandhi, accompanied by formidable campaigner and poet, Sarojini Naidu.

The police dogged public assemblies, often brutally beating the audience.

The Cellular Jail, Andaman Islands
Hundreds of freedom fighters were shipped here by the British. Many were hanged, some died of diseases such as malaria. Now a national monument, the jail's popular name, Kala Pani ("black waters"), recalls its dark past.

TIMELINE

Rabindranath Tagore

1906 Muslim League formed at Dacca

1907 Congress splits at Surat between the moderates and extremists

1908 Tilak, a prominent nationalist, sentenced to six years transportation on charges of sedition

1910

1913 Rabindranath Tagore wins the Nobel Prize for Literature

1917 Gandhi takes up the cause of indigo farmers at Champaran, Bihar

1914 Canada refuses Indians aboard the ship *Kamagata Maru* permission to land

1915 Home Rule League started by Annie Besant

1919 Police fires at unarmed crowd at Jallianwala Bagh in Amritsar, Punjab

1920 Non-cooperation Movement launched by Gandhi

1920

New Delhi
New Delhi was declared the Raj's capital in 1911. This early photo shows Parliament House, then the Legislative Assembly building.

Nehru and Jinnah
Brilliant lawyers who joined Gandhi's national movement, they enjoyed an iconic status in India and Pakistan after Independence.

Gandhi delivered his powerful message of freedom at public meetings.

WHERE TO SEE THE FREEDOM MOVEMENT

The National Archives *(see p71)* and the Gandhi Smriti *(see p78)* have a permanent exhibition on the Freedom Movement. Panels on this theme are also displayed at the Jawahar Pavilion in Pragati Maidan *(see p85)*. Teen Murti House *(see p78)* offers a view of Nehru's life.

Gandhi Samadhi, Rajghat *(see p97)*

The Partition (1947)
A huge displacement of people across the borders took place at the division of the subcontinent into India and Pakistan, leading to an eruption of violent communal riots.

MAHATMA GANDHI
Called Mahatma ("great spirit"), MK Gandhi returned to India from South Africa in 1915 as a protest against apartheid. He travelled across the subcontinent, launching a moral crusade that encouraged non-violent Civil Disobedience against colonial rule.

1930–32 Gandhi leads the Dandi Salt March and Civil Disobedience Movement

Subhash Chandra Bose and members of the Indian National Army

1948 Assassination of Mahatma Gandhi

1940 Muslim League adopts the Pakistan Resolution

1930

1940

1942 Quit India Movement

1939 Resignation of the Congress Ministers

1947 India attains Independence

Bungalow designed for a new capital at Delhi in the 1930s

Nehru is sworn in as the first Prime Minister by Lord Mountbatten

India Today

Cell-phones are a familiar sight

INDIA CELEBRATED 50 YEARS of independence in 1997. Nehru, the first prime minister, laid the foundations for a modern nation state with a democratic, secular polity, a strong industrial base and a planned economy, with non-alignment as the keystone of its foreign policy. India's one billion people speak 18 languages, and though many of them are illiterate and unemployed, a vigorous and free press and electoral system ensure that their interests and rights are safeguarded and well represented. The two major national political parties are the Congress, and the more right-wing Bharatiya Janata Party.

1,000 million
700 million
400 million

1941   1961   1981   2001

POPULATION FIGURES

☐ *Growth of population*

New Delhi
was built between 1911 and 1933 by Lutyens and Baker.

Rural India
More than half the country's population lives in its villages. An adult literacy programme is under way to educate the disadvantaged, particularly women.

The Nehru Family
Jawaharlal Nehru is seen here with his daughter Indira Gandhi (who was not related to Mahatma Gandhi), and her son Rajiv Gandhi. All three were prime ministers of India. Rajiv's Italian-born widow, Sonia, now heads the Congress Party.

The Indian flag
is a tricolour of saffron, white and green, with a *chakra* (wheel) in the centre.

TIMELINE

1952 First General Election
1953 Mount Everest scaled by Hillary and Tenzing
1964 Death of Jawaharlal Nehru, first prime minister
1971 War with Pakistan, birth of Bangladesh
1977 Janata Party, the first non-Congress coalition, takes power
Indian flag

| 1960 | 1965 | 1970 | 1975 | 1980 |

1955 Bandung Conference on Non-Alignment
1962 India-China War
1966 Indira Gandhi becomes prime minister
1965 War with Pakistan
1974 First nuclear test, Pokhran
1975 Indira Gandhi declares the unpopular Emergency
1980 Indira Gandhi returns as prime minister
1982 India sends scientific team to Antarctica
1950 India becomes a Republic

Industrial Development
Nehru, the architect of the country's industrial base, hailed factories as the new temples of modern India. India is now a major industrial power with a huge workforce of skilled workers.

Cricket
Introduced by the British, this game is now a national obsession. Sachin Tendulkar, the "little master", is regarded by many as the greatest batsman since Donald Bradman.

The Indian Army is one of the largest in the world.

South Block and its twin, North Block, were designed to flank Raisina Hill.

Protest Rallies
India's vibrant democracy expresses itself through popular protest (dharna) in which women figure prominently. The Narmada Bachao activists, seen here, have mobilized women and displaced tribal people against the World Bank-funded Narmada Dam.

Amartya Sen
He won the Nobel Prize for Economics in 1998 for his work on development economics, based on studies of India's literacy, population, famine and the status of women.

THE REPUBLIC DAY PARADE
A magnificent parade on 26 January celebrates the day when India became a republic in 1950. A colourful flypast, folk dances and floats celebrate its pluralistic society, and the president, as head of the republic, takes the salute at Rajpath.

1984 Indira Gandhi assassinated, her son Rajiv Gandhi succeeds her as prime minister

1990 VP Singh becomes prime minister; announcement of reservation for backward classes

1998 The right-wing Bharatiya Janta Party (BJP) comes to power for the first time

AB Vajpayee becomes prime minister in 1998

1985	1990	1995	2000	2005

A woman casts her vote

1992 Destruction of Babri Masjid in the state of Uttar Pradesh leads to communal riots

1991 Rajiv Gandhi assassinated; New Liberalization Policy under Prime Minister Narasimha Rao

2001 Earthquake in Gujarat

1999 Conflict with Pakistan over Kashmir at Kargil; 13th General Elections re-elect a BJP-led government

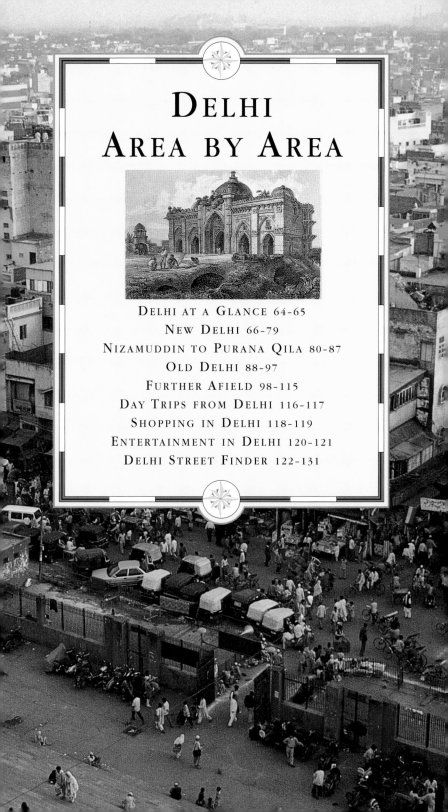

DELHI
AREA BY AREA

Delhi at a Glance

Situated along the yamuna river, New Delhi was built by the British in the 1930s and is the youngest of several historic cities that have occupied this site. Now a noisy and chaotic metropolis of 14 million people and a mélange of shanty settlements and smart colonies, it is still dotted with the remains of its interesting past. There are museums and art galleries with impressive collections, and its shops offer a tempting array of handicrafts. Delhi is a major cultural centre of the country with music, dance and art events held throughout the year.

The Jami Masjid *(see p92) is the largest congregational mosque in Asia with lively bazaars in the surrounding lanes.*

Connaught Place *(see p76), was built in the 1930s as the business centre of New Delhi, in concentric circles round a central park. Its stately colonnaded corridors contain shops and offices.*

NEW DELHI *(see pp66–79)*

Rashtrapati Bhavan *(see pp68–70) is the official residence of the President of India. Called Viceroy's House in colonial times, it was designed by Edwin Lutyens and occupies the crest of Raisina Hill. Its forecourt is the venue for colourful state pageantry.*

The National Museum *(see pp72–5) houses the most comprehensive collection of antiquities in the country. This 2nd-century Sunga panel of a grieving woman is part of a stunning section on sculpture from various periods and places.*

0 kilometres   1

0 miles   1

◁ **Swirling traffic in the narrow lanes of the old city around Jami Masjid**

OLD DELHI
(see pp88–97)

Red Fort (see pp94–5), *an impressive fort-palace built by Shah Jahan, was the seat of Mughal power. After the Indian Mutiny of 1857, the British converted it into a garrison and it was stripped of many precious treasures.*

The Crafts Museum (see pp86–7) *complex offers an insight into India's cultural, craft and rural traditions. The museum exhibits textiles, folk art and objects of everyday use in terracotta, metal and wood.*

NIZAMUDDIN TO PURANA QILA
(see pp80–87)

Humayun's Tomb (see p83) *is where the second Mughal emperor Humayun is buried. This garden tomb with its imposing double dome is considered by many to be the first great Mughal mausoleum in this region.*

NEW DELHI

T HE BRITISH BUILT New Delhi, between 1911 and 1931, to be the showcase of the Empire. On Independence, this grand imperial capital became the official and bureaucratic centre of the new Indian nation. Today, Viceroy's House is the president's residence, and ministers and civil servants live nearby in spacious bungalows along the tree-lined

Gargoyle

avenues. Kingsway, the east-west processional avenue leading to India Gate, is now Rajpath, where every 26 January the Republic Day Parade is held *(see p71)*. The National Museum is on Janpath. To the north are Connaught Place, the Birla Mandir and the cultural complex at Mandi House. Despite strict security restrictions, New Delhi is the city's most impressive area.

SIGHTS AT A GLANCE

Historic Buildings, Streets and Plazas
India Gate **6**
Rajpath **4**
Rashtrapati Bhavan **1**
Vijay Chowk **2**

Churches and Temples
Lakshmi Narayan Mandir **11**
Church of Redemption **3**

Museums
Gandhi Smriti **14**
National Gallery of Modern Art **7**
National Museum **5**
Nehru Memorial Museum and Library **13**

Monuments
Jantar Mantar **12**
Ugrasen's Baoli **9**

Gardens
Lodi Gardens **15**

Shops and Markets
Connaught Place **10**
Khan Market **16**

Theatres and Art Galleries
Mandi House Complex **8**

GETTING THERE

This area is well served by buses and taxis. Once there, the best vistas are from Vijay Chowk.

KEY

▨	Street-by-Street map *See pp68–9*
🚉	Railway station
Ⓜ	Metro station
🚌	Bus station
🅿	Parking
🚓	Police station
⊠	Post office
✚	Hospital
🛕	Temple
卐	*Gurudwara*
✟	Church
🏛	Tomb

0 metres   750
0 yards   750

◁ **India Gate and the elegant statue canopy designed by Lutyens**

Street-by-Street: Around Vijay Chowk

T HE BARREN, TREELESS GROUNDS around Raisina Hill were
selected as the site of the new capital city. Now a
well-guarded verdant area, it houses India's president,
ministers and officials, as well as its Parliament and
ministries. Imperial hierarchical conventions, both
spatial and political laid down by the British are still
followed, so that even today, Indian ministers and
officials live in spacious bungalows on broad tree-
shaded avenues around Rashtrapati Bhavan where no
high-rise buildings are allowed. From Vijay Chowk,
Lutyens's grand central vista lies ahead – large trees
and fountains line the lawns of Rajpath
up to India Gate, the Canopy and the
National Stadium at the far end.

★ Vijay Chowk
*A pair of red sandstone
obelisk-shaped fountains
flank this forecourt that
overlooks a grand vista* ❷

North Block
has an imposing
Central Hall
which is open
to the public.

Sansad Bhavan is
also known as
Parliament House.

The Iron Gates
*Copied from a pair
Lutyens saw in
Chiswick, England,
these are held by
highly ornamental
sandstone gateposts.
Rashtrapati Bhavan
lies to the west of them.*

KEY

– – – – Suggested route

EDWIN LANDSEER LUTYENS

**Building the Secretariats
on rocky scrubland**

Architect Edwin Landseer
Lutyens (1869–1944), President
of the Royal Academy from 1938
to 1944, was commissioned to
design India's new capital in
1911. With Herbert Baker, his
colleague, it took him 20 years to
build the city in a unique style
that combined Western
Classicism with Indian decorative
motifs. The result is classical in
form and English in manner with
Neo-Mughal gardens and grand vistas meeting at verdant
roundabouts. Delayed by World War I and quarrels
between Baker and Lutyens, spiralling costs met by Indian
revenues led Mahatma Gandhi to term it a "white elephant".
Ironically, the British lived here for only 16 years.

★ South Block
*The Prime Minister's Office
and the Defence Ministry
are located within this
block, a high security zone.*

Sunehri Bagh
This gently curving street leads to a picturesque roundabout with a simple 18th-century mosque built by a pir called Sayyid Sahib. Shady trees are a standard feature of all Lutyens's avenues.

LOCATOR MAP
See Street Finder map 4

Roundabout
Beautifully landscaped road intersections are a haven for workers during lunch.

India Gate

Vayu Bhavan

Udyog Bhavan

ILAL NEHRU MARG

KAMARAJ ROAD

SUNEHRI BAGH ROAD

LEIX ROAD

KRISHNA MENON MARG

0 metres   25
0 yards   25

Statue of Kamaraj
He was Congress Party President (1963–6).

★ **Bungalow-lined Avenues**
Strict building bylaws preserve the original architecture of the colonial bungalows in the tree-lined avenues of this area.

STAR SIGHTS

★ **Vijay Chowk**

★ **Bungalow-lined Avenues**

★ **South Block**

Rashtrapati Bhavan seen through Lutyens's ornate iron gates

Rashtrapati Bhavan ❶

Map 4 E2. ☎ *(011) 2301 5321*. 🚫 *to the public. Visit permits can sometimes be obtained from the Deputy Military Secretary to the President of India.* **Change of Guard Ceremony** *Apr–Oct: 6:30am; Nov–Mar: 7am Sat.* **Mughal Gardens** 🚫 *Feb–Mar.*

Dᴇsɪɢɴᴇᴅ by Edwin Lutyens *(see p68)* to be the focal point of New Delhi during British rule, the house built for the viceroy, which is today the President of India's official residence, stands at the crest of Raisina Hill. This 20th-century architectural masterpiece covers an area of 4.5 acres (2 ha) of land. The cupola of its copper and sandstone dome rises 55 m (180 ft) above the ground.

Within are courtyards, banqueting halls, state apartments and private living quarters. The *pièce de résistance* is the grand Durbar Hall, where all important Indian state and ceremonial occasions are held. Situated directly beneath the dome and forming the centrepiece of the "H"-shaped building, this circular hall was originally the Throne Room and contains the two gold and crimson thrones Lutyens designed for the viceroy and vicereine. To the west, the beautifully landscaped grounds include the formal **Mughal Gardens**. These terraced gardens with their watercourses and fountains built on three levels, end with Lutyens's "butterfly garden", where the flowers particularly attract butterflies.

Jaipur Column

Vijay Chowk ❷

Map 4 F2. **N Block** 🚫 *9am–6pm Mon–Fri.* **Sansad Bhavan** 🚫 *11am–5pm. Visit is subject to Parliament not being in session.*

Tʜᴇ ᴀʀᴇᴀ where Rajpath meets Raisina Hill, known as Vijay Chowk, was planned as a commanding approach to the Viceroy's House. This is where the unforgettable "Beating Retreat" ceremony takes place each year on 29 January *(see p41)*.

Rising impressively from the levelled top of Raisina Hill are the two virtually identical **Secretariat** buildings designed by Herbert Baker and known as the North and South Blocks. These long classical edifices house the Home and Finance ministries and the Ministry of Foreign Affairs. The stately Central Hall of North Block (to the left, if facing Vijay Chowk) is open to the public.

Sited to the north of Vijay Chowk, Baker's circular **Sansad Bhavan** (Parliament House) was a later addition following the Montagu-Chelmsford Reforms of 1919, to house the Legislative Assembly. The Constitution of India was drafted here in the early days of Independence. Today, both the Rajya Sabha (Upper House) and the Lok Sabha (House of the People) meet here when Parliament is in session. The Lok Sabha's often boisterous debates take place in the Central Hall.

Sansad Bhavan (Parliament House), where the Constitution of India was drafted

Cathedral Church of the Redemption ❸

Church Rd. **Map** 4 E1. 🔲 *(011) 2309 4229.* ⭘ *7am–noon; 4–6pm daily.*

HENRY ALEXANDER MEDD (1892–1977), the architect of this magnificent church, was inspired by Palladio's Church of II Redentore in Venice, from which it also derives its name. Consecrated in 1931, the cathedral formed an integral element of the plan for the imperial capital complex, and was built as the main Anglican church for senior British officials in New Delhi. Today, it is the diocese of the Bishop of the Church of Northern India. Among the many memorial tablets inside the church, there is one in honour of its architect.

The Neo-Classical Cathedral Church of the Redemption

Rajpath ❹

Map 5 A2. **National Archives** 🔲 *(011) 2338 5000.* ⭘ *9am–6pm Mon–Fri.* ⬤ *Sat, Sun & public hols.* **Indira Gandhi National Centre for the Arts** 🔲 *(011) 2338 9216.*

THIS TWO-MILE-LONG avenue, used for parades and lined with ornamental canals and fountains along the lawns on either side, is very popular with the residents of Delhi on steamy summer evenings.

The **National Archives**, situated at the intersection with Janpath, houses a major collection of state records and private papers. Opposite is the **Indira Gandhi National Centre for the Arts** (IGNCA) which has an archive of rare manuscripts, and holds national and international exhibitions and symposia.

National Museum ❺

See pp72–3.

India Gate ❻

Map 5 B2.

AT THE EASTERN end of Rajpath, the 9-m (30-ft) wide India Gate was built to commemorate the Indian and British soldiers who died in World War I and those who fell in battle in the North-West Frontier Province and the Third Afghan War. An eternal flame burns in memory of unknown soldiers who died in the 1971 Indo-Pakistan war. Facing India Gate is the sandstone canopy where King George V's statue was installed after his death in 1936. The statue is now at Coronation Park *(see p103).* Around India Gate are the stately homes of erstwhile Indian princes, including Hyderabad House where official state banquets are held, and Jaipur, Bikaner, Patiala and Baroda Houses.

India Gate

National Gallery of Modern Art ❼

Jaipur House, near India Gate. **Map** 5 C2. 🔲 *(011) 2338 2835.* ⭘ *10am–5pm Tue–Sun.* ⬤ *Mon & public hols.* 🔲 🔲

JAIPUR HOUSE, the former residence of the Jaipur maharajas, is one of India's largest museums of modern art. Its vast collection includes graphics, paintings and sculptures dating from the mid-19th century to the present day. The galleries display works of British landscape painters such as the Daniells, and early Indian artists such as the Tagores, Jamini Roy, Amrita Shergill and Raja Ravi Varma. Works of contemporary artists such as MF Husain, Ram Kumar, KG Subramanyam and Anjolie Ela Menon are also seen here. Reproductions of paintings are sold at the gallery shop.

REPUBLIC DAY PARADE

Indians love parades and ever since 1950, when India became a republic, the Republic Day parade on 26 January has always attracted large crowds despite the often chilly weather. The president, the prime minister and other dignitaries watch as soldiers in dashing uniforms from the many regiments and squadrons of the Army, Navy and Air Force march smartly past. Brightly dress-ed schoolchildren, civil defence services personnel and others quick-step down the grand vistas of Rajpath to the rousing percussion of military bands. Most popular are the Camel Corps and the inventive floats representing each state of the country. A ceremonial fly-past by the Indian Air Force signals the end of the parade.

Republic Day Parade

The National Museum ❺

Dancing girl from 2500 BC

FIVE MILLENNIA OF INDIAN HISTORY can be explored at the National Museum, with a collection of more than 150,000 pieces of Indian art. The nucleus collection of about 1,000 artifacts was sent to London in the winter of 1948–9 for an exhibition at the Royal Academy's Burlington House. After its return, it was housed in the Durbar Hall of Rashtrapati Bhavan until the present building, built of the same beige and pink stone as the imposing new capital, was complete in 1960. The Museum's collection of Indus Valley relics and Central Asian treasures from the Silk Route is considered among the finest in the world.

★ Dara Shikoh's Marriage Procession
An 18th-century Mughal miniature painting in gold and natural pigments.

★ Nataraja
This 12th-century Chola statue of the cosmic dance of Lord Shiva is the centre-piece of the museum's South Indian bronzes.

The Coins and Indian Scripts Gallery displays an impressive collection of coins and the evolution of the Indian script.

Jewellery Gallery

Ground floor

★ Kubera
A rare example of a Hindu god shown as a 2nd-century Kushana (see pp46–7) grandee with marked Central Asian features is among a large collection of Mathura Art.

Entrance

Silk painting, 7th–8th century

THE SERINDIAN COLLECTION

Almost 700 years after the Silk Route fell into disuse, Sir Aurel Stein, a British archae-ologist, led a series of expeditions (1900–16) to un-cover its treasures. On view at the National Museum, Stein's Central Asian collec-tion of the artifacts he found in the Taklamakan Desert has silk paintings, Buddhist manuscripts and valuable records of life along this ancient trade route.

Terracotta Mask
This unusual human mask made of terracotta dates back to 2700 BC, and was unearthed in Mohenjodaro in the early 20th century.

Aurangzeb's Sword

The personal sword of the Mughal emperor Aurangzeb, crafted in 1675 in the Indo-Persian style, has quotations from the Koran inscribed on it.

VISITORS' CHECKLIST

Janpath. **Map** 5 A2. ☎ (011) 2301 9272. ⏰ 10am–5pm Tue–Sun. ⬤ Mon & public hols. 📷 📸 extra charges. 🎥 11:30am, 2:30pm, 4pm. 🚻 🔲 ♿ 🔳 **Film shows, lectures, presentations and special exhibitions.**

Gold Brocade

This 19th-century silk wedding sari woven in Varanasi is embellished with motifs in gold thread.

Wood carvings in the form of religious statues, carved doors and lintels are some of the exhibits here.

Second floor

First floor

★ Illuminated Koran

A superb example of the elegant Islamic art of calligraphy, this gilded 18th-century Koran is one of a collection that also has a 8th-century Koran in the ancient Kufic script. The latter is among the oldest of its kind in the world.

GALLERY GUIDE

The collection is displayed on three floors, grouped according to theme, epoch and style. The central foyer itself has a display of sculptures from various parts of the country. The museum also has a library and auditorium where film shows and lectures are regularly held. Information on these is published in the newspapers. Information regarding catalogues and souvenirs can be had at the ticket office in the foyer. The display is changed from time to time for variety, and special exhibitions are also mounted.

KEY TO FLOORPLAN

- ☐ Indus Valley Culture
- ☐ Ancient and Medieval Sculpture
- ☐ Chola Bronzes
- ☐ Buddhist Art
- ☐ Indian Miniatures
- ☐ Decorative Arts
- ▦ Manuscripts and Wall Paintings
- ☐ Central Asian Antiquities
- ☐ Textiles, Arms and Armour, Musical Instruments

STAR EXHIBITS

- ★ **Dara Shikoh's Marriage Procession**
- ★ **Nataraja**
- ★ **Kubera**
- ★ **Illuminated Koran**

Exploring the National Museum Collection

SPREAD OVER THREE FLOORS radiating from an octagonal courtyard, the museum has 30 galleries (some closed for renovation or devoted to temporary exhibitions). The impressive collection includes sculpture, paintings, jewellery, decorative arts and textiles. These represent the finest examples of each style and period from all over the country.

2nd-century Kushana sculpture

INDUS VALLEY CULTURE

EXCAVATIONS in the 1920s at Harappa and Mohenjodaro (now in Pakistan) revealed the remains of a sophisticated urban culture that existed between 2500–1500 BC along the Indus Valley (see pp44–5). The museum's collection of relics from these sites is among the finest in the world. Although the Indus copper and bronze instruments are less opulent than the later Mesopotamian and Egyptian ones, other items, such as the figure of a dancing girl and a headless female torso, show enormous artistic skill.

Also on display are soapstone seals, used perhaps by merchants and officials, whose pictographic script remains undeciphered. Particularly notable is the display of Harappan pottery which ranges from functional items such as pots to charming toys, beads, necklaces and weights.

ANCIENT AND MEDIEVAL SCULPTURE

SIX GALLERIES on the ground floor trace the growth of Indian sculpture over 1,500 years. Among the earliest pieces is a rare terracotta fertility goddess from Mathura dating to the 3rd century BC. From Amaravati in Andhra Pradesh (1st century AD), is a superb sculpted panel depicting its now vanished reliquary mound (stupa). The 2nd-century AD Kushana frieze of Vasantasena, an inebriated courtesan (see pp46–7), is an amusing comment on court life, while the splendid collection of Gandhara art, with its marked Hellenistic style, shows the evolution of the human form in North Indian sculpture after the 1st century. Its delicately draped statues are the first representations of the Buddha in human form. After the great stone-carved Hindu temples and images of the Gupta period (3rd–5th centuries), regional styles emerged in the south and the east. Successive galleries trace sculptural developments of the Pallava, Chalukya and Hoysala dynasties.

2nd-century Jain votive plaque from Mathura

BRONZES

INDIAN BRONZES, executed through the cire perdue or "lost wax" process as an alternative to stone temple sculptures, developed in South India under the Chola and Pallava dynasties. Idols made of bronze, an alloy of eight metals with copper as the base, were less weighty than stone and could either be worshipped at home or taken out for festive processions. The gallery's collection covers 600 years (5th–11th centuries). The pride of place belongs to a 10th-century Chola Nataraja, the name given to the Lord of Dance, Shiva. This shows him dancing the Chaturatandava, a classic representation of his cosmic dance of life and death. The circle of flames that surrounds the dancer represents the entire cosmos.

Another 11th-century Chola bronze, Kaliyamardan Krishna, is a superb study of the balance and poise of the young Lord Krishna as he dances on the hood of the five-headed serpent, Kaliya, holding his tail in triumph.

Devi, 15th-century bronze

MANUSCRIPTS AND WALL PAINTINGS

AMONG THE WEALTH of rare manuscripts in the museum are the Bustan-e-sadi (1502), one of the few dated and illustrated manuscripts of pre-Mughal India. Leaves from the 16th-century Babur Nama, a biography of the first Mughal emperor, illustrate the style of early Mughal painting. A Rig Veda Samita (1514) and a beautiful 18th century cloth scroll of the Bhagvat Purana are also part of this collection.

Also on display is an unparalleled Hunting Scene (c.1810) from the Kota School of Painting, salvaged from the Jhala Jhalim Singh Haveli in Kota, Rajasthan.

Mandi House Complex ❽

Map 2 D5.
Triveni Kala Sangam Tansen Marg.
📞 (011) 2371 8833. 🕐 9am–5pm
Mon–Sat. ⬤ public hols. 🚻 ♿
Rabindra Bhavan Ferozeshah Rd.
📞 (011) 2338 6626.
Kamani Auditorium Copernicus
Marg. 📞 (011) 2338 8084.
Sri Ram Centre Safdar Hashmi Marg.
📞 (011) 2371 4307. 🚻 ♿
National School of Drama Bhagwan
Das Rd. 📞 (011) 2338 9402.
*For **Tickets** see **Entertainment**
pp120–21.*

MANDI HOUSE, once the
palace of the ruler of a
small principality in Himachal
Pradesh and today the offices
of the state-owned television
centre, lends its name to this
cultural complex encircling
the roundabout.
Triveni Kala Sangam's
various art galleries hold
regular contemporary art
exhibitions. A pleasant open
air auditorium here stages
dance and theatre per-
formances. Well-known
artists and writers can often
be glimpsed in the popular
café, and there is also a
bookshop specializing in
Indian arts publications.
　The state-sponsored arts
complex, **Rabindra Bhavan**,
houses the three national
academies of literature
(Sahitya Akademi), fine arts
and sculpture (Lalit Kala
Akademi), and the performing
arts (Sangeet Natak Akademi)
in separate wings. All have
libraries and display galleries
which also sell reproductions
and postcards. The Lalit Kala
is the site of the international
Triennale exhibition in which
painters and sculptors from
more than 30 countries
participate. Exhibitions of
photography, graphics and
ceramics are also held here.
　Kamani Auditorium, the
Sri Ram Centre and the
National School of Drama
host theatrical, classical music
and dance events in their
auditoria. The latter two have
their own repertory companies which stage plays in
Hindi, Urdu and other
regional Indian languages.

**Ugrasen's Baoli in the heart of
New Delhi**

Ugrasen's Baoli ❾

Off Hailey Rd. **Map** 2 D5.

THIS STEPWELL (*see p27*) is
reached by turning left on
Hailey Road into a narrow
lane without a signpost just
before the Consul-
ate General of
Malta. A little way
along on the right
are the remains of
an old stone wall;
the *baoli* is behind
them and can be
entered through a
narrow buttressed
gateway, usually
locked, but the *chowkidar*
will open the gate. Con-
sidered one of Delhi's finest
stepwells, its architectural
features suggest a 15th-
century date, though popular
myth holds that it was built in
the 14th century by Raja
Ugrasen, an ancestor of the
mercantile Aggarwal
community, to provide water
and shelter for travellers.

**Mirror-work skirts on
sale at Janpath**

Connaught Place ❿

Map 1 C4.
Shops 🛍 10:30am–7:30pm
Mon–Sat. ⬤ Sun & public hols.

ROBERT TOR RUSSELL, one of
New Delhi's architects,
designed this imperial plaza
named after the Duke of
Connaught, an uncle of King
George V. Noble Palladian
archways and stuccoed
colonnades deliberately
recalled the very English
terraces of Cheltenham and
Bath; and when the first
shops raised their shutters in
1931, they had names like
"Empire Stores" to distinguish
them from the local shops
selling Indian goods in
shopping areas like Gole
Market and Chandni Chowk.
Today there are as many
offices as shops in the central
circle, officially
renamed Rajiv
Chowk. (The
outer circle is now
Indira Chowk.)
The shops are an
eclectic mix of
travel agencies,
banks, outlets for
several leading
international
brands and the ubiquitous gift
kiosks. Though Connaught
Place has, in recent years, lost
out to other local markets, its
shaded arcades offer a
pleasant atmosphere to stroll
in and to browse through the
pavement book stalls. There
are many restaurants also
located here, as well as a
number of cinema halls
showing the latest Hindi

Connaught Place, the British-built shopping complex in New Delhi

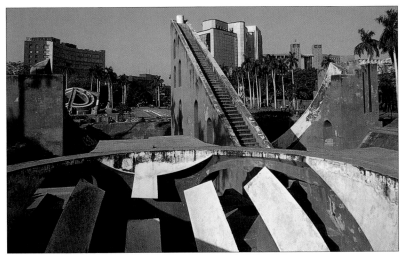

The brick and plaster astronomical instruments in Jantar Mantar

potboilers. The central lawns, earlier a venue for street theatre, shoeshine boys and self-styled "ear cleaners", have made way for the Delhi Metro. Other popular shopping centres in the area are the state emporia at Baba Kharak Singh Marg and the stalls along Janpath, especially the Tibetan Market.

Lakshmi Narayan Mandir ⓫

Mandir Marg. **Map** 1 A4. ✍

T HE PROMINENT industrialist GD Birla built this temple dedicated to Lakshmi Narayan in 1938. Mahatma Gandhi attended its first *puja* as this was among the country's first temples that had no caste restrictions. Popularly known as Birla Mandir, it is a fairly typical example

of contemporary Indian temple architecture.

Approached by a flight of marble stairs, the main shrine has images of Vishnu and his consort, Lakshmi. It is surmounted by ochre and maroon *shikharas* (temple towers). Subsidiary shrines dedicated to Radha-Krishna, Hanuman, Shiva and Durga *(see pp22–3)* are set around the courtyard. On the walls are inscriptions from Hindu scriptures, often with English translations. They are also decorated with paintings from the *Mahabharata (see p141)* and *Ramayana (see p37)*.

Surrounded by a peaceful park with a pleasant marble pavilion on one side and a large *dharamshala* (resthouse) on the other, this popular temple is a good place to visit as it is spotlessly clean and very well-maintained.

Jantar Mantar ⓬

Sansad Marg. **Map** 1 C5.

S AWAI JAI SINGH II of Jaipur built this observatory in 1724 when commissioned by the then Mughal emperor Muhammad Shah. A keen astronomer, the maharaja felt that the existing instruments were not accurate enough to calculate the eclipses and planetary positions required to set the timings of his *pujas* and other sacred rituals. To solve the problem he erected five observatories *(see pp192–3)* with instruments that were sufficiently large and fixed to the site to be both exact and not prone to vibration. The instruments are the Samrat Yantra, a right-angled triangle whose hypotenuse is parallel to the earth's axis. This is, in fact, a gigantic sundial, and there are two brick quadrants on either side which measure its shadow. The others are the Jai Prakash Yantra, Jai Singh's invention, which, among other functions, verifies the time of the spring equinox; the Ram Yantra which reads the altitude of the sun; and the Misra Yantra, a group of instruments for a variety of purposes. Today, the observatory lies obsolete, in the centre of a pleasant park, surrounded by high-rises.

The popular Lakshmi Narayan Mandir

The Nehru Memorial Museum and Library at Teen Murti Bhavan

Nehru Memorial Museum and Library ⑬

Teen Murti Marg. **Map** 4 E3. ☏ *(011) 2301 5191.* ◷ *9am–5pm Tue–Sun.* ⬤ *Mon & public hols.* **Nehru Planetarium** ☏ *(011) 2301 2994.* 🎞 *Shows 11:30am, 3pm.*

JAWAHARLAL NEHRU lived in this house, then called Teen Murti Bhavan, while he was India's first prime minister (1947–64). On his death, the house was converted into a national memorial comprising a museum and a library for research scholars.

Originally the residence of the Commander-in-Chief of British Forces in India and located directly south of Rashtrapati Bhavan, the house was designed by Robert Tor Russell, the architect of Connaught Place and the Eastern and Western Courts on Janpath. Its design follows the established Lutyens-style classicism with a teak panelled interior and vaulted reception rooms. Nehru's bedroom and study, still exactly as he left them, are an austere centre in a grand house. Especially interesting are the bookshelves that line the corridors, containing Nehru's private collection, an eclectic mix of English classics, Left Book Club editions and treatises on the Cold War.

This home has a special place in modern Indian history as it once housed, not just the incumbent prime minister, but two future ones as well, his daughter, Indira Gandhi, and grandson, Rajiv. Both mother and son were assassinated *(see pp60–61)*.

The extensive grounds are home to the **Nehru Planetarium** and the square, three-arched **Kushak Mahal**, a 14th-century hunting lodge built by the Tughlaq sultan, Feroze Shah *(see p97)*.

On the roundabout, in front of the house, is the memorial known as Teen Murti ("three statues") dedicated to the men of the Indian regiments who died in World War I. It was from this landmark that the house derived its name.

Teen Murti Memorial

Gandhi Smriti ⑭

Tees January Marg. **Map** 4 F3. ☏ *(011) 2301 1480.* ◷ *10am–5pm daily.* 🚫 📷 ⬤ *Mon & public hols.*

ON 30 JANUARY 1948, at 11am, Nathuram Godse assassinated Mahatma Gandhi as he was going to his daily prayer meeting in the gardens of this house, once the residence of the Birla family *(see p77)*. A simple sandstone pillar marks the spot.

Now a museum commemorating Gandhi's life and final hours, the ambience here reflects Gandhi's philosophy of lofty political principles and down to earth common sense. A series of appealing dioramas made up of dolls in glass cabinets, tell the story of his eventful life through such defining moments as bidding farewell to his parents while going to England and the death of Kasturba, his beloved wife. The rooms where he used to stay when in Delhi are memorably austere and do convey a sense of his history. In the garden, footsteps, cast in red sandstone, lead to the site of his final martyrdom.

The museum complex has shops selling inexpensive editions of Gandhi's writings as well as items made from khadi, the simple homespun cloth he always wore, and which became one of the important symbols of the Freedom Movement *(see pp58–9)*.

Lodi Gardens 15

Map 5 A4. ○ *sunrise–sunset daily.*

LODI GARDENS, located in the heart of residential New Delhi, was built at the behest of Lady Willingdon, the Vicereine, in 1936. Originally the site of two villages, their inhabitants were shifted elsewhere and lawns and pathways were laid out around the tombs belonging to the 15th-century Sayyid and Lodi dynasties. Inside, the bridge called **Athpula**, literally "eight piers", near the entrance on South End Road, is said to date from the 17th century. To the west of it are the ramparts of the **tomb of Sikandar Lodi** (r.1489–1517) which enclose an octagonal tomb at the centre of some rather overgrown gardens. Inside it, traces of turquoise tilework and calligraphy are just about visible.

To the south of Sikandar Lodi's Tomb are the **Bara Gumbad** ("big dome") and **Sheesh Gumbad** ("glazed dome"). The names of the nobles buried within have long been forgotten, but the Bara Gumbad is an imposing structure with an attached mosque built in 1494, and a *mehmankhana* (guesthouse). The Sheesh Gumbad derives its name from the glazed turquoise tiles that still cling to its outer walls along with blue calligraphic panels.

Recent research claims that this is Bahlol Lodi's tomb. The **tomb of Muhammad Shah** (r.1434–44), the third ruler of the Sayyid dynasty, is said to be the oldest in the garden. The dome of this octagonal structure is surrounded by *chhatris,* and *jaalis* once filled the spaces between the pillars. The graves inside are said to be those of the sultan himself and some of the most favoured nobles of his court.

Today, with its tree-lined pathways and well-kept lawns and flower beds, the park acts as a "green lung" for the people of Delhi. It is one of the city's most picturesque parks and a favourite haunt of joggers, yoga-enthusiasts and families who come here to picnic on weekends. Vendors selling balloons, ice-creams and snacks from handcarts are popular with children.

Muhammad Shah's Tomb

Khan Market 16

Subramaniam Bharti Marg. **Map** 5 B3. **Shops** ○ *10am – 7:30pm Mon–Sat.* ● *Sun & public hols.*

THIS MARKET WAS BUILT in the early 1940s to serve the needs of the British forces living in the hurriedly constructed barracks at Lodi Estate. Its name, Khan Market, is in honour of the prominent Pathan nationalist and social reformer, Dr Khan Sahib, the brother of Khan Abdul Gaffar Khan, the "Frontier Gandhi". Both men were revered for their role for independence among the warlike tribes of the North-West Frontier Province (now in Pakistan).

This popular market is much frequented by Indians and foreigners alike because of the wide range of Indian and Western merchandise on offer. Crockery, clothes and cakes, dog leashes, exotic (for India) vegetables, such as red peppers, avocadoes and asparagus, are just some of the goods available here. There are traditional sari shops, and also Anokhi *(see p266),* selling blockprinted linen and garments in both Western and Indian style. There are also a number of excellent places to buy shoes, as well as bookshops, such as Bahri & Sons, The Book Shop and Faqir Chand's, one of the oldest shops in the market. Its other charming features are the groceries and the flower shops. A number of fast-food outlets are located here for shoppers in search of a quick snack, and one of Delhi's best delicatessens, Sugar & Spice.

Athpula, the 17th-century bridge near the entrance to Lodi Gardens on South End Road

NIZAMUDDIN TO PURANA QILA

THE NIZAMUDDIN AREA, named after the famous 14th-century Sufi saint, Nizamuddin Auliya, is bisected by Mathura Road and has a clearly visible split personality. East Nizamuddin is the quieter half, with Humayun's Tomb *(see p83)* resting peacefully at the centre of a Persian garden. West Nizamuddin, the old Muslim quarter around the saint's *dargah,* is a lively *basti* which still retains its medieval character. This important pilgrim centre also has the graves of famous poets such as Amir Khusrau and Mirza Ghalib, as well as the tombs of Jahanara, the daughter of Shah Jahan *(see pp154–5),* and the dilettante Muhammad Shah Rangila,

A *jaali* **screen**

a later Mughal emperor. In this neighbourhood, the medieval and modern co-exist harmoniously. Busy Mathura Road swirls past the Subz Burj with its blue-tiled dome, today a traffic island. Humayun's Tomb and the Sundar Horticulture Nursery is off to the west. Further north is the up-market residential colony of Sundar Nagar with antique shops, Delhi Zoo and Purana Qila, the "old fort", *(see p84).* The crumbling battlements of the fort overlook the Crafts Museum, the small shrine of Matka Pir, a Sufi saint, and the exhibition grounds of Pragati Maidan. To the east stands the Khair-ul-Manazil Mosque, built by Maham Anga in the mid-16th century.

SIGHTS AT A GLANCE

Historic Site
Nizamuddin ❶

Tomb
Humayun's Tomb p83 ❷

Monuments
Purana Qila ❸
Khair-ul-Manazil Mosque ❹

Museums
Crafts Museum pp86–7 ❺

Exhibition Grounds
Pragati Maidan ❻

GETTING THERE
Take a taxi or auto-rickshaw to Nizamuddin to visit both the village and Humayun's Tomb. To get to Purana Qila, hire another taxi or auto from one of the many stands. Once at Purana Qila, most of the sights are easily accessible by foot.

KEY

🚉	Railway station
🚌	Bus station
🅿	Parking
🛕	Temple
🅲	Mosque
🔱	Tomb

◁ **Inlaid marble and tiles decorating the façade of Atgah Khan's Tomb in Nizamuddin**

Nizamuddin Complex ❶

West of Mathura Rd. **Map** 6 D5.
Dargah ⬜ *daily*. **Qawwali** *6:30pm
Thurs*. 🔶 *Urs (Apr)*.

THIS MEDIEVAL settlement, or *basti*, is named after Sheikh Hazrat Nizamuddin Auliya, whose grave and hospice are located here. Nizamuddin belonged to a fraternity of Sufi mystics, the Chishtiyas *(see p319)*, respected for their austerity, piety and disdain for politics and material desires. His daily assemblies drew both the rich and the poor, who believed that he was a "friend of God" and so a master who would intercede on their behalf on Judgement Day. Nizamuddin died in 1325 but his disciples call him a *zinda pir*, a living spirit, who heeds their pleas and alleviates their misery.

Colourful stalls lining the alley leading to Nizamuddin's *dargah*

Congregational area, Nizamuddin

The Urs *(see p38)* is held on the anniversary of his birth and death, and celebrated by his disciples with qawwalis and offerings of *chadors*.

A winding alley leads to the saint's grave. It is crowded with mendicants and lined with stalls selling flowers and *chadors*, polychrome clocks and prints of Mecca. The main congregational area is a marble pavilion (rebuilt in 1562) where, every Thursday evening, devotees sing devotional songs composed by the celebrated Persian poet, Amir Khusrau (1253–1325). Women are denied entry beyond the outer verandah but may peer through *jaalis* into the small, dark chamber where the saint's grave lies draped with a rose petal-strewn cloth and where imams continuously recite verses from the Koran. The complex also contains the graves of several eminent

Tomb of the famous poet Mirza Ghalib

disciples, such as Jahanara Begum and Amir Khusrau.

Across the western side of the open courtyard is the red sandstone Jama't Khana Mosque, built in 1325. To its north is a *baoli*, secretly excavated while Tughlaqabad *(see p114)* was being built because Ghiyasuddin Tughlaq had banned all building activities elsewhere. Legend has it that labourers worked here at night with the help of lamps lit, not by oil, but water blessed by Nasiruddin, Nizamuddin's successor *(see p108)*. The mid-16th-century tomb of Atgah Khan, Akbar's minister and the husband of one of his wet nurses, who was murdered by Adham Khan *(see p113)*, is to the north. An open marble pavilion, the Chaunsath Khamba ("64 pillars"), is close by. Just outside, is an enclosure containing the simple grave of Mirza Ghalib (1786–1869). One of the greatest poets of his time, Ghalib wrote in both Urdu and Persian, and his verses are still recited today. Nearby is the Ghalib Academy, a repository of paintings and manuscripts.

Always crowded, the *basti* preserves with miraculous serenity, the legend of this *pir*, who was called "a king without throne or crown, with kings in need of the dust of his feet" by his disciple, Amir Khusrau.

NIZAMUDDIN COMPLEX

One of Delhi's historic necropolises, many of the *pir's* disciples, such as Amir Khusrau and Jahanara Begum, Shah Jahan's favourite daughter, are buried close to their master. Jahanara's epitaph echoes her master's teachings: "Let naught cover my grave save the green grass, for grass well suffices as a covering for the grave of the lowly".

Humayun's Tomb ❷

Marble star inlaid on panel

Humayun, the second Mughal emperor *(see p84)*, is buried in this tomb, the first great example of a Mughal garden tomb and inspiration for several later monuments, such as the incomparable Taj Mahal. Built in 1565 by a Persian architect Mirak Mirza Ghiyas, it was commissioned by Humayun's senior widow, Haji Begum. Often called "a dormitory of the House of Timur", the graves in its chambers include Humayun's wives and Dara Shikoh, Shah Jahan's scholarly son. Also in the complex are the Afsarwala Tomb, the octagonal tomb and mosque of Isa Khan, a noble at Sher Shah's court, and the tomb of Humayun's favourite barber. The Arab ki Sarai housed the Persian masons who built the tomb.

VISITORS' CHECKLIST

Off Mathura Rd. **Map** 6 D4.
📞 *(011) 2435 5275.*
🕐 *sunrise–sunset daily.*
🎫 *free on Fri.* 📷

The tomb as seen from the entrance

The Dome
This imposing white marble double dome is a complete half-sphere, and is surmounted by a finial with a crescent in the Persian style. Later Mughal finials, such as the one at the Taj Mahal, used a lotus.

Geometric designs inlaid on panels

Jaalis
Such fine trellis work in stone later became a signature Mughal feature.

The imposing plinth is decorated with red sandstone arches and consists of multiple chambers, a departure from the single chamber of previous tombs.

The Tomb Chamber
The plain white marble sarcophagus stands on a simple black and white marble platform. The grave itself lies in the rather dark, bat-filled basement below.

Purana Qila ❸

Mathura Rd. **Map** 6 D2. *(011)
2435 4260.* sunrise–sunset daily.
Son et Lumière Sept–Oct & Feb–
–April: 8:30–9:30pm; Nov–Jan:
7:30– 8:30pm; May–Aug: 9–10pm.
Tickets: from site and the Delhi
Tourism office. *(011) 2331 5322.*

Purana Qila, literally "old
fort", stands on an ancient
mound. Excavations near its
eastern wall reveal that the
site has been continuously
occupied since 1000 BC. It is
also believed to be the place
where Indraprastha, the
Pandava capital mentioned in
the epic, the *Mahabharata
(see p141),* once stood.

It was here that Humayun,
the second Mughal emperor,
began to construct his city,
Dinpanah ("Asylum of Faith"),
just four years after his father
Babur established the Mughal
dynasty in 1526 *(see pp52–3).*
However, his reign was short-
lived and, in 1540, he was
dispossessed of his kingdom
by the ambitious Afghan
chieftain, Sher Shah Sur
(r.1540–45). When Sher Shah
took possession of the citadel,
he strengthened its fortifications, added several new
structures and renamed it
Shergarh. After his death, his
successors were defeated by
Humayun who recaptured his
domains in 1555. Today, of
the many palaces, barracks
and houses that once existed,
only Sher Shah's mosque and
the building said to be
Humayun's library remain.

The Yamuna once flowed
on the fort's eastern side and
formed a natural moat: a small
lake to the west facing busy

Boating outside Purana Qila

Mathura Road is all that
remains today. The present
entrance, an imposing red
sandstone gate on the western
wall called the **Bara
Darwaza**, is one of the
three principal gates of
Shergarh. Its double-
storeyed façade,
surmounted by
chhatris and
approached by a
steep ramp, still
displays traces of tiles
and carved foliage.
Humayun's Gate, on
the southern wall, has
an inscription
bearing Sher Shah's
name and the date
950 AH (1543–4). To
the north, the **Taliqi Darwaza**
(the so-called "forbidden
gate") has carved reliefs, and
across the road is the red
sandstone **Lal Darwaza**, or
Sher Shah Gate, one of the
entrances to the township that
grew around the fort.

**Chhatri with
decorative tilework**

The single-domed **Qila-i-
Kuhna Mosque**, built by Sher
Shah in 1541, is an excellent
example of a pre-Mughal
design. Its prayer hall inside
has five elegant arched niches
or mihrabs set in its western
wall. Marble in shades of red,
white and slate is used for the
calligraphic inscriptions and
marks a transition from Lodi
to Mughal architecture. A
second storey provided space
for female courtiers to pray,
while the arched doorway on
the left wall, framed by ornate
jharokhas, was reserved for
members of the royal family.

The **Sher Mandal** stands to
the south of the mosque. This
double-storeyed octagonal
tower of red sandstone was
built by Sher Shah and was
used as a library by
Humayun after he
recaptured the fort.
The tower is topped
by an octagonal
chhatri, supported
by eight pillars and
decorated with white
marble. Inside, there
are remnants of the
decorative plasterwork
and traces of the
stone shelving
where, presumably,
the emperor's books
were placed. This was also
the tragic spot where, on 24
January 1556, on hearing the
muezzin's call, the devout
Humayun hurried to kneel on
the stairs, missed his footing
and tumbled to his death. His
tomb can be seen from the
southern gate. Purana Qila
flourished as the sixth city of
Delhi *(see p107)* and traces of
walls still stand in the area.

Sher Shah's mosque at Purana Qila

The single dome surmounting the prayer hall at Khair-ul-Manazil

Khair-ul-Manazil ❹

Mathura Rd. **Map** 5 C2.
◯ sunrise–sunset.

THIS MOSQUE, "the most auspicious of houses", was constructed in 1561 by Akbar's influential wet nurse, Maham Anga, and a courtier, Shiha-bu'd-Din Ahmed Khan. An imposing, double-storeyed red sandstone gateway leads into a large courtyard ringed by cloisters, two storeys high, one of which was used as a *madrasa*. The prayer hall with its five-arched openings is topped by a single dome. Above the central archway, a marble inscription mentions Maham Anga's and Shiha-bu'd-Din's names. Inside, the central mihrab is decorated with bands of blue and green calligraphy. Maham Anga is buried in Mehrauli with her son, Adham Khan (*see p113*), who was killed by Akbar.

Crafts Museum ❺

See pp86–7.

Pragati Maidan ❻

Mathura Rd. **Map** 6 D1. ▐ (011) 2331 8143. ▐FAX▐ (011) 2331 8142. ◯ 10am–5:30pm daily. ▨ ◙ ▣ ▮
Hamsadhwani, Falaknuma and **Shakuntalam** ▐ (011) 2337 1849. **National Science Centre** ◯ 10am–6pm Tue–Sun. ● Mon & public hols. ▨

INDIA'S LARGEST exhibition centre, covering nearly 150 acres (61 ha), is the venue for exhibitions and trade fairs organized by the India Trade Promotion Organization. The work of some of India's most eminent architects can be seen here. Raj Rewal has designed the Hall of Nations and Industries and Joseph Allen Stein, the World Trade Centre. Among other notable buildings are those by Charles Correa, Achyut Kanvinde and Satish Grover. All the Indian states have pavilions spread across the fair's extensive grounds, linked by 16 km (10 miles) of roads.

Exhibitions are held here throughout the year and cover a range of products from textiles, jewellery, automobiles to mining equipment and food products. Every two years the World Book Fair and the India International Travel and Tourism Show are held, drawing international delegates. Within the grounds are Appu Ghar, a children's amusement park, and the National Science Centre (*see p271*). Two theatres, the Falaknuma and Shakuntalam, screen a cross-section of Indian and foreign films, while the Hamsadhwani Auditorium is the venue for various cultural events.

A view of Pragati Maidan from Purana Qila

MATKA PIR

Rows of *matkas* (earthenware pots) line the entrance to the shrine of Matka Pir, a Sufi saint. According to legend, a man and his wife came to the saint to seek his help for the birth of a son. Being poor, they could only offer a humble pot of dal and jaggery. The saint asked them to place the pot in the courtyard and leave the rest to God. A year later, their wish fulfilled, they returned with another pot, a tradition that has continued since then. The pot motif leads all the way up the wide marble stairs to the *dargah*, standing on a ridge overlooking Mathura Road. The saint's powers still attract many pilgrims.

The shrine of the Sufi saint, Matka Pir

Crafts Museum ❺

**Wooden doll
on toy swing**

FOR CENTURIES, Indian craftsmen, such as potters and weavers, masons and carvers, have created a range of objects of everyday use that are both beautiful and practical. A unique project was started in 1956 to promote indigenous artisans by displaying their work in one place, and by the early 1980s, over 20,000 objects had been collected. This was the core around which grew India's first Crafts Museum.

Sarota
A late 19th-century betel nut cracker from South India.

★ Bandhini Odhni
This exquisite veil is the work of the Bhansali tribe in Kutch, Gujarat. In tie-and-dye (bandhini), grains are used to set the pattern. Threads are tied around them and the cloth dyed in different colours.

Mukhalinga
A rare, late 19th-century brass and silver phallic image (linga) with a human face (mukha). Tiny snakes as earrings and the third eye are symbols of Shiva.

Amphitheatre

STAR EXHIBITS

★ Bandhini Odhni

★ Bhuta Figure

★ Charrake

Crafts Demonstration Area
Artisans from all over India set up workshops each month (barring the monsoon) to display their skill to visitors.

KEY

- ☐ Gallery of Aristocratic Arts
- ☐ Gallery of Ritual Arts
- ☐ Gallery of Folk and Tribal Cultures
- ☐ Gallery of Popular Culture
- ☐ Gallery of Textiles
- ☐ Administration Block
- ☐ Temporary Exhibition Gallery
- ☐ Visual Store

Yashoda and Krishna

This mid-20th-century plaster cast statuette from South India is an interesting example of popular kitsch, inspired by gods and mythology. It is cheap and easy to reproduce for use in a domestic shrine.

★ Charrake

These enormous, circular vessels are cast of an alloy known as bell metal. They are still used in Kerala for wedding feasts or at temples for making payasam (a type of rice pudding) for devotees during festivals.

Madhubani Painting

A stunning wall painting in natural pigments depicting a wedding scene by Ganga Devi, a famous woman painter of this traditional art form from Bihar in Eastern India.

Library

★ Bhuta Figure

These life-sized wooden figures were made 200 years ago as part of the Bhuta cult of spirit worship in the southern state of Karnataka.

Entrance

GALLERY GUIDE

The museum's display is spread over two floors of the complex, divided into separate areas by courtyards that also double up as exhibition spaces. A large open area is designated for live art displays by visiting artisans each month, except during the rainy season.

The Crafts Museum Shop

Located on the premises of the Crafts Museum, the shop sells a wide selection of fine Indian folk crafts and textiles.

OLD DELHI

W HAT IS KNOWN as Old Delhi today was originally the Mughal capital of Shahjahanabad, built by Shah Jahan when he moved the imperial court from Agra to Delhi. Construction began in 1638, and ten years later the Red Fort, Jami Masjid, Chandni Chowk and the surrounding residential and mercantile quarters were ready for occupation.

The city was surrounded by a rubble wall pierced by 14 gates of which three – Delhi, Turkman and Ajmeri – survive. An elegant, mannered lifestyle flourished, enriched by the courtiers and merchants, artists and poets who lived in the lanes and

Detail of a door in Red Fort

quarters, called *galis* and *katras*, of the walled city. In 1739, the Persian freebooter Nadir Shah came to plunder the city of Shahjahanabad and left a bleeding ruin behind him. The final deathblow was, however, dealt when the British troops moved into the Red Fort after the Mutiny of 1857, turning it into a military garrison, while a railway line cut the walled city in half. Yet, the spirit of the place has survived all these vicissitudes and its busy *galis* continue to support a vibrant life. Modernity has brought a new urgency to the pace of the traditional traders who still live and operate from here.

SIGHTS AT A GLANCE

Mosques
Jami Masjid ❶
Zinat-ul Masjid ❻

Historic Streets and Sites
Ajmeri Gate ❹
Chandni Chowk ❷
Turkman Gate ❺

Monuments
Feroze Shah Kotla ❽
Red Fort pp94–5 ❸

Memorial
Rajghat ❼

GETTING THERE
The most convenient way to get to Red Fort and Chandni Chowk is by car or autorickshaw. You may also join one of the many day tours to the Old City. Once there, explore the area by foot or cycle-rickshaw.

KEY
- 🚉 Street-by-Street map *See pp90–91*
- 🚉 Railway station
- Ⓜ Metro station
- 🅿 Parking
- 🚓 Police station
- ⊠ Post office
- ➕ Hospital
- 🛕 Temple
- Ⓒ Mosque
- 𝔾 *Gurudwara*
- ✝ Church

0 metres 750
0 yards 750

◁ **The white marble throne-balcony, Diwan-i-Aam, Red Fort**

Street-by-Street: Chandni Chowk

NOW A BUSY COMMERCIAL CENTRE, Chandni Chowk was once a grand processional thoroughfare that led from Red Fort to Jami Masjid. When it was laid out in 1648 by Jahanara Begum, Shah Jahan's favourite daughter, a canal ran down the centre of the tree-lined stately avenue. Chandni Chowk, or the "silvery, moonlit square", was then lined with merchants' shops and the grand residences or *havelis* of noblemen and merchants.

Sisganj Gurudwara
Guru Tegh Bahadur, the ninth Sikh guru, was beheaded at this site. The gurudwara marks the site of his martyrdom.

Sunehri Masjid
The "Golden Mosque", with three gilt domes, was built in 1722. On 22 March 1739, Nadir Shah stood on its roof to watch the massacre of Delhi's citizens.

Fatehpuri Masjid

CHANDNI CHOWK

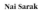
KINARI BAZAAR

Nai Sarak

DARIBA KAL

★ **Kinari Bazaar**
Tightly packed stalls sell all manner of glittering gold and silver trimmings such as braids, tinsel garlands and turbans for weddings and festivals.

CHEL PURI

BAZAAR GULIYA

Karim's
Tucked away in a narrow lane to the south of Jami Masjid is Delhi's most authentic Mughlai eatery. Named after a legendary 19th-century chef, the restaurant is now run by his descendants.

Shiv Temple

STAR SIGHTS
★ Jami Masjid
★ Lahore Gate
★ Kinari Bazaar

★ Lahore Gate

This imposing red sandstone gateway is the main entrance to Red Fort. The Prime Minister addresses the Independence Day rally here.

LOCATOR MAP
See Street Finder map 2

Dariba Kalan

Gold and silver ornaments are sold in this lane. Gulab Singh's famous attar shop (see p119) is located here.

Charity box at the Bird Hospital

★ Jami Masjid

India's largest mosque stands on a mound. Its two slender minarets flank three marble domes **1**

Govt Girls Senior Secondary School

Karim's

0 metres   25

0 yards   25

KEY

– – – Suggested route

Jami Masjid, built by Shah Jahan, the largest mosque in India

Jami Masjid ❶

Off Netaji Subhash Marg. **Map** 2 E2.
⬤ for non-Muslims during times of prayer and after 5pm.

THIS GRAND MOSQUE, built in 1656 by the Emperor Shah Jahan on a natural rocky outcrop, took six years and 5,000 workmen to construct at the cost of nearly a million rupees. A magnificent flight of red sandstone steps leads to the great arched entrances where, in Aurangzeb's time, horses were sold and jugglers performed. Today, sweet-sellers, shoe-minders and beggars mill around here. The huge 28 m (300 ft) square courtyard accommodates up to 20,000 people at prayer times, especially during Friday prayers and on Id, when it looks like a sea of worshippers. Next to the ablution tank in the centre is the *dikka* platform where, before loudspeakers took over, a second prayer leader echoed the imam's words and actions for worshippers too far from the pulpit.

Three imposing black and white marble domes surmount the enormous prayer hall, and two minarets frame the great central arch. From the top of the southern minaret, a steep climb of 20 minutes, there are remarkable views of the roof-line of Old Delhi giving way to the high-rises of New Delhi. Women require a male escort to enter the minaret.

Chandni Chowk ❷

Map 2 D2.

ONCE SHAHJAHANABAD'S most elegant boulevard, this wide avenue extending from Red Fort to Fatehpuri Masjid, is still the heart of Old Delhi, where both religious activity and commerce mix happily together. All along its length are shrines sacred to various communities. The first is the Digamber Jain Mandir. Next to it is the Bird Hospital for sick and wounded birds. Loud chants, clanging bells and calls of vendors selling flowers and vermilion powder surround the Gauri Shankar Mandir, dedicated to Shiva and Parvati, which has a linga said to be 800 years old. Still further, close to the Sisganj Gurudwara, is the Kotwali (police station), the scene of British reprisal after 1857 *(see p55)*. Nearly a century before, another gruesome spectacle took place nearby when one afternoon in 1739, the Persian chieftain Nadir Shah stood on the roof of the Sunehri Masjid and watched his men kill nearly 30,000 of Delhi's citizens. The actual Moonlit Square (Chandni Chowk), is the open space in front of the very British Town Hall, now the Hardayal Library. Just behind it is the Mahatma Gandhi Park, which was called Begum Bagh in Mughal times. Further down, and commanding the end of this charming quarter, stands the Fatehpuri Masjid, constructed in 1650 by Fatehpuri Begum, one of Emperor Shah Jahan's wives. Nearby are the spice markets of Khari Baoli.

Swami Shraddhanand's statue, Chandni Chowk

Chandni Chowk, a vibrant centre of commerce and religious activity

Bazaars of Old Delhi

A cycle-rickshaw puller

OLD DELHI'S BAZAARS are legendary. An English visitor to these bazaars over a hundred years ago, wrote in praise of the "Cashmere shawls, gold and silver embroidery, jewellery, enamels and carpets" to be found here. Today, the great wholesale *katras* of Chandni Chowk and Jami Masjid still retain that souk-like quality. Their narrow streets are lined with shops whose goods spill out onto the pavement; and shopping still means vigorous bargaining for a bewildering array of goods.

Khari Baoli is Asia's biggest spice market. It spills across this street which derives its name from a stepwell that no longer exists.

Katra Neel is reminiscent of Middle Eastern souks. The tiny shops sell a wide variety of textiles, such as brocades from Varanasi, silk, cotton and voile.

Kinari Bazaar specializes in tinsel accessories, and attracts trousseau shoppers.

Katra Neel

Dariba Kalan is the jewellers' lane where artisans have worked for over two centuries.

Nai Sarak is very popular among students as school and college textbooks and stationery are sold on this street.

Chawri Bazaar has every conceivable variety of paper, sold here by weight.

Churiwali Gali has garlands of glass bangles strung along rods to match every sari or lehenga. It is popularly called the "lane of bangle-sellers".

The Red Fort ❸

RED SANDSTONE BATTLEMENTS give this imperial citadel its name, Red Fort (Lal Qila). Commissioned by Shah Jahan in 1639, it took nine years to build and was the seat of Mughal power until 1857, when the last emperor, Bahadur Shah Zafar, was dethroned and exiled. Lahore Gate, one of fort's

A panel in Diwan-i-Aam

six gateways, leads on to the covered bazaar of Chatta Chowk, where brocades and jewels were once sold. Beyond this lies the Naqqar Khana, from where musicians played three times a day.

Detail of a Gilded Pillar
The Mughal love of opulence is visible in the lavish use of marble and gold in the fort.

Moti Masjid
Named after the pearly sheen of its marble, the tiny "pearl mosque" was added by Emperor Aurangzeb in 1659.

★ **Hamams**
The royal bath has three enclosures. The first provided hot vapour baths, the second sprayed rose-scented water through sculpted fountains, and the third contained cold water.

★ **Diwan-i-Aam**
The emperor gave daily audiences to all his subjects in this 60-pillared hall. The intricately carved throne canopy stands on a platform, while the low marble bench was for the chief minister (wazir).

STAR FEATURES

★ **Diwan-i-Khas**

★ **Diwan-i-Aam**

★ **Hamams**

★ Diwan-i-Khas
The legendary Peacock Throne, one of Shah Jahan's seven jewelled thrones, was housed in this exclusive pavilion where the emperor met his most trusted nobles. The walls and pillars were once inlaid with gems and the ceiling was of silver inlaid with precious stones.

VISITORS' CHECKLIST

Chandni Chowk. **Map** 2 D2.
(011) 2327 7705.
6am–7pm daily.
public hols.
Son et Lumière Apr–Oct: 8pm;
Nov–Mar: 7pm.
Museum 10am–5pm. Fri.

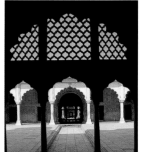

Khas Mahal
The royal apartments were divided by the "Stream of Paradise". The emperor's prayer room (Tasbih Khana) was flanked by his sleeping chamber (Khwabgah) and sitting room (Baithak). This overlooked the Yamuna and led to a balcony where he appeared before his subjects at sunrise.

Rang Mahal
Inside these gilded chambers, once exclusively for women, is an inlaid marble fountain shaped like an open lotus.

THE RED FORT
1 Delhi Gate
2 Lahore Gate
3 Naqqar Khana
4 Diwan-i-Aam
5 Rang Mahal
6 Moti Mahal
7 Khas Mahal
8 Diwan-i-Khas
9 *Hamams*
10 Shah Burj (Tower)
11 Sawan (Pavilion)
12 Bhadon (Pavilion)
13 Zafar Mahal
14 Moti Masjid

KEY
Area illustrated above

0 metres 200
0 yards 200

Ajmeri Gate ❹

Ajmeri Gate Rd. **Map** 1 C3.

THIS IS ONE OF THE 14 gates encircling Shahjahanabad that has survived more than 300 years and today stands in the midst of the city's congested commercial centre. Diagonally opposite Ajmeri Gate is **Ghazi-ud-Din's Tomb** and **Madrasa**. Ghazi-ud-Din Khan was an eminent courtier during the reign of the sixth Mughal emperor Aurangzeb, and his son, Mir Qamar-ud-Din, established the dynasty that ruled the southern state of Hyderabad until Independence in 1947.

The imposing, red sandstone *madrasa* has several arcades and a mosque on its western side. Founded in the late 17th century, this was at one time Delhi's foremost *madrasa* and after 1824 came to be known as the Anglo-Arabic School. English classes were held here, and British teachers also introduced mathematics and science texts to students, which were then translated into Urdu. Ghazi-ud-Din's grave is in a marble enclosure at the mosque's southern end. Athough this complex is surrounded by today's urban congestion, it still performs the noble function it was meant to. The three-domed mosque is in regular use and students crisscross the courtyard, while

Ghazi-ud-Din's *madrasa*

striped towels hang from the hostel balconies where glorious silks may once have billowed. Until recently, the esteemed Delhi College, now the Zakir Husain College, was also located on the premises.

A cycle-rickshaw from Ajmeri Gate will take you past tiny shops to the teeming lanes of Lal Kuan Bazaar where the **Zinat Mahal** is situated. Built in 1846, this was the eponymous home of the favourite wife of the last Mughal emperor Bahadur Shah Zafar. Today, it houses a school, lawyers' offices and shops. The original façade was wonderfully carved and arcaded with an oriel window. The beautiful verse by Bahadur Shah Zafar that was inscribed over the arched gateway can still be seen.

Turkman Gate ❺

Asaf Ali Rd. **Map** 2 D3.

THE SOLID, square-shaped, red sandstone Turkman Gate stands in splendid isolation among the modern high-rise buildings of busy Asaf Ali Road. It marked the southern boundary of Shahjahanabad and was named after a Muslim *pir,* Hazrat Shah Turkman Bayabani, whose 13th-century tomb and *dargah* stand to the east. The serpentine lanes behind the gateway are home to two medieval monuments. **Kalan Masjid** ("black mosque"), in the Bulbulekhan area, was built in 1387 by Khan-i-Jahan Junan Shah, Feroze Shah Tughlaq's prime minister. This is one of the seven mosques he built in Delhi; the others are at Khirkee and Begumpuri *(see p109).* A short walk away lies what is believed to be the **grave of Sultana Razia** Delhi's only medieval woman ruler *(see pp50–51).* Her brief reign was bedevilled by revolts and she was killed at Karnal in 1240 while fleeing from Delhi. Her plain rubble-stone grave lies open to the sky in a cramped enclosure amidst houses and shops. The atelier of the last practising craftsman of Delhi's blue pottery, Hazarilal, is situated in the congested alleys of Hauz Suiwalan, located behind Turkman Gate.

Traffic swirling around the Mughal Turkman Gate

Zinat-ul Masjid ⑥

Daryaganj. **Map** 2 F3.

Tis mosque was built in
1710 by Princess Zinat-un-
Nisa Begum, one of Emperor
Aurangzeb's daughters. The
gracefully proportioned red
sandstone mosque has a
spacious courtyard built over
a series of basement rooms.
Its seven-arched prayer hall is
surmounted by three domes,
with alternating stripes of
black and white marble. The
locals who worship here have
a more lyrical name for it, the
Ghata ("Cloud") Mosque
because its striped domes
simulate the monsoon sky.

Zinat-ul Masjid, also known as the Ghata or "Cloud" Mosque

Rajghat

Rajghat ⑦

Mahatma Gandhi Rd. **Map** 2 F3.
◯ *sunrise–sunset daily.* **Prayer
meetings** *5pm Fri.*
National Gandhi Museum ☎ *(011)
2331 1793.* ◯ *9:30am–5:30pm
Tue–Sun.* ⬤ *Mon & public hols.*
Film shows *4–5pm Sat & Sun.*

Rajghat, India's most revered
symbol of nationalism, is
the site of Mahatma Gandhi's
cremation. A sombre black
granite platform inscribed
with his last words *He Ram!*
("Oh God!") now stands here.
The only splash of colour
comes from the garlands of
orange marigolds draped over
it. Devotees sing *bhajans* and
the steady beat of the *dholak*
lends the scene a dolorous
melancholy. All visiting heads
of state are taken to this
samadhi ("memorial") to lay
wreaths in memory of the
"Father of the Nation". On
Gandhi's birthday (2 Oct) and
death anniversary (30 Jan),
the nation's leaders gather
here for prayer meetings.

Just across the road is the
Gandhi National Museum,
crammed with memorabilia
connected with Gandhi's life,
including his letters and
diaries. A framed plaque on
the stairs explains his simple
philosophy: "Non-violence is
the pitting of one's whole
soul against the will of the
tyrant… it is then possible for
a single individual to defy the
might of an unjust empire."

Feroze Shah Kotla ⑧

Bahadur Shah Zafar Marg. **Map** 2 F4.

Only some ramparts and
ruined structures remain
of Feroze Shah Kotla, the
palace complex of Ferozabad,
Delhi's fifth city erected by
that indefatigable builder,
Feroze Shah Tughlaq *(see
p107)*. Entry is from the gate
next to the Indian Express
Building. Towards the very
end of the walled enclosure
stand the partial ruins of the
Jami Masjid. Roofless, with
only the rear wall still extant,
this was at one time Delhi's
largest mosque where as
legend says, Timur the Lame,
the Mongol conqueror who
sacked Delhi in 1398, came to
say his Friday prayers. Next to
the Jami Masjid is a rubble
pyramidal structure topped by
one of the Mauryan emperor
Ashoka's polished stone
pillars *(see pp46–7)*, brought
from the Punjab and installed
here in 1356 by Feroze Shah.
It was from the inscriptions
on this pillar that James
Prinsep, the Oriental linguist,
deciphered the Brahmi script,
a forerunner of the modern
Devanagari, in 1837.
     Khuni Darwaza (the
"bloodstained gate"), opposite
the Indian Express Building,
was built by Sher Shah Sur as
one of the gates to his city
(see p84). This was where
Lieutenant Hodson shot
Bahadur Shah Zafar's sons
after the Mutiny of 1857 was
quashed. Across the road is
Delhi's main cricket stadium,
named after the palace
complex, where world-class
test matches are held.

The Ashokan Pillar at Feroze Shah Kotla

FURTHER AFIELD

Detail, Moth ki Masjid

THERE IS MUCH to see and explore beyond the city centre. An undulating wooded area, the Ridge, sweeps across Delhi from the southwest to the north. The north contains the university campus and Civil Lines, an orderly civilian enclave created by the British, and the west houses the army Cantonment. South Delhi, juxtaposed between the old cities of Siri, Jahanpanah and Tughlaqabad, is a more recent addition, with many affluent suburbs, smart residential colonies, shops, cinemas and restaurants. Further south, the historic Mehrauli Archaeological Park encompasses 19th-century hunting lodges, tombs, pavilions and the towering Qutb Minar. This picturesque area was the site of Delhi's first city, Qila Rai Pithora built around Lal Kot, a Tomar Rajput fortress.

SIGHTS AT A GLANCE

Historic Buildings and Sites
Chiragh Delhi ⑰
Civil Lines ⑤
Delhi Cantonment ⑩
Delhi University ⑧
Hauz Khas ⑮
Jahanpanah ⑲
Khirkee ⑱
Mehrauli Archaeological Park pp110–13 ⑳
Old Delhi GPO ②
Siri Fort ⑯
Tughlaqabad ㉓

Temples, Churches and Mosques
Baha'i House of Worship ㉕
Kalkaji Temple ㉔
Moth ki Masjid ⑭
St James's Church ①

Cemeteries
Nicholson Cemetery ③

Parks and Gardens
Northern Ridge ⑦
Qudsia Gardens ④
The Ridge ⑨

Monuments
Coronation Memorial ⑥

Museums
National Rail Museum ⑪
Sanskriti ㉑

Tombs
Safdarjung's Tomb ⑫
Sultan Ghari ㉒

Markets
INA Market ⑬

GETTING THERE
A private car, taxi or auto-rickshaw is the best way of exploring the area. Private tour operators also run coaches to some sites.

0 kilometres 3
0 miles 3

	Delhi city centre
	Built-up area
	Greater Delhi
🚉	Railway station
	Major road
	Minor road

SIGHTS OUTSIDE THE CENTRE

Street-by-Street: Around Kashmiri Gate

A local bakery sign

D ELHI'S KASHMIRI GATE area resonates with memories of 1857. Many of the dramatic events between the months of May and September took place on the short stretch between Kashmiri Gate and the Old Delhi General Post Office (GPO). In the 1920s, this was also a favourite watering hole of the British residents living in nearby Civil Lines. Then the street was lined with smart shops and restaurants, few of which survive now.

Shop Façades
The grand old shops are now shabby and derelict.

★ Kashmiri Gate
The Mughals used to set off from this gate to spend the summer in Kashmir. In 1857, it was the scene of a bitter battle and a plaque on the western side honours "the engineers and miners who died while clearing the gate for British forces on September 14, 1857".

Nicholson Cemetery ❸

NICHOLSON RD

CHURCH ROAD

LOTHIAN RO

RAMLAL CHANDHOK MARG

BARA BAZA

Fakr-ul-Masjid
The domes and minarets of this small mosque rise above the rows of shops and offices along this busy street. Local residents come here to worship every Friday.

0 metres   15
0 yards   15

Old Hindu College

Old St Stephen's College

KEY

− − − Suggested route

STAR SIGHTS

★ Kashmiri Gate

★ St James's Church

★ St James's Church
Delhi's oldest and most historic church, consecrated in 1836, is an impressive edifice, painted yellow and white ❶

Northern Railways Office
This Indo-Saracenic fantasy was once the residence of the British Commissioner, William Fraser, one of Skinner's closest friends.

CHURCH ROAD

Delhi College of Engineering

Dara Shikoh's library

Old Delhi GPO ❷

St James's Church ❶

Lothian Rd. 📞 (011) 2386 2539.
🕐 8am–12 noon; 2–5pm daily.
Services 9am Sun.

A TABLET in the church founded by Colonel James Skinner explains: "This church is erected at the sole expense of Colonel James Skinner" in fulfilment of a vow made on the battlefield. Built at the cost of Rs 80,000, the church is in the shape of a Greek cross, surmounted by an imposing eight-leafed dome. The two stained-glass windows were installed in the 1860s. Skinner died at Hansi *(see p140)*. A marble tablet, in front of the altar, marks his simple grave.

The imposing Old Delhi General Post Office

Old Delhi GPO ❷

Lothian Rd. 🕐 9:30am–6pm
Mon–Fri; 9:30am–1pm Sat.

TO THE SOUTH of Kashmiri Gate is the Old Delhi General Post Office, an old fashioned establishment caught in a time warp. This stucco-fronted colonial edifice is significant because it faces a traffic island on which stand two structures dating to the Indian Mutiny of 1857. The Telegraph Memorial is a memorial obelisk dedicated to the officers of the Telegraph Department. The inscription on it honours the telegraph operators, Brendish and Pilkington, who flashed news of the Indian Mutiny to the British garrison at Ambala. Nearby lies the ruined British Magazine. It was blown up by a Captain Willoughby on 11 May 1857 to prevent it from falling into the hands of the rebelling sepoys.

JAMES SKINNER

One of the Empire's most swashbuckling adventurers, Skinner was the son of a Scotsman and a Rajput. Rejected by the British Army because of his mixed parentage, he raised his own cavalry regiment, Skinner's Horse, whose flamboyant yellow uniforms gave rise to the name Yellow Boys. His troops fought with distinction and are still part of the Indian Army. On his death he was honoured as a Commander of the Order of the Bath. His descendants still live on an estate in Mussoorie, Uttar Pradesh.

James Skinner (1778–1841)

Graves at Nicholson Cemetery

Nicholson Cemetery ❸

Lala Hardev Sahai Marg.
⏱ 10am–5pm.

IN A RATHER tumbledown walled cemetery named after him, surrounded by brisk traffic and overlooked by the huge Inter State Bus Terminus (ISBT), lies the flamboyant Brigadier General John Nicholson, the British commander. The headstone on his grave, which is to the right of the entrance, records that he "led the assault on Delhi but fell mortally wounded and died 3rd September 1857, aged 35". The surrounding graves belong to others like him who died at the time of the Indian Mutiny, between 10 May and 30 September 1857. The saddest, though, are the tiny graves of children, such as the headless angel mourning over Alfred and Ida Scott's little daughter: "We gave her back to bloom in heaven".

To enter the cemetery, knock on the gate and the *chowkidar* will open it. Though there are no entrance charges, a small tip (10–20 rupees) to the *chowkidar* and a donation to the Church of North India will be welcome.

Qudsia Gardens ❹

Shamnath Marg. ⏱ *sunrise–sunset.*

QUDSIA BEGUM, the dancing girl who became the wife of Emperor Muhammad Shah (r.1719–48), laid out these gardens in around 1748, and although the Inter State Bus Terminus and the Tourist Park now occupy much of the original site, the imposing gateway still stands. The rest of the present park is more modern with a children's playground and a rather formidable statue of the great Rajput king, Maharana Pratap. North of the gardens is the children's home run by Mother Teresa's Missionaries of Charity, where abandoned children are cared for.

Civil Lines ❺

Bounded by Shamnath Marg and Mahatma Gandhi Marg.

OLD DELHI'S Civil Lines were inhabited by the British civilian population while the Cantonment *(see p104)* was the military enclave. They lived in spacious bungalows, shopped at the Exchange Stores, dined at Maidens Hotel and worshipped at St James's Church. The old "temporary" Secretariat (built in 1912) is also located here on Mahatma Gandhi Marg. This long white building with its two towers, where the former Legislative Assembly once sat, also housed the offices of the Delhi Administration at one time. When the British moved into New Delhi, established Indian professional and merchant families settled here. Several old bungalows have been redeveloped as modern blocks of flats, yet some areas, such as Rajpur Road, still retain their essential colonial character.

To the east of Civil Lines, near the Delhi-Chandigarh bypass, is Metcalfe House, a sprawling mansion built in the 1830s by Sir Thomas Metcalfe, Delhi's eccentric British Resident from 1835–53. This house, once the hub of British social life, can be seen from the highway. It is now owned by the Defence Ministry and not open to the public.

White-plastered façade of the Oberoi Maidens Hotel in the Civil Lines area

Statues of former viceroys in the Coronation Durbar site

still visible. Feroze Shah also had a large hunting estate here where he built a lodge called Kushak-i-Shikar, a mosque, as well as a double-storeyed mansion, the Pir Ghaib, now in the grounds of the Hindu Rao Hospital (enter the main gate and turn right at the Cardiac Unit). The name, Pir Ghaib, derives from the tale of a resident *pir* who one day, simply vanished *(ghaib)* while meditating at this site. A cenotaph in one of the rooms marks the spot.

Coronation Memorial ❻

S of NH1 Bypass. ⭘ *sunrise–sunset.*

THIS WAS THE SITE of the Royal Durbar held in 1911 to proclaim the accession of George V as King Emperor of India. A red sandstone obelisk records that the King Emperor proclaimed his coronation to the "governors, princes and peoples of India" (in that order) and "received their dutiful homage". He also announced the transfer of the capital from Calcutta to Delhi and two days later laid the foundation stones for the new city *(see pp68–9).* On 12 December 1911, more than 100,000 people thronged the site where the King Emperor and Queen Empress sat beneath a golden dome mounted on a crimson canopy. Today, the site is a flat, dusty and forlorn spot, and ranged round in a pathetic semi-circle are statues of former viceroys, evicted from their perches in the city to make way for later Indian leaders. These include Lords Hardinge and Willingdon (distinguished for their role in the construction of New Delhi).
Towering over them all is the 22 m (73 ft) statue of the King Emperor himself, draped in his Durbar robes, which was removed from the canopy at India Gate *(see p71)* and installed here in the 1960s.

Coronation Memorial

The Northern Ridge ❼

Rani Jhansi Rd, Ridge Rd, Magazine Rd. ⭘ *sunrise–sunset.*

THE NORTHERN END of the Ridge is a forested park cut through by Ridge Road and Rani Jhansi Road, with the small clearing of Bara Hindu Rao in the middle. This area still resounds with memories of 1857. It was around Flagstaff Tower, to the far north, that British women and children took shelter before they were evacuated to Karnal near Panipat *(see p140).*
The Mutiny Memorial (known locally as Ajitgarh), at the southern end, is a red sandstone Victorian Gothic spire built by the British to commemorate "the soldiers, British and native … who were killed" in 1857, and lists separately the names of those who died. At the entrance is a plaque, dated 1972, which points out: "The enemy of the in-scriptions were those who fought bravely for national liberation in 1857". There are pano-ramic views of Old Delhi from the platform at the base of the tower. Nearby is a 3rd-century Ashokan Pillar, one of the two Feroze Shah Tughlaq *(see p97)* brought from Meerut in 1356. Faint inscriptions in Brahmi, extolling the virtues of practising *dhamma* (the Buddhist Way of Truth), are

St Stephen's College

Delhi University ❽

Vishwavidyalaya Marg.

THE UNIVERSITY area runs parallel to the Northern Ridge, and colleges dot the vast campus. Arguably the most attractive of these is St Stephen's College, designed by Walter George in 1938. With its long corridors built in quartzite and its well-kept gardens, it has some deliber-ately cultivated Oxbridge associations. At one time this was one of India's premier institutions, with renowned scholars such as the historian Percival Spear on its staff. The office of the Vice Chancellor was once the guesthouse for British officials. It was here, in what is now the registrar's office, that the young Lord Louis Mountbatten proposed to, and was accepted by, Edwina Ashley. A plaque celebrates the event. They eventually became India's last viceroy and vicereine.

The image of the Buddha installed at Buddha Jayanti Park

The Ridge ❾

Upper Ridge Rd. ◯ sunrise–sunset.

DELHI'S RIDGE, the last outcrop of the Aravalli Hills extending northwards from Rajasthan, runs from southwest to northeast. The area was originally developed by Feroze Shah Tughlaq, some 600 years ago as his hunting resort. He erected many lodges, the ruins of which can still be seen here and towards the northern end of the Ridge (see p103). This green belt of undulating, rocky terrain is covered by dense scrub forest consisting mainly of laburnum (Cassia fistula), kikar (Acacia arabica) and flame of the forest (Butea monosperma) trees, interspersed with bright splashes of bougainvillea.

A large portion in the southwest is now the **Buddha Jayanti Park**, a peaceful, well-manicured enclave, criss-crossed with paved paths. Pipal (Ficus religiosa) trees abound, and on a small ornamental island is a simple sandstone pavilion shading the large gilt-covered statue of the Buddha, installed by the 16th Dalai Lama in October 1993. An inscription nearby quotes the Dalai Lama: "Human beings have the capacity to bequeathe to future generations a world that is truly human". Every May, Buddhist monks and devotees celebrate Buddha Jayanti (see p38) here.

Delhi Cantonment ❿

Bounded by NH8, MG Rd and Sadar Bazaar Marg. **St Martin's Church** Church Rd. 📞 (011) 2569 4632. **War Graves Cemetery** Brar Square. 📞 (011) 2569 1958. ◯ 8am–5pm daily.

THE CANTONMENT in Delhi was planned by John Begg and built by the Military Works Department in the 1930s. With its straight roads, neat, whitewashed walls, well-clipped hedges, parade ground and shooting-range, it epitomizes the quint-essential spit and polish of the military. The garrison **Church of St Martin's**, probably the most original modern church in India, was designed by Lutyens's close associate, Arthur Gordon Shoosmith (1888–1974). Consecrated in 1931 and built from three and a half million bricks, it rises straight-walled with small,

A memorial tablet

recessed windows and a 39 m (128 ft) tower, the lines between the bricks being the only ornamentation. Within is a stark classical interior with a plaque in honour of the architect and a haunting tablet in memory of the three children of Private Spier who died within days of each other at Abbottabad (now in Pakistan) in 1938. If the church is locked, contact the Presbyter-in-Charge who lives in the adjacent cottage.

A short distance from Dhaula Kuan Circle is the **War Graves Cemetery** where lie the Commonwealth soldiers and airmen who died on the Eastern Front in World War II. A monument at the entrance proudly declares: "Their Name Liveth Ever-more". The graves are set in neat rows with matching headstones; only the regi-mental insignia and biblical texts are different. Every Remembrance Day (11 Nov), wreaths are laid at the Memorial Column, followed by a short prayer.

The National Rail Museum ⓫

Chanakyapuri. 📞 (011) 2688 1816. ◯ 9:30am–5pm Tue–Sun. ● 1:30–2:30pm & public hols. 🎥 extra for video and train rides. 📷

INDIA'S RAILWAY NETWORK gives rise to astonishing statistics. It has a route length of 63,360 km (39,370 miles) and tracks that cover 108,513 km (67,427 miles). There are about 7,150 stations, 12,600 passenger trains, and 1,350 goods trains

The War Graves Cemetery

that run every day. The railways employ 1.6 million people, while 13 million passengers travel by train each day and eat 6 million meals through the journey.

This museum encapsulates the history of Indian railways. Steam locomotive enthusiasts will appreciate the collection that traces the development of the Indian railways from 1849, when the first 34 km (21 miles) of railway between Bombay (now Mumbai) and Kalyan was planned. The wealth of memorabilia on display inside includes the skull of an elephant which collided with a mail train at Golkara in 1894, and a realistic model of an 1868 first-class passenger coach with separate compartments for accompanying servants. Outside, are several retired steam locomotives built in Manchester, Glasgow and Darlington in the late 19th century, and the splendid salon that carried the Prince of Wales (later King Edward VII) on his travels during the 1876 Royal Durbar.

A "toy train" offers rides around the compound, and the shop sells model loco-motives, ranging from Rs1,000 to 3,000.

Safdarjung's Tomb ⑫

Aurobindo Marg. ◯ *sunrise–sunset.* 🎥 📷 *extra charges for video photography.* ☎ *(011) 2301 7293.*

THIS IS THE LAST of Delhi's garden tombs and was built in 1754 for Safdarjung, the powerful prime minister of Muhammad Shah, the emperor between 1719–48. Marble was allegedly stripped from the tomb of Abdur Rahim Khan-i-Khanan in Nizamuddin *(see p82)* to construct this rather florid example of late Mughal architecture. Approached by an ornate gateway, the top storey of which houses the Archaeological Survey of India's library, the tomb, with its exaggerated onion-shaped dome, stands in a *charbagh* cut by water channels. Its red and buff stone façade is extensively ornamented with well-preserved plaster carving, and the central chamber itself is unusually light and airy with some fine stone inlay work set into the floor.

A well-stocked shop at INA Market

INA Market ⑬

Aurobindo Marg. **Shops** ◯ 9am–9pm Tue–Sun. ● Mon.

THIS LIVELY BAZAAR retains all the trappings of a tradi-tional Indian market but also sells imported foodstuffs such as cheese, pasta and exotic varieties of seafood. The stalls are crammed together under a ramshackle roof, mostly corrugated iron and oilcloth. Shops selling stainless steel utensils, spices, ready-made garments, live chickens and tiny restaurants offering Indian fast food, co-exist cheek by jowl. Ingredients for regional Indian cuisine, such as South Indian *sambhar* (curry) powder, Bengali spices or massive red chillies from Kashmir are also available. Great pots of Punjabi pickles, made from cauliflower, carrots, radish and mustard seeds are sold by weight. Diplomats, out-of-town shoppers and locals all patronize this market for its reasonable prices and variety of products.

The name derives from Indian National Airports, as people working at nearby Safdarjung Aerodrome lived in the adjacent colony. The aerodrome, further down Aurobindo Marg, was built in the 1930s. During World War II, it was the headquarters of the South Eastern Command Air Wing. It now houses offices of the Ministry of Civil Aviation and the Delhi Gliding Club. Indian Airlines also has a 24-hour booking office here *(see p293).*

A steam engine at the National Rail Museum

CANTONMENT TOWNS

After the 1860s, over 170 cantonments (pronounced "cantoonment") were built on the outskirts of major towns to impress Indians with the seriousness of British military might. Each was a self-contained world, with symmetrical rows of barracks, finely graded bungalows, clubs and regimental messes, bazaars, hospitals and churches. Military hierarchies, too, were rigidly followed. Even after Independence, the military is mostly stationed in cantonment areas.

Indian cavalry officer, pre-World War II

Moth ki Masjid ⑭

South Extension, Part II.

BUILT IN 1505 by Miyan Bhuwa, Sikander Lodi's prime minister, the design of this graceful red sandstone structure with its five-arched, three-domed prayer hall was developed further in later Mughal mosques. Over the central arch is a fine *jharokha* with traces of the original plaster decoration. The red sandstone gateway and the ornate decorations on the mosque's façade are also noteworthy. It is said that Sikander Lodi gave Miyan Bhuwa a *moth* (lentil seed) which reaped him such rich returns that he was able to endow this mosque. Sadly, he annoyed Sikander's successor, Ibrahim Lodi (r.1517–26), who had him put to death.

Detail of Moth ki Masjid

\Hauz Khas ⑮

W of Aurobindo Marg.

BEYOND THE BOUTIQUES, art galleries and restaurants that have taken over the former village of Hauz Khas, are the medieval monuments from Feroze Shah Tughlaq's reign. In 1352, the sultan constructed a number of buildings on the banks of Hauz Khas, the large tank (now dry) excavated by Alauddin Khilji for his city of Siri *(see p108)*. Contemporary accounts claim that Feroze Shah was a prolific builder, and during his 37-year reign he constructed an astounding 40 mosques, 200 towns, 100 public baths and about 30 reservoirs.

Among the buildings here are a *madrasa*, Feroze Shah's tomb and the ruins of a small mosque at the extreme north of the complex. The double storeyed *madrasa* was built so that the tank and lower storey were at the same level, while the upper floor was at ground level. Refreshing breezes across the water must have once cooled the theological discussions held there by scholars. The low domes, colonnades and *jharokhas* relieve the severity of its façade, while plaster carvings and deep niches for books embellish the interior. The *chhatris* in the entrance forecourt are said to cover the teachers' burial mounds. The tomb of Feroze Shah lies at one end of the *madrasa*. Wine-red painted plaster calligraphy decorates the interior of the austere tomb.

The complex is best viewed in the afternoon when sunlight filters through the *jaalis* carved into the linteled archway, to cover the graves of the sultan, his sons and grandson with delicate star-shaped shadows.

East of Hauz Khas, off Aurobindo Marg, is a small rubble-built tapering structure called **Chor Minar** ("tower of thieves") with a staircase, now locked, leading to the top. This dates to the 14th-century Khilji period and its walls, pockmarked with holes, are said to have held the severed heads of thieves to deter others from crime.

Close by, to the northwest, is the **Nili Masjid** ("blue mosque"), named after the blue tiles above its *chhajja*. The inscription on the central of its three arches reveals that it was built in 1505 by one Kasumbhil, the nurse of the son of the governor of Delhi. Nearby is an Idgah, whose remaining long wall is carved with 11 mihrabs and an inscription proclaiming that it was built in 1404–5 by Iqbal Khan, a Tughlaq noble.

The double-storeyed *madrasa* at Hauz Khas

Early Capitals of Delhi

ELHI'S FAMOUS "seven cities" range from the 12th-century Qila Rai Pithora, built by Prithviraj Chauhan *(see p48)*, to the imperial Shahjahanabad, constructed in the 17th century. Each of these cities comprised the settlements that grew around the forts and palaces erected by powerful sultans with territorial ambitions. As the Sultanate was consolidated, the rulers moved their capitals from those defensively situated in the rocky outcrops of the Aravallis, northwards towards the open plains by the banks of the Yamuna. Today, Delhi is an amalgam of medieval citadels, palaces, tombs and mosques, and a spreading, modern concrete jungle.

Purana Qila

Shabjahanabad *was Delhi's seventh city, built between 1638 and 1649 by Shah Jahan who shifted the Mughal capital here from Agra (see pp150–51).*

Ferozabad, *stretching north from Hauz Khas to the banks of the Yamuna, is Delhi's fifth city built by Feroze Shah Tughlaq (r.1351–88).*

Shabjahanabad

Ferozabad

New Delhi

Purana Qila

Siri, *Delhi's second city can still be seen near the Siri Fort Auditorium and the adjacent village of Shahpur Jat (see p108). The once prosperous city of Siri was built by Alauddin Khilji in 1303.*

Purana Qila, *the citadel (see p84) of Delhi's sixth city, was built by Humayun. It was captured and occupied by the Afghan chieftain, Sher Shah Sur (r.1540–45) who called it Shergarh.*

Siri

Jahanpanah

Qila Rai Pithora

Tughlaqabad

Jahanpanah *was built by Muhammad-bin-Tughlaq (r.1325–51) as a walled enclosure to link Qila Rai Pithora and Siri. The ruined battlements of Delhi's fourth city stand near Chiragh (see p108).*

Qila Rai Pithora *was the first of Delhi's seven cities, built by the Chauhans in about 1180. In 1192, it was captured by Qutbuddin Aibak who established his capital here (see pp110–11).*

Tughlaqabad, *a dramatic fortress (see p114) on the foothills of the Aravallis, was Delhi's third city built during Ghiyasuddin Tughlaq's four-year reign (1321–5).*

Ruins of Siri, Delhi's second city built by Alauddin Khilji

Siri Fort 16

Siri Fort Rd. **Siri Fort Auditorium**
☎ *(011) 2649 3370.*

SOME CRUMBLING ramparts are all that remain of Alauddin Khilji's 14th-century city of Siri *(see p107)*. The ruins of mosques and tombs can be found in the adjoining village of Shahpur Jat, today a shopper's paradise with many up-market boutiques, offices and a few art galleries. Siri Fort is commonly associated with the Siri Fort Auditorium which regularly hosts concerts and film festivals. It is directly adjacent to the Asian Games Village complex where there are speciality restaurants serving Indian, Chinese and Mexican cuisine.

Chiragh Delhi 17

Bordered by Outer Ring Rd & LB Shastri Marg.

THE DARGAH of the Sufi saint Nasiruddin Mahmud (died 1356), who succeeded Hazrat Nizamuddin Auliya *(see p82)* as spiritual leader of the Chishti sect, lies in the once secluded village of Chiragh Delhi. This saint, known as Raushan Chiragh-i-Dehlvi ("illuminated lamp of Delhi"), was buried here and the village that grew around his tomb was named after him. Muhammad-bin-Tughlaq, the sultan at that time, built the original village walls in the 14th century.

The shrine itself is small and should be approached on foot through the narrow, congested village lanes, past rows of tailoring establishments (including one specializing in *burqas*) and shops selling varieties of *mithai* ("sweetmeats"), *chadors*, flower garlands and other religious offerings. Some ruined *havelis*, which must have once been very beautiful, also line the street. A huge arched doorway leads to the *dargah*, a quieter and simpler shrine than that of Hazrat Nizamuddin. Shaded by trees, the tomb is set in a 12-pillared square chamber, enclosed by *jaali* screens and surmounted by a large plastered dome rising from an octagonal drum. Small domed turrets stand at the four corners. The roof inside has been embellished with fine painted plaster carvings set with mirrors, clearly a recent addition. Within the enclosure are several smaller mosques and halls, added over the years for religious discourses.

At the far end from the gateway is a partially ruined tomb that is locally claimed to be that of Bahlol Lodi (r.1451–88), the founder of the Lodi dynasty. The *chhajja* has collapsed, but the square chamber is still surmounted by five domes, the central being the largest. The arches have engraved inscriptions.

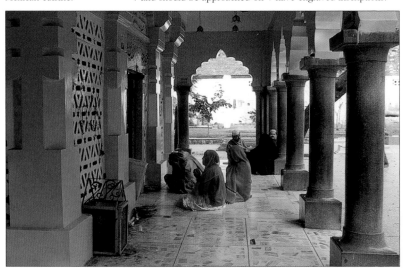

Women devotees worshipping at Chiragh Delhi

Covered corridors with arches in the 14th-century Begumpuri Mosque

Khirkee ⓲

N of Press Enclave Marg.

THE VILLAGE adjacent to Chiragh Delhi is called "Khirkee" after the huge mosque built by Feroze Shah Tughlaq's prime minister, Khan-i-Jahan Junan Shah *(see p96)* in the mid-14th century. Standing today in a declivity and surrounded by village houses, is the unusual two-storeyed Khirkee ("windows") Mosque. It has a sombre fortress-like appearance with bastions on all four corners, and its severe façade is broken by rows of arched windows that are covered by portcullis-like *jaalis* which give the mosque its name. Built on a high plinth, flights of stairs lead up to imposing gateways on the north, south and east sides. The inner courtyard is partly covered, its roof supported by monolithic stone pillars, and crowned by nine sets of nine small domes. Only four courtyards remain open to the sky. This was the first example of this type of mosque design. But the division of open space by pillars was found

Detail of an arched window with *jaali*

unsuitable for large congregations, so this design was never repeated.

Satpula ("seven-arches"), the dam and stone weir built by Muhammad-bin-Tughlaq in 1326, is located a few metres down the same road. It formed part of the reservoir which was used for irrigation, and the grooves, meant for sliding the shutters that regulate the flow of water, can still be seen on the seven arches. The weir also formed a portion of the fortified wall enclosing the city of Jahanpanah *(see p107)*. Its upper storey was used during Muhammad-bin-Tughlaq's time as a *madrasa*.

The fortress-like Khirkee Mosque

Jahanpanah ⓳

S of Panchsheel Park.

IN THE HEART of Jahanpanah, Muhammad-bin-Tughlaq's capital, stands **Begumpuri Mosque**, also built by Khan-i-Jahan Junan Shah. (When asking for directions, it is advisable to specifically ask for the old mosque, as a new one is located nearby.) Built on a high plinth with massive, typically Tughlaq walls, the mosque has a single imposing doorway at the head of a flight of stairs leading into the vast rectangular courtyard surrounded by arched cloisters, surmounted by 44 small domes. The prayer hall has 24 arched openings, the central one surmounted by a large dome. It is said that in times of need, this mosque also functioned as a treasury, granary and meeting place.

Nearby, to the north, is the palace of **Bijay Mandal**, a derelict, brooding octagonal structure rising from a high plinth. It is worth climbing the broken stone-cut stairs to the upper platform to get a sense of its size. According to the famed 14th-century Arab traveller, Ibn Batuta, it was from these very bastions that Muhammad-bin-Tughlaq held public audience and reviewed his troops. Later, in the early 16th century, the palace is believed to have been used as a residence by Sheikh Hasan Tahir, a much revered saint who visited Delhi during the reign of Sikandar Lodi. Panoramic views of the city of Delhi, extending from the Qutb Minar to Humayun's Tomb and beyond, can be seen from its upper platform.

Mehrauli Archaeological Park ⓴

Chhatri outside **Jamali-Kamali**

BEST KNOWN FOR the Qutb Minar, a World Heritage monument, Mehrauli was built over Rajput territories known as Lal Kot and Qila Rai Pithora. In 1193, Qutbuddin Aibak made this the centre of the Sultanate of Delhi and by the 13th century a small village, Mehrauli, had grown around the shrine of the Sufi saint, Qutb Sahib. Later, Mughal princes came to Mehrauli to hunt and some 19th-century British officials built weekend houses here, attracted by its orchards, ponds and abundant game *(shikar)*. It is still a popular weekend retreat for Delhi's rich and famous.

Dargah Qutb Sahib
This 13th-century dargah *is still a pilgrim point.*

Zafar Mahal is a palace named after the *nom de plume* of the last Mughal emperor, Bahadur Shah Zafar.

Mehrauli village

Hauz-i-Shamsi is a large reservoir built in 1230 by Iltutmish, who is supposed to have been guided to this site by the Prophet in a dream.

★ **Jahaz Mahal**
Venue of the Phoolwalon ki Sair (see p40), *this square pleasure pavilion, built during the Lodi era (1451–1526), seems to float on the Hauz-i-Shamsi tank.*

Jharna (waterfall) was so-called because after the monsoon, water from the Hauz-i-Shamsi would flow over an embankment into a garden.

Bagichi Masjid

STAR FEATURES

- ★ **Qutb Minar**
- ★ **Jamali-Kamali Mosque and Tomb**
- ★ **Jahaz Mahal**

Madhi Masjid
Surrounded by bastions and a high wall, this fortress-like mosque has a large open courtyard and a three-arched, profusely ornamented prayer hall.

Adham Khan's Tomb
Built by Akbar in the 16th century, this was rescued from decay by Curzon (see pp56–7).

VISITORS' CHECKLIST

Delhi–Gurgaon Rd.
○ sunrise–sunset daily.
🚻 🚹 🍴 📷 🎫 *Phoolwalon ki Sair (early Oct).*

★ Qutb Minar
The Qutb (Arabic for pole or axis) area saw the advent of Islamic rule in India. The world's highest single tower, this is the focus of an early Islamic complex (see p112).

0 metres   250
0 yards   250

Dilkusha
New Delhi

Rajon ki Bain
This dramatic three-storeyed stepwell was also called Sukhi Baoli (dry well). Nearby is the five-storeyed Gandhak ki Baoli, named after its strong sulphur (gandhak) smell. These baolis once supplied fresh water to the area.

Balban's Tomb
Balban's 13th-century tomb lies in a square rubble-built chamber, open to the sky.

★ Jamali-Kamali Mosque and Tomb
The tomb of Jamali (the court poet during the late Lodi and early Mughal age) is inscribed with some of his verses. Its well-preserved interior has coloured tiles and richly decorated painted plasterwork. The second grave is unidentified but is widely believed to be that of his brother, Jamali.

The Qutb Complex

Floral motif

THE QUTB MINAR TOWERS over this historic area where Qutbuddin Aibak laid the foundation of the Delhi Sultanate *(see pp50–51)*. In 1193, he built the Quwwat-ul-Islam ("the might of Islam") Mosque and the Qutb Minar to announce the advent of the Muslim sultans. Later, Iltutmish, Alauddin Khilji and Feroze Shah Tughlaq added other buildings, bringing in a new architectural style *(see p24)*. The fusion of decorative Hindu panels and Islamic domes and arches shows the mingling of two cultures.

Iron Pillar
This 4th-century pillar, originally made as a flagstaff in Vishnu's honour, is a tribute to ancient Indian metallurgy.

Qutb Minar
The five-storeyed Victory Tower started by Qutbuddin Aibak was completed by his successor, Iltutmish.

Alauddin Khilji's Tomb

Iltutmish's Tomb

Carved Panels
Panels, carved with inscriptions from the Koran, embellish the gateway.

Alai Darwaza
This gateway to the complex, erected in 1311 by Alauddin Khilji, is one of the earliest buildings in India to employ the Islamic principles of arched construction (see p24).

Imam Zamin's Tomb

Iltutmish's Tomb
Built in 1235 by Iltutmish himself, its dome has vanished. The interior is carved with geometric and calligraphic patterns.

To Entrance

Quwwat-ul-Islam Mosque
Hindu motifs, such as tasselled ropes and bells, are clearly visible on the carved pillars of this mosque.

Dargah Qutb Sahib, shrine of the Sufi saint Qutbuddin Bakhtiyar "Kaki"

Exploring Mehrauli

Clustered round the *dargah* of Qutb Sahib, Mehrauli became a sylvan retreat for the later Mughals and top officials of the East India Company. Its medieval bazaar survives despite its recent conversion into boutiques and cafés, popular with Delhi's "smart set".

Medallion with calligraphy

ꙮ Dargah Qutb Sahib

In the heart of the Mehrauli bazaar, lies the *dargah* of a Sufi saint called Qutbuddin Bakhtiyar or "Kaki", after the small sugared cakes *(kaki)* he was fed when he fasted. It has been rebuilt several times since his death in 1235, so that today many mosques, tanks and chambers surround it, among them the lovely Moti Masjid ("pearl mosque") built in 1709. A domed marble pavilion contains his grave, which women may only view through the marble *jaalis*. A royal necropolis in the same area has the graves of some later Mughal kings, such as Bahadur Shah I (1707–12) and Akbar II (1806–36). The *dargah* and the Jogmaya Temple are the starting point for the Phoolwalon ki Sair *(see p40)*, the procession of flower-sellers which began in the 1720s as a floral tribute to the Mughal emperor. Revived by Nehru after 1947, it is now an important cultural event.

ꙮ Adham Khan's Tomb

Near the bus terminus, at the approach to Mehrauli village, is an imposing, single-domed structure standing on a high platform. This is believed to be the last of the octagonal tombs built in Delhi and its shaded colonnades are much favoured by local youth for their siestas. Adham Khan, the son of Akbar's wet nurse, Maham Anga *(see p85)*, was considered a foster-brother of the emperor. In 1562, Adham Khan killed a rival, Atgah Khan, the husband of another wet nurse *(see p82)*. A furious Akbar ordered Adham Khan's execution, but was so moved by the death of his mother, Maham Anga, 40 days later, that he had a tomb built for both mother and son.

By far the largest building here, the tomb is locally known as the *bhulbhulaiyan* (maze) because of the narrow passages concealed within its walls. In the 1800s, the British used the tomb as a rest-house, police station and residence for minor officials.

A corridor in Adham Khan's Tomb

Sanskriti Museum

Sanskriti ㉑

Anandgram, Mehrauli-Gurgaon Rd.
📞 (011) 2650 1125. ⏱ 10am–5pm
Tue–Sun. ⬤ Mon & public hols.

THIS UNUSUAL MUSEUM is set amidst beautifully land-scaped spacious grounds where exhibits are displayed both in the garden and in specially constructed rural huts. The collection, too, is equally unusual. It is devoted to traditional objects of everyday use, exquisitely crafted by the unknown, unsung, rural artisan. OP Jain, whose personal collections gave birth to this museum, has donated exquisite combs, nutcrackers, lamps, foot-scrubbers and kitchenware. Terracotta objects from all over India are also on display. The pots are especially dazzling, particularly as their production techniques have not changed for centuries.

Sultan Ghari ㉒

Off Mahipalpur-Mehrauli Rd.

SULTAN GHARI was the first Islamic tomb to be built in Delhi and among the earliest in India. The Slave king, Iltutmish erected this tomb in 1231 for his eldest son and heir, Nasiruddin Muhammad, who was killed in battle. Today, its fortress-like exterior appears out of place in the midst of one of Delhi's largest residential complexes, Vasant Kunj. Inside is a raised courtyard, and the tomb itself is an octagonal platform, forming the roof of the crypt (ghar) below. Like many monuments of this early medieval period, Sultan Ghari was constructed from pillars and stones taken from temples nearby. Fragments of these are visible in the surround-ing colonnades, which may have once housed a *madrasa*. The mihrab on the west side has some fine calligraphic decoration and, interestingly, there is a marble *yonipatta*, the base of a Shiva linga *(see p319)* embedded in the floor.

The tomb, located on the road from Andheria More to Delhi Airport, is reached after turning left from the Spinal Injuries Centre and taking the next left after that.

Tughlaqabad ㉓

Off Mehrauli-Badarpur Rd.

THIS SPECTACULAR fortress, built by Ghiyasuddin Tughlaq in the 14th century *(see p107)*, was completed in just four years. The quality of its construction was influenced by building techniques in Multan where Ghiyasuddin had served as governor. It was so sturdy that the rubble-built walls clinging to the shape of the hill, survive intact all along the 6.5 km (4 mile) perimeter. To the right of the main entrance is the citadel from which rise the ruins of the Vijay Mandal ("tower of victory"). To the left is a rectangular area where arches are all that remain of a complex of palaces and halls. Beyond these, houses were once laid out in a neat grid pattern. Legend has it that when Ghiyasuddin tried to prevent the building of the *baoli* at Hazrat Nizamuddin Auliya's *dargah (see p82)*, the saint cursed him by saying that one day only jackals and the Gujjar tribe would inhabit his capital. Perhaps the saint forgot to add tourists and monkeys to that list!

A good view of the fort and of the adjoining smaller one of Adilabad is possible from the

Ghiyasuddin Tughlaq's Tomb

The crumbling ramparts of Tughlaqabad Fort

The lotus-domed Baha'i House of Worship, one of Delhi's most spectacular sights

walls. Adilabad was built by Muhammad-bin-Tughlaq (r.1325–51), who is believed to have killed his father Ghiyas-uddin by contriving to have a gateway collapse on him. They are both buried in Ghiyasuddin's Tomb, joined to the Tughlaqabad Fort by a causeway that crossed the dammed waters of a lake.

The tomb was the first in India to be built with sloping walls, a design that was repeated in all subsequent Tughlaq architecture. Its severe red sandstone walls, relieved by white marble inlay, are surmounted by a white marble dome. The red sandstone *kalasha* (urn) which crowns it and the lintel spanning the arched opening decorated with a lotus bud fringe, are both influenced by Hindu architecture.

Kalkaji Temple ㉔

Nehru Place. ⬚ *Navaratri (Mar–Apr & Sep–Oct).*

THIS TEMPLE is a good place to see Hinduism in bustling, popular practice. It is approached through a narrow winding alley, lined with stalls selling laminated religious prints, bangles, *sindur* (vermilion powder) and fruit, while devotional hymns blast from rival cassette stalls. The 12-domed temple, with a heavily decorated pillared pavilion, was built in the mid-18th century on an older site by Raja Kedarnath, prime minister of Emperor Akbar II. Thereafter, many contemporary additions, financed by rich merchants, have been made. The goddess Kali or Kalka, draped in silks, sits under silver umbrellas and a marble canopy. Legend has it that a farmer, on discovering that his cow regularly offered her milk to the goddess, built this temple in her name.

Baha'i House of Worship ㉕

Bahapur, Kalkaji. █ *(011) 2644 4029.* ⬚ *Apr–Sep: 9am–7pm; Oct–Mar: 9:30am–5:30pm Tue–Sun.* ⬛ *Mon & public hols.* **Prayer services** *10am, noon, 3pm & 5pm.*

JUST OPPOSITE the Kalkaji Temple is the Baha'i House of Worship, a world where silence and order prevails. The arresting shape of its unfurling 27-petalled white marble lotus has given it its more popular name, the Lotus Temple. The edifice, circled by nine pools and 27 acres (92 ha) of green manicured lawns, is one of Delhi's most innovative modern structures.

The Baha'i sect originated in Persia and this temple was designed by Iranian architect, Fariburz Sahba. Construction began in 1980 and was completed in 1986. Inside, the lofty auditorium can seat 1,300 and all are welcome to meditate there and attend the daily 15-minute services. The temple looks spectacular after dark when the lighting gives the marble panels a luminous, ethereal quality.

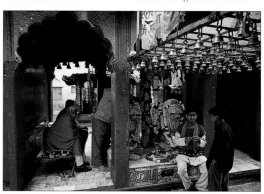

Inside view of Kalkaji Temple

Day Trips from Delhi

IF YOU WANT A BREAK from the hustle and bustle of Delhi and wish to explore the surrounding countryside, there are several interesting sights to visit, all within a 50-km (30-mile) radius of the city. The lake at Sultanpur is a haven for migratory birds in winter, and in Pataudi is a beautiful palace which belongs to its cricket-loving nawabs, now open to tourists. Surajkund, with its vast medieval reservoir, is the venue of a popular crafts fair held every February. All these excursions take about eight hours. Since they are not particularly easy to reach by public transport, it is best to hire a car and driver for the day, which can be organized by your hotel or local taxi rank and is relatively inexpensive.

SIGHTS AT A GLANCE

Pataudi ❷
Sultanpur Bird Sanctuary ❶
Surajkund ❸

0 kilometres   50

0 miles   25

KEY

▦	City centre
☐	Greater Delhi
✕	International airport
═	National highway
═	Major road
═	Minor road

Sultanpur Bird Sanctuary ❶

46 km (27 miles) W of Delhi.
🛈 Haryana Tourism, Chanderlok Building, Janpath, Delhi (011) 2332 4911. ◯ sunrise–sunset daily.
◻ ▨ ☐ ✗

THIS SANCTUARY, a two-hour drive from Delhi, has been developed around a low-lying marshy area that is dry in summer, but fills up during the monsoon to form a shallow lake (jheel). Sultanpur is at its best in the winter when this shallow sheet of water provides a haven for migratory birds.

Several pleasant walks, including a paved pathway which runs around the small lake, allow one to explore the 35-km (22-mile) area, while the many hides or machans, mounted on stilts, provide a good view of the birdlife on the lake. The Sarus crane, the world's tallest flying bird, breeds in the mud spits covered with reeds that rise above the waters. Often, on late winter evenings, large, noisy flocks of demoiselle cranes descend on the lake. The other birds that visit the lake include egrets, herons, kingfishers, pelicans and painted storks.

The rolling tree-shaded lawns, home to herds of friendly deer, have beautifully sited picnic spots. The sanctuary shop has a good selection of books and posters on Indian birdlife.

Sultanpur, home to a variety of deer and many migratory birds

Pataudi ❷

60 km (37 miles) S of Delhi.
Ibrahim Kothi 🍴 *Advance
reservations are essential.* 📞 *(011)
2301 3549.* ♿

THE TWO-AND-A-HALF hour drive to Pataudi is a pleasant one, particularly after crossing Gurgaon when the road runs through open wheat fields and occasional villages. Pataudi, a typical North Indian town with a tangle of narrow lanes and a congested bazaar, is famous for its cricket-playing nawabs who claim descent from a 16th-century Afghan noble.

The old palace, built about 200 years ago, is now derelict, but still retains its romantic charm. The new palace, known as **Ibrahim Kothi**, was built in 1939. The elegant white, double-storeyed building, set amidst 10 acres (4 ha) of flowering gardens, has deep, pillared verandahs and is surmounted by a small dome. The well-maintained interior includes polished

Elegant interior of Ibrahim Kothi

parquet floors, pink Venetian chandeliers and chintz furnishings. The walls are lined with portraits and sepia photographs of the present nawab's ancestors. One is of his father as a member of the famous "bodyline" English cricket team which toured Australia in the 1930s.

A section of the palace has now been refurbished and opened as a hotel for tourists who want to spend a relaxed holiday in royal splendour.

Ibrahim Kothi at Pataudi

Surajkund ❸

21 km (13 miles) S of Delhi.
ℹ️ *Haryana Tourism, Chanderlok
Building, Janpath, Delhi (011) 2332
4911.* 🎫 🖥 ⛵

KING SURAJPAL of the Rajput Tomar dynasty *(see p48)*, hero of many legends, built this reservoir some time in the late 10th or early 11th century. An embankment of stone terraces was built round a pool which trapped rain water running down from the hills. A sun temple is thought to have stood on the western side. Tomar Rajputs trace their descent from the sun, hence the name: *suraj* (sun) *kund* (pool). Today, the embankment is more or less intact, though there is no trace of the temple and the pool itself is none too clean. The nearby artificial lake is picturesque and is best enjoyed from the paddle or rowing boats on hire. You might even glimpse a pale green water snake swimming alongside.

About 2 km (1.5 miles) to the west is **Anangpur Dam** built by the Tomar king, Anangpal. A rather impressive quartzite stone stucture, it blocks a narrow ravine to create an artificial lake. The dam is reached on foot, but it is an extremely brambly and rocky walk and best avoided in the rainy weather.

This area is a popular picnic spot for Delhi's residents. Haryana Tourism and the Delhi Transport Corporation run special daily buses to Surajkund during the annual crafts *mela (see p41).*

SURAJKUND CRAFTS MELA

For two weeks in early February, Surajkund comes alive with the sounds and colours of one of India's largest arts and crafts fair. Craftsmen and artisans from every part of the country sell their wares at a specially created village, under thatched canopies decorated with *rangoli*. Here, mirrorwork from Gujarat, painted puppets from Jaipur, fanciful bell-metal beasts from Orissa and Madhubani paintings from Bihar can be found at a wide range of prices. There are balloon sellers and food stalls to give the *mela* a carnival air, while folk dancers and musicians in colourful costumes weave in and out of the crowds. The evenings, given over to folk theatre, dance and music performances, attract huge crowds.

A performance by folk singers at the Surajkund Crafts Mela

Shopping in Delhi

THE HALLMARK of shopping in Delhi is the fabulous variety of styles, merchandise and markets. Besides Connaught Place, almost every residential colony boasts a market. Old, established shops and bazaars co-exist happily with glitzy high-end boutiques and department stores, and one can buy

Logo of Dastkar

anything from seasonal vegetables, fruits and traditional handicrafts to designer clothes and the latest imported electronic items. Be prepared to bargain where required, even a small success will make your shopping spree in Delhi a complete and satisfying experience. For practical information, see page 264.

SHOPS AND MARKETS

NEW DELHI's main shopping centres are in Connaught Place and Janpath where the Central Cottage Industries offers an exciting and varied range of textiles, jewellery and souvenirs at fixed and reasonable prices. Indian handicrafts and handlooms are available at the state emporia on Baba Kharak Singh Marg, Dilli Haat and the Crafts Museum Shop (see pp86–7). In the north is Chandni Chowk (see p93), the traditional market, while to the south are Khan Market, Sundar Nagar and Santushti. The old urban villages of Hauz Khas, Shahpur Jat and Mehrauli have trendy boutiques where shoppers rub shoulders with loitering cows. The South Extension, Lajpat Nagar and Sarojini Nagar markets are popular with local shoppers. The five-star hotels, too, have shopping arcades that sell carefully-selected goods.

ANTIQUES, CARPETS AND SHAWLS

GENUINE ANTIQUES are rare to come by and cannot be taken out of the country unless certified by the ASI (see p279). However, hotel shops, Sundar Nagar and the **Crafts Museum Shop** stock excellent reproductions of miniature paintings, wood-carving and bronzes made by artisans today. Contemporary silverware is available at **Cooke & Kelvey** and **Frazer & Haws**. For Afghan and Kashmiri carpets and shawls, such as the paisley jamawar and pashmina, the best outlets are **Cottage Industries** and **Khazana**.

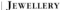

Silver fruit bowl

JEWELLERY

SUPERB PIECES of traditional jewellery, such as *kundan* and *meenakari*, are available at **Bharany's**. The best places for silver jewellery are Dariba Kalan, in Chandni Chowk, and Sundar Nagar market.

Poster displaying a selection of cotton *dhurries* from Fabindia

TEXTILES AND QUILTS

INDIAN SILKS AND COTTON are famous throughout the world. Cottage Industries and the state emporia have a good selection of textiles from different parts of India. **Fabindia**, **The Shop** and **Anokhi** are fine places to shop for good quality ready-made garments, linen and light cotton quilts, while **Shyam Ahuja** sells *dhurries* and linen. The best selection of designer clothes and accessories is available at **Abraham & Thakore**.

LEATHER

LEATHER GOODS, in particular shoes and bags, are found in most major shopping areas. For quality handmade shoes and jackets, the Chinese-owned outlets such as **John Brothers**, still set the standards for comfort and durability. For trendier goods there is **Hyde Out**, a miniscule shop that is quite chaotically piled high with bags and footwear.

Abraham & Thakore, one of Delhi's most exclusive boutiques

HANDICRAFTS AND GIFTS

INDIAN HANDICRAFTS are available at the state emporia, the Crafts Museum Shop, **Dastkar** and **Dilli Haat** on Aurobindro Marg. **Tibet House** has *thangkas*, carpets, woollen shawls and jackets. **The Neemrana Shop**, **Tulsi** and **Good Earth** have a good selection of gift items, such as candles, handmade paper products and artifacts in ceramics, wood and metal.

BOOKS, MUSIC AND NEWSPAPERS

EVERY LOCAL MARKET has stalls selling newspapers, magazines, music cassettes and bestsellers. The largest number of books and music shops are in South Extension and Khan Market. **The Book Shop**, **Bookworm** and **Timeless Book Gallery** stock a wide variety of books by international publishing houses. **Motilal Banarsidas** in Old Delhi specializes in books on Indology. Every

Embroidered textiles sold on Janpath

Sunday, a bazaar selling old and second-hand books is held on the pavements of Daryaganj where one can pick up interesting bargains.

SPECIALITY SHOPS

IN CHANDNI CHOWK'S Dariba Kalan is **Gulab Singh Johari Mal**, a marvellous old-fashioned shop where one can test Indian perfumes from cut-glass bottles. Their attar soaps are also worth buying. Herbal cosmetics by **Shahnaz**

Herbal and **Biotique** are found at most chemists, and Ogaan *(see Textiles)* also stocks herbal products.

Spices and fresh seasonal fruit are found at INA Market while **Sugar & Spice** and Steak House stock a variety of cheese, cold cuts and other delicious food stuffs. Indian tea, from the gardens of Assam, is sold in a small shop in Sundar Nagar (near the Oberoi Hotel on Zakir Hussain Marg), Khan Market and at **Aapki Pasand**.

DIRECTORY

ANTIQUES

Cooke & Kelvey
Janpath. **Map** 1 C5.
(011) 2372 1081.

Cottage Industries
Janpath. **Map** 1 C5.
(011) 2332 0439.

Crafts Museum Shop
Pragati Maidan.
Map 6 D2.
(011) 2337 1887.

Frazer & Haws
Green Park.
(011) 2651 1666.

Khazana
Taj Mansingh. **Map** 5 B3.
(011) 2302 6162.

JEWELLERY

Bharany's
Sundar Nagar Market.
Map 6 D3.
(011) 2435 8528.

TEXTILES

Abraham & Thakore
1 MG Rd.
(011) 2680 1856.

Anokhi
Khan Market. **Map** 5 B3.
(011) 2460 3423.

Fabindia
Greater Kailash I.
(011) 2621 2183.

Shyam Ahuja
Santushti. **Map** 4 E4.
(011) 2467 0112.

The Shop
Connaught Place. **Map** 1 C5. (011) 2374 6050.

Tulsi
Santushti. **Map** 4 E4.
(011) 2687 0339.

LEATHER

Hyde Out
Khan Market. **Map** 5 B3.
(011) 2462 2100.

John Brothers
B Block, Connaught Place.
Map 1 C4.
(011) 2335 2812.

HANDICRAFTS AND GIFTS

Dastkar
45–B, Shahpur Jat.
(011) 2640 5920.

Good Earth
M 1, Hauz Khas.
(011) 2685 1757.

The Neemrana Shop
Khan Market.
(011) 2462 0262.

Tibet House
Lodi Rd. **Map** 5 B5.
(011) 2461 1515.

BOOKS AND MUSIC

Motilal Banarsidas
Jawahar Nagar.
(011) 2391 1985.

The Bookshop
Khan Market.
Map 5 B3.
(011) 2469 7102.

The Bookworm
B Block, Connaught Place.
Map 1 C4.
(011) 2332 2260.

Timeless Book Gallery
South Extension Part I.
(011) 2463 2903.

SPECIALITY SHOPS

Aapki Pasand
15, Netaji Subhash Marg.
Map 2 E3.
(011) 2326 0373.

Gulab Singh Johri Mal
Dariba Kalan, Chandni Chowk. **Map** 2 E2.
(011) 2327 1345.

Sugar & Spice
Khan Market. **Map** 5 B3.
(011) 2462 8504.

ENTERTAINMENT IN DELHI

DELHI, AS THE CAPITAL OF INDIA, has a rich and varied cultural life, mainly because the government has, over the last 50 years, consciously promoted a revival of traditional art forms. As a result, dancers, musicians and folk artistes from all over India deem it an honour to perform here before discerning audiences. Although Delhi is still a culturally conservative city, jazz, theatre and rock concerts are frequent, and there are several good bars and discotheques.

The city's cultural calendar livens up between October and March when the season is in full swing. The number of events multiply as all major festivals of music, dance, theatre and cinema are held at this time.

Logo of the
International Film
Festival of India

India International Centre, Delhi

ENTERTAINMENT GUIDES AND TICKETS

ALL NEWSPAPERS list the day's entertainment on their engagements page. Other useful sources of information on events, restaurants, sports and related activities are the weekly *Delhi Diary* and monthly magazines such as *Delhi City Guide* and *First City*.

At several venues in the city, such as the India International Centre *(see Lectures and Discussions)*, there is free entry. At others, such as the Indian Council for Cultural Relations, it is by invitation. Tickets for selected music and dance festivals and theatre, however, are advertised and sold at certain bookshops or at the box office.

MUSIC AND DANCE

DELHI IS THE BEST PLACE TO experience the range and richness of classical dance and music. Performances by the best exponents of the major dance styles of Bharata Natyam, Kathak, Odissi and Kathakali take place in the high season. The same is true of concerts of Hindustani and Carnatic music, the two major streams of classical music. During the season, shows are held mainly at **Siri Fort Auditorium** and **Kamani**. Some venues, such as **Triveni Kala Sangam** and the **India Habitat Centre,** have performances all the year round. The state-run **Indian Council for Cultural Relations** also organizes shows at Azad Bhavan and the FICCI auditorium.

Colourful folk dances from all over India can be seen during the annual Trade Fair at **Pragati Maidan** *(see p85)*.

City magazines

THEATRE

THE MAIN THEATRE repertory company is the **National School of Drama** which presents plays in its own open air auditorium and at Kamani Auditorium near by. In 1999, the company began a National Theatre Festival, to be held every May–Jun. Its performances are in Hindi and Urdu and include works by contemporary Indian and Western playwrights.

Several amateur theatre groups perform in both Hindi and English, contributing to a hectic theatre season in the winter. The main venues are **Shri Ram Centre,** Kamani, and the India Habitat Centre *(see Music and Dance)*.

FILMS

DELHI PLAYS HOST to an international film festival which is held in the January of every even year at the Siri Fort complex. Tickets can be obtained from the box-office.

Other film festivals, organized by the Directorate of Film Festivals, are held here as well. These are mainly regional Indian cinema and foreign films that are not usually screened on the commercial circuit. Documentary films, presenting the works of up-and-coming filmmakers, are screened at the India International Centre, **Max Mueller Bhavan** and the **British Council**. Many foreign cultural centres, like the Alliance Française and the **French Cultural Centre** also have regular film shows.

Popular Indian and foreign films are screened at the many cinema halls dotted all over

Shubha Mudgal, a well-known classical singer

the city. Among the better-equipped halls are **3Cs, PVR Anupam, Priya** and **Chanakya**. All daily newspapers carry details of film shows. The tickets should be bought in advance as cinema, both Indian and foreign, continues to be a major form of popular entertainment.

EXHIBITIONS

IN THE PAST FIVE YEARS the number of art galleries has grown in response to an increased interest in contemporary Indian art. Regular exhibitions present the work of painters, sculptors and photographers. Certain well known galleries such as **Art Heritage** and others located at Triveni Kala Sangam, India Habitat Centre, India International Centre and Max Mueller Bhavan are in the city

centre. Others, such as **Vadehra Art Gallery**, are in South Delhi. The **National Gallery of Modern Art** *(see p71)* and the **National Museum** *(see pp72–5)* both organize major exhibitions.

LECTURES AND DISCUSSIONS

LECTURES, DISCUSSIONS and seminars covering a wide range of subjects, such as international and current affairs, wildlife and ecology, mountaineering and Indian culture are regularly held at the **India International Centre**. These are announced in the daily newspapers and are open to all. Other venues where such programmes are held are the **Indira Gandhi National Centre of the Arts** (IGNCA), British Council and the India Habitat Centre.

A popular bar in a five-star hotel

NIGHTLIFE

DELHI'S NIGHTLIFE is becoming livelier by the minute. The five-star hotels house most of the better bars and discotheques, such as **Club Lounge, Djinns, Dublin, Patiala Peg** and others. These are popular with the young crowd, especially on Saturday nights. Clubs are open only to their registered members.

DIRECTORY

MUSIC AND DANCE

India Habitat Centre
Lodi Rd. **Map** 5 B5.
(011) 2468 2222.

Indian Council for Cultural Relations
Azad Bhavan, IP Estate. **Map** 1 C4.
(011) 2337 9199.

India Trade Promotion Org.
Pragati Maidan. **Map** 6 D1.
(011) 2331 4857.

Kamani Auditorium
Copernicus Marg. **Map** 2 D5.
(011) 2338 8084.

Siri Fort Auditorium
Asian Village Complex.
(011) 2649 3370.

Triveni Kala Sangam
205 Tansen Marg. **Map** 2 D5.
(011) 2371 8833.

THEATRE

National School of Drama
Bhawalpur House. **Map** 2 E5.
(011) 2338 9402.

Shri Ram Centre
Mandi House. **Map** 2 D5.
(011) 2371 4307.

FILMS

British Council
Kasturba Gandhi Marg. **Map** 1 C5.
(011) 2371 0111.

Chanakya
Chanakyapuri. **Map** 4 D5.
(011) 2467 4009.

3 C's
Lajpat Nagar.
(011) 2692 7846.

French Cultural Centre
Aurangzeb Rd. **Map** 5 A3.
(011) 2301 4682.

Max Mueller Bhavan
3 Kasturba Gandhi Marg. **Map** 2 D5.
(011) 2332 9506.

Priya Cinema
Vasant Vihar.
(011) 2614 0048.

PVR Anupam
Community Centre, Saket.
(011) 2686 5999.

EXHIBITIONS

Art Heritage
Triveni Kala Sangam. **Map** 2 D5.
(011) 2371 9470.

National Gallery of Modern Art
Jaipur House. **Map** 5 C2.
(011) 2338 5378.

National Museum
Janpath. **Map** 5 A2.
(011) 2301 9272.

Vadehra Art Gallery
D 40 Defence Colony.
(011) 2461 5368.

LECTURES AND DISCUSSIONS

India International Centre
40 Lodi Estate, Max Mueller Marg. **Map** 5 A4.
(011) 2461 9431.

Indira Gandhi National Centre for the Arts
Janpath. **Map** 5 A4.
(011) 2338 9216.

NIGHTLIFE

Club Lounge
The Oberoi, Dr Zakir Hussain Marg. **Map** 6 D4.
(011) 2436 3030.

Djinns
Hyatt Regency.
(011) 2679 1234.

Dublin
Maurya Sheraton.
(011) 2611 2233.

Patiala Peg
Hotel Imperial, Janpath. **Map** 5 A1.
(011) 2334 5678.

Pegasus
Nirula's Hotel. **Map** 1 C4.
(011) 2332 2419.

Someplace Else
The Park, Sansad Marg. **Map** 1 C5.
(011) 2374 3000.

Thugs
Hotel Broadway, **Map** 2 E3. (011) 2327 3821.

DELHI STREET FINDER

DELHI IS A confusing city to get around. New Delhi and the adjoining Nizamuddin to Purana Qila area are fairly well marked out, whereas Old Delhi is a maze of narrow lanes *(galis)* and bylanes. The city has extended far beyond the main city centre, in keeping with its burgeoning population, and the vast complexes of residential housing add to the confusion of getting around. Navigating the city's roads and streets *(margs)* is challenging. Signposts are often hard to find and most of the names have changed in recent years or are known by more than one name. Connaught Place is now officially Rajiv Gandhi Chowk, Connaught Circus is Indira Gandhi Chowk and Sansad Marg is also known as Parliament Street. The Street Finder covers the city centre area and lists the major sights, hotels, restaurants, shops and entertainment venues. The Further Afield map is on page 99 and covers the area north, west and south of the city centre.

Ashokan lions

Shops at the entrance to the Dargah at Nizamuddin

KEY TO STREET FINDER

- Major sight
- Place of interest
- Other buildings
- Railway station
- **M** Metro station
- Bus terminus
- Tourist information
- Hospital
- Police station
- Temple
- *Gurudwara*
- Church
- Mosque
- Tomb
- Post office
- **P** Parking
- Railway line
- One-way street

Scale for Street Finder pages

◁ **The President's Bodyguard at the Republic Day Parade**

3

A   B   C

1

2

CENTRAL RIDGE
RESERVED FOREST

VANDE MATARAM MARG

BUDDHA
JAYANTI
PARK

Malcha
Mahal

SIMON BOLIVAR MARG

3

UPPER RIDGE ROAD

BHAGWAN
MAHAVIR
VANASTHALI

SARDAR PATEL

DHARAM MARG

PANCHSHEEL MARG

RAJDOOT MARG

MALCHA MARG

4

SARDAR PATEL MARG

Welcomgroup
Maurya
Sheraton

American
Embassy

CHANAKYAPURI

Sardar Patel
Railway Station

The Taj
Palace

Austrian
Embassy

French
Embassy

CROSS ROAD 3

Delhi
Airport

Bulgarian
Embassy

Swedish
Embassy

Russian
Embassy

CHANDRAGUPTA MARG

NYAYA MARG

CROSS ROAD 4

SAN MARTIN ROAD

Chanakyapuri
Railway Station

5

MAHATMA GANDHI MARG

JHEEL PARK

Italian
Embassy

SATYA MARG

Canadian
High
Commission

SHANTI

NATIONAL
ROSE
GARDEN

SMRITI
VATIKA

BENITO JUAREZ MARG

SERVICE ROAD

NYAYA MARG

SATYA MARG

National Rail
Museum

SATYA MAR

A   B   C

Appu
Ghar

Pragati
Maidan

Shakuntalam
Theatre

Hamsadhwani
Theatre

Shringar
Theatre

Crafts
Museum

National
Science Centre

BHAIRON MARG

Floating
Lake

Purana Qila

Maharani
Guest House
La Sagrita
Tourist Home

Jukaso
Inn

Sundar
Nagar
Market

NATIONAL
ZOOLOGICAL
PARK

RING ROAD

Yamuna River

NIZAMUDDIN BRIDGE

MAHATMA GANDHI MARG

MATHURA ROAD

SUNDAR
NURSERY

The
Oberoi

LAL BAHADUR SHASTRI ROAD

Subz Burj

Mirza
Ghalib's
Tomb

Hazrat Nizamuddin
Aulia Dargah

BHARAT SCOUTS & GUIDES MARG

Isa Khan's
Tomb

Humayun's
Tomb

Afsar
Wala
Masjid

Arab Ki Sarai Road

NIZAMUDDIN
WEST

NALWA ROAD

MATHURA ROAD

NIZAMUDDIN
EAST

MUKLI MARG

HARSHA LANE

HARSHA ROAD

RAHIM KHAN ROAD

Nizamuddin
Railway Station

ISBT
Sarai Kale
Khan

JANGPURA

Drain

→ Agra

Baha'i
House of
Worship

BRIDGE OF BOATS (NOV TO JUNE)

Street Finder Index

BEYOND DELHI
AREA BY AREA

Beyond Delhi at a Glance

Inlaid panel

THE REGION beyond Delhi is bounded by the snow-capped Himalayas in the north and the ravines of the River Chambal in the south. The rich alluvial plains of the Ganges and Yamuna lie at its heart, and to the west are the Aravalli Range and Thar Desert. The Rajputs and Mughals enriched the area with architectural gems of which the finest are in and around Agra and Jaipur. Mighty fortresses, luxurious palaces, mosques, tombs and temples are what draw tourists to the Delhi, Agra and Jaipur region. Away from the cities are wildlife sanctuaries, and to the north are rivers, ideal for white-water rafting and adventure sports.

Alwar *(see pp206–7), a former princely state, is dominated by a large hilltop fort, at the base of which lie elegant palaces, cenotaphs and gardens. Alwar is also a convenient base to explore forgotten forts and cities in and around the Sariska National Park.*

Ajmer *(see pp218–19) is best known for the shrine of the Sufi saint Khwaja Moinuddin Chishti and the ancient and stately Adhai Din ka Jhopra. The pilgrim city of Pushkar, where the annual camel fair is held, is a short distance away.*

DELHI

JAIPUR AND ENVIRONS
(See pp178–225)

Jaipur *(see pp182–99), was built by Sawai Jai Singh II in the early 1700s. In 1949 it became the capital of Rajasthan. A popular tourist desti-nation, it is visited for its historic palaces, observatory, hilltop forts, palace-hotels and tempting markets.*

0 kilometres   100

0 miles   50

Haridwar (see p144), *one of North India's holiest cities, stands on the banks of the Ganges as it descends to the plains. The Kumbh Mela is held here every 12 years.*

NORTH OF DELHI
(See pp136–45)

Roorkee (see p143), *a small town on the way to Haridwar, lies in the heart of a rich horticultural belt. Its famous Engineering College, established in 1847, is housed in an elegant colonial building.*

AGRA AND AROUND
(See pp146–77)

Agra (see pp150–59), *the imperial Mughal capital during the 16th and 17th centuries, is best known for the Taj Mahal, built by Shah Jahan for his favourite wife, Mumtaz Mahal. Other Mughal monuments can be seen within and outside the city.*

Orchha (see pp176–7), *the early capital of the Bundela kings, is picturesquely situated on the banks of the Betwa. Its temples, palaces and cenotaphs are architectural gems.*

NORTH OF DELHI

L YING BETWEEN THE GANGES AND YAMUNA RIVERS, *this agriculturally prosperous region is believed to be the cradle of Indian civilization. Its historical and mythological past extends from the ancient brick cities of the Indus Valley and the early Aryan settlements to the later Muslim and European forts and cities. Each culture has enriched the region and given it its remarkable diversity.*

This vast plain, from about the second millennium on, has remained one of India's most densely populated areas. As time went on, ancient fortified city states developed into medieval walled towns which contained prosperous agricultural lands and flourishing markets. Many of these are today important industrial centres. Since the area had such a diverse history, its architectural remains are an eclectic mixture of styles so that ancient brick structures, Mughal monuments and colonial churches rub shoulders with modern factories.

To the north are the pilgrim towns of Haridwar and Rishikesh, where the Ganges, India's most holy river, enters the plains. With the splendid backdrop of the Shivalik Hills, this area, rich in flora and fauna, offers exciting places for adventure sports such as white-water rafting.

To most Indians, however, this is the sacred territory of the *Mahabharata (see p141)*, where gods and epic heroes fought a legendary battle at Kurukshetra and where Krishna *(see pp162–3)* expounded the famous *Bhagavad Gita*. The development of ideas that led to the later compilation of the *Vedas* and *Upanishads*, the bedrock of Hindu philosophy and ethics, are believed to have taken place here as well. Panipat, the site of three decisive battles that changed the history of North India, lies close by.

To the northeast and northwest lie the now forgotten towns of Narnaul, Hansi and Sardhana, associated with the medieval Tughlaq and Sur dynasties, and European freebooters and nabobs such as Skinner, Reinhardt and his wife, Begum Samroo. Meerut, the epicentre of the Indian Mutiny, is now a busy market and trading centre.

Roadside stalls selling religious paraphernalia, a common sight outside temples

◁ **The famous Har-ki-Pauri ghat at Haridwar, seen from the Ganga Temple**

Exploring North of Delhi

BEYOND DELHI, the landscape changes dramatically. The way to Haridwar, at the foothills of the Himalayas, is lined with mango and litchi orchards. The canal network around Roorkee sustains an agriculturally prosperous rural region. On the other hand, the busy Grand Trunk Road that leads beyond Panipat and Kurukshetra all the way to the Punjab, has always been an important artery of trade and commerce. Rolling fields of paddy and wheat are dotted with electricity pylons that service this important industrial belt. Yet the odd *kos minar* and medieval fort recall another age when this was the scene of important battles and the road to the north.

St Andrew's Church at Roorkee

KURUKSHETRA ❹

Sirsa ←

PANIPAT ❸

HISSAR ●

❷ HANSI

SONIPAT ●

GETTING AROUND

This area is well served by roads, including the famous Grand Trunk Road (now National Highway 1). There are good tourist lay-bys with clean toilets and cafés along it. The high-speed Shatabdi Express between New Delhi railway station and Dehra Dun, as well as the overnight Mussoorie Express to Haridwar, are other ways to reach Haridwar. The New Delhi-Kalka Shatabdi Express stops at Ambala from where a taxi can be taken to Kurukshetra. Taxis and tourist buses also ply at regular intervals between New Delhi and Haridwar, and New Delhi and Chandigarh.

ROHTAK

NH10

DELHI

GURGAON

MAHENDERGARH ●

KEY

■	Major road
■	Minor road
	River
☼	Viewpoint

❶ NARNAUL ●

Jaipur

SEE ALSO

- *Where to Stay* pp237–9
- *Where to Eat* pp259–60

Grazing sheep tended by Gujjar tribesmen near Panipat

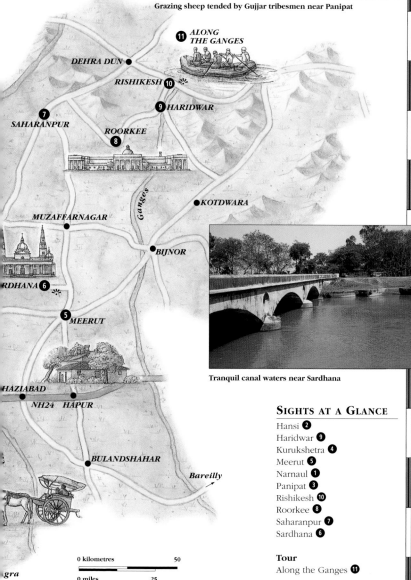

⑪ ALONG THE GANGES

DEHRA DUN ●

RISHIKESH ⑩ ☀

⑨ HARIDWAR

⑦
SAHARANPUR

ROORKEE
⑧

Ganges

●**KOTDWARA**

MUZAFFARNAGAR ●

●**BIJNOR**

RDHANA **⑥** ☀

⑤ MEERUT

Tranquil canal waters near Sardhana

HAZIABAD

NH24   **HAPUR** ●

● **BULANDSHAHAR**

Bareilly ↗

gra

0 kilometres   50

0 miles   25

SIGHTS AT A GLANCE

Hansi **②**
Haridwar **⑨**
Kurukshetra **④**
Meerut **⑤**
Narnaul **①**
Panipat **③**
Rishikesh **⑩**
Roorkee **⑧**
Saharanpur **⑦**
Sardhana **⑥**

Tour
Along the Ganges **⑪**

Narnaul ●

Narnaul district. 132 km (82 miles) W of Delhi. **Road map** C3.

BELIEVED to have been founded by the Pandava Sahdev, the town of Narnaul is historically significant as the birthplace of the great ruler Sher Shah Sur *(see p84)* whose grandfather, Ibrahim Shah Sur, is buried here in a magnificent Afghan-style mausoleum. The Jal Mahal ("water palace"), situated in what was once an artificial lake built by Shah Quli Khan in 1591, is a Mughal-style structure; so is the Birbal ka Chatta, with its projecting balconies and pavilions. In the town's old section are some magnificent, but neglected *havelis* with murals in the Shekhawati style *(see p212)*.

Hansi ●

Narnaul district. 137 km (85 miles) W of Delhi. **Road map** C2.

THIS NONDESCRIPT TOWN is associated with two soldiers of fortune. At the end of the 18th century, the Irish adventurer, George Thomas, repaired the city's defensive wall, remodelled the ruined fort and made it his headquarters. Some 30 years later, Colonel James Skinner *(see p101)* of Skinner's Horse, built a large mansion (now derelict) here where he spent his last years. The town is scattered with monuments dating to the 12th century, including the shrine called Char Qutbs, a Sufi *dargah* of the Chishtiya order, and the 19th-century tomb of Begum Skinner, one of Skinner's 12 Indian wives.

Memorial of the Third Battle of Panipat

ENVIRONS: Hissar, 26 km (16 miles) west of Hansi, was the favourite retreat of Feroze Shah Tughlaq *(see p97)*. He built many palaces and forts here, now in ruins. An oddity from that time is an edifice called the Jahaz, so named as it resembles a ship *(jahaz)*.

Qalandar Shah's *dargah* at Panipat, built 700 years ago

Panipat ●

Panipat district. 85 km (53 miles) N of Delhi on NH1. **Road map** C2. Ⓜ *Urs of Qalander Shah (Jan–Feb).*

ON THE FLAT, DUSTY PLAINS of Panipat, three decisive battles were fought that changed the course of Indian history. The Mughal empire *(see pp52–3)* was established in 1526 after Babur defeated the Delhi sultan, Ibrahim Lodi, and was consolidated 30 years later when his grandson Akbar triumphed over Sher Shah's general in 1556. Finally, in 1761, the Marathas, the Mughal emperor's military arm, were routed by Afghan invader, Ahmad Shah Abdali, paving the way for the British *(see pp54–5)*. Today, Panipat is a busy town well known for its furnishing fabrics and carpets. The 700-year-old Sufi *dargah* of Qalander Shah is situated here. On its outskirts are *kos minars* (milestones) indicating that Panipat was part of the Grand Trunk Road *(see p160)*.

Kurukshetra ●

Kurukshetra district.175 km (109 miles) N of Delhi on NH1. **Road map** C1. Ⓜ *Gita Jayanti (Nov–Dec).*

LINKED WITH 360 legendary sites of the *Mahabharata*, this strategic plain was ruled by the Kuru tribe in the later Vedic period. The 18-day epic battle between the Pandavas and Kauravas was fought on this "field of righteousness". The town of Kurukshetra is also the start of a pilgrimage circuit of 128 km (80 miles) undertaken during the solar eclipse and at Gita Jayanti in November or December, when lighted clay lamps are set afloat on the sacred waters of the tanks during a ceremony called the *deepdan*.

The main bathing tanks are the Brahmasar, with a small temple on an island, and the smaller, more sacred Sannahit Sarovar, lined with ghats and temples. Hindus believe that a dip here during the solar eclipse is very sacred for it is when the twin planets, the malefic Rahu and Ketu, try to swallow the sun to spread terror in the world. However, the sun defeats their machinations, so, after a holy dip, pilgrims donate food equal to their body weight as thanksgiving. The last solar eclipse of the 20th century occurred in August 1999, and the next, the first of the new millennium, is due on 31 May 2003.

The Krishna Museum and Gita Research Centre in the town has a large collection that brings out the pervasiveness of the Krishna cult in Indian art down the ages.

Sacred tank at Kurukshetra

The Mahabharata

Ganjifa card of Arjuna

CONSIDERED an inexhaustible fund of knowledge and ideas, the *Mahabharata* is about an eponymous battle between the Pandavas and Kauravas. Said to be first narrated by a sage, Ved Vyas, the epic was written down only between the 6th and 7th centuries BC. Eight times the length of the *Iliad* and *Odyssey* put together, the subtle moral subtext of its legends and stories codifies notions of theology and statecraft that inspired rulers down the ages.

The *Bhagavad Gita,* a later insertion of 700 stanzas, records the sermon that was given by the divine charioteer, Lord Krishna, to the Pandava prince Arjuna on the epic battlefield of Kurukshetra. It extols the virtues of performing one's moral duty without seeking reward, and condones the use of violence against injustice. Its philosophy of righteous living and the importance of one's *dharma* (duty, calling) continues to guide the lives of millions of Indians. A few years ago, a television serial on the *Mahabharata* became so popular that life came to a virtual standstill when it was transmitted.

The battle is an allegory for the war between right and wrong. The epic's didactic tone made it an authoritative manual on moral rules and righteous conduct.

Folk art often uses the epic as a theme. This *patachitra* from Eastern India is used as a visual aid by minstrels, while *ganjifa* playing cards similarly use Arjuna as the icon for a king.

Krishna is seen as the divine charioteer who steers the mind (chariot) and five senses (the five horses that pull Arjuna's chariot) to follow the right path through life.

THE BATTLE OF THE MAHABHARATA AT KURUKSHETRA
The kingdom of Hastinapur and Queen Draupadi were lost by the five Pandavas when their evil cousins, the Kauravas, tricked them in a game of dice. After a long exile, the Pandavas, though outnumbered by the hundred Kauravas, were led by Krishna to victory in the Battle of the Mahabharata.

Arjuna, the skilled archer, shoots the eye of a fish reflected in water. This act won him the hand of Draupadi and the envy of the Kaurava princes.

Lord Krishna gives the sermon of the Gita *to Arjuna on the battlefield of Kurukshetra. As the charioteer of the Pandavas in the war, this god plays a crucial role in the epic.*

A cantonment house in Meerut

Meerut ❺

Meerut district. 72 km (44 miles) NE of Delhi on NH24. **Road map** D2.
🏙 1,074,000. 🚌 Mon.
🎪 Nauchandi Mela (Mar).

A N IMPORTANT commercial and administrative town, Meerut is better known as the place where the sepoys first mutinied on 10 May 1857 igniting the Indian Mutiny *(see pp54–5)*. Today, this bustling town swirls around architectural monuments dating to the 11th and 12th centuries, such as the Jami Masjid (1019), Salar Masa-ud Ghazi's *maqbara* (1194), the tomb of Makhdum Shah Wilayat and the *maqbara* of Shah Pir (1628). Meerut's colonial heritage is, however, preserved in its manicured cantonment to the north of the old city. This is one of the country's best-planned cantonments with a broad, tree-lined mall or main road

and colonial bungalows *(see p25)* with sprawling gardens along its length. The cantonment's Neo-Classical St John's Church (1821), where British residents had gathered for refuge when the revolt broke out, was the scene of a bloody massacre that fateful May day. Memorial tablets with their names and histories lie inside. The old Central Jail, associated with the worst excesses of the Mutiny and its aftermath, is now converted into a public park.

Sardhana ❻

Meerut district. 85 km (57 miles) NE of Delhi. **Road map** D2. 🎪 Feast of Our Lady of Graces (2nd Sun of Nov). 🏛 (to Cathedral) 🚩

S URROUNDED BY a network of canals, Sardhana's history is inextricably linked with two flamboyant European adventurers, Walter Reinhardt and

George Thomas, who had come to India to seek their fortunes in the mid-18th century *(see pp54–5)*.

Reinhardt deserted the French army in 1750 and organized a band of fierce, well-trained mercenaries who fought for various local chiefs. Called "Sombre" or "Samroo" for his swarthy complexion, he settled in Sardhana on land gifted by Najaf Khan, a nobleman of Delhi. Reinhardt was succeeded by his wife, Begum Samroo, a formidable and wily lady who converted to Catholicism in 1781. She was known throughout the region as the only Roman Catholic "queen" in India, as she led her husband's troops until her death in 1836. Her military skills, matched by her piety and philanthropy, made her popular with the locals, who still respect her memory.

Begum Samroo's palace, the grand Dilkusha Kothi, with its impressive hallway, is situated within a garden of almost 75 acres (30 ha). It now houses a charity school and orphanage. The Cathedral nearby has a white marble altar inlaid with semi-precious stones and a Carrara marble monument to the Begum sculpted by Tadolini of Rome. Now raised to the status of a basilica, this is still an important centre for Catholics. Both the palace and cathedral, built between 1822 and 1834 in a hybrid colonial style, reflect the spirit of that adventurous era.

The classical façade of Dilkusha Kothi at Sardhana

Saharanpur ❼

Saharanpur district.165 km (103 miles) NE of Delhi on NH24. **Road map** D1. 🏛 *453,000.*

SAHARANPUR was founded in 1340 during the reign of Muhammad-bin-Tughlaq *(see p107)*. During the Mughal period it was a popular summer resort for nobles attracted by its cool climate and plentiful game. Many of the gardens that were laid out 200 years ago, such as the Company Bagh in the centre of town, were transformed into nurseries and botanical gardens in the 19th century, laying the foundation for the town's eventual growth into an important horticultural centre. Today, Saharanpur is one of North India's largest producers of luscious mangoes, while the sprawling Government Botanical Gardens, on its outskirts, is an important centre for research on the medicinal properties of plants.

Within the old city, highly skilled artisans craft items of intricately carved furniture, ornamental screens, panels and trays, brass-inlaid with traditional geometric and floral designs. Some of the finest examples of Saharanpur's woodcraft can be seen in St Thomas's Church. Also of interest are the old Jami Masjid (1530), Zabita Khan's Mosque (1779) and the old Rohilla Fort in Nawabganj.

Stone lion at the head of the aqueduct in Roorkee

Roorkee ❽

Haridwar district. 198 km (123 miles) from Delhi on Delhi-Haridwar Rd. **Road map** D1. 🎪 *Roorkee Flower Show (Mar).*

AN IMPORTANT university and cantonment town, this was originally a sleepy village on the banks of the River Solani. It gained importance when the Ganga Canal Workshop was set up in 1843 as part of the massive Ganga Canal Irrigation Project. This transformed the surrounding arid region into the highly productive agricultural area of today. To the north of the town is a magnificent brick aqueduct, marked with two enormous stone lions. It was considered a major engineering feat of the 19th century, and carries the water of the Ganga Canal over the River Solani. The Thomson Civil Engineering College (now the University of Roorkee) was established in 1847 and is the oldest technical institution in the country. The pleasantly sited campus, located within extensive wooded areas, has several important research institutions. Some of the structures from the colonial period are exceptional, such as the Church of St John the Baptist (1852), with beautiful stained-glass windows. The town is also renowned for high quality replicas of 18th- and 19th-century engineering and survey equipment.

Interior of the Roorkee University

Saharanpur's Botanical Gardens, a repository of rare plants

MANGO

The mango or *aam* is the best-loved fruit of the country. The Mughal emperor Babur called it the "finest fruit of Hindostan." Hundreds of varieties, with exotic names and pedigrees, are available from May to July, before the monsoon arrives. Savoured most for the sweet pulp of the ripe fruit, the raw mango is also valued for its medicinal properties, as well as its sharp tang, and is made into pickles and chutneys eaten through the year. The popular design motif of the paisley is derived from the shape of its fruit, and mango leaves, considered auspicious, are used as buntings at festive occasions.

Langra **mangoes**

Pilgrims taking a dip in the holy Ganges at Haridwar

A good way to experience Haridwar's ambience, which has changed little since ancient times, is to stroll along the riverside bazaar, lined with stalls full of ritual paraphernalia – small mounds of vermilion powder, coconuts wrapped in red and gold cloth, and brass idols. The most popular items with the pilgrims, however, are the jars and canisters sold here. These are used to carry back water from the Ganges *(Gangajal)*, a vital part of Hindu worship which, the faithful believe, remains ever fresh.

Haridwar ●

Haridwar district. 214 km (133 miles) N of Delhi. **Road map** D1. 𝄞 175,000. ⓘ *Regional Tourism Office, Rahi Motel (01334) 22 6430.* 🚆 *Railway Rd.* ✦ *Kumbh Mela (every 12 years; Feb–Mar); Ardh Kumbha Mela (every 6 years; Feb–Mar); Haridwar Festival (Oct); Dusshera (Oct–Nov).*

T HE GANGES, India's holiest river, descends from the Himalayas to the plains at Haridwar. This gives the town such a unique status that a pilgrimage to Haridwar is every devout Hindu's dream.

Remarkably bare of ancient monuments, Haridwar's most famous "sight" and a constant point of reference is the Ganges and its numerous bathing ghats, tanks and temples. These bustling sites

Chotiwala, a popular restaurant

of ritual Hindu practices, performed by pilgrims for the salvation of their ancestors and for their own expiation, demonstrate their deep faith in the power of the river. The main ghat, Har-ki-Pauri, is named after a supposed imprint of Vishnu's feet here. Hundreds attend the daily evening *aarti* at this ghat, when leaf boats are filled with flowers, lit with lamps and set adrift on the Ganges. Further south, a ropeway connects the town to the Mansa Devi Temple across the river with a panoramic view of Haridwar. South of the town, the famous Gurukul Kangri University is renowned as a centre of Vedic knowledge, where students are taught in the traditional oral style. It also has a section displaying archaeological exhibits.

Rishikesh ●

Haridwar district. 238 km (148 miles) N of Delhi. **Road map** D1. 𝄞 60,000. ⓘ *UP Tourist Bureau, Railway Station Rd (0135) 243 0131.* ✦ *International Yoga Week (Feb).*

T HIS TWIN CITY of Haridwar, situated at the confluence of the Chandrabhaga and the Ganges, is the start of the holy Char Dham pilgrim route to the Himalayas. Muni-ki-Reti (literally "sand of the sages"), lies upstream from the Triveni Ghat and is believed to be a blessed site since ancient sages meditated here. It has several famous ashrams, such as the Sivanand, Purnanand and Shanti Kunj ashrams, which offer courses to those interested in India's ancient knowledge systems. Maharishi Mahesh Yogi, a cult figure during the 1960s, when the Beatles were his followers, also has an ashram here.

KUMBH MELA

According to Hindu mythology, four drops of the immortal nectar *(amrit)* wrested by the gods from the demons, spilled over Haridwar, Allahabad, Ujjain and Nasik. A Kumbh Mela is held once every 12 years by rotation at these venues in Magh (Feb–Mar), when the sun transits from Pisces to Aries, and when Jupiter is in the sign of Aquarius (Kumbh in Hindu astrology). Hindus believe that they can imbibe the immortal *amrit* and wash away their sins by bathing in the Ganges at this propitious time. The *mela* is regarded as the largest congregation of human beings in one place anywhere in the world, when millions come for a holy dip, and to attend the seminars, discourses and debates held in the camps of leading Hindu sages and theologians. Haridwar's last Kumbh Mela, held in 1997, attracted over ten million people. A smaller celebration, called the Ardh Kumbh (half-Kumbh), is held every six years.

Pilgrims thronging the ghats at the Kumbh Mela

River Tour along the Ganges ⓫

FROM SEPTEMBER TO APRIL, the Ganges, swollen by the monsoon rains of the upper catchment areas, becomes a torrent gushing over the rocky boulders as it hurtles out of the mountains to the plains. This is the time when a few stretches of rapids, where the flow is rough but safe, become a popular circuit for enthusiasts of white-water rafting (see p275). Only organized tours, run by certified experts are allowed. For the less adventurous, a driving tour offers a panorama of this valley of the sages whose ashrams nestle in the surrounding forests along the holy river.

The Ganges flowing serenely through a forested valley

Kaudiyala ①
The starting point of the river tour, it has scenic camp sites on the river bank.

Marine Drive ②
This early camp site is named after a Bombay promenade famous for its view.

Devaprayag

The Wall

Three Blind Mice

Golf Course

Shivpuri ③
The beautiful Glass House on the Ganges (see p239) offers a spectacular view of the river and the surrounding countryside.

Ganges

Brahmapuri ④
An ashram, one of many along the Ganges, is located here.

KEY

▦	Tour route
⩵	Roads
〰	River
⚡	Viewpoint
🏔	Rapids
🄰	Camping

Lakshman Jhula ⑤
A modern suspension bridge replaced the old rope bridge in 1929. This leads to the quieter east bank of Rishikesh where most ashrams are situated.

TIPS FOR RIVER RAFTERS

Length: 36 km (22 miles).
Stopping-off points: White-water rafting can be done in leisurely stages, over two days, with a night halt at the Kaudiyala Camp. Stopover points are provided at Marine Drive, Shiv-puri and Brahmapuri. However, a shorter tour of the same stretch can also be covered in one day.

Rishikesh ⑥
An ancient spiritual centre, Rishikesh is serenely located on the banks of the Ganges amid lush, wooded hills.

0 kilometres 10

0 miles 5

AGRA AND AROUND

A GRA WAS THE IMPERIAL CAPITAL *of the Mughal court during the 16th and 17th centuries before it was shifted to Delhi. The Mughals were prolific builders and nowhere is this more evident than in the picturesque riverine region along the Yamuna which is the backdrop for its palaces, tombs, forts and gardens. Three of these, the Taj Mahal, the Agra Fort and Akbar's abandoned capital of Fatehpur Sikri, have been declared World Heritage Sites by UNESCO.*

The imperial Mughal highway which still runs along the Yamuna between Delhi and Agra is a link to the region's historical past. The rich pastoral and agricultural land around Brindavan, the supposed homeland of Krishna *(see p163)*, was the main axis of the Mughal empire. The outer fringes of this area, formed by Mathura, Bharatpur and Deeg, have wetlands that attract many rare migratory birds, such as the Siberian crane, who come each winter to the World Heritage Site of the Keoladeo Ghana National Park.

As one goes further west and south, the greens and gold of the Yamuna lands give way to the scrub and ravines along the River Chambal. This is the centre of the subcontinent: hot, dusty and vast. These awesome ravines were the preferred habitat of robbers, dacoits and bandits. After the decline of the Mughals, some of the more ambitious bandits declared themselves kings and built for themselves small, but powerful kingdoms with magnificent fortresses in this harsh area. Their architecture, that is a happy amalgam of traditional Hindu with Muslim building styles, can be seen in Datia, Orchha and Deeg.

Itinerant poets and musicians in this area still sing of daring kings and queens such as Laxmibai, the Rani of Jhansi. Her spirited resistance to the British forces during the Indian Mutiny of 1857, made her a popular icon during the Freedom Movement. Close by lies Gwalior. This important princely state has a magnificent fort that goes back to the 3rd century, and splendid palaces built by its Scindia rulers.

The three-domed mosque to the west of the Taj Mahal

◁ Ablution tank in the *namazgah* of Fatehpur Sikri's Jami Masjid

Exploring Agra and Around

AGRA LIES IN THE CENTRE of a rich and varied cultural territory. At one end of this region are the pastoral fields around Yamuna, and at the other, the stark and awesome ravines of the Chambal River. Between these two rivers are a number of towns, monuments and sanctuaries, making this one of the most popular travel circuits in North India. In mythology, Mathura was the sacred territory of Krishna *(see p163)* while in history, it was the centre of an important Buddhist kingdom, and the imperial Mughal highway ran through it. Later, Jat and Rajput Bundela kings built forts and palaces in nearby Bharatpur, Deeg, Jhansi, Datia and Orchha. Thus, this region contains some of the best examples of Indian art and architecture, while the riverine wetlands around Bharatpur provide a natural habitat for a range of wildlife and migratory birds.

Delhi

Yamuna

NH2

BRINDAVAN

BRAJBHUMI 5

GOVARDHAN

6

DEEG

BHARATPUR 7

8

Jaipur NH11 **KEOLADE**

11

BARI

Chambal

SHIVPUR

Guna

Cows near Brindavan, where they enjoy sacred status

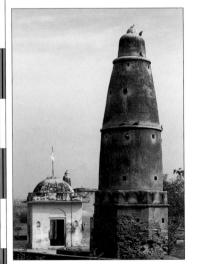

A Mughal *kos minar* on the Grand Trunk Road

KEY

	Major road
	Minor road
	River
☀	Viewpoint

0 kilometres   50

0 miles   25

Temples and bathing ghats along the Yamuna at Mathura

SEE ALSO

- **Where to Stay** pp238–43
- **Where to Eat** pp260–61

GETTING AROUND

The best way to explore this region is by car. The National Highway (NH2) which runs from Delhi to Agra goes through Mathura. A network of smaller roads links the region beyond Mathura and Brindavan. Except in patches, particularly after the monsoon, these are generally in a good condition. Once in Mathura, a boat trip along the Yamuna is a good way to see the ghats. The Keoladeo Ghana Sanctuary provides tourists with cycle-rickshaws and guides on payment. The area is also well serviced by trains, including the high speed Shatabdi Express, which goes from Delhi to Bhopal via Gwalior and Jhansi and the Taj Express between Delhi and Agra. Several trains pass through Jhansi, from where easy car trips can be made to Datia and Orchha. Agra and Gwalior also have domestic airports.

SIGHTS AT A GLANCE

Agra ❶

**Detail of *jaali*,
Musamman Burj**

AGRA was the imperial Mughal capital during the 16th and 17th centuries. It was from here that the emperors Akbar, Jahangir and Shah Jahan governed their vast empire. The city flourished under their patronage, attracting artisans from Persia and Central Asia, and also from other parts of India, who built luxurious forts, mausoleums and gardens. Agra's strategic location on the banks of the Yamuna as well as on the Grand Trunk Road linking eastern India with the west, made it a trading station, visited by merchants and travellers from all over the world. With the decline of the Mughals, Agra was captured by the Jats, the Marathas, and finally the British.

**A riverside view of the
Jahangiri Mahal**

🏛 Agra Fort
⬜ 6am–6pm daily. 📷
⬜ **Son et Lumière** 7:30pm daily.

Situated on the west bank of the Yamuna, Agra Fort was built by Akbar between 1565 and 1573. Its imposing red sandstone ramparts form a crescent along the riverfront, and encompass an enormous complex of courtly buildings, ranging in style from the early eclecticism of Akbar to the sublime elegance of Shah Jahan. The barracks to the north are 19th-century British additions. A deep moat, once filled with water from the Yamuna, surrounds the fort.

The impressive **Amar Singh Gate** to the south leads into the fort. To its right is the so-called Jahangiri Mahal, the only major palace in the fort that dates to Akbar's reign. This complex arrangement of halls, courtyards and galleries with dungeons below was the zenana or main harem

building. In front of Jahangir Mahal is a large marble pool which, as legend says, in Nur Jahan's time used to be filled with thousands of rose petals so that the empress could bathe in its scented waters.

Along the riverfront are the **Khas Mahal**, an elegant marble hall with an exuberantly painted ceiling, characteristic of Shah Jahan's style of architecture, and two golden pavilions with typical *bangaldar* roofs (*see p319*). These pavilions were supposedly associated with the princesses Jahanara and Roshanara, and have narrow niches where jewels could be concealed. Facing them is **Anguri Bagh** ("grape garden") with its lily-pools and candle-niches. The **Sheesh Mahal** and royal baths are to the northeast near the gloriously

inlaid **Musamman Burj**, the double-storeyed octagonal tower with clear views of the Taj. This was where Shah Jahan, imprisoned by his son Aurangzeb, spent the last years of his life. **Mina Masjid** ("gem mosque"), probably the smallest in the world and the emperor's private mosque, is nearby. To the side of Musamman Burj is the **Diwan-i-Khas**, a lavishly decorated open hall where the emperor met his court. Two thrones, in white marble and black slate, were placed on the terrace for the emperor to watch elephant fights below. Opposite is the **Machchhi Bhavan** ("fish house"), once a magnificent water palace. To its west is the **Diwan-i-Aam**, an arcaded hall within a large courtyard. Its throne-alcove of inlaid marble provided a sumptuous setting for the fabled Peacock Throne. To the northwest is the graceful **Nagina Masjid** ("jewel mosque") built by Shah Jahan for his harem, and the **Moti Masjid** ("pearl mosque").

Beyond is the **Meena Bazaar**, the fort's shopping centre, overlooked by a fine marble balcony where, according to legend, the beautiful Mumtaz Mahal first met Shah Jahan. The bazaar street led directly to Delhi Gate, the original entrance, and to the Jami Masjid in the old city. Both the gate and bazaar street are now closed to the general public.

Musamman Burj

Colonnaded arches of the Diwan-i-Aam

Jami Masjid, built by Shah Jahan's favourite daughter Jahanara

VISITORS' CHECKLIST

Agra district. 223 km (139 miles) SE of Delhi. **Road map** D3. 1,260,000. Kheria 16 km (10 miles). Agra Cantonment (0562) 131; Raja ki Mandi (0562) 235 4477. Idgah (0562) 236 4557. UPTDC 64 Taj Rd, (0562) 222 6431; ITDC 191 Mall Rd, (0562) 222 6368. Kailash Fair (Aug–Sep).

Jami Masjid
daily.

A magnificently proportioned building in the heart of the medieval town, the "Friday Mosque" was sponsored by Shah Jahan's favourite daughter, Jahanara Begum, who also commissioned a number of other buildings and gardens, including the canal that once ran down Chandni Chowk in Delhi *(see pp90–91)*. Built in 1648, the mosque's sandstone and marble domes with their

A detail of the minaret

distinctive zigzag chevron pattern dominate this section of the town. The eastern courtyard wing was demolished by the British in 1857 *(see pp54–5)*. Of interest are the tank with its *shahi chirag* ("royal stove") for heating water within the courtyard, and the separate prayer chamber for ladies.

ENVIRONS: The area around Jami Masjid was a vibrant meeting place, famous for its kabab houses and lively bazaars. A stroll or rickshaw ride through the captivating network of narrow alleys can be a rewarding experience, offering glimpses of a close-knit way of life reminiscent of Mughal Agra. This is also the city's crafts and trade centre, where a staggering array of products such as jewellery, *zari* embroidery, *dhurries*, dried fruit, sweets, shoes and kites are available.

Some of the main bazaars are Johri Bazaar, Kinari Bazaar, Kaserat Bazaar and Kashmiri Bazaar. The quieter back lanes such as Panni Gali have many fine buildings with decorative upper storeys and imposing gateways leading into secluded courtyards, where the thriving workshops of master craftsmen still exist.

AGRA CITY CENTRE

Agra Fort ①
Jami Masjid ②
Railway Station ③
Roman Catholic Cemetery ⑤
St John's College ④

KEY

Railway station
Bus station
Post office
Temple
Mosque
Church

Exploring Agra: The Outer Sights

A *pietra dura* motif

A GRA'S EUROPEAN LEGACY dates to the reign of Akbar, when the first Jesuit missionaries from Portuguese-governed Goa visited his court to participate in religious debates. This marked the advent of Christianity in North India, and paved the way for future European traffic in the region. In the 18th and 19th centuries this was a great cosmopolitan centre where priests and scholars, merchants and mercenaries employed by the Scindias of Gwalior *(see p174)*, lived, traded or set up schools, colleges and impressive churches.

The monument in memory of John Hessing

Auto-rickshaws parked outside the Fort Railway Station

🚉 Fort Railway Station
(*(0562) 132.*
This memorable colonial building was constructed in 1891 as a stopover for colonial tourists visiting Agra's monuments. The octagonal bazaar *chowk* that originally connected the Delhi Gate and Agra Fort to the old city and the Jami Masjid was demolished and the many-towered station with its French château-style slate roofed platforms was built in its place. This is still one of Agra's most frequently-used stations; the other two are located in the cantonment and at Raja ki Mandi.

🚉 St John's College
NH2 (Drummond Rd/Mahatma Gandhi Rd). **(** *(0562) 252 0123.*
St John's College, started by the Church Missionary Society, has been described as "an astounding mixture of the antiquarian, the scholarly and the symbolic". It consists of a group of red sandstone buildings, including a hall and library, arranged around a quadrangle, all designed in a quasi-Fatehpur Sikri style by Sir Samuel Swinton Jacob *(see p194)*. The building was inaugurated in 1914 by the viceroy, Lord Hardinge, and it remains one of the region's highly lauded institutions.

✝ Roman Catholic Cemetery
Opp Civil Courts. 🕐 *daily.*
Towards the north of the town is the Roman Catholic Cemetery, the oldest European graveyard in North India. It was established in the 17th century by an Armenian merchant, Khoja Mortenepus, on a piece of land purchased from the church as the burial ground for Agra's large Armenian trading community.

A number of Islamic-style gravestones, with inscriptions in Armenian, survive today, and include the graves of the cannon expert, Shah Nazar Khan, and Khoja Mortenepus himself. The cemetery also contains tombs of European missionaries, traders, and adventurers such as Walter Reinhardt *(see p140)*.

One of the oldest tombs belongs to the English merchant, John Mildenhall (d.1614), envoy of Elizabeth I, who arrived at the Mughal court in 1603 seeking permission to trade. Other interesting graves include those of the Venetian doctor,

St John's College, designed by Sir Samuel Swinton Jacob

St George's Church in Agra Cantonment

Bernardino Maffi, and Geronimo Veroneo (once wrongly regarded by some as the architect of the Taj).

Near the chapel is the tall obelisk marking the grave of the four children of General Perron, French commander of Scindia's forces. Another Frenchman, a member of the Bourbon family and kinsman of Henry IV of France, is also buried at this site.

The largest and most impressive grave is that of John Hessing (d.1803) who first ventured out East as a soldier with the Dutch East India Company at Kandy (Sri Lanka). He came to India in 1763 and joined the service of the Nizam of Hyderabad in the South, before moving northwards to be a mercenary with Scindia's forces. His red sandstone tombstone, interestingly modelled on the lines of the Taj Mahal, was built by a local architect.

One of the tombs, in memory of Father Santos, is enclosed by a trellis frame where Hindus and Muslims tie threads, praying for the fulfillment of their wishes.

To its south, on Wazirpura Road, is the **Roman Catholic Cathedral**, constructed in the 18th century at the expense of Walter Reinhardt. An old, derelict church from Akbar's time stands next to it.

Cantonment
Bounded by Mahatma Gandhi Rd, Grand Parade Rd and the Mall Rd.
The pleasant, tree-shaded army cantonment area, with its own railway station and orderly avenues has many interesting public buildings,

churches, cemeteries and bungalows in a medley of styles dating from the British days. **St George's Church** (1826), a yellow ochre plastered building, visible even from the Taj, is a typical example of the North Indian cantonment style of architecture. JT Boileau, the architect, also built the Christ Church in Shimla.

Havelock Memorial Church (1873) constructed in a "trim Classical style" commemorates one of the British generals of the 1857 mutiny. **Queen Mary's Library** and the **Central Post Office** are other buildings in the area.

Structures such as the **Agra Club**, once the hub of British cantonment social life, and the hybrid Indo-Saracenic government Circuit House which used to accommodate officials of the Raj, are also located in the cantonment.

Firoz Khan Khwajasara's Tomb
S of Agra, on Gwalior Rd.
□ daily.
A signpost on the Gwalior Road indicates the turning to this unusual 17th-century octagonal tomb, standing on the edge of a lake. This is where Firoz Khan, natural-born eunuch and custodian of Shah Jahan's palace harem, is buried. The red sandstone structure stands on a high plinth and has a gateway attached to the main building. Steps lead to the upper storey where a central pavilion containing the cenotaph is located. Highly stylized stone carvings decorate the surface. Interestingly, unlike other buildings of the period, there is an absence of calligraphic inscriptions. If the tomb is closed, the *chowkidar* from the village will open the gate.

The central pavilion where Firoz Khan is buried

GOLD THREAD AND BEAD ZARDOZI
Agra's flourishing local craft tradition of elaborate gold thread and bead embroidery is known as *zardozi*. This technique was Central Asian in origin and came to the region with the Mughal emperors. Local craftsmen in the old city added further refinements to create garments and accessories for the Imperial court. However, with the decline of court patronage, the skill languished and almost vanished. It owes its recent revival to encouragement from contemporary fashion designers. The delicate stitches and complicated patterns in genuine gold thread and coloured beads are now widely used for both traditional and contemporary garments and accessories, including shawls and scarves, bags and shoes.

Detail of a *zari*-embroidered textile

Taj Mahal

Carved dado on outer niches

ONE OF THE WORLD'S most famous buildings, the Taj Mahal commemorates both the Mughal emperor Shah Jahan, and Mumtaz Mahal, his favourite wife. Its perfect proportions and exquisite craftsmanship have been described as "a prayer, a vision, a dream, a poem, a wonder." This sublime garden-tomb, an image of the Islamic garden of paradise, cost nearly 41 million rupees and 500 kilos of gold. Around 20,000 workers laboured for almost 22 years to complete it in 1653.

The Dome
The 44-m (144-ft) double dome is capped with a finial.

★ Marble Screen
The filigree screen delicately carved from a single block of marble was meant to veil the area around the royal tombs.

Four minarets, each 40 m (131 ft) high and crowned by a *chhatri*, frame the tomb, highlighting the perfect symmetry of the complex.

Plinth

★ Tomb Chamber
Mumtaz Mahal's cenotaph, raised on a platform, is placed next to Shah Jahan's. The actual graves, in a dark crypt below, are closed to the public.

River Yamuna

STAR FEATURES
★ Marble Screen
★ Tomb Chamber
★ Pietra Dura

The Charbagh was irrigated by the waters of the River Jamuna.

Main entrance

VISITORS' CHECKLIST

Tajganj. ☎ (0562) 233 0498.
🕐 6am–7:30pm Tue–Sun.
● Fri. 🎟 🚻
🎭 Taj Mahotsav (Feb).
Museum 🕐 10am–5pm.
● Mon, Fri & public hols. 🎟

The Lotus Pool
Named after its lotus-shaped fountain spouts, the pool reflects the tomb. Almost every visitor is photographed sitting on the marble bench here.

Pishtaq
Recessed arches provide depth while their inlaid panels reflect the changing light to give the tomb a mystical aura.

★ Pietra Dura
Inspired by the paradise garden, intricately carved floral designs inlaid with precious stones embellish the austere white marble surface to give it the look of a bejewelled casket.

TAJ MAHAL

1 Main Tomb
2 *Masjid* (mosque)
3 *Mehmankhana* (guesthouse)
4 *Charbagh*
5 Gateway

KEY

☐ Central illustration
☐ *Charbagh*

Calligraphic Panels
The size of the Koranic verses increases as the arch gets higher, creating the subtle optical illusion of a uniformly flowing script.

Decorative Elements of the Taj

Stylized floral motif

IT IS WIDELY BELIEVED that the Taj Mahal was designed to represent an earthly replica of one of the houses of paradise. Its impeccable marble facing, embellished by a remarkable use of exquisite surface design, is a splendid showcase for the refined aesthetic that reached its height during Shah Jahan's reign. Described as "one of the most elegant and harmonious buildings in the world", the Taj indeed manifests the wealth and luxury of Mughal art as seen in architecture and garden design, painting, jewellery, calligraphy, textiles, carpet-weaving and furniture.

Detail of the marble screen with an inlaid chrysanthemum

PIETRA DURA

The Mughals were great naturalists who believed that flowers were the "symbols of the divine realm". In the Taj, *pietra dura* has been extensively used to translate naturalistic forms into decorative patterns that complement the majesty of its architecture.

Flowers such as the tulip, lily, iris, poppy and narcissus were depicted as sprays or arabesque patterns. Stones of varying degrees of colour were used to create the shaded effects.

Inlaid marble above the mosque's central arch

White marble, black slate and yellow, red and grey sandstone are used for decoration

PIETRA DURA

A contemporary inlaid marble platter

The Florentine technique of *pietra dura* is said to have been imported by Jahangir and developed in Agra as *pachikari*. Minute slivers of precious and semi-precious stones, such as carnelian, lapis lazuli, turquoise and malachite, were arranged in complex stylized floral designs into a marble base. Even today, artisans in the old city maintain pattern books containing the intricate motifs used on the Taj and can still re-create 17th-century designs in contemporary pieces.

A single flower often had more than 35 variations of carnelian

CARVED RELIEF WORK

Decorative panels of flowering plants, foliage and vases are realistically carved on the lower portions of the walls. While the *pietra dura* adds colour to the pristine white marble these highlight the texture of the polished marble and sandstone surface.

Floral sprays, carved in relief on the marble and sandstone dado levels, are framed with pietra dura and stone inlay borders. The profusion of floral motifs in the Taj symbolizes the central paradise theme.

Jaali patterns on the octagonal perforated screen surrounding the cenotaphs are a complex combination of the floral and geometric. The filtered light captures the intricate designs and casts mosaic-like shadows on the tombs.

CALLIGRAPHY

Inlaid calligraphy in black marble was used as a form of ornamentation on undecorated surfaces. The exquisitely detailed panels of inscriptions of Koranic passages, that line the recessed arches like banners, were designed by the Persian calligrapher, Amanat Khan.

Exploring the East Bank

THE PICTURESQUE east bank of the Yamuna is dotted with the remains of gardens, palaces, pavilions and the exquisite tomb of **Itimad-ud-Daulah**. North of Itimad-ud-Daulah is **Chini ka Rauza**, (literally, "China tomb" after its tiled exterior) built by Afzal Khan, a poet-scholar from Shiraz who was Shah Jahan's finance minister. This large square structure is Persian in style, and at one time its surface was covered with glazed tiles from Lahore and Multan, interspersed with calligraphic panels in graceful Naskh characters. The burial chamber within has painted stucco plaster design that once must have comple-mented the tiled exterior.

Further upriver is the quiet, tree-shaded **Rambagh** or Aram Bagh ("garden of rest"). This is said to be the first Mughal garden laid out by Babur in 1526 (*see p167*), and his temporary burial place before his body was taken to Kabul to be interred. The spacious walled garden, divided by walkways leading to a raised terrace with open pavilions overlooking the river, was further developed by Nur Jahan.

Chini ka Rauza
1 km (less than a mile) N of Itimad-ud-Daulah. ⬤ *daily.* 🎟

Rambagh
3 km (2 miles) N of Itimad-ud-Daulah. ⬤ *daily.* 🎟

Riverside pavilion at Rambagh

Itimad-ud-Daulah's Tomb

A stylized floral motif

LYRICALLY DESCRIBED AS a "jewel box in marble", the small, elegant garden tomb of Itimad-ud-Daulah, the "Lord Treasurer" of the Mughal empire, was built over a period of six years from 1622 by his daughter Nur Jahan, Jahangir's favourite wife. This tomb is a brilliant combination of white marble, coloured mosaic, stone inlay and lattice work. Stylistically too, this is the most innovative 17th-century Mughal building and marks the transition from the robust, red sandstone architecture of Akbar to the sensuous refinement of Shah Jahan's Taj Mahal.

Tapering pinnacles with lotus mouldings crown the minarets.

Upper Pavilion
The replica tombs of Itimad-ud-Daulah and his wife are placed in the marble-screened upper pavilion.

Mosaic Patterns
Panels of geometric designs created by inlaid coloured stones decorate the dado level of the tomb.

★ Marble Screens
Perforated marble screens with complex ornamental patterns are carved out of a single slab of marble.

STAR FEATURES

★ Pietra Dura

★ Tomb Chamber

★ Marble Screens

The dome with its canopy-like shape is different from the conventional domes of this period.

The Tomb
The square two-storeyed tomb stands in the centre of a charbagh. At the four corners of the low platform are four squat attached minarets.

The marble latticed balustrade

★ **Tomb Chamber**
The roof has incised, painted and gilded stucco and stalactite patterns. The yellow marble caskets appear to have been carved out of wood.

Chhatri
The open-pillared domed chhatri above the minaret.

★ **Pietra Dura**
The polished marble surface is covered with stone inlay, the first time this technique was extensively used in Mughal architecture.

Entrance

Painted Floral Patterns
Niches with painted floral bouquets, fruit, trees and wine decanters embellish the interior of the central chamber of the main tomb.

The entrance to Akbar's mausoleum at Sikandra

Sikandra ❷

Agra district. 8 km (5 miles) NW of Agra on NH2. **Road map** D2. 🚗
Akbar's Mausoleum ☎ (0562) 237 1230 (contact for prior permission to go to the tomb terrace). ⏰ 7am–5:15pm daily. 📷 📹 ⛔ 🎫 Urs at Akbar's tomb (mid-Oct).

T HE MUGHAL EMPEROR, Akbar, is buried in this small village on the outskirts of Agra. Named after Sikander Lodi, one of the last of the Delhi sultans (see pp50–51), this was a pleasant garden suburb during Agra's golden age. It is widely believed that Akbar designed and started the construction of his own mausoleum which, after his death, was modified and completed by his son and successor, Jahangir. The result is this impressive, perfectly symmetrical complex with the tomb, located in the centre of a vast, walled garden.

The main gateway (see p25) to the south is a magnificent red sandstone structure with a colossal central arch, finished with an exuberant polychrome mosaic of inlaid white marble, black slate and coloured stones. On each corner of the gateway are four graceful marble minarets, considered to be forerunners of those found later on the Taj Mahal (see pp154–5).

The garden, where deer and monkeys frolic, is a typical charbagh (see p167). The wide sweep of stone causeways leading to the tomb divides the area into four quadrants, each with its own fountain and sunken pond, fruit trees and bushes, now a derelict tangle.

The main tomb is a distinct departure from the conven-tional domed structure of the tomb of Akbar's father, the second Mughal emperor, Humayun, at Delhi (see p83). The first three storeys of this majestic, four-tiered composition, comprise red sandstone pavilions. Above them is an exquisite marble-screened terrace enclosing the replica tomb, which is profusely carved with floral and arabesque designs, Chinese cloud patterns, and the 99 names of Allah. The upper levels are now closed and permission is required to view the terrace.

Detail of a panel on the entrance gateway at Sikandra

The actual tomb is within a domed sepulchre in the heart of the building, illuminated by shafts of light from an arched window. A low door at the end of the ramp

ensures that every visitor bows his head with respect on entry. Just outside the complex is the **Kanch Mahal**, a double-storeyed red sandstone mansion with an ornamented façade and fretted balconies. Further down, on Mathura Road, is **Mariam Zamani's Tomb**, where one of Akbar's wives is buried in a square building set on a high plinth within a small garden. It was used as an orphanage by the Church Missionary Society in 1812. A church has been constructed in the compound. Further along the Agra-Delhi highway is **Guru-ka-Tal**, a unique example of the many tanks constructed by Jahangir for collecting rainwater. Broad flights of steps lead down to the water. The reservoir is now part of a guru-dwara complex dedicated to the ninth Sikh guru, Tegh Bahadur (see p90).

ENVIRONS: About 4 km (2 miles) south of Sikandra stands a lifesize red sandstone horse on the spot where Akbar's favourite steed supposedly died. Located opposite, is the gateway of **Kachi-ki-Sarai**, a historic rest house along this route.

THE GRAND TRUNK ROAD

A roadside dhaba

The Grand Trunk Road, Rudyard Kipling's "stately corridor" that linked Calcutta in the east with Kabul in the northwest, was laid out by Sher Shah Sur (see p84) in the 16th century. In those days, it resounded with the movement of armies on campaign, and in times of peace, with the pomp and pageantry that accompanied the Mughal emperors as their court moved from Agra to Delhi.

This is still one of Asia's great roads and North India's premier highway. Some of the ancient shade-giving trees still stand, but the old caravanserais are now in ruins. Instead, at frequent intervals along the highway, there are dhabas for long-distance travellers, especially lorry-drivers, to stop for a cheap and filling meal of dal and roti, washed down with glasses of hot tea or cooling lassi, and to snatch a quick nap on string cots thoughtfully provided by the owner.

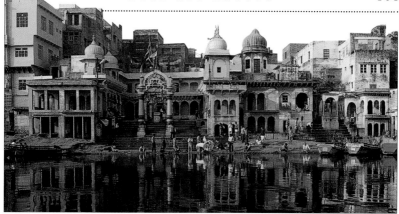

Vishram Ghat at Mathura where every evening at sunset oil lamps are floated on the river

Mathura ❸

Mathura district. 62 km (39 miles) from Agra on NH2.
Road map D3. 🚉 *300,000.*
🚌 🚃 🛈 *Old Bus Stand, Mathura.*
🎏 *Hariyali Teej (July), Janmashtami (Aug–Sep), Annakut (Sep–Oct), Kansa Vadha (Sep), Holi (Feb–Mar).*

MATHURA, on the west bank of the Yamuna, is where the story of Krishna begins. A dark, cell-like room in the complex of the rather modern Sri Krishna Janmabhoomi Temple on the periphery of the city, is revered as the birthplace of one of India's most popular gods. Further away, along the riverfront, the city's 25 ghats form a splendid network of temples, pavilions, trees and steps leading to the water. Teeming with colourful shops selling traditional items, such as its delicious *pedas* (milk sweets), this is the heart of the town.

The evening *aarti,* when small oil lamps are floated on the river, is performed at **Vishram Ghat**, where legend says Krishna rested after he killed the tyrant Kamsa. Close by is the **Sati Burj**, a red sandstone pavilion built in the 1570s, and **Kans Qila**, the site of the old fort where Sawai Jai Singh II of Jaipur constructed one of his five observatories *(see pp192–3).*

The **Jami Masjid**, with its striking tile-work, and a number of other interesting buildings with elaborately carved façades, lie behind the riverfront. A charming oddity is the Roman Catholic Church of the Sacred Heart, built in 1860 in the army cantonment. It combines Western elements with details taken from local temple architecture.

Mathura's ancient history predates the better known legend of Krishna. From about the 5th century BC until the 4th century AD, the city prospered as a major centre of Buddhism. Under the powerful Kushana and Gupta dynasties, it was renowned throughout the ancient world as North India's cultural capital. During this period the Mathura School of Art flourished *(see pp46–7),* and superb pieces of sculpture, made from the distinctive local white-flecked red sandstone, were carved by artisans in workshops here and exported to far off places.

The **Government Museum** collection highlights the Mathura School of Art and

A religious icon from Mathura

has some exquisite pieces. These include a perfectly preserved Standing Buddha, the famous headless statue of the great Kushana king Kanishka, as well as a huge collection of carved columns, railings and fragments of narrative panels, excavated from nearby archaeological sites, depicting court scenes and religious imagery.

Also on view are artifacts from the other centres of Buddhist art, such as Gandhara (now in Pakistan), showing Graeco-Roman influences after Alexander's invasion of the northwest. There are also sections on terracotta pottery and figurines dating from the 2nd–1st centuries BC, coins and medieval stone, brass and metal objects.

🏛 **Government Museum**
Dampier Nagar. 📞 *(0565) 250 0847.*
🕐 *10:30am–4:30pm Tue–Sun.* ⬤
Mon & public hols. 📷 *extra charges.*

A boat carrying pilgrims along the Yamuna

Brindavan ❹

Mathura district. 68 km (42 miles)
N of Agra off NH2. **Road map** D3.
🏯 57,000. 🚌 ℹ️ *Old Bus Stand,
Mathura.* 🎭 *Holi (Feb–Mar), Rath ka
Mela (Mar), Hariyali Teej (Jul),
Janmashtami (Aug–Sep).* 🏛️ *daily.*

Pilgrims on the *chaurasi kos ki yatra*

SITUATED ALONG the River
Yamuna, Brindavan
(literally, "forest of fragrant
basil") became an important
pilgrim centre after the early
16th century when Chaitanya
Mahaprabhu, a Vaishnava
saint from Bengal, revived the
Krishna cult. He encouraged
Bengali devotees, especially
widows, to settle here in
ashrams endowed by wealthy
Hindu merchants. However,
the town's mythic origins are
much older, as devout Hindus
believe that the young Lord
Krishna once lived here as a
humble cowherd with his
foster parents. So "his" cows
still have the run of the streets
and his name is continuously
chanted in prayer halls. Stalls
outside temples sell elaborate
flower garlands and milk
sweets called *pedas*, believed
to have been loved by
Krishna. All this gives the
feeling that the people of
Brindavan live in an
enchanted time warp.

This charming phenomenon
is best seen in Brindavan's
numerous temples and ghats,
built by the Hindu kings of
Amber, Bharatpur and Orchha
and by rich merchants. The
edge of the old town has the
historic **Govindeoji Temple**,
originally a seven-storeyed
structure built in 1590 by Raja
Man Singh I of Amber. The
presiding deity is now in
Jaipur *(see p182)*. Across this
temple is the 19th-century **Sri
Ranganathji**, an imposing
Dravidian-style temple with a
gold-plated ritual pillar and a
fascinating museum of temple
treasures. Beyond these, and
within the narrow streets of

Brajbhumi Driving Tour ❺

DEVOTEES BELIEVE that the area around
Braj is composed of sacred *mandalas*
(circuits) that map the idyllic pastoral
landscape of Krishna's early life. Divided
by the Yamuna, this tour partly follows
the *chaurasi kos ki yatra*, a traditional
pilgrimage of about 300 km (112 miles),
undertaken around Janmashtami.

Kosi ⑥
This was the
treasure-house of
Krishna's foster
father, Nand.

DELHI

NH2

Barsana ④
With its 17th-century
Ladliji temple, Barsana is
believed to be the home
of Radha.

Nandgaon ⑤
Krishna lived here
with foster parents
Nand and Yashoda
after his escape
from Gokul and
the evil Kamsa.

Govardhan ③
This pilgrim town has grown
around the hill that legend says
Krishna lifted on his finger to shield
the people of Braj from torrential
rain. Nearby is Kusum Sarovar.

the old town, are the sacred walled groves of Seva Kunj, linked with the Raslila dance of the region *(see p28)*.

The **Shahji Temple** with its spiral columns, lies on the way to Nidhivana where Swami Haridas, the guru of Tansen *(see p174)*, developed the classic musical tradition of Dhrupad in the 16th century. Other notable temples are the **Madan Mohan Temple**, built in 1580 with local red sandstone, on a hill next to the river. A little further are the popular **Banke Bihari Temple**, which can be approached from the main bazaar street, and the 16th-century **Jugal Kishore Temple**, adjoining the main pilgrim route to the ghats. The **Gopinath** and **Radha Raman** temples are located close to each other near Keshi

Gopuram **of the South Indian-style Ranganathji Temple**

A Vaishanavite sadhu

Ghat. The ISKCON Temple and the Brindavan Research Institute, on the outskirts of the town, are recent additions to the town's skyline.

At Holi and Janmashtami *(see pp36–7)*, Brindavan is a riot of colour and dance as people celebrate the god who still enchants them and where his *lila* (divine sport) is still a living presence.

Deeg ❻

Bharatpur district. 98 km (61 miles) N of Agra on NH2. **Road map** D3. *RTDC Hotel Saras, Agra Rd, Bharatpur (05644) 22 3700. Holi (Feb-Mar), Rath ka Mela (Mar).*

ONCE THE CAPITAL of the Jat kings of Bharatpur *(see p166)*, Deeg rose to prominence after the decline of the Mughal empire in the 18th century. Its square fort, a massive edifice, has mud and rubble walls which are buttressed by 12 bastions and a shallow moat. The fortified town outside the fort once had grand mansions, lush gardens and pools, that now lie unkempt and forlorn. Deeg's Raja Suraj Mal and his son, Jawahir Singh, were also builders of lavish pleasure palaces. Of these, the most remarkable is the **Water Palace** *(see pp164–5)*, built in celebration of the monsoon. This was a favourite summer retreat of the Bharatpur kings.

Radhakund ②
Said to be Radha's personal bathing pool, it has a special sanctity for her devotees.

Brindavan ①
An important pilgrim centre, it is separated from Mathura by the River Yamuna.

KEY

Tour route
Roads
Rivers

0 kilometres 5
0 miles 2

TIPS FOR DRIVERS
Length: 105 km (65 miles).
Stopping-off points: Brindavan has good hotels and restaurants and is the ideal base for the tour. Both Radhakund and Barsana have UPSTDC tourist bungalows, and Govardhan and Kosi have petrol stations. However, private transport will be a more convenient way to explore this region.

THE KRISHNA CULT

A peacock feather, a flute and the colour blue announce the presence of Krishna. Named after his dark skin, this most human of gods still haunts the glades and forests along the Yamuna. A naughty child who was passionately fond of milk and butter, Krishna is also the charming flute-player whose flirtatious dalliance with Radha is a metaphor for the complex metaphysics of temporal and spiritual love, widely celebrated in art and literature.

Sanjhi, **Brindavan's paper stencil craft**

Deeg Water Palace

Sandstone carving on Singh Pol

THE MAGIC OF THE MONSOON and the traditions of music and dance associated with it inspired the Bharatpur kings to build a romantic "water palace" at their summer capital, Deeg. A lyrical composition of sandstone and marble pavilions, gardens and pools, this late 18th-century marvel, built by Raja Suraj Mal, used a number of innovative special effects that simulated monsoon showers, even producing rainbows. The skilful cooling system drew water from a huge reservoir that originally took two days to fill. The coloured fountain-jets are now played only during the Jawahar Mela.

Nand Bhavan
Huge terracotta water pitchers placed inside its innovative double roof insulated its interior against the heat of summer.

The main entrance, Singh Pol, is named after the two lions (*singh*) sculpted on its front arch.

★ **Sawan Pavilion**
Shaped like an upturned boat, its ingenious water system created a semi-circle of falling water.

Gopal Sagar Tank

Bhadon Pavilion

Mughal Marble Swing
This was a part of Suraj Mal's war booty, now placed in front of Gopal Bhavan.

★ **Gopal Bhavan**
This elegant complex is flanked by the boat-shaped Sawan-Bhadon pavilions. Its numerous overhanging kiosks and balconies are reflected in Gopal Sagar from which it seems to rise. The interior still retains the original furnishings and objets d'art of this palace.

VISITORS' CHECKLIST

Bharatpur district. 95 km (59 miles) NW of Agra. **Road map** D3. 🚌 🕐 8am–5pm daily. ● the day after Holi (Mar). Jawahar Mela (Aug). 🚪 Mon. 📷

★ Keshav Bhavan
Heavy lithic balls were placed on the roof here. When water gushed up the hollow pillars and pipes inside the arches, the balls rolled on the roof to produce "thunder".

Lotus Quoins
Placed at each corner of the plinth, these urns were inspired by Mughal designs.

Rup Sagar Tank

Suraj Bhavan
A pillared, secluded pavilion with a splendid view of the charbagh, *it was part of the zenana enclosure.*

Kishan Bhavan

The roof-level reservoir had water drawn to it from four wells. Pipes led from holes in its sides to supply the chutes and fountains with a continuous stream of water.

Charbagh

MONSOON ARCHITECTURE

In the dry areas of North India, light and wind direction guided architecture. Underground rooms, water channels, fountains, latticed screens, terrazzo floors and open courtyards were devices to keep homes cool before the advent of electricity. The Sawan-Bhadon pavilions at Deeg, named after the months of the monsoon (July–August), are an architectural style inspired by the rainy season. Built to savour the thunder and rain of the monsoon, such pavilions adorned forts and palaces.

Coloured water fountains at Deeg

STAR FEATURES

★ Gopal Bhavan

★ Sawan Pavilion

★ Keshav Bhavan

Bharatpur **❼**

Bharatpur district. 55 km (34 miles) from Agra. **Road map** D3.
🚶 204,500. **ℹ** opp RTDC Hotel Saras, Agra Rd (05644) 22 3700. 🚌
🎪 Jaswant Mela (Oct).

The State Museum at Lohagarh Fort, Bharatpur

M OST FAMOUS for its bird sanctuary, the kingdom of Bharatpur, on the eastern edge of Rajasthan, came into prominence during the declining years of the Mughal Empire. It was founded by the fearless Jats, a community of landowners. Their most remarkable leader was Raja Suraj Mal (r.1724–63), who in 1733 captured and fortified the city of Bharatpur, thereby laying the foundations of his capital. This powerful ruler defied the reigning Mughal emperor, stormed Delhi and Agra and brought home the massive gates of Agra Fort and installed them at his own fort at Deeg's Water Palace (see pp164–5), near Bharatpur. A prolific builder as well, he used the loot from Mughal buildings, including a swing (now in Deeg), to embellish the forts and palaces he built throughout his kingdom.

In the centre of the town is **Lohagarh** ("iron fort"), which withstood repeated attacks by the Marathas and the British until it was finally captured by Lord Lake in 1805. When built, it was a masterpiece of construction with massive double ramparts made of solid packed mud and rubble that were surrounded by impressive moats. Most of the outermost ramparts have disintegrated, but the inner ones are intact and are distinguished by two towers, the Jawahar Burj and Fateh Burj, built to mark successive Jat victories over the Mughals and British. The Victory Column at Jawahar Burj carries an inscription with the genealogy of the Jat kings. Both its north and south gates were part of the loot from the imperial Mughal capital at Delhi.

Three palaces were built in the fort by the rustic Jats in a surprisingly fine mix of Mughal and Rajput stylistic detail. The royal apartments, in Mahal Khas, had unusual octagonal chambers in the corners with colourful painted walls, but these are now the site of a pharmaceutical college. The other two palaces were located around the Katcheri (court) Bagh, and now house the **State Museum**, where a rare collection of 1st- and 2nd-century stone carvings and terracotta toys from nearby excavations can be seen. An interesting sunken *hamam* is close by.

Figure of Krishna, State Museum

In 1818, Bharatpur became the first Rajput state to sign a treaty of alliance with the British East India Company. A later maharaja was a keen collector of Rolls Royce cars, which he converted for use on tiger and duck shoots.

🏛 State Museum
Near Nehru Park. **📞** (05644) 22 8185.
⏰ 10am–5pm. ● Fri & public hols.
🎟 free on Mon. 📷 extra charges.

Keoladeo Ghana National Park **❽**

See pp 168-9.

Fatehpur Sikri **❾**

See pp 170-71.

Dholpur **❿**

Dholpur district. 54 km (34 miles) S of Agra. **Road map** D3. 🚶 92,000.
ℹ Bharatpur, (05644) 22 3700. 🚌

S ITUATED ON THE BANKS of the River Chambal, the small town of Dholpur was strategically located on the

The moat and ramparts of Lohagarh

The lakeside temples of Machkund

route from Delhi to the Deccan, making it the target of invading armies. In 1504, Sikandar Lodi (see pp50–51) set up camp here for a month on his march against Gwalior. Some 20 years later, Babur made this a royal domain of his new empire. The ruined Shergarh Fort, said to be 1,000 years old, is in Dholpur and so is a modest 19th-century palace (closed to the public) which can only be seen through an ironwork railing. The palace has a number of art deco rooms covered with European tiles. Dholpur is today associated with the beige-coloured sandstone quarried nearby, used in buildings all over Rajasthan and made famous by Lutyens, who used it for the building of New Delhi (see pp68–9).

ENVIRONS: Dholpur town is a convenient base to explore a number of fascinating neighbouring sites. **Machkund** (3 km/2 miles west), has over 100 temples along its lake. Its waters are said to heal all skin diseases. **Damoh**, a popular picnic spot, has 76 waterfalls. **Talab Shahi** (40 km/25 miles) has the remains of hunting lodges developed by the Jat rulers of Dholpur for their numerous European guests. Off the beaten track is **Jhor** (16km/10 miles), where in 1978, Babur's 400-year-old Lotus Garden was discovered.

Bari ⓫

Dholpur district. 84 km (68 miles) SW of Agra. **Road map** D4.
i Bharatpur, (05644) 22 3700. 🚌

Shah Jahan's palace gate, Bari

THE SITE of an old 100-acre garden once so dense that sunlight could not reach the ground, Bari was where Emperor Shah Jahan built a number of pleasure pavilions. Located nearby is the Vana Vihar Ram Sagar Wildlife Reserve, home to crocodiles, sambhar, wild boar and several species of migratory bird. Remains of an old fort built by Feroze Shah Tughlaq (see p97) can also be seen here.

BABUR AND THE PARADISE GARDEN

The Garden of Fidelity in the *Babur Nama*

The concept of the Paradise Garden, the hallmark of Mughal landscape design, was introduced by the first Great Mughal, Babur. Yearning for the natural beauty of Ferghana, his homeland in Central Asia, he recreated the Persian paradise garden based on Islamic geometric and metaphysical concepts of design.

The *charbagh* was an enclosed garden divided into four quarters, representing the four quarters of life, by a system of raised walkways, sunken groves and water channels. Water was the central element, for it was regarded by the rulers of Central Asian desert kingdoms as the source of life. The intersecting water channels met at a focal point which contained a pavilion for the emperor, seen as a representative of God on earth.

The Mughals used their gardens as living spaces, and also as settings for their garden tombs (see p27). The Jhor garden of paradise, sometimes referred to as the Lotus Garden, was laid out in 1527, barely a year after Babur invaded India. Three water channels, Babur's hot bath, a tank and a pavilion are all that remain of the original garden, which once covered several acres.

Keoladeo Ghana National Park ❽

A WORLD HERITAGE SITE regarded as one of the world's most important bird sanctuaries, Keoladeo Ghana derives its name from a Shiva temple (Keoladeo) within a dense *(ghana)* forest. This once-arid scrubland was first developed by the Bharatpur rulers in the mid-18th century by diverting the waters of a nearby irrigation canal to create a private duck reserve. Extravagant shooting parties for viceroys and other royal guests were held here, and horrifying numbers of birds were shot in a single day. Today, the park spreads over 29 sq km (11 sq miles) of wetlands, and attracts a wide variety of migrant and water birds who fly in each winter from places as distant as Siberia. Keoladeo's dry area has a mixed deciduous and scrub vegetation and is home to many mammals such as the nilgai.

Bharatpur's wetlands, which hold one of the world's finest heronries

Around the Park
Expert boatmen navigate the wetlands and point out bird colonies. Bicycles and cycle-rickshaws are also available for touring the forest paths.

Dry scrubland provides good grazing for many species of deer and cattle.

NH11

JAIPUR

Forest Lodge ★

★ Shanti Kutir

Mrig Tal

Ramnagar

Sapanm

Lala Pyare ka Kund

Chiksana Canal

• Aghapur

KEY

▬	Main road
═	Minor road
–·–	Park boundary
▬	Walk/cycle trail
▨	Marshland
☀	Viewpoint
▣	Jetty
⬆	Boating area
⌂	Police station
⛩	Temple

BIRDS, RESIDENT AND MIGRANT

The male Sarus crane dances to attract his mate

The park attracts over 375 bird species belonging to 56 families. Egrets, darter cormorants, grey herons and storks hatch nearly 30,000 chicks every year. The park's most eagerly awaited visitor is the Siberian crane, now an endangered species. Other birds include the peregrine falcon, steppe eagle, garganery teal, snake bird and the white ibis. Among the large variety of storks are the open-bill stork, the painted stork and the black-necked stork, considered to be the world's tallest stork. When standing on its coral-coloured legs, the bird rises to a height of 2 m (6 ft), with a wing spread of 2.5 m (8 ft). The Sarus crane, a symbol of fidelity in Indian mythology, woos its partner for life with an elaborate mating dance.

Baby cormorants

VISITORS' CHECKLIST

Bharatpur district. 52 km (32 miles) S of Agra. **Road map** D3.
🛈 *RTDC, opp Hotel Saras, Agra Rd, Bharatpur (05644) 22 3700.*
🚌 *near Anah Rd, off NH11.*
○ *6am–6pm daily.* 🚫 🚭 ▫
🍴 🏠 🚻 📷 ♿
Bicycles and cycle-rickshaws available to rent.

Painted Storks
Between July and October, the trees become nesting sites for nearly 5,000 pairs of these birds named after their colourful beaks and plumage which is "painted" with black bands.

Turtle
Other living species include turtles, otters, foxes and reptiles such as the rock python.

Nilgai (Blue Bull)
The largest of all Asiatic antelopes, these avid crop grazers are protected against hunting because of their resemblance to the holy cow. Their broad backs offer comfortable resting places to birds.

Siberian Crane
The subcontinent's only winter habitat for this rare bird, Keoladeo was visited by a lone pair in 2001. Poachers on the 6,400 km (3,977 miles) route have decimated their migrant flocks.

Nesting
With the arrival of the monsoon (late June), thousands of birds set up nesting colonies. As many as 60 noisy nests on one tree may be seen during this season.

A stone plaque near the temple records figures of past bird shoots.

Fatehpur Sikri ❾

Fretwork *jaali*

BUILT BY MUGHAL Emperor Akbar in 1571 in honour of the famous Sufi saint, Salim Chishti, Fatehpur Sikri was the Mughal capital for 14 years. An example of a Mughal walled city with defined private and public areas and imposing gateways, its architecture, a blend of Hindu and Islamic styles, reflects Akbar's secular vision as well as his style of governance. After the city was abandoned, some say for lack of water, many of its treasures were plundered (*see pp54–5*). It owes its present state of preservation to the initial efforts of Lord Curzon (*see pp56–7*), a legendary conservationist.

Pillar in the Diwan-i-Khas
The central axis of Akbar's court, supported by carved brackets, was inspired by Gujarat buildings.

Haram Sa complex

Jami Masjid

Khwabgah
The emperor's private sleeping quarters, this "chamber of dreams" with murals and Persian calligraphy has an ingenious ventilating shaft near his bed.

Anoop Talao or pool is associated with Akbar's legendary court musician Tansen who, it is said, could light oil lamps with the magic of his voice.

Abdar Khana

Entrance

★ Turkish Sultana's House
The elaborate dado panels and delicately sculpted walls of this ornate sandstone pavilion make the stone seem like wood. It is topped with an unusual stone roof with imitation clay tiles.

Diwan-i-Aam
This large courtyard with an elaborate pavilion was originally draped with rich tapestries and used for public hearings, receptions and celebrations.

★ Panch Mahal

A five-storeyed open sandstone pavilion, it overlooks the Pachisi Court, where Akbar's queens savoured the cool evening breezes. Its decorative screens were probably stolen after the city was abandoned.

Birbal's House

★ Diwan-i-Khas

Perhaps a debating chamber, the real function of this unique structure is still unknown.

Jodha Bai's Palace

Maryam's House

Ankh Michauli

Sometimes identified as the treasury, this building has mythical guardian beasts carved on its stone struts. Its name means "blind man's buff".

Pachisi Court is named after a ludo-like game played here by the ladies of the harem.

PLAN OF FATEHPUR SIKRI

Fatehpur Sikri's royal complex contains the private and public spaces of Akbar's court, which included the harem and the treasury. The adjoining sacred complex containing the Jami Masjid, Salim Chishti's tomb and the Buland Darwaza, are separated from the royal quarters by the Badshahi Darwaza, an exclusive royal gateway.

KEY

☐ Area illustrated above

☐ Other buildings

☐ Sacred complex (Jami Masjid)

STAR FEATURES

★ Diwan-i-Khas

★ Panch Mahal

★ Turkish Sultana's House

Exploring Fatehpur Sikri

Detail of a carved panel

Tʜᴇ ᴘʀɪɴᴄɪᴘᴀʟ ʙᴜɪʟᴅɪɴɢs of the imperial palace complex, clustered on a series of terraces along the sandstone ridge, formed the core of Akbar's city. Stylistically, they marked the absorption of Gujarat into the Mughal Empire and reveal a successful synthesis of pre-Islamic, Hindu and Jain architecture (as in the carved brackets) with the elegant domes and arches of Islamic buildings. The concentric terraces clearly divide the public spaces from the private royal quarters. The buildings, mostly in Akbar's favourite red sandstone, were quarried from the ridge on which they stand.

Stone "tusks" at the Hiran Minar

Aerial view of Fatehpur Sikri

Eᴠᴇɴ ᴛᴏᴅᴀʏ, the access to the city that was Akbar's capital is provided by a straight road he built, then lined with exotic bazaars. It leads visitors through the Agra Gate to the triple-arched **Naubat Khana**, where the emperor's entry used to be announced by a roll of drums. The imperial palace complex is entered from the west through the Naubat Khana and opens into the spacious cloistered courtyard of the **Diwan-i-Aam**, where Akbar gave public audiences. A passage behind it leads into the so-called "inner citadel" which contains the **Diwan-i-Khas**, **Khwabgah** and **Anoop Talao**, along with the the treasuries and the **Abdar Khana** where water and fruit for the royal household were stored. It also contains the curiously named **Turkish Sultana's House**. Though probably built for one of Akbar's wives, the identity of the "Turkish Sultan" is

unclear. The great courtyard in front of the Diwan-i-Khas is the **Pachisi Court**, named after the central open space that resembles the board game of *pachisi*, similar to ludo.

The **Haram Sara**, or harem complex, was a maze of interconnected buildings beyond Maryam's House or **Sunehra Makan** ("golden house"), named after its rich frescoes and gilding. The massive and austere exterior of the harem leads to **Jodha Bai's Palace**, a large inner courtyard, surrounded by pavilions decorated with azure glazed tiles on the roof. A screened viaduct, presumably for privacy, connected the palace to the **Hawa Mahal** facing a small formal garden. The **Nagina Masjid**, adjoining the garden, was the royal ladies' private mosque. The two-storeyed pavilion popularly said to be

Birbal's House, situated to the east of Jodha Bai's palace, has spectacular carving on the exterior and interior of its unusual layout. Beyond this lies a large colonnaded enclosure surrounded by cells, meant probably for the servants of the harem, and the royal stables.

The **Hathi Pol** and **Sangin Burj**, the original gateways to the harem, lead to the outermost periphery of the palace complex. This was laid out in concentric circles around the inner citadel and is made up of ancillary structures, such as the caravanserais, the *hamams* and waterworks. The **Hiran Minar** ("deer tower"), believed to be a memorial to Akbar's favourite elephant, was probably an *akash deep* ("heavenly light") with lamps suspended from stone "tusks" to guide visitors.

Entrance to Birbal's House

Jami Masjid

An inlaid panel

Tᴴɪꜱ ɢʀᴀɴᴅ ᴏᴘᴇɴ mosque towers over the city of Fatehpur Sikri and was the model for several Mughal mosques. Flanked by arched cloisters, its vast *namazgah* has monumental gates to the east and south. However, the spiritual focus of the complex is the tomb and hermitage of the Sufi mystic, Salim Chishti, as popular today as it was in the days of its Mughal patrons.

Tomb of Sheikh Salim Chishti
Exquisite marble serpentine brackets and almost transparent screens surround the inner tomb which has a mother-of-pearl canopy inlaid with sandalwood.

Hujra
Symmetrically flanking the main mosque, this pair of identical cloistered prayer rooms has flat-roofed pillared galleries that run round the complex.

Badshahi Darwaza
Akbar used the steep steps of this royal gateway to enter the complex. The view of the sacred mosque directly across, greeted his entry.

Corridors

Buland Darwaza
Erected by Akbar, the huge 54 m (177 ft) gateway later inspired other lofty gates. Young boys dive from its ramparts into the pool below to fish for coins.

Mᴀᴋɪɴɢ ᴀ Wɪꜱʜ ɪɴ Cʜɪꜱʜᴛɪ'ꜱ Tᴏᴍʙ

Ever since Akbar's childlessness was ended by the remarkable prediction of Salim Chishti in 1568, the saint's tomb has become the haunt of those in search of a miracle. The *dargah*, lavishly endowed by both Akbar and his son Jahangir, attracts crowds of supplicants who make a wish, tie a small cotton thread on the screen around the tomb, and go back confident that the saint will make it come true.

A thread tied to a screen in Chishti's tomb

The strikingly ornamental façade of Gwalior Fort

Gwalior ⓬

Gwalior district. 118km (73 miles) S of Agra on NH3. **Road map** D4. 827,000. Hotel Tansen, M G Rd (0751) 234 0370. Tansen Music Festival (Oct–Nov).

THIS ROYAL SEAT of the Scindias is dominated by a massive hill **fort**. The interior owes some of its finest features to the Tomar musician-king, Man Singh (r.1486–1517). Near the ornate Hindola Gate, one of three gateways located near the old city, is the romantic Gujari Mahal (1510) built by Man Singh for his tribal wife, the beautiful Mrignayani, and it now houses the outstanding **Archaeological Museum**. His main palace, the Man

Frieze in Gwalior fort

Mandir, with an amazing variety of ornamental glazed tile patterns, is considered the most remarkable example of an early Hindu palace. In the city below the fort, the 19th-century Italian palazzo-style **Jai Vilas Palace** houses the Scindia Museum. Famous for a magnificent crystal staircase and furniture, its vast Durbar Hall has Venetian chandeliers that weigh three tons. A silver model train, laden with brandy and cigars, once used to serve guests at the spectacular royal feasts held here.

Other notable sights are the tombs of Tansen and Muhammad Ghaus, as well as early temples such as Teli ka Mandir *(see p24)* and the Sas-Bahu ka Mandir.

Gwalior Fort
8am–6pm daily.

Son et Lumière daily.
Archaeological Museum
10am–5pm Tue–Sun. Mon & public hols.
Jai Vilas Palace
S of Fort. 9am–5pm Tue–Sun. Wed & public hols.

Datia Palace

Datia ⓭

Datia district. 187 km (116 miles) S of Agra. **Road map** D4. 83,000. UPTDC, Hotel Veerangana, Shivpuri Rd, Jhansi (0517) 244 2406.

THE MAIN FOCUS of this ghostly town is the five-storeyed Datia Palace, an outstanding building of great structural complexity. Built by the Bundela king Bir Singh Deo in 1620, its sinister underground chambers still exude an eerie ambience. The finely painted royal apartments within the main courtyard are connected to the galleries around them by double-storeyed bridges.

Another important historic building is the later Rajgarh Palace, which offers a panoramic view of the entire walled town.

GWALIOR GHARANA OF MUSIC

Akbar, Tansen and Guru Ramdas

The Gwalior Gharana is one of the oldest schools of North Indian classical music. Its greatest achievement was the adaptation of folk music into the orthodox Dhrupad mode, a contribution of Raja Man Singh and Mrignayani, whose tribal music wove a spell on the king. This form was given lively expression by Gwalior-born Tansen, Akbar's court musician, who developed a range of lyrical new *ragas (see p28)*.

A Tour of Bundelkhand ⑭

GWALIOR AND THE ADJOINING REGION of Bundelkhand, named after the Bundela Rajputs, make up a culturally distinctive area in Central India. Innumerable forts and monuments, situated in a boulder-strewn landscape of great beauty, still echo with stories of the valour and pageantry of the Bundela Rajput courts, and warriors such as the Rani of Jhansi. The area's glorious history and refined cultural traditions are reflected in the architectural treasures of Gwalior, the magical, medieval town of Orchha, and the hilltop temples of Sonagiri.

Gwalior ①
The capital city of many great dynasties since its origins in the 1st century AD, Gwalior is the most splendid of the "gateways" to the Bundelkhand region.

Pawaya ②
The remains of an ancient fort can be seen in this capital of the Nag kings (3rd century AD) from the highway at Dabra.

AGRA

Sonagiri ③
This impeccably maintained complex of 77 Jain temples is approached through a thriving pilgrim settlement.

Dabra

Sind

Datia ④
This erstwhile Bundela capital surrounded by numerous small lakes, has scenically located palaces on hillocks.

KEY

 Tour route
Other roads
Rivers

B U N D E L K H A N D

Betwa

LALITPUR

Jhansi ⑤
The town is best known for its impressive fort and the heroic Rani Laxmi Bai, who died leading her troops in the 1857 Indian Mutiny.

0 kilometres 20
0 miles 10

Orchha ⑥
The temples, cenotaphs and tiered palaces here are perfect examples of Bundelkhand architecture *(see pp176–7)*.

see pp176–7

TIPS FOR DRIVERS

Length: *120 km (75 miles).*
Stopping-off points: *Gwalior, Sonagiri, Datia, Jhansi, Taragram, Orchha. After Gwalior, there is a petrol pump at Dabra on NH3. Accommodation in the form of state tourism hotel and guesthouses is available at Gwalior, Jhansi and Orchha. Local buses run between the major stops.*

Taragram ⑦
Its fascinating handmade paper factory is an interesting experimental centre aimed at upgrading local craftsmanship.

The 16th-century Chaturbhuj Temple at Orchha

Orchha ⑭

Tikamgarh district. 238 km (148 miles) S of Agra. **Road map** E5. 🛈 *MPTDC, Sheesh Mahal.* 🎉 *Ramnavami (Mar–Apr), Dussehra (Sep–Oct).*

Orchha is dramatically positioned on a rocky island, enclosed by a loop of the River Betwa. Founded in 1531, it was the capital of the Bundela kings until 1738, when it was abandoned in favour of Tikamgarh.

Crumbling palaces, pavilions, *hamams*, walls and gates connected to the town with an impressive 14-arched causeway, are all that remain today. Three main palaces, **Raj Mahal** (1560), **Jahangiri Mahal** (1626) and **Rai Praveen Mahal** are massed symmetrically together. Rai Praveen Mahal was named after a royal paramour and Jahangiri Mahal after the Mughal prince who spent a mere night here.

There are three beautiful temples in the old town, the Ram Raja, the Chaturbhuj and the Laxminarayan. A unique blend of fort and temple styles, the **Chaturbhuj Temple**, dedicated to Vishnu, has huge arcaded halls for massed singing and a soaring spire towering over the area.

Lying along the Kanchana Ghat of the Betwa are 14 hauntingly beautiful *chhatris* of the Orchha rulers. Along with the many *sati* pillars in Jahangiri Mahal's museum, these are reminders of Orchha's feudal past when *sati* queens jumped into their husband's funeral pyres.

Jahangiri Mahal

Flower motif in turquoise stone

Named after the Mughal emperor Jahangir who spent one night here with his Bundela ally Bir Singh Deo, this is an excellent example of Rajput Bundela architecture. The many-layered palace has 132 chambers off and above the central courtyard and an almost equal number of subterranean rooms. The square sandstone palace is extravagantly embellished with lapis lazuli tiles, graceful *chhatris* and ornate *jaali* screens. The palace also has a modest museum.

Chhatris
These give a delicate and airy feel to the roofline of the palace.

Carved niches line the outer walls.

Entrance

★ **Entrance Gateway**
The impressively fringed entry gate, flanked by stone elephants, offers a good view of River Betwa.

STAR SIGHTS

★ **Entrance Gateway**

★ **Screened Corridor**

★ Screened Corridor
A screened corridor runs round the fourth level which has eight pavilions with lavishly painted interiors, separated by courts.

VISITORS' CHECKLIST

Palace Complex. ⬤ 8am–6pm
daily. ⬤ public hols. ⓘ MPTDC,
Sheesh Mahal. 🖼 📷 🍴 📷
🖼 **Museum** ⬤ 10am–5pm.

Glazed Tilework
Geometric lapis motifs decorate the outer façade at the upper levels.

Jahangir's bedroom

Fortified bastions
protect the palace.

PLAN OF ORCHHA

The fortified town of Orchha encloses three major palaces and ruined ancillary structures.

1 Jahangiri Mahal
2 Sheesh Mahal
3 Raj Mahal
4 Rai Praveen Mahal
5 *Hamam*
6 Stable

KEY

☐ Area illustrated above

The central courtyard can be viewed from each part of the palace and has a small museum in a set of rooms that run along it.

JAIPUR AND ENVIRONS

THE JAIPUR REGION *of Rajasthan lies on the eastern fringes of the Thar Desert, a semi-arid land cut southwest to northeast by the craggy Aravalli Hills. Studded by hilltop and jungle forts, its valleys and plains glitter with palaces and pavilions, pleasure gardens and temples. Once ruled by proud Rajput princes, this territory is still sustained by memories of a feudal past that is kept alive by its splendid architectural remains and deep-rooted traditional culture.*

At the end of the 11th century, the Kachhawahas of Jaipur established their kingdom at Amber. In the region around it lay other Rajput kingdoms – the Chauhan stronghold of Ajmer that would soon fall to Muslim forces, and the massive Rathore jungle fort of Ranthambhore, which would later become a Mughal preserve. By the 18th century the fierce feudal lords of Shekhawati would become vassals of Amber-Jaipur, while Jat kings would rule over Bharatpur, the only non-Rajput kingdom in the area.

The early Rajput states engaged in bitter internecine clan wars, but with the rise of the Delhi sultans *(see pp50–51)*, their energies were directed at keeping their lands safe from the marauding Muslim troops. Finally, under the Mughal emperor Akbar, military and matrimonial alliances paved the way for peace in the region. The result was a cultural and social synthesis which produced some outstanding art and architecture. The British also followed this policy of appeasement and offered the princes military protection in return for their loyalty. The rule of the princely states ended when, after Independence, they were incorporated into the modern Indian state of Rajasthan, with Jaipur as the administrative capital.

But despite democracy, the Rajput feudal tradition, with its code of loyalty to the local chieftain, and immense pride in their past, remains alive. This is perhaps what has preserved the extraordinary culture of the region, so that for many it still remains the romantic land of forts, palaces and kings it was in medieval times.

Devotees thronging the sacred ghats at Pushkar during Kartik Purnima

◁ **Jaipur's signature building, the fanciful Hawa Mahal or "Palace of Winds"**

Exploring Jaipur and Environs

THIS HISTORICALLY RICH TERRITORY is centred around the old capital of Amber and the "newer" city of Jaipur with its palace, observatory, temples and bazaars and impressive modern buildings. To Jaipur's north are the attractive Samode palace and Shekhawati areas, while to its northeast is the wooded area of the Aravallis, where Alwar, a former princely state, and the Sariska National Park are situated. To the southwest, past the textile towns of Sanganer and Bagru, are the religious sites of Ajmer and Pushkar. Southeast of Jaipur lies Chaksu, a pilgrim centre, and the important medieval kingdom of Tonk, beyond which is the spectacular tiger sanctuary of Ranthambhore, nestling beneath the grand ramparts of a historic medieval fort.

A roadside tea stall

KEY

▦	Major road
▭	Minor road
▭	River
✹	Viewpoint

```
0 kilometres    30
0 miles         25
```

Bikaner

SHEKHAWATI 13

NH11

SAMODE 12
CHOMU 11
Luni

MAKRANA 15

SAMBHAR SALT LAKE 14

JAIPUR 1

4
BAGRU **SANGAN...**

PUSHKAR 17 16
KISHANGARH

18 **AJMER**

NH8

● **BEAWAR**

Udaipur

20
TONK

✹ *Kota*

Pushkar's spectacular cattle fair in progress

SEE ALSO

• *Where to Stay* pp243–7
• *Where to Eat* pp261–3

GETTING AROUND
Jaipur's airport is at Sanganer *(see p204)*, and two superfast trains (the Pink City Express and Shatabdi Express) connect the city to Delhi. Air-conditioned luxury coaches from Delhi to Jaipur are run by Rajasthan Tourism. The rest of the region is best explored by road. The Palace on Wheels *(see p295)*, a luxury rail tour through the region, is for the well-heeled tourist who wishes to savour the trip through the desert in royal comfort.

A sacred tank at Galta

Delhi

NH8

SILISERH ⑥   ⑤ **ALWAR**

SARISKA ⑧

⑨   ⑦ **RAJGARH**

BAIRAT

⑩

BHANGARH

●**RAMGARH**

ER

Agra

NH11

AKSU

Banas   *Chambal*

⑫

RANTHAMBHORE

㉑

SAWAI
MADHOPUR

INDERGARH

㉓

Sagar Lake in front of Amber Fort

SIGHTS AT A GLANCE

Tours

Printed textiles drying in the sun at Sanganer

Jaipur **①**

Stone guardian at Hawa Mahal

A LABYRINTH OF fascinating bazaars, opulent palaces and historic sights, Jaipur offers a chance to see the medieval alongside the modern. On its colourful streets camels jostle for space with motorbikes, and turbaned village elders rub shoulders with youngsters in blue jeans. Often called the Pink City because its prominent buildings are washed with this colour, Jaipur's old walled area has the City Palace Museum, a medieval astronomical observatory and bazaars that sell everything from precious jewellery to camel skin shoes. Recent additions include a multi-arts centre, yet the city's focal point is still the myriad-windowed pink Hawa Mahal, the Palace of Winds.

Govind Dev Temple, dedicated to Krishna

🏛 City Palace Museum
See pp188–91.

🛕 Govind Dev Temple
Jaleb Chowk, behind City Palace.
⭘ 5–11am, 6–8pm daily. 🎭 Holi (Mar), Janmashtami (Jul–Aug), Annakut (Oct–Nov).

The presiding deity of this unusual temple is the flute-playing Krishna (also known as Govind Dev). This image, originally from the Govindeoji Temple in Brindavan (see p162), was brought to Amber in the late 17th century to save it from the iconoclastic zeal of Aurangzeb. It is believed that this temple was once a garden pavilion called Suraj Mahal where Sawai Jai Singh II lived while his dream-city Jaipur was being built. Legend has it that one night, the king awoke from his sleep to find himself in the presence of Krishna who demanded that his *devasthan* ("divine residence") be returned to him. Jai Singh then moved to the Chandra Mahal, at the opposite end of the garden, and installed the image as the guardian deity of Jaipur's rulers. Devotees are allowed only a brief glimpse of their god seven times a day, and on special festivals such as Janmashtami (see p39).

🌿 Jai Niwas Bagh
⭘ 6am–10pm daily.
Just behind the temple is the 18th-century Jai Niwas Bagh, planned as a private leisure ground for the ladies of the royal household. Inspired by the classic Mughal *charbagh*, it has features such as water channels, fountains and neat flower beds. Towards the north is the **Badal Mahal**, a five-arched hunting pavilion on the banks of the Talkatora. Its ceilings still bear faint traces of the cloud (*badal*) pattern in blue and white.

Railway station

MIRZA ISMAIL ROAD

ASHOK MARG

SARDAR PATEL ROAD

BHAGWAN DAS ROAD

MAHAVIR MARG

Raj Mahal Palace

Statue Circle & Birla Planetarium

CHANDPOL BAZAAR

INDIRA BAZAAR

NEHRU BAZAAR

KISHANPOL BAZAAR

Naharga Fort

| 0 metres | 500 |
| 0 yards | 500 |

Rambagh Palace

Jawahar Kala & Sanganer

A view of the walled city of Jaipur

Sights at a Glance
Chaugan Stadium ⑤
City Palace Museum ①
Govt Central Museum ⑨
Govind Dev Temple ②
Hawa Mahal ⑧
Jai Niwas Bagh ③
Jantar Mantar ⑦
Talkatora ④
Tripolia Bazaar ⑥

♣ Talkatora

N of Jai Niwas Bagh. ○ *daily.* ⛴

The Talkatora is an artificial tank that existed before Jaipur was built. This may have been one of the reasons why this site was chosen for the new city. When excavated, it was surrounded on three sides by a lake known as Rajamal ka Talab, making it look like a *tal-katora*, literally a "bowl in a lake". Sawai Jai Singh II was particularly fond of this rather secluded spot and used to breed crocodiles here. The original lake was later filled in and developed as a residential area.

⬛ Chaugan Stadium

Brahmpuri. ○ *5am–8pm daily.*

This large open area near the City Palace derives its name from *chaugan*, an ancient Persian form of polo played with a curved stick. In the past, this area was used for festival processions, wrestling matches, as well as elephant and lion fights. The maharajas and nobility watched from the pavilions of Chini ki Burj (which still retains some of the old blue and white tilework), Moti Burj, Chatar ki Burj and Shyam ki Burj, all located here. *Chaugan* is not played any more, but the stadium is the venue for the famous Elephant Festival held at the time of Holi *(see p38).*

Caparisoned elephant at a festival

Brahmpuri & Gaitor

MANGALA MARG

Amber & Jaigarh

Ramgarh

AMBER ROAD

DAYANAND MARG

MOTIKATLA BAZAAR

RAMGANJ BAZAAR

JOHARI BAZAAR

GHATADARWAZA BAZAAR

SURAJPOL BAZAAR

Galta

RASTA

LIA BAZAAR

PU BAZAAR

R A

ROAD

AGRA

Sisodia Bagh

NH8 BYPASS

MOTI DOONGRI ROAD

Museum of Indology & Moti Doongri

KEY

⬛	Street-by-Street *See pp182–3*
🚌	Bus stand
⬛	Tourist information
⊠	Post office
⬛	Police
⬛	Temple
⬛	Church

THE BUILDING OF JAIPUR

Sawai Jai Singh II (r.1700–43)

Sawai Jai Singh II, a brilliant statesman, scholar and patron of the arts who ruled for 40 years, was awarded the title of "Sawai" ("one-and-a-quarter"), a metaphor for one who is extraordinary, by Mughal emperor Aurangzeb when he was just 11 years old. Along with a talented Bengali scholar and engineer, Vidyadhar Chakravarty, Jai Singh supervised the building of a new capital south of Amber and named it Jaipur ("city of victory"). Work started in 1727 and took six years to complete. Surrounded by a crenellated wall pierced by seven gates, Jaipur is one of North India's finest examples of a planned urban city. Its grid of nine rectangular sectors, believed to represent the nine cosmic divisions of the universe, is actually based on a geometric and pragmatic plan with a system of main streets, intersected by spacious market squares. Jai Singh encouraged traders and artists to settle here, giving tax incentives to merchants to ensure its economic prosperity.

Street-by-Street: Around Badi Chaupar

THE BADI CHAUPAR ("large square") is at one end of the colourful Tripolia Bazaar. There have been few changes to the original 18th-century plan of streets and squares. Narrow pedestrian lanes branch out of the main streets where artisans fashion puppets, silver jewellery, and other local crafts in tiny workshops. Behind are the *havelis* of eminent citizens, some used as schools, shops and offices. The area is a hub of activity, rich with pungent smells and vibrant colours, with temple bells adding to the cacophony of street sounds.

Gangaur Festival
A colourful procession of bullock carts marks Gangaur festivities.

Ishwar Lat
Ishwari Singh built this tower in 1749 to commemorate his victory over his stepbrother, Madho Singh I.

★ **Jantar Mantar**
Jai Singh II's observatory of astronomical instruments looks like a set of futuristic sculptures (see pp192–3).

City Palace

Tripolia Gate

Chandpol

Chhoti Chaupar ("small square") leads to Kishanpol Bazaar, famous for its shops selling rose-, saffron-, almond- and vetiver-flavoured sherbets.

Maharaja Arts College

Flower Sellers
Marigolds and other flowers made into garlands, sell briskly as offerings to beloved deities in temples and roadside shrines.

Lac Bangles
Maniharon ka Rasta is full of tiny workshops of lac bangle-makers.

★ **Hawa Mahal**
An unfamiliar rear view of the Hawa Mahal, seen from the City Palace.

Badi Chaupar

★ **Johari Bazaar**
Vegetable sellers sit at one end of this street where the big gem dealers also have their offices and shops.

→ **Surajpol**

JOHARI BAZAAR

ZAAR

MAURA RASTA

GOPALJI KA RASTA

| 0 metres | 100 |
| 0 yards | 100 |

KEY

– – – Suggested route

Tarkeshwar Temple

Jami Masjid
Tall minarets define the "Friday Mosque", its three storeys fronted by arched screens.

Pottery Shop
Large terracotta urns, pots of all sizes, bells, statues, foot-scrapers and oil lamps made by traditional craftsmen are sold here.

STAR SIGHTS

★ **Jantar Mantar**

★ **Hawa Mahal**

★ **Johari Bazaar**

▥ Hawa Mahal

Sireh Deori Bazaar. ☏ *(0141) 261 8862.*
🕒 *9am–4:30pm.* ⬤ *Holi & public hols.*
📷 📷 *extra charges.* ▨

A whimsical addition to Rajasthan's rich architectural vocabulary, the fanciful Hawa Mahal or "Palace of Winds" was erected in 1799 by the aesthete Sawai Pratap Singh (r.1778–1803). Its ornate façade has become an icon for the city, a tiered baroque-like composition of projecting windows and balconies with perforated screens. Though five storeys high it is just one room deep, with walls no thicker than 20 cm (8 inches). Built of lime and mortar and painted pink, this structure was so designed to enable the purdahed ladies of the harem to watch unnoticed the colourful street scenes and state processions on Sireh Deori Bazaar below. Visitors are permitted to climb up the winding ramp to the top.

Pratap Singh was a poet, composer and patron of the arts. A devotee of Krishna, he dedicated the Hawa Mahal to him, and many believe that when seen from afar, the building looks like the *mukut* (crown) that often adorns Lord Krishna's head.

A gateway towards the west leads into the complex and to

Façade of Hawa Mahal

the administrative offices and **Archaeological Museum**.

▥ Archaeological Museum

Tripolia Bazaar. 🕒 *9am–5pm.*
⬤ *Fri & public hols.*

▥ Tripolia Bazaar

To the south of the City Palace is one of the walled city's busiest streets and bazaars. The shops here mainly sell an enormous range of metal goods and kitchenware. The pavements outside the shops attractively display utensils in brass, copper, aluminium and steel as well as crowbars, chisels and other assorted hardware. Sometimes, handicrafts, plastic and paper products, such as the traditional red cloth-bound *bahi khathas* (account books) still used by merchants and moneylenders, are also available. At Badi Chaupar, towards the end of the street, are flower-sellers with baskets full of fragrant roses, marigolds, tube-roses and jasmine, and shops selling silver jewellery, hand-embroidered *jootis* (slippers) and feather-light cotton quilts.

Detail of a painted gate

In the centre of this lively commercial artery stands the majestic Tripolia ("triple-arched") Gate. Constructed in 1734, this was once the main entrance to the palace and on festive occasions, crowds watched the royal entourage of the maharaja and his nobles *(thakurs)*, clad in ceremonial robes, seated on elephants and horses, pass through this impressive gate. Today, its use is confined to members of the royal family and their special guests, and a guard on duty reminds visitors that this is not a public thoroughfare.

A short distance from Tripolia Gate, towards the east, is the well-maintained **Nawab Saheb ki Haveli**, named after Nawab Faiz Ali Khan, Ram Singh II's *(see p194)* prime minister. This 18th-century mansion was once the residence of Vidyadhar Chakravarty *(see p183)*, who is believed to have chosen this site to supervise the building of the new city of Jaipur. Its enclosed terrace offers some marvellous views of the city. Other *havelis* of eminent citizens can be seen in the narrow alleys off the main street. Some of these gracious old buildings are still occupied by descendants of the original owners, others have been rented out to schools, shops and offices.

▥ Nawab Saheb ki Haveli

🕒 *10am–6pm daily.* 📷

A view of Tripolia Gate with Ishwari Singh's victory tower seen in the distance

Jewellery

BE IT THE fabulous emeralds and rubies sported by former maharajas and their queens or the splendid silver and bone ornaments worn by peasants, jewellery is an integral part of Rajasthani culture. Even camels, horses and elephants are adorned with specially designed anklets and necklaces. Jaipur is one of the largest ornament-making centres in India, and *meenakari* (enamelling) and *kundankari* are two traditional

A kundankari pendant

techniques for which it is most famous. In the 16th century, Man Singh I *(see p49)*, influenced by the prevailing fashions of the Mughal court, brought the first five Sikh enamel workers from Lahore to his state. Since then, generations of highly skilled jewellers have lived and worked here. Jaipur caters to every taste, from chunky silver ornaments to elegant designs intricately set in gold with precious stones.

A jewelled trinket box *with a* kundankari *lid, the lower portion of this box is worked in fine* meenakari *and has traditional floral patterns in red, blue, green and white.*

Sarpech, *the cypress-shaped turban ornament, was a fashion statement introduced by the Mughal emperors in the early 17th century to display their finest gems. Rajput rulers, impressed by Mughal flamboyance, sported dazzling ornaments like this piece of enamelled gold set with emeralds, rubies, diamonds and sapphires with a pearl drop.*

The skill of setting stones *can be seen in the crowded alleys of Haldiyon ka Raasta, Jadiyon ka Raasta and Gopalji ka Raasta. An inherited art, the trade of jewellery is in the hands of artisans' guilds.*

Meenakari *embellishes the obverse side of* kundan *jewellery, for the Rajasthani love of adornment decrees that even the non-visible back of a piece of jewellery, which touches the wearer's skin, must be as beautiful as the front.*

Kundankari *uses a highly refined gold as the base, which is then inlaid with lac and set with precious and semi-precious stones to provide the colour and design. Purified gold wire outlines the design and also conceals the lac background.*

Jaipur *is now a centre of lapidary, specializing in the cutting of emeralds and diamonds that come from Africa, South America, and parts of India. Gem-cutters learn their skill by cutting garnets.*

8

City Palace Museum

Jaipur's coat-of-arms

OCCUPYING THE HEART of Jai Singh II's city, the City Palace has been home to the rulers of Jaipur since the first half of the 18th century. The sprawling complex is a superb blend of Rajput and Mughal architecture, with open, airy Mughal-style public buildings leading to private apartments. The opulence and exquisite craftsmanship is a tribute both to the wealth of the former maharajas and their lavish patronage of the arts. Today, part of the complex is open to the public as the Maharaja Sawai Man Singh II Museum, popularly known as the City Palace Museum, but the beautiful Chandra Mahal remains the residence of the erstwhile maharaja.

★ Pritam Chowk
The "Court of the Beloved" has four delicately painted doorways representing the seasons.

Sileh Khana
The erstwhile armoury houses the museum's collection of weapons, some lavishly decorated, and is considered among the finest in India.

Crafts demonstration area

★ Mubarak Mahal
This sandstone "Welcome Palace" was built in 1900 by Madho Singh II to receive guests, hence the name. It is now the costume and textile gallery.

STAR FEATURES
★ Pritam Chowk
★ Mubarak Mahal
★ Rajendra Pol
★ Silver Urns

★ Rajendra Pol
Flanking the gateway are two large elephants, each carved from a single block of marble.

Chandra Mahal

Each floor of this seven-storeyed palace is extravagantly decorated and has a specific name according to its function. The palace is closed to the public.

Riddhi-Siddhi Pol

★ Silver Urns

Two giant silver urns in the Diwan-i-Khas, listed in the Guinness Book as the largest silver objects in the world, carried sacred Ganges water for Madho Singh II's visit to London in 1901.

Shops

Transport gallery

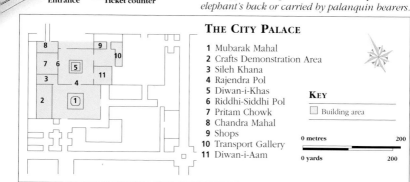

Entrance

Ticket counter

Diwan-i-Aam

In the Art Gallery is this "golden throne" (Takth-e-Rawan) on which the maharaja sat when he appeared in public. It was either put on an elephant's back or carried by palanquin bearers.

THE CITY PALACE

1 Mubarak Mahal
2 Crafts Demonstration Area
3 Sileh Khana
4 Rajendra Pol
5 Diwan-i-Khas
6 Riddhi-Siddhi Pol
7 Pritam Chowk
8 Chandra Mahal
9 Shops
10 Transport Gallery
11 Diwan-i-Aam

KEY

☐ Building area

0 metres 200

0 yards 200

Exploring the City Palace Museum

Archery ring

THE MAHARAJA SAWAI MAN SINGH II Museum provides a splendid introduction to the arts and crafts and the courtly pomp and ceremony of Jaipur in the old days. In their long reign, which spanned almost a thousand years, the Kachhawaha rulers amassed a fabulous collection of treasures – rare manuscripts, miniature paintings, carpets, textiles, costumes and weaponry, palanquins and chariots. These are some of the royal and historical memorabilia displayed here. Initially a private collection open only to select visitors and dignitaries, in 1959 it was formally declared a state museum that is open to the public.

A detail of a gold-embroidered skirt belonging to one of the queens

TEXTILES AND COSTUMES GALLERY

A GLITTERING COLLECTION of textiles and costumes from the royal *toshakhana* is displayed on the first floor of **Mubarak Mahal**. On view are rich, gorgeous brocades, known as *kimkhabs*, from Surat, Aurangabad and Varanasi, exquisitely embroidered and handloom-woven shawls from Kashmir, embroidered silks, embossed velvets and light, gossamer muslins typical of

A tissue *ghaghara*, early 20th century

Dhaka (today in Bangladesh), which collectively represent India's great textile tradition. The expert and refined craftsmanship that existed in Jaipur almost three centuries ago is visible in the wide variety of hand blockprinted textiles from nearby Sanganer and tie-and-dye *(bandhini)* pieces specially produced by the printers and dyers from the palace workshops. Equally breathtaking is the

incredible range of well-preserved royal garments. Dazzling gathered skirts and long, flowing veils *(odhnis)*, decorated with delicate *zari* (gold thread embroidery) and *gota* (gold or silver frill), worn by the ladies of the court, vie for attention with the brocaded robes, waist-bands *(patkas)*, pyjamas and turbans that comprised the male attire. The most striking of these royal robes is the enormous pale pink *atamsukh* ("comfort of the soul") of Sawai Madho Singh I (r.1750–68), who was 2 m (7 ft) tall and 1.23 m (4 ft) in girth, and weighed about 230 kg (500 lbs)! This long, quilted cloak-like robe, worn usually by men in winter, is embossed with gold work.

Other exhibits include a range of royal paraphernalia including rich tent hangings, curtains, carriage and dish covers dating back to the 17th century. Among these is a rare gold brocaded velvet throne cover bearing seal marks that date to 1605, and an intricately woven gold and silk circular *thal-posh* (dish-cover).

The lattice screens that run round the balcony here once enabled royal ladies to view the hall without being seen.

ART GALLERY

THE DIWAN-I-AAM or Sabha Niwas, built on a raised, pillared platform, was once used by the maharajas for formal durbars, ceremonies and receptions. This has now been converted into an art gallery, displaying some of the museum's greatest treasures. Exhibits include an excellent collection of 17th-century Mughal and Indo-Persian floral carpets, woven in Lahore, Herat and Agra during the reign of Emperor Shah Jahan. Also displayed here are the maharajas' valuable and fine collection of miniatures from the late Mughal, Rajput and Deccani courts, depicting both religious and secular themes. Some of the treasures include *Krishna Playing Holi* (Amber-Jaipur, 1737), *Lord Krishna's Cosmic Dance* (Jaipur, late 18th century), *Allah-Wirdi Khan with Attendants in a Garden* (Deccan, early 18th century), *Madho Singh I on a Boat* (Jaipur, 18th century) and *Nari Kunjar* (Jaipur, 18th century), an unusual composton of female figures entwined imaginatively to

One of the rare Mughal miniatures in the Art Gallery

Manuscript of the *Geet Govinda* in the Art Gallery

create an elephant. There is also a large selection of *Ragamala* and *Baramasa* sets depicting the seasons, as well as some superb paintings from Kishangarh *(see p215)* by Nihal Chand.

This gallery also has rare palm leaf manuscripts and books bound with painted wood covers, and scrolls of religious texts. Of particular interest are the two priceless Persian manuscripts of the Hindu epics, the *Ramayana* and the *Mahabharata*. The latter, known as *Razmnama*, was specially prepared, at huge cost, for Emperor Akbar by Abu'l Fazl, his biographer, and profusely illustrated by his court painters. Sadly, this unique manuscript is never displayed. Sawai Jai Singh II's large personal collection of astronomy books in Arabic, Persian, Latin and Sanskrit, which formed the basis for his study and understanding of the movement of the planets, is also kept in the art gallery.

Other interesting items are an ivory howdah, a silver mobile throne and a selection of old cameras and black and white prints dating to the reign of Ram Singh II (1835–80), a versatile ruler and passionate photographer.

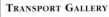
Mughal helmet

ARMS GALLERY

THIS GALLERY known as the Sileh Khana is located near the Mubarak Mahal. Some of the exhibits, displayed under exuberantly painted ceilings, are reputed to be the finest examples of weapons used in medieval India and are a tribute to the Rajput warrior's worship of arms. Whether specially commissioned, or acquired by the maharajas, the weapons in the royal armoury were both lethal and exquisitely crafted. On view are a range of swords, daggers and *katars*, a two-sided blade with a grip handle. Some are of green or white jade and are carved, while others are studded with jewels. Hilts are engraved with hunting

Diamond-studded dagger with pistols

scenes, images of gods and goddesses, or topped with the heads of exotic birds and animals. Among the swords on display is one belonging to Raja Man Singh I (r.1590–1619) weighing about 5 kg (11 lbs). Another, made by Abdullah Isfahani, bears the emblem of the Shah of Persia. There are two swords of Jahangir and Shah Jahan and also Akbar's gold-encrusted helmet, shaped like a turban. A fascinating section displays gunpowder containers, some made of ivory, others decorated with mother-of-pearl inlay on shell.

The gallery's collection also contains such gut-wrenching exhibits as a lotus-shaped steel mace belonging to Jai Singh I. When rammed into the enemy's stomach, it would spring into a deadly fan of sharp spikes and disembowel the victim.

TRANSPORT GALLERY

A COMPARATIVELY recent addition is the Transport Gallery situated near the Art Gallery. It exhibits a selection of palanquins, chariots, *ikkas*, buggies and carriages from the old Buggi Khana which fell into disuse after the motor car became popular with the maharajas. Don't miss the gigantic Indra Vamaa carriage, which used to be pulled by four elephants. Until it was installed here, it was used only for ceremonial occasions. Now it conjures up some of the pomp of a bygone era.

Fragment of a 16th-century Persian carpet

Jantar Mantar

Kantivrita Yantra

O F THE FIVE OBSERVATORIES built by Sawai Jai Singh II, the one in Jaipur is the largest and best preserved; the others are in Delhi *(see p77)*, Ujjain, Mathura and Varanasi. A keen astronomer himself, Jai Singh was aware of the latest astronomical studies in the world, and was most inspired by the work of Mirza Ulugh Beg, the astronomer-king of Samarkand. Built between 1728 and 1734, this observatory resembles a giant sculptural composition of 16 instruments and has been described as "the most realistic and logical landscape in stone". Some of the instruments are still used to forecast how hot the summer months will be, the expected date of arrival, duration and intensity of the monsoon, and the possibility of floods and famine.

Narivalaya Yantra
Inclined at 27°, these represent the two hemispheres and are sundials that calculate time by following the solar cycle.

Unnatansha Yantra was used to determine the positions of stars and planets at any time of day or night.

Laghu Samrat Yantra
This "small sundial" is constructed on Latitude 27° North (Jaipur's latitude) and calculates Jaipur's local time up to an accuracy of 20 seconds.

City Palace Museum

Entrance

Floating Pic label 6/7 Garamond Bold

Chakra Yantra
A brass tube passes through the centre of two circular metal instruments through which the angle of stars and planets from the equator can be observed.

★ Ram Yantra
Vertical columns support an equal number of horizontal slabs in two identical stone structures that comprise this instrument. The readings from these determine the celestial arc from horizon to zenith, as well as the altitude of the sun.

Jantar Mantar
The complex of stone and metal instruments was repaired with the addition of marble inlay by Madho Singh II in 1901.

VISITORS' CHECKLIST

Chandni Chowk, outside City
Palace. 🕻 (0141) 261 0494.
⬤ 9am–4:30pm daily. ⬤ Holi
& public hols. 📷 extra
charges. 🖊

★ Samrat Yantra
Jai Singh believed that gigantic instruments would give more accurate results. This 23-m (75-ft) high sundial forecasts the crop prospects for the year.

Hawa Mahal

Rashivalaya Yantra
This is composed of 12 pieces, each of which represents a sign of the zodiac and so faces a different angle and constellation. This unique yantra is used by astrologers to make accurate horoscopes.

★ Jai Prakash Yantra
Two sunken hemispheres map out the heavens. This instrument is believed by some historians to have been invented by Jai Singh himself to verify the accuracy of all the others in the observatory.

STAR FEATURES

★ Ram Yantra

★ Samrat Yantra

★ Jai Prakash Yantra

South of the Walled City

Jaali detail

BY THE END OF THE 19TH CENTURY, Jaipur had spread far beyond the boundaries established by Sawai Jai Singh II. Much of the area outside the walled city was developed by the enlightened ruler, Sawai Ram Singh II (r.1835–80). This able administrator also modernized the city by adding many civic amenities such as good roads, street lighting and running water. As Jaipur expanded, it incorporated the pleasure palaces and hunting lodges existing on its outskirts. The still-gracious city we see today is a harmonious blend of the old and the new.

The Indo-Saracenic-style Government Central Museum (Albert Hall)

🏛 Government Central Museum
Ram Niwas Bagh. **(** (0141) 256 5124. **⏰** 10am–4:30pm Sat–Thur. **⚫** Fri & public hols. 🎫 free on Mon.

Designed by Sir Samuel Swinton Jacob, Albert Hall or the Government Central Museum was commissioned by Sawai Ram Singh II to honour the visit of Albert, the Prince of Wales, in 1876. Swinton Jacob had perfected the Indo-Saracenic style of architecture *(see p25)*, a hybrid form that combined modern European with traditional Indian elements to create a highly ornamental style used for many public buildings during the Raj.

This grand multi-layered building, with its domes, parapets and balustrades, is located in the centre of the Ram Niwas Gardens. Its ground floor displays decorative shields and embossed salvers in Jaipur's famed metalware, life-sized models of rural scenes, good examples of Jaipur's glazed pottery, and even an Egyptian mummy. A 30-ft (9-m) long *phad* (painted cloth scroll), depicts the life of Pabuji, a 14th-century Rajasthani folk hero. The first floor has a fine collection of Mughal and Rajput miniature paintings.

The museum's greatest treasure, one of the world's largest Persian garden carpets (1632) housed in the Durbar Hall, can be seen on request.

🏛 Museum of Indology
Nilambara, Prachaya Vidya Path, 24 Gangwal Park. **(** (0141) 260 7455. **⏰** 10am–5pm, daily. 🎫 📷 🚫

The large mansion of the reputed scholar, Acharya RC Sharma "Vyakul", is now home to a privately owned museum that displays his unusual personal collection. Among the exhibits are impressive displays of maps and coins, manuscripts, textiles and jewellery, fossils, gems and clocks. The museum's charm, however, lies in its idiosyncrasies, such as a map of India painted on a grain of rice, a copy of Rajasthan's oldest newspaper (1856), and letters written, incredibly, on a single strand of hair.

🏛 Moti Doongri
Jawaharlal Nehru Marg. **⚫** to the public.

Moti Doongri owes its florid exterior to Sawai Man Singh II who converted the old fort of Shankargarh into a palace, and added turrets in the style of a Scottish castle. In 1940 he married the beautiful Princess Gayatri Devi of Cooch Behar, and this palace with its modernized interior became the venue for glittering parties hosted by the glamorous couple for their wide circle of friends. After his death in 1970, the maharani, by then a Member of Parliament, lived here for some years to keep in touch with her constituency. The palace, a private property, is perched on a low hillock, with only its ramparts and the tall spire of an ancient Shiva temple visible from the road.

At the foot of Moti Doongri is the white marble **Lakshmi Narayan Temple**. This generously endowed building was erected in 1979 on a piece of land sold by the Jaipur royal family for a token sum to the Birlas, an important industrial family. Though the sale was disputed and created a huge uproar in the local press, the temple is now a popular place of worship, admired for its carvings.

Lakshmi Narayan Temple, a white marble addition to the Pink City

The luxurious interior of Rambagh Palace

♔ Statue Circle
Bhagwan Das Rd.
This popular landmark is a traffic roundabout, circling an imposing white marble statue of Sawai Jai Singh II, commissioned by the Sawai Jai Singh Benevolent Trust. It was installed in 1968 and is now a lunch-hour recreation spot for office workers and for evening joggers.

Facing the statue to the left is the **Birla Planetarium**. The complex comprises two modern buildings: the science museum with an auditorium, and the planetarium. The main entrance of the building is a replica of Amber Fort's Ganesh Pol *(see pp200–201)*. Exhibitions and sales of Rajasthani handicrafts are held here periodically.

Statue of Sawai Jai Singh II

♔ Birla Planetarium
Statue Circle, Prithviraj Rd.
🕐 10am–8pm daily. 📞 (0141) 238 1594. 📷 🚫

♔ Rambagh Palace
Bhawani Singh Rd. 📞 (0141) 238 1919. 🍴 open to non-residents.
The Rambagh Palace, now a splendid hotel, has had a colourful past. From its modest origins in 1835 as a small, four-roomed garden pavilion for Ram Singh II's wet nurse, it was used as a hunting lodge after she died in 1856. Later, when Ram Singh II's son, Madho Singh II returned from England, he transformed it with the help of Swinton Jacob into a royal

playground with squash and tennis courts, a polo field and indoor swimming pool. In 1933 it was selected as the official residence of Madho Singh's adopted son and heir, Man Singh II, who invited Hammonds of London to re-do the interiors, adding an exotic red and gold Chinese room, black marble bathrooms and fabulous Lalique crystal chandeliers, fountains and an illuminated dining table. Surrounded by fairy-tale gardens, this was the perfect setting for Man Singh and his lovely wife. Rambagh became the official residence of the Head of State of the new Rajasthan Union in 1949, and a hotel in 1957.

♔ Raj Mahal Palace
Sardar Patel Marg. 📞 (0141) 238 3260. 🍴 open to non-residents.
Now a grand heritage hotel, this pleasant 18th-century palace, less opulent than the Rambagh Palace, occupies a

special place in the history of Jaipur. Built in 1739 for Sawai Jai Singh II's favourite queen, Chandra Kumari Ranawatji, it was used as a summer resort by the ladies of the court. In 1821, it was then declared the official home of the British Resident in Jaipur. However, the most glamorous and memorable phase of its colourful history dates to the time when Man Singh II and Gayatri Devi moved here from Rambagh Palace in 1956. Among the celebrities they entertained were Prince Philip, a polo player like Man Singh, and Jackie Kennedy.

Jawahar Kala Kendra

🏛 Jawahar Kala Kendra
Jawaharlal Nehru Marg. 📞 (0141) 270 6501. 🕐 10am–5pm. 📷 🚻
Designed by Indian architect Charles Correa in 1993, this remarkable building offers tribute to contemporary Indian design. Imaginatively patterned after the famous grid system of the city, each of the nine squares or courts houses a *mahal* named after a planet. Each *mahal* displays selected exhibits of textiles, handicrafts and weaponry, while in the centre there is a grand open air plaza where performances of traditional Rajasthani music and dance are held.

POLO – THE GAME OF KINGS
Polo, said to be Central Asian in origin, was brought to India by the Muslim conquerors. Its requirement of superior cavalry skills made it a popular sport among Rajput royalty and the army. Man Singh II was a dashing polo player and formed the Jaipur polo team and club in the 1930s. Ironically, he died in England in 1970, playing the game he loved so well. Jaipur is still a well-known venue, and international celebrities such as Prince Philip and Prince Charles have played polo here.

A Jaipur polo player in action

Beyond Jaipur: East

Wall painting

ENCLOSING A NARROW VALLEY, a parallel range of hills runs along Jaipur's eastern periphery from Sanganer in the south up to Amber and beyond. This combination of rocky terrain and thickly wooded slopes provided an attractive environment for the rulers and nobility who built temples, garden pavilions and palaces here for themselves. The area is also known for its wildlife, particularly monkeys, after whom the valley is fittingly named the Valley of Monkeys.

One of Galta's sacred tanks

Galta

10 km (6 miles) E of Jaipur on Agra Rd.

The picturesque Galta gorge plunges down the hillside to join the Jaipur-Agra road. A great sage, called Galav, is supposed to have lived and performed penance here. Deep within the gorge is Galta Kund, an 18th-century religious site with two main temples dedicated to Ram and Vishnu; the Achariyon ki Haveli; and a number of smaller shrines and now derelict buildings. High on the ridge is the Surya Temple. At different levels are seven sacred tanks, fed throughout the year by natural spring water flowing from a rock resembling a cow's mouth. The water is said to have curative powers. The two *baradaris* on either side of the complex have fairly well preserved frescoes depicting legends from Krishna's life, including a ceiling profusely painted with gorgeous lotus blooms. From the summit there are spectacular views of Jaipur, but do beware of monkeys in search of food.

Sisodia Rani ka Bagh

Purana Ghat. 6 km (4 miles) E of Jaipur on Agra Rd. (0141) 268 0494. 8am–6pm daily.

This terraced garden was laid out in the 18th century for Sawai Jai Singh II's second wife, a Sisodia princess from Udaipur. The marriage was one of convenience, to foster better relations between the two powerful princely states, and one of the conditions was that the new queen's son would succeed to the Jaipur throne. To escape the ensuing and inevitable palace intrigues, the queen decided to shift to a more private home outside the walled city.

Her little double-storeyed palace is surrounded by beautiful gardens artfully planted with fragrant bushes of jasmine, where peacocks dance amid the spray of fountains and gurgling water channels. The interiors are decorated with lively murals depicting episodes from Krishna's life, hunting scenes and polo matches, mythical beasts and heroic events. Not surprisingly, this enchanting place has become a popular location for Indian films.

ENVIRONS: Opposite Sisodia Rani ka Bagh is **Vidyadhar ka Bagh**, a small and once beautiful 18th-century garden dedicated to the courtier traditionally credited with designing Jaipur *(see p183)*.

Ghat ke Balaji

1 km (4 miles) N of Sisodia Rani ka Bagh towards Galta.

Behind Sisodia gardens a double flight of steps ends in a pair of tall gateways leading to a small temple dedicated to the monkey-god Hanuman (also known as Balaji). This endearing deity is cherished by the local people who treat him with tender care, and in winter wrap his image in a muffler and quilt to keep him warm. The monkeys that inhabit the area are equally well looked after. Every evening at 4pm, a charming ritual takes place when, to the call of the priests, hordes of silver grey langurs with black faces and long tails descend on the temple for a meal specially cooked for them. Then, swishing their tails, they head back to the valley that bears their name.

Ghat ki Guni

6 km (4 miles) E of Jaipur on Agra Rd.

In the 18th and 19th centuries the ministers and dignitaries of the Jaipur court created a tranquil summer retreat in this valley, when the area would bustle with the constant to and fro of aristocracy. Now, the deserted *havelis*, temples

Sisodia Rani ka Bagh, laid out as a formal Mughal *charbagh*

Elegant *chhatris* of deserted buildings lining the Ghat ki Guni road

and bathing ghats are all that remain of this once exclusive resort. On either side of the road today, are dense rows of niched façades perforated by tiny windows and arched *chhatris*, elegant eaves and domes, while among the ruins and winding alleys, a number of tea-stalls and little shops selling trinkets and souvenirs have sprung up.

🛕 Ramgarh

40 km (25 miles) E of Jaipur.
Ramgarh, on the banks of a man-made lake, is the site of one of the earliest fortresses of the Kachhawahas. It was built by the dynasty's founder, Duleh Rai (r.1093–1135), after he defeated the local Meenas by attacking them on a Diwali night when they were forbidden to carry weapons. A temple dedicated to the goddess Jamvai Mata, whose divine intervention is said to have led to his victory, was also constructed by him. This temple is visited by thousands of devotees all through the year. The lake itself was created in the late 19th century when Sir Samuel Swinton Jacob planned the construction of a dam across the Banganga River, and was, until recently, Jaipur's main source of drinking water. On its northern bank is Ramgarh Lodge, an elegant French villa-style hunting lodge built in 1931 for the Jaipur royal family, and now a pleasing heritage hotel. Ramgarh is a tranquil retreat for those who wish to escape from the city and its Polo Club is one of the best in the country.

The man-made Ramgarh Lake

HANUMAN – THE MONKEY GOD

A much loved figure in the pantheon of Hindu gods *(see pp22–3)*, Hanuman appears wherever Rama is worshipped. In the *Ramayana (see p37)*, this loyal trooper and his monkey army play a crucial role in the defeat of Ravana and the rescue of Sita. To this day, warriors, acrobats and wrestlers regard him as their patron deity. The cult of Hanuman as a martial god and protector is so widespread that even a simple stone daubed with orange vermilion paste *(sindur)* signals his presence.

Yet, he has another more loveable side which widens the circle of his devotees. They believe this fearless warrior, who set Lanka afire and decimated Ravana's army, is ignorant of his own miraculous powers. Not only can he cure disease and exorcise evil spirits; he can cure infertility because his celibacy gives him that power. Others believe he also knows the secrets of yoga and the finer points of music and Sanskrit grammar. By combining the might of a martial god with the endearing qualities of the monkey he resembles, Hanuman becomes a link between warrior princes and simple peasants.

Hanuman statue

Beyond Jaipur: North

TOWERING ABOVE JAIPUR are the two dramatic fortresses of Nahargarh and Jaigarh that guard the approach from the north to both Amber and the new capital of Jaipur. Today, they recall a bygone age when warrior clans fought for supremacy. The surrounding rocky terrain also has the remains of fortified walls, temples and shrines, *havelis* and the ornate marble cenotaphs of the Kachhawaha kings.

Mural motif

Nahargarh

9 km (5 miles) NW of Jaipur on Amber Rd. (0141) 244 8044. 9am–4:30pm daily. public hols.

The forbidding hill-top fort of Nahargarh ("tiger fort") stands in what was once a densely forested area. The fierce Meena tribe ruled this region until they were defeated by the Kachhawahas. Legend says that this was the site of the cenotaph of Nahar Singh, a martyred Rathore warrior, and when Sawai Jai Singh II ordered that its fortifications be strengthened to defend the newly-built Jaipur, the warrior's spirit resisted all construction until a priest performed tantric rites. Successive rulers further expanded the fort. Madho Singh II added a lavish palace called Madhavendra Bhavan for his nine queens. Laid out in a maze of terraces and courtyards, it has a cool, airy upper chamber from which the ladies of the court could view the city. Its walls and pillars are an outstanding example of *arayish*, a plaster-work technique that is hand-polished with a piece of agate to produce a marble finish.

Pundarik ki Haveli

Shastri Chowk, Brahmpuri. (0141) 232 1534. 8am–5:30pm daily.

Lying to the east of Nahargarh, on the way to Gaitor, is the Brahmpuri area where the grand *havelis* of the pundits and scholars of the Jaipur court once stood. One mansion was the residence of Pandit Ratnakar Pundarik, a Brahmin courtier during the reign of Sawai Jai Singh II who, it is said, conducted the *puja* that appeased the spirit of Nahar Singh. Fortunately, this *haveli* has survived the ravages of time and is partly occupied. A portion is now a protected monument to preserve the superb frescoes decorating the walls and ceilings of the living rooms. These lively paintings depict gods and goddesses, courtly scenes and festival processions. One also portrays life on the different floors of the seven-storeyed Chandra Mahal (*see pp188–9*).

Gaitor

Brahmpuri. 9am–4:30pm. public hols.

The marble cenotaphs of the Kachhawaha kings are enclosed in a walled garden just below Nahargarh Fort. Sawai Jai Singh II chose this to be the new cremation site after Amber was abandoned (*see p203*). Ornate, carved pillars support the marble *chhatris* erected over the platforms where the maharajas were cremated. One of the most impressive cenotaphs is that of Jai Singh II himself. It has 20 marble pillars, carved with mythological scenes and

Maharani ki Chhatri

One of the exquisite, well preserved murals at Pundarik ki Haveli

The picturesque Jal Mahal seemingly afloat in the monsoon

topped by a white marble dome. Another is that of Sawai Ram Singh II, with stone pillars and dome panels carved with images of Hindu deities and scenes from Krishna's life. There is another sandstone and marble *chhatri* in memory of Madho Singh II. The most recent cenotaph was erected in 1997 in memory of Jagat Singh, the only son of Sawai Man Singh II and Gayatri Devi.

ENVIRONS: The *chhatris* of the official wives of the Jaipur kings are located in a separate enclosure called **Maharani ki Chhatri**, outside the Jorawar Singh Gate of the walled city, on the road to Amber. Set in a pleasant garden, the complex with its cupolas and carved pillars was restored in 1995.

⛩ Maharani ki Chhatri
Amber Rd. ◯ *9am–4:30pm daily.* ⬤ *public hols.* ▨

⛩ Jal Mahal
Amber Rd, opp Trident Hotel. ◯ *restricted entry.*
During the monsoon when water fills the Man Sagar, the Jal Mahal or "water palace" seems to float serenely on the calm waters of the lake. Built in the mid-18th century by Madho Singh I, it was based on the Lake Palace at Udaipur where the king spent his childhood. Later it was used as a lodge for duck shooting parties, and even today, a large number of waterbirds can be sighted here. A terrace garden is enclosed by arched passages, and at each corner is a semi-octagonal tower capped by an elegant cupola.

ENVIRONS: Sawai Jai Singh II performed a number of Vedic *yagnas* on the western banks of Man Sagar. Dating to that period are traces of a **Yagna Stambha** ("pillar") where he performed a horse sacrifice, and the **Kala Hanumanji**, a temple dedicated to the well-known monkey god.

To the north of Jal Mahal is the splendidly restored **Kanak Vrindavan Temple** dedicated to Krishna, where the image of Govind Dev *(see p182)* was lodged before it was taken to the City Palace. This picturesque complex with its well-landscaped gardens, fountains and pavilions, makes a popular picnic spot.

⛩ Jaigarh
Amber Rd. ◼ *(0141) 267 1848.* ◯ *9am–5pm daily.* ⬤ *public hols.* ▨
Legendary Jaigarh, the "victory fort", watches over the old capital of Amber, its great, crenellated outer walls delineating the edge of a sharp ridge for 3 km (2 miles)

from north to south. Located within the fort is one of the world's few surviving cannon foundries. Its most prized possession is the monumental Jai Van, cast in 1726 and believed to be the world's largest cannon on wheels. Its 6-m (20-ft) long barrel has fine carvings of elephants, birds and flowers. Ironically, despite its impressive size, the cannon remained a work of art and was never fired.

An interesting sight is the massive Diva Burj, a tower on whose uppermost seventh storey a huge oil lamp would be lit on the king's birthday and during Diwali, until the top two storeys were struck down by lightning. The fort has two temples and a large palace complex built over 200 years by different rulers. Located here are the Subhat Niwas (audience hall), the profusely painted Aram Mandir (an airy pleasure pavilion), the residential Laxmi Niwas with baths, and a small theatre for music, dance and puppet shows. The fort's intricate system of collecting and storing rainwater in huge tanks located in the courtyard is unique. Legend has it that Man Singh I's vast treasure, amassed during his military campaigns, was hidden within these tanks. In 1976, the government carried out a massive but unsuccessful hunt, even to the extent of draining the water tanks to locate this legendary trove.

The famous Jai Van

The ramparts of Jaigarh Fort, a feat of military engineering

Amber Fort ❷

Detail of door at Shila Devi

THE FORT PALACE OF AMBER WAS the Kachhawaha citadel until 1727, when their capital moved to Jaipur. However, successive rulers continued to come here on all important occasions to seek the blessings of the family deity, Shila Devi. The citadel was established in 1592 by Man Singh I on the remains of an earlier 11th-century fort, but various buildings added by Jai Singh I (r.1621–67) constitute its magnificent centrepiece.

Elephant ride on the cobbled pathway to the fort

★ Sheesh Mahal
The flame of a single candle, reflected in the tiny mirrors embedded in this chamber, transforms it into a starlit sky.

Aram Bagh, the pleasure garden.

Jas Mandir
This hall of private audience has latticed windows, a floral ceiling of elegant alabaster relief work and glass inlay. A marble screen here overlooks the Maota Lake and wafts in cool air.

Jai Mandir

Location of Amber Fort
Protected by Jaigarh Fort, the massive ramparts of Amber Fort follow the contours of a natural ridge.

STAR FEATURES
★ Sheesh Mahal
★ Ganesh Pol
★ Shila Devi Temple

VISITORS' CHECKLIST

Jaipur district. 11 km (6 miles) N of
Jaipur. **Road map** C3. [(0141)
253 0044. 🕐 9am–4:30pm.
⬤ public hols.

★ **Ganesh Pol**
*The shimmering three-storeyed
gateway built in 1640 leads to
the private apartments,
connected by the
screened upper-
most level for
ladies in
purdah.*

Sukh
Niwas

★ **Shila Devi Temple**
*Behind this wall is the
temple dedicated to
Shila Devi.*

Sattais
Katcheri

Diwan-
i-Aam

PLAN OF AMBER FORT

KEY
☐ Area illustrated above
☐ Man Singh's palace
☐ Jaleb Chowk

0 metres   100
0 yards   100

1 Suraj Pol   **4** Diwan-i-Aam   **6** Sheesh Mahal
2 Chand Pol   **5** Ganesh Pol   **7** Sukh Niwas
3 Shila Devi   **6** Jai Mandir   **8** *Baradari*
   Temple   **6** Jas Mandir   **9** Zenana

Exploring Amber (the Old Capital)

Painting detail on Ganesh Pol

CROWNING THE CREST of a hill, Amber Fort and its ramparts offer a panoramic view of Maota Lake, two exquisite formal gardens, and the historic old town at the base of the hill, dotted with the remains of an older capital before it shifted to the precincts of the fort. Some of the old *havelis* and numerous temples here are remarkably well-preserved, while stepwells and lakes point to the existence of a self sufficient township where even the great Mughal emperor Akbar stopped on his annual pilgrimage to Ajmer.

Sattais Katcheri, where the revenue records were written

The Fort Complex
The main entrance to the historic Amber Fort is through the imposing **Suraj Pol** ("sun gate"), so called because it faces the direction of the rising sun, the Kachhawaha family emblem. This gate leads into a huge flagged courtyard, **Jaleb Chowk**, literally, "the square where elephants and horses are tethered". Originally the fort's parade ground, its central area is surrounded on three sides by guard rooms, now souvenir and refreshment shops. A flight of steps leads to the **Shila Devi Temple**, which contains the image of the Kachhawaha family deity, a stone *(shila)* goddess Kali, brought here by Man Singh I from Bengal in 1604. The temple has ornately carved silver doors presented by the second wife of the last maharaja in 1939, silver oil lamps and grand pillars of green marble carved to look like banana trees.

The next courtyard has the **Diwan-i-Aam**, the space for public audience. Near it are 27 *(sattais)* airy colonnades, called the **Sattais Katcheri**, where scribes once sat to record revenue petitions.

The magnificent **Ganesh Pol** is the gateway to three private palaces built around a Mughal-style garden *(see p167)*, **Aram Bagh**. Each of these pleasure-palaces has some special feature. Sukh Niwas has doors carved from fragrant sandalwood, and water cascades over marble chutes to cool the interior. The marble Jai Mandir, at the other end of the garden, has the superb **Sheesh Mahal** studded with mirrors. The adjoining **Jas Mandir** has a marble screen across its eastern façade that overlooks the Maota Lake.

The lake, which provided water to the fort, is surrounded by two exquisite gardens. The **Kesar Kyari Bagh** has star-shaped flower beds once planted with saffron *(kesar)* flowers, while **Dilaram Bagh**, built in 1568 as a resting place for Emperor Akbar on his way to Ajmer, is a clever pun on the name of its architect, Dilaram ("heart's ease"). A small archaeological museum is located near Dilaram Bagh.

The furthermost end of the fort, which was also its oldest section, was converted into the **Zenana** ("women's quarters") by Man Singh I to house his 12 wives and concubines. The apartments bear the distinct stamp of Mughal zenana architecture, with screens and covered balconies for the protection and purdah of the royal ladies. Faint traces of frescoes are still visible on the walls. In the centre of the courtyard is a colonnaded pavilion called the **Baradari**.

Kesar Kyari Bagh, named after rare saffron flowers once planted in its star-shaped flower beds

Bharmal ki Chhatri, the old cenotaphs of the Kachhawaha rulers

The Township

The **Chand Pol** ("moon gate"), directly opposite Suraj Pol, leads to the old town outside the fort. The **Narsimha Temple**, built in the early 15th century by the Kachhawaha king Narsingh Dev, is the first of many on this route. The temple itself is only a small part of a derelict palace complex which was the site of past coronations before the Amber rulers abandoned it for the fort.

East of this lies the beautiful **Jagat Shiromani Temple**, erected in the early 17th century by Man Singh I in memory of his eldest son, Jagat Singh. A remarkable *toran* (carved lintel) adorns the doorway of the temple which has images of Vishnu, Radha and Krishna. Legend says that the Krishna image was brought here in the 16th century by the saint-poetess Mira Bai, famous for her devotion to Lord Krishna, from Chittorgarh, her home in southern Rajasthan.

Moving further east is the **Sanghi Jutharam Temple** which at one time had a beautiful 12-sided well, a small garden and several chambers. It is now protected by the Archaeological Survey of India (ASI). To its northeast lies the **Ambikeshwar Mahadev Temple**, dedicated

Marble carving in Narsimha Temple

to a manifestation of Shiva. One of the oldest temples here, it now stands 3 m (10 ft) below ground level and is said to be slowly sinking.

North of the Ambikeshwar Temple is **Panna Mian ka Kund**, built in the 17th century by a eunuch Panna Mian, a leading figure at the court of Raja Jai Singh I. From here, there is a cobbled path winding eastwards past further ruins and out through **Kheri Gate**, one of the old gates of Amber, leading to a popular picnic spot called **Sagar**, with its two terraced lakes. These were once important sources of water supply during times of siege. Located in a depression formed by the surrounding hills, just behind Jaigarh Fort, the site still bears traces of an elaborate water transport system in which elephants were used to carry water up to the fort.

These monuments lie to the west of the main Jaipur-Delhi highway that cuts across the town. The main market and the Amber bus stand are also located along this road, which is

now almost entirely occupied by tiny wayside eateries and souvenir shops. Further along this road, to the north, stands the **Akbari Mosque**, built by Emperor Akbar in 1569 at one of the spots where he stopped to pray on his way to Ajmer *(see pp218–19)*. The basic structure of the mosque remains intact even though it has been often repaired.

Further westwards down this road is **Bharmal ki Chhatri**, a walled enclosure containing a group of memorials. This was the old cremation site for the rulers of Amber until a new spot was established at Gaitor *(see pp198–9)* after the capital moved from Amber to Jaipur.

Steps criss-crossing down to the water in the partly restored Panna Mian ka Kund

Marble statue of a Jain *tirthankara* at Sanganer's Sanghiji Temple

Sanganer ❸

Jaipur district. 16 km (10 miles) SW of Jaipur. **Road map** C3. ✈ 🏠 *daily.*

Two ornate triple-arched gateways lead into Sanganer, a colourful town renowned for its blockprinted cotton textiles. According to local lore this tradition of blockprinting goes back to the 16th century when Sanga, one of the 18 sons of Prithviraj, the Kachhawaha ruler of Amber, re-established the town. Printers from nearby villages were asked to migrate to this new settlement to develop a range of textiles for the Jaipur court. It was Sanganer's river with its mineral powers of fixing the colours of the dyes that gave this printing village its fame and wealth. Today, the town resounds with the thud of printing, as craftsmen work in their sheds amidst bolts of cloth, dye-soaked pads and wooden blocks. Most of the printers and dyers in the town belong to a guild with retail outlets that sell reasonably priced fabric, tailored linen and accessories.

Sanganer is also a centre of handmade paper, a spin-off from textile printing, and Jaipur's famous Blue Pottery *(see p266).* Raja Man Singh I of Amber *(see p49)* set up the first workshops here to

Frieze at Sanghiji Temple

produce this special type of hand-painted pottery inspired by Persian and Chinese blue and white tiles so popular at the Mughal court.

Tucked away in the old walled town is an impressive 11th-century Jain temple. The **Sanghiji Temple** was probably built by a Jain trader with additional donations from the town's other wealthy merchants. Like other Jain temples found elsewhere in Rajasthan, this too is lavishly decorated with ornate stone carvings that include images of all the 24 Jain *tirthankaras* (saints) and a beautiful statue of Mahavira, the founder of Jainism, in the innermost sanctuary.

Sanganer is now a busy suburb of Jaipur city and the location of its airport.

Bagru ❹

Jaipur district. 32 km (20 miles) SW of Jaipur past Sanganer on Ajmer Rd. **Road map** C3. 🚌 🏠 *daily.*

The small village of Bagru is yet another traditional textile printing centre. Unlike the refined prints of Sanganer, Bagru's are bolder and more earthy, and originally had a limited colour palette of red and black. The indigo, yellow and green that we see today are later additions. The origins of blockprinting in Bagru date back some 300 years, when the first few printing families were brought to this village by the then *thakur* of Bagru, an important fiefdom of the Jaipur kings. Over time, more printers settled here, lured by state patronage as well as the abundant supply of water, so essential for printing.

Bagru's printers *(chhipas)* supplied the fabric that was used by the local farming communities as both stitched and unstitched garments. As the demand for blockprinted textiles increased, their clientele became more varied and their range of products more diversified. Yet, in many ways, little has changed and this is one of the few places to see the printing process at work. Craftsmen still follow the traditional methods of resist-printing, blockprinting and bleaching, and though the use of synthetic dyes has crept in, some colours, such as black and yellow, are still extracted from vegetable and mineral matter.

Faded wall paintings outside the palace at Bagru

Blockprinted Textiles

DELICATE FLOWERS and foliage, paisleys, birds and animals on a white background are Sanganer's typical motifs. Handed down from father to son, these designs were inspired by the flower studies of miniature paintings *(see pp30–31)* and Mughal *pietra dura* motifs *(see pp156–7)*. Blockprinting can be seen in the workshops of the city's Chhipa Mohalla, where each stage of this ancient technique, from

An intricate paisley motif

chiselling intricate patterns on wooden blocks, to dyeing the fabric in huge copper vats on wood-fed fires, and printing, is all done by hand. In the more complex designs, a single motif may use up to ten different colours with as many blocks, each with a different design. In the final stage, swathes of printed cloth are spread on riverbanks or hung on huge frames to dry under the sky.

Sanganeri motifs *of stylized flowers* (phool) *and leaves* (buti) *in soft colours re-create a field of dainty flowers.*

Textile printing *is done with wooden blocks. These are dipped in dye to print the cloth stretched across a low stool. Earlier, colours were extracted from vegetable and mineral matter. Pomegranate rinds, saffron, madder root, turmeric and the indigo plant were some natural sources. Chemicals have now replaced natural dyes.*

Wooden printing blocks *are carved by hand with popular design motifs. Traditional designs have today been enlivened by inputs from modern Indian fashion designers.*

Bagru's *floral, figurative and geometric motifs are printed on a coarse cotton cloth that is made into blouses and gathered skirts worn by local women. However, in recent years, these earthy prints have become popular in urban centres too.*

HANDMADE PAPER

The Kagazi Mohalla, the colony of papermakers, recycles scraps of cloth and silk thread to produce an impressive range of decorative and functional paper products. Fabric is first converted into pulp and then flattened on a wire mesh. The thin sheets of paper are finally peeled off and hung up to dry. These craftsmen jealously preserve their trade secrets and seldom marry outsiders.

Sheets of handmade paper hung to dry

Alwar ⑤

Gate of Fateh Jang's Tomb

SITUATED between Mughal and Rajput territories, Alwar's place in history was manipulated by its rulers who made shrewd alliances to gain political leverage. Alwar's growth from a vassal state of the Kachhawaha kings to a significant Rajput state came about after Pratap Singh captured the fort of Bala Qila in 1775. Later, as the British cultivated it as a friendly base in Rajputana, there followed a burst of architectural extravagance that went along with a lavish round of tiger shoots, as its rulers tried to rival the glittering lifestyle of their cousins in Jaipur. Today, Alwar is a dusty provincial town with some remarkable monuments, mostly visited by tourists on their way to the Sariska National Park.

From the *Gulistan*, an 18th-century Mughal manuscript

🏛 City Palace

Near Collectorate. ⏱ *10am–4:30pm.*
A stunning profusion of architectural features marks this palace, with Rajput *bangaldar* eaves and elegant *chhatris* alongside Mughal floral tracery and *jaalis*. Built in 1793, the District Collectorate and Police Headquarters now occupy most of the palace, so it is best viewed from the large central courtyard. A stairway flanked by two marble kiosks leads from here to the gorgeous Durbar Hall and Sheesh Mahal, to see which special permission is needed.

A door on the right of the courtyard leads to the **City Palace Museum**, spread over three halls of the upper storey. These contain some treasures of the erstwhile rulers, such as their famed collection of miniature paintings of the Alwar, Jaipur and Mughal schools. The 7,000 rare manuscripts in Persian, Arabic,

Dagger, City Palace Museum

Urdu and Sanskrit include an illuminated Koran, a version of the rare and precious *Gulistan* of the great Persian poet Sa'adi, as well as the *Babur Nama* or "Memoirs of Babur" (1530). The awesome armoury display includes the swords of Mohammed Ghori, Akbar and Aurangzeb, and a macabre coil called *nag-phas*, used for strangling enemies. The first room contains a silver dining table with dividers, through which moving metal shoals of swimming fish can be seen. Behind the palace, across a magnificent *kund*, is the cenotaph of Maharaja Bakhtawar Singh (r.1790–1815). It is locally known as **Moosi Maharani ki Chhatri** after his mistress who performed *sati* here when he died. One of Rajasthan's most elegant monuments, blending brown sandstone and white marble, its carved pavilion has domed arches with exquisite

floral tracery, and ceilings adorned with fading gold leaf paintings of mythological characters and courtly scenes.

🏛 City Palace Museum
⏱ *10am–4:30pm.* ⬤ *Fri & public hols.* 🎫 🚫

🏛 Moosi Maharani ki Chhatri
⏱ *10am–4:30pm.* ⬤ *Fri & public hols.* 🎫 *Shoes not allowed.*

🏛 Bala Qila
⏱ *daily. Written permission is needed from the office of the Superintendent of Police, City Palace.*
Perched on a steep hill above the city, easily accessible by car, the Bala Qila was originally a 10th-century mud fort. Several additions were made to it by the Jats and Mughals (Babur is said to have spent a night here) until it was finally captured in 1775 by Pratap Singh of Alwar. Now a police wireless station, this sprawling fort was defended by 66 large and small towers. The frescoed palace within, the Nikumbh Mahal, was named after its first occupants, the Nikumbh Rajputs. The entire city can be seen from the fort's extensive ramparts, which give an idea of its scale and of the engineering skills that went into its building. Also visible are the ruins of Salim Mahal, named after Jahangir (Salim), who was exiled here after he plotted to kill Abu'l Fazl, Akbar's official biographer and one of the "nine gems" of his court.

The elegant marble pavilion at Moosi Maharani ki Chhatri

The aqueduct which brought water from Siliserh to the Company Bagh

VISITORS' CHECKLIST

Alwar district. 150 km (93 miles)
NE of Jaipur. **Road map** C3.
🚶 260,000. 🚉 Nehru Marg. 🚌
Manu Marg. 🛈 TRC, near
Railway Station, Alwar (0144) 234
7348; Paryatan Bhavan, MI Road,
Jaipur (0141) 511 0595. 🔓 daily.
📅 Jagannathji Fair (Mar–Apr),
Laldas Mela (May), Sawan Teej
(Jul–Aug), Diwali (Oct–Nov).

♣ Company Bagh
Vivekanand Marg. ⏰ 6am–6pm.
A lovely garden when it was
laid out in 1868, the Company
Bagh is now a shadow of its
former self. It was originally
named after Alwar's British
ally and protector, the East
India Company. Later, it was
christened Purjan Vihar by
Maharaja Jai Singh. An enchanting greenhouse here is
named "Simla", because it
reminded the maharaja of the
British summer capital in
North India. A three-km (two-
mile) long aqueduct, made of
solid stone masonry, brought
water from a reservoir at
Siliserh to this garden.

🏛 Fateh Jang's Tomb
Near Railway Station.
⏰ 9:30am–4:30pm.
The tomb of Fateh Jang, one
of Shah Jahan's ministers, is a
five-storeyed monument,
constructed in 1647. Dominated by an enormous dome, its
walls and ceiling have raised
plaster reliefs, and fine calligraphic inscriptions can be
seen on the first floor. A
school now occupies the
tomb's compound.

ENVIRONS: To the north of
Alwar, located at the edge of
Vijay Sagar Lake, is the 105-
roomed **Vijay Mandir
Palace**, built to look like an

anchored ship by Jai Singh
(r.1892–1937). A great builder
of palaces, the eccentric Jai
Singh had the famous 100-
roomed Moti Doongri palace-
fortress to the south of the
Company Bagh blown up
because it offended his
sensibilities. Vijay Mandir was
his last official residence and
he lived here for many years.
The former ruling family still
occupies it and reserves the
right of admission to it.

Alwar is full of apocryphal
stories of Jai Singh's strange
tastes. His Bugatti cars were
"buried" after he tired of
them, and he once ordered a
custom-made gold Lancaster
car that resembled the King of
England's coronation coach,
minus the horses!

ALWAR TOWN MAP

Bala Qila ①
City Palace Complex ②
Company Bagh ③
Fateh Jang's Tomb ④

KEY

🚉 Railway station
🚌 Bus stand
🛈 Tourist information
✉ Post office
🛕 Temple
🛕 *Gurudwara*
C Mosque

0 kilometres   1

0 miles   1

Siliserh ❻

Alwar district. 13 km (8 miles) SW of
Alwar. **Road map** C3. TRC, near
Railway Station, Alwar (0144)
234 7348.

THIS ENCHANTING SPOT is
midway between Alwar
and Sariska National Park *(see
pp210–11)*. The 10.5 sq km
(4 sq miles) Siliserh Lake, in a
valley bounded by low
forested hills, is still the main
reservoir supplying water to
Alwar and the surrounding
area. Perched on a hillock
overlooking the lake is the
water palace built in the mid-
19th century by the king of
Alwar, Vinay Singh, for his
beautiful wife, a local village
girl, so that she could be near
her family home. This once-
grand palace is now a hotel
and an ideal place for a quiet
getaway, as the only sounds
one hears are those made by
cormorants, ducks and other
waterbirds. Pathways lead up
the foothills and around the
lake where the remains of old
cenotaphs still stand. From
the palace's open terrace
there are wonderful views of
the sun setting over the lake.

Rajgarh Fort, once the capital of the Alwar kings

Rajgarh ❼

Alwar district. 35 km (22 miles) S of
Alwar. **Road map** C3. TRC, near
Railway Station, Alwar (0144)
234 7348.

OVERLOOKING a picturesque
valley, with green fields
and citrus groves, is the grand
hilltop fort of Rajgarh, the old
capital of the Alwar rulers.
Built by the founder of the
dynasty, Pratap Singh, in the
mid-18th century, its status as
the capital was brief, and in
1775, when Pratap Singh
captured Bala Qila *(see p206)*,
the court moved to Alwar.
The fort, however, with its

once beautiful Sheesh Mahal,
frescoed walls and secret
passages, was maintained as a
summer residence, but over
time it fell into disuse until
finally it was abandoned. The
town, too, at the foot of the
hill, wears a desolate look.

Sariska National Park ❽

See pp210–11.

Bairat ❾

Alwar district. 64 km (40 miles) SW of
Alwar. **Road map** C3. TRC, near
Railway Station, Alwar (0144)
234 7348.

NOWHERE IS THE AGE and
majesty of the Aravalli
Hills as apparent in the region
as it is at Bairat. The striking
topography of giant rocks,
variously textured and
shaped, provides a dramatic
backdrop for an excavated,
ancient archaeological site
that dates back to the 3rd
century BC. One of the cities
along the main north-south
trade route, this was a major
Buddhist centre. A rock edict
of Emperor Ashoka (273–232
BC) was found here, and at
one end of the village, off a
dirt track, high on a hillock
locally known as Bijak ki
Pahadi, are the remnants of a
Buddhist monastery and
circular temple. It is believed
to be India's oldest free-
standing structure. Historians
have identified it as a *chaitya*
hall or chapel which was
once supported by 26
octagonal wooden columns.

Siliserh Palace, built on a hillock overlooking the lake

Bairat's history, however, goes back to the time of the *Mahabharata* (around the 9th century BC), when this land formed part of a kingdom comprising much of eastern Rajasthan, and was ruled by King Virat from his capital of Viratnagar (present Bairat). It was here that the Pandavas *(see p141)* spent the 13th year of their exile. Locals believe that one of the Pandava brothers, the mighty Bhim, lived at **Bhim ki Doongri** ("Bhim's hillock"), and that Arjuna created the River Banganga when he struck an arrow into the earth. King Virat joined the Pandavas in the battle at Kurukshetra, and his daughter married Arjuna's son, Abhimanyu.

On the other side of town, near the rock edict, is an early 17th-century garden mansion dating to Jahangir's reign. Within the compound is a Jain temple, and just outside is the charming 16th-century hunting lodge where Akbar camped on his way to Ajmer. Locally known as the Chhatri, it was built on a raised platform, with five well-sculpted pavilions.

Remains of the circular temple dating to the Buddhist period, Bairat

Bhangarh 🔟

Alwar district. 56 km (35 miles) S of Sariska via Thana Gazi. **Road map** C3. ℹ️ *TRC, near Railway Station, Alwar (0144) 234 7348.* 🚌

A BUMPY RIDE from Sariska will take you to the abandoned city of Bhangarh, a fascinating site said to be a Kachhawaha clan citadel before Amber. Local legend says that the place was deserted when cursed by an evil magician, and many of its structures were transported to the new capital, Ajabgarh.

Built in the early 17th century by Madho Singh, the younger brother of Amber's Raja Man Singh I *(see p49)*, Bhangarh, also known as the "City of Ten Thousand Homes", exemplifies the hierarchy of traditional town planning.

A stone colonnaded pathway lined with market kiosks, stables or residences leads to the inner sanctum at the foot of the hills where a ruined palace, derisively called Randiyon ka Mahal ("palace of the prostitutes") remains, overlooking the Someshwar Temple, still in use. Three other temples dot the sprawling site, of which the Mangala Devi Temple, with a corbelled dome and finely carved exterior, is by far the most imposing.

ENVIRONS: On the road to Bhangarh is Ajabgarh, built by Madho Singh's grandson as a new settlement for the people of Bhangarh, by erecting a wall to separate the two cities. Part of the old town is under water, but a fort and some ruins may still be seen.

Carved bracket from the Mangala Devi Temple, Bhangarh

THE PANDAVAS IN EXILE

The great epic, the *Mahabharata (see p141)*, describes how, after losing the Pandava kingdom and wife Draupadi to the wicked Kauravas at a game of dice, Prince Yudhishthira, along with his brothers, Bhim, Arjuna, Nakul and Sahdev, were banished to 13 years of exile. The last year was the most crucial and had to be spent in complete anonymity for, if recognized, it meant another 12 years of exile. Forced to accept these rigid terms, the Pandavas roamed the country, spending their 13th year in disguise at the court of King Virat. The story of the Pandavas, their exile and the final battle are important components of the land's folklore, while sites such as Kurukshetra *(see p140)*, associated with their adventures, are venerated pilgrim spots.

The five Pandava brothers, from a popular TV serial

Sariska National Park ❽

Silk cotton flower

DESIGNATED A TIGER RESERVE under Project Tiger *(see p223)* in 1979, the park sprawls over 800 sq km (308 sq miles) with a core area of 480 sq km (185 sq miles). The Aravallis branch out at Sariska, forming low plateaux and valleys that harbour a wide spectrum of wildlife in the dry jungles. Formerly the private hunting ground of Alwar State, Sariska owes a debt to the strict game and protection laws laid down by its conservation-conscious rulers, which preserved its natural habitat and wildlife. A 17th-century fortress and several ancient temple ruins, such as the Pandupol Temple, also lie within the park.

Langur Monkeys
These black-faced primates with long tails are known as Hanuman langurs.

Sariska Palace
A turn-of-the-century hunting lodge of the Alwar rulers, this splendid palace, now a luxury hotel, has a collection of vintage photographs of past hunts, and period furnishings.

Endangered Species
Forest guides who keep track of where a tiger was last seen can lead you to spot this elusive predator.

Water Holes
To combat the chronic shortage of water in the region, the Forest Department has laid out a series of water holes at Pandupol, Bandipol, Slopka, Kalighati and Talvriksha. These make good vantage points to view wildlife, especially at sunset, when herds of animals flock to them to quench their thirst.

Flora

The dry deciduous forests of Sariska come to life during the brief spring and early summer when the flowering dhak *(Butea monosperma) and laburnum bloom. The date palm begins to bear fruit, while berries, locally known as* kair *(Capparis decidua) appear on the bushes.*

VISITORS' CHECKLIST

Alwar district. 103 km (22 miles) NE of Jaipur. **Road map** C3. 🚌 *Alwar.* 🛈 *Field Director, Project Tiger Sanctuary, Sariska (0144) 284 1333.* ⏱ *7–11am, 3–6pm.* ⬤ *Jul–Aug.* 🎫 *extra for personal vehicles or jeeps.* 🎫 📷 🍴

Jackal

Jackals and hyenas often lead trackers to a tiger kill. Along with panthers and jungle cats, these carnivores feed on the many species of deer, nilgai or blue bull, wild boar and porcupine in the forest. Tiger sightings are, however, rare in Sariska.

| 0 kilometres | 5 |
| 0 miles | 2 |

Cheetal

The gentle cheetal or spotted deer, like the sambar, is commonly seen at the park's water holes, or resting under the trees. The other deer species, the chowsingha (four-horned antelope), is specific to Sariska and can be seen around Pandupol.

ALWAR

ıpol
• Umri
a

KEY

═══ Major road

═══ Minor road

──── Park border

☀ Viewpoint

──── Trails

∩ Archaeological sight, ruin

🏰 Palace

🛕 Temple

🛈 Information centre

Grey Partridge

The hides at Kalighati and Slopka are ideal for observing the park's birdlife, such as the crested serpent eagle, the great Indian horned owl, wood-peckers, kingfishers and partridge.

Chomu ⓫

Jaipur district. 32 km (20 miles) NW of
Jaipur. **Road map** C3. 🏠 *Govt
Hostel, MI Rd, Jaipur (0141) 236
0238.* ⌂ *daily.*

THE SMALL TOWN of Chomu
links Jaipur with the
Shekhawati region. Traces of
a grander past are visible in
its once impressive fort,
handsome *havelis* and stepwells. But Chomu's charm lies
in its rural ambience, where
bullocks and camels plough
the fields, and the unique
four-pillared well is the main
source of water. In the
market, tractor spare parts
and tubewell pump-sets vie
for attention with hand-carts
spilling over with mounds of
cucumbers and *ber (Zizyphus
mauritiana)*, a berry for
which the region is famous.

Samode ⓬

Jaipur district. 42 km (26 miles) NW of
Jaipur. **Road map** C3. 🏠 *Govt
Hostel, MI Road, Jaipur (0141) 236
0238.* ⌂ *daily.* 📷 *Gangaur festival
(Mar–Apr).*

SAMODE'S romantic palace,
immortalized in films such
as *The Far Pavilions*, is the
main reason why this minor
Rajput hamlet is now a

The fairy tale Samode Palace, a luxurious retreat set amidst rugged hills

luxurious tourist destination.
Erected in the late 19th
century by a powerful noble
of the Jaipur state, this jewel-
like palace nestles among the
hills below an older hill fort.

A flight of stairs leads up to
a massive gateway and into
the palace. Its simple exterior
is highly deceptive for, surrounding the vast central
courtyard, are spacious rooms
on three levels. Of these, the
chambers on the uppermost
level are the most opulent.
The Durbar Hall, Sheesh
Mahal and Sultan Mahal are
embellished all over with
dazzling mirrorwork and
elaborate murals that depict
courtly life, hunting scenes
and religious themes, along
with floral and geometric

motifs. The murals represent
the best of the Jaipur style
and are said to rival those at
Jaipur's Chandra Mahal *(see
pp188–9)* and Tonk's Sunehri
Kothi *(see p222)*. However,
entrance is restricted since it
is now a luxury hotel.

A short distance away is
Samode Bagh where the more
adventurous can stay in one
of the 50 deluxe tents pitched
in the formal garden. Other
points of interest are the
abandoned old fort at the end
of a strenuous walk up 376
steps, and the quaint little
village where a wide variety
of local handicrafts such as
colourful hand-woven
dhurries, tie-and-dye fabric,
lac bangles and *jootis*
(slippers) are available.

THE PAINTED HAVELIS OF SHEKHAWATI

In the many little towns of Shekhawati are the ancestral
homes of some of India's leading industrialist families, such
as the Birlas, Dalmias and Goenkas. These sprawling old
havelis with their exuberantly frescoed walls *(see p27)* were
built between the late 18th and
early 20th centuries by the local
Marwari merchants who had
migrated to the port-cities of
Bombay and Calcutta to seek
their fortunes. Their interaction
with the British and exposure to
modern urban and industrial trends influenced their lifestyles,
and their homes reflected the new ideas they brought back with
them, as well as their new-found wealth and social status.

The style and content of the Shekhawati frescoes are a telling
comment on the urbanization of a traditional genre. The local
artists still followed the one-dimensional realism of traditional
Indian painting *(see pp30–31)*, but juxtaposed among the gods,
goddesses and martial heroes are images from a changing world.
In their celebration of contemporary "pop" themes, the frescoes
of British ladies, top-hatted gentlemen, brass bands and soldiers,
trains, motor cars, aeroplanes, gramophones and telephones,
symbolize the emerging industrial society of the late 19th century.

A "pop art" view of Rajput
chieftains

The entrance to Biyani
Haveli, Sikar

A Tour of Shekhawati ⓭

Northeast of jaipur, situated along the old camel caravan trade route, lies Shekhawati, or the "garden of Shekha", named after Rao Shekha, a fiercely independent ruler who consolidated the region in the 15th century. Today, the region resembles a vast open-air museum full of frescoed mansions. A network of excellent roads through semi-arid scrubland connects most towns and villages where the painted *havelis* of India's leading merchant families stand today in ghostly splendour.

Gods and goddesses frolic on the wall of Biyani Haveli, Sikar

Mandawa ④
The fort-palace is now a charming hotel and a convenient base from which to visit the neighbouring towns.

Dundlod ⑤
Its fort-palace and two splendid Goenka *havelis* are worth a visit.

Fatehpur ③
This picturesque mid-15th century town is best known for the Singhania, Goenka and Jalan *havelis*.

JHUNJHUNU

0 kilometres   20

0 miles   10

Mukundgarh

Key

⬛ Tour route

— Roads

≋ Rivers

Lachhmangarh ②
This 19th-century town is based on Jaipur's grid plan. The Char Chowk ("four coutyards") Haveli, owned by the Ganeriwala family, is said to be the grandest in the region.

Nawalgarh ⑥
The Poddar and the Aath ("eight") *havelis* are renowned for their frescoes.

NAGAUR

JAIPUR

Tips for Drivers

Length: *111 km (69 miles).*
Stopping-off points: *Mandawa, Dundlod, Mukundgarh, Fatehpur and Nawalgarh have good hotels. Petrol pumps are at regular intervals on the main road. Apart from NH11, the lesser roads towards Jhunjhunu are poor, but there are roadside eateries at intervals selling mineral water, hot and cold drinks and snacks.*

Sikar ①
Sikar's charm lies in its *havelis*, bazaars and rural ambience.

Sambhar Salt Lake ⑭

Jaipur district. 70 km (44 miles) NE of Ajmer. **Road map** B3. 🚌 📷
Sambhrai Mata Mela (Oct).

SAMBHAR LAKE is among the six important sites in India designated by the World Wide Fund for Nature (WWF) as a wetland of international importance. This vast inland saline lake spreads over an area of roughly 230 sq km (89 sq miles) and is fed by five rivers. During November and December, several species of migratory bird, especially flamingoes, can be seen here. A number of local legends are connected with the lake's origin, and a Shiva temple and two sacred tanks dedicated to mythological princesses are an indication of the lake's antiquity. The place, however, came into prominence after it was noticed by Babur in the 16th century. Since then, it has been a major source of salt for the country. One of the reasons for this is that after a good monsoon, the water level can rise by up to 3 ft (1 m), but over winter, the lake turns brackish due to capillary action caused by evaporation, drawing up salt from underground deposits. The little township that has grown around the lake survives on the extraction and packaging of salt. Men, women and even children can be seen working away at the countless trenches and mounds that are spread across the ghostly-white terrain. This has now become a highly commercial business, and though only one state-owned company has the monopoly, there has been an unprecedented growth in the numbers of private manufacturers. Many *bunds* (small dams) have been illegally constructed in the catchment area to retain rainwater for small-scale operations. This has affected not only the flow of water into the lake but has also put a considerable strain on its ecosystem.

Flamingoes in flight over Sambhar Lake

Makrana ⑮

Nagaur district. 80 km (50 miles) N of Ajmer. **Road map** B3. 🏯 *83,000.*
🏨 *Khadim Hotel, Ajmer.* 🛒 *daily.*

GREAT SLABS of hewn marble indicate that Makrana is a highly commercial stone-quarrying centre. The quarries stretch over a distance of

Marble quarrying at Makrana

20 km (12 miles) and produce the highly-prized luminous white marble that was used to build the Taj Mahal (*see pp154–5*). Quarrying began several centuries ago, and traditional open-pit methods are still used to excavate the stone. The demand for good quality marble has not lessened, and nearly 50,000 tons are mined annually and transported throughout the country. The town is also a good place to pick up gifts and souvenirs. Many small workshops have sprung up where artisans carve statues, pillars, vases, lamps and other objects for local sale and export. Objects are also sent to Agra where marble inlayers recreate the same delicate floral patterns as seen in the Taj Mahal (*see pp156–7*).

Salt packaging at Sambhar Salt Lake

Phool Mahal Palace in a picturesque setting

Kishangarh 🔟

Ajmer district. 30 km (19 miles) NE of Ajmer on NH 8. **Road map** B4. 🎪 116,000. 🛏 *Khadim Hotel, Ajmer.*

O**F ALL RAJPUTANA'S** princely states, this was the smallest. It was established in the early 17th century by Kishan Singh, a Rathore prince from Jodhpur, on lands near Ajmer. The king's sister was one of Jahangir's wives *(see pp52–3)*, a privilege that gave him a special status at the Mughal court. An obvious outcome of this proximity was that the Kishangarh kings tried to emulate the cultured lifestyle of the Mughal emperors, and when the arts lost imperial patronage under the leadership of the austere

Aurangzeb, this tiny state became a haven for several migrant miniature painters.

The old city is certainly worth exploring as it remains much as it was in the past. The narrow streets are lined with *havelis*, some of which have been converted into shops, and on the pavements

Roopangarh Fort

are vendors selling all kinds of merchandise, including red chillies for which the region is famous. The **Phool Mahal**, a privately-owned palace which is now a heritage hotel, has an idyllic setting on the banks of a lake that attracts a variety of waterbirds. Shady balconies, courtyard gardens and brass doors flanked by paintings hint at its past glory.

🏠 **Phool Mahal**
📞 *(01463) 24 7405.*

ENVIRONS: The 17th-century Roopangarh Fort, 25 km (15 miles) from Kishangarh, was once the capital of the state. Among the riches of this splendid heritage hotel is a rare collection of the famous Kishangarh miniatures.

THE KISHANGARH SCHOOL (1735–70)

In the mid-17th century, many miniature painters left the imperial atelier and moved to the Rajput, Central Indian and Punjab hill states, where each court evolved its own distinct regional style. Kishangarh's School of Painting flourished under the reign of Raja Sawant Singh (r.1748–64) who was a mystic, poet and Krishna devotee. His talented court painter, Nihal Chand, immortalized the love story of the king and his court singer in lyrical, romantic paintings where they are portrayed as Radha and Krishna. They are often surrounded by animals and birds, also in pairs, celebrating the union of the gods. The most famous painting is the portrait of Bani Thani, as the court singer was known. She is depicted in profile with a sharp nose and very elongated eyes and tapering wrist and fingers. This highly stylized form of portraiture became the hallmark of the Kishangarh School.

Portrait of Bani Thani

Street-by-Street: Pushkar ⓘ

A turtle shrine

APEACEFUL PILGRIM TOWN of lakes and 400 temples, Pushkar derives its name from *pushpa* (flower) and *kar* (hand) after a legend that says that its lakes were created from the petals that fell from the divine hands of Brahma, the Creator *(see pp22–3)*. Today, life revolves around its lakeside ghats, temples and vibrant, colourful bazaars, and it is this harmonious mix of the spiritual and commercial that draws people to Pushkar.

Villagers at the Fair
Hundreds of thousands of people, camels and cattle attend the annual fair, said to be one of Asia's largest.

Dhanna Bhagat Temple

Residential area

SADAR BAZAAR

0 metres 100
0 yards 100

← **To Savitri Temple**

★ Brahma Temple
This is one of the few temples in India dedicated to Brahma who, as myth says, was cursed by his wife Savitri when, in her absence, he invited Gayatri, a tribal girl, to take her place in an important ritual.

Badi Ganeshji Temple

PARIKRAMA MARG

Parshuram Temple

KEY

— — — Suggested route

STAR SIGHTS

★ **Brahma Temple**

★ **Ghats**

Pushkar Lake
On top of a hill, by the sacred lake at Pushkar, is the temple of Savitri. Across the lake, on another hill, is the Gayatri Temple.

Rangaji Temple

This temple is conspicuous for its South Indian style of architecture. Its gopuram (pagoda), intricately carved with over 360 images of deities, towers over the area.

Camel race at the Pushkar fair

Women at Sadar Bazaar

Digambar Jain Dharamshala

Mosque

To the fair ground

Rangaji Temple

SADAR BAZAAR

To Ajmer bus stop

Chhatri

Pushkar Mela

In the Hindu month of Kartik (Oct–Nov), ten days after Diwali, this quiet town and its environs come alive as the much-anticipated annual cattle fair gets going. Temporary tents and campsites suddenly appear to accommodate the thousands of pilgrims, tourists and villagers who come here with herds of cattle, horses and camels to participate in this spectacular event.

Pushkar has always been the region's main cattle market for local herdsmen and farmers buying and selling camels and indigenous breeds of cattle. Over the years, this trade in livestock has increased in volume and has become one of Asia's largest cattle fairs.

In the vast, specially-built amphitheatre on the outskirts of the town, camel, horse and donkey races and contests take place amid lusty cheers from a huge audience.

A festive funfair atmosphere prevails over Pushkar during the Mela's two-week duration. Giant Ferris wheels and open air theatres offer amusement, while food and souvenir stalls do brisk business. In the evenings, people huddle round campfires, listening to the haunting strains of Rajasthani folk ballads.

The fair reaches a crescendo on the night of the full moon (*purnima*), when pilgrims take a dip in the holy lake. At dusk, during the beautiful *deepdan* ceremony, hundreds of clay lamps on leaf boats are lit and set afloat in a magical tableau.

★ Ghats

Pushkar has 52 ghats. Devout Hindus make at least one pilgrimage to Pushkar and bathe at the holy ghats to wash away their sins and thereby earn themselves salvation.

Ajmer ⑱

Calligraphy, Adhai Din ka Jhonpra

FAMOUS THROUGHOUT the subcontinent as the holiest Muslim pilgrim centre after Mecca, Ajmer's prominence in history is connected to the *dargah* of a Sufi saint, Khwaja Moinuddin Chishti. The Mughals made Ajmer the provincial capital of their territories in Rajputana, and it was here that Sir Thomas Roe, the first British ambassador, presented his credentials to Jahangir in 1615. Although the *dargah* is still its most important landmark, Ajmer is also known for its proximity to another famous pilgrim centre, Pushkar. The town is framed by undulating hillocks dotted with interesting ruins. The picturesque environs of Anasagar Lake with charming pavilions, are popular with picnickers.

♜ Taragarh Fort
○ *9:30am–4:30pm.*
This rugged, sprawling 7th-century "Star Fort" occupies the summit of Beetli Hill. A series of five gateways lead into this once-impregnable citadel, said to be the earliest hill fort in the country. Many ruined buildings lie within it, among which are a mosque, still in use, and the shrine of Miran Sayyid Hussain, a 12th-century governor of the fort. The later structures were added by the British whose troops occupied the fort in the 19th century.

⛩ Dargah Sharif
See pp220–21.

⛩ Adhai Din ka Jhonpra
N of Dargah Sharif, Nalla Bazaar.
○ *9:30am–4:30pm.*
This impressive complex of pillared cloisters is all that remains of a mosque built around AD 1200 by the Slave king, Qutbuddin Aibak. Some say that the mosque's name, which means "a hut of two-and-a-half days", indicates the time taken to build it.

The Dargah Sharif dome rising above the surrounding houses

However, it is more likely that it refers to the duration of a religious fair held during the Urs in the 18th century. Like the Quwwat-ul-Islam mosque at Delhi's Qutb complex (*see p112*), also built at the same time, pillars and fragments from nearby Hindu and Jain temples were used for its construction. The mosque

itself, said to have been built over a demolished Jain college, stands on a platform cut out of the hillside, with ten shallow domes supported by 124 columns. The glory of the structure is an exquisite seven-arched screen in front of the many-pillared hall. Each arch is different from the next, and every column is ornamented with delicate engravings and calligraphic inscriptions in both Kufic and Tughra (early Arabic scripts). The sheer exuberance of the decoration and ingenious use of materials led Cunningham, the first Director-General of the Archaeological Survey of India, to describe it as "one of the noblest buildings the world has produced".

🏛 Rajputana Museum
Near bus stand. ☎ *(0145) 262 0637.*
○ *9:30am–4:30pm daily.* ● *public hols.*
Akbar's fort and palace, in the heart of the old city, has had a chequered history. The first seat of Mughal power in Rajasthan, it was later used by the British as an arsenal. Finally, on the orders of the Viceroy Lord Curzon, the fort was converted into a museum in 1908. Its varied collection highlights the sculpture and other antiquities gathered from sites all over Rajasthan. The most impressive exhibits are the sculptures dating from the 4th to 12th centuries, of which the most remarkable are the four-armed Vishnu seated on Garuda, and a door-frame from the ancient site of Baghera, depicting the ten *avatars* of Vishnu. Other important displays include antique coins, inscriptions, copper plates, paintings and weapons.

The exquisitely carved seven-arched façade of the Adhai Din ka Jhonpra

The Aravalli Range, picturesquely framing the Anasagar Lake

Nasiyan Temple

Anok Chowk, Seth Moolchand Soni Marg. ◐ summer: 8am–5pm; winter: 8:30am–5pm daily.

Built in the 19th century, the "Red Temple" in the heart of Ajmer is a fine example of a Jain religious building. Just behind the main temple (closed to non-Jains) is the double-storeyed Svarna Nagari Hall. It is elaborately decorated with coloured glass mosaics, and large gilded wooden figures re-create scenes from Jain mythology, such as the birth and life of Rishabhdeva, the first Jain *tirthankar* (saint).

Anasagar Lake

Circular Rd. ◐ 7am–10pm.

This tranquil lake to the north of the city is named after Anaji (r.1135–50), the grandfather of Prithviraj Chauhan. Charmed by its scenic beauty, Jahangir laid out a garden, Daulat Bagh, and Shah Jahan built the marble pleasure pavilions.

Overlooking this popular picnic spot is a grand colonial building, now the Circuit House, where the British Resident once lived.

VISITORS' CHECKLIST

Ajmer district. 135 kilometres (112 miles SW of Jaipur). **Road map** B4. 485,000. *RTDC Hotel Khadim (0145) 262 7490.* Near Hotel Khadim. *Station Rd.* Sanganer. *Urs (Oct–Nov).*

Mayo College

Can visit with Principal's permission.
Set up in 1875 by Lord Mayo as an "Eton of the East" for Rajput princes, the school's main building, designed by Charles Mant, is a jewel of Indo-Saracenic architecture *(see p25).* Its early students were allowed to live in their individual "houses" with English private tutors and family retainers. Some, such as the prince of Alwar, would ride to school after vacations on an elephant. After 1947, commoners were allowed entry, and today, along with its girls' section, Mayo is rated as one of India's best public schools.

Lord Mayo

AJMER TOWN MAP

Adhai Din ka Jhonpra ②
Anasagar Lake ⑤
Dargah Sharif ①
Rajputana Museum ③
Mayo College ⑥
Nasiyan Temple ④

0 metres 500
0 yards 500

ANASAGAR CIRCULAR ROAD
ANASAGAR LAKE
PUSHKAR
JAIPUR
PRITHVIRAJ MARG
JAIPUR ROAD
KUTCHERY ROAD
DARGAH BAZAAR
NAYA BAZAAR
NALLA BAZAAR ROAD
Taragarh Fort
MADAR GATE
STATION ROAD
BEECHLA TANK
CIRCULAR ROAD
NASIRABAD ROAD
NASIRABAD
UDAIPUR

KEY
🚉 Railway station
🚌 Bus station
ℹ Tourist information
✉ Post office
🛕 Temple
⛪ Church

Dargah Sharif

Shahjahani Gate

Aᴿᴱᴠᴱᴿᴱᴅ Muslim pilgrim centre since the 12th century, the Dargah Sharif contains the tomb of the famous Sufi saint Khwaja Moinuddin Chishti (1143–1236), popularly called Garib Nawaz, or "protector of the poor". Reputed to possess miraculous powers, the saint draws people of every faith to his *dargah* to seek favours and blessings. It is said that the saint entered his cell to pray in seclusion until his death on the sixth day. Each year, six days in the seventh lunar month (October) are marked as his Urs (death anniversary celebrations). Over the years, the saint's royal devotees built grand extensions to the tomb, so that today the *dargah* complex, teeming with pilgrims and tourists, is virtually a township in itself.

★ Mehfil Khana
Built in 1888 by the fabulously wealthy Nizam of Hyderabad, this is the venue for all-night qawwalis.

★ Shahjahani Masjid
Emperor Shah Jahan built this marble mosque. The Mughals made many such generous endowments.

Qawwali Singers
Qawwalis (see p28), always sung by a group, are specially composed to sing the saint's praises in front of his tomb.

Ibadat Khana,
(prayer hall)

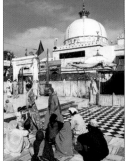

★ Mazar Sharif
Chishti's tomb, begun during the saint's lifetime by Iltutmish, was completed in the 16th century by Emperor Humayun. Later Mughal princes added to it. A marble dome surmounts the simple brick tomb, enclosed by a silver railing and a marble lattice screen.

Sᴛᴀʀ Fᴇᴀᴛᴜʀᴇs

★ **Mazar Sharif**

★ **Shahjahani Masjid**

★ **Mehfil Khana**

Akbar's Mosque
Akbar, Chishti's most illustrious devotee, walked from Agra to Ajmer twice: once for enabling his conquest of Chittor, and again after the birth of his heir, Prince Salim, the future Jahangir.

Pilgrims
People of every faith come to seek favours and bring flowers and chadors as thanksgiving offerings.

Nizam Gate

Dargah Bazaar

Shahjahani Gate

Buland Darwaza
This imposing entrance doorway was erected by one of the Khilji rulers. A flag is hoisted over its ramparts to mark the start of the Urs ceremony held each October.

Degs
Two enormous degs (iron cauldrons), one nearly 10 ft (3 m) in diameter, are used during the Urs for cooking a special rice pudding, tabarrukh. *After they have been emptied, professional divers "loot" the degs by jumping in and scooping out the dregs.*

Dargah Bazaar
The long road that lies outside the Nizam Gate, the main entrance to the complex, is the location of a bustling market. Colourful stalls and kiosks sell baskets of rose petals as well as chadors for devotees to offer at the dargah.

A 15th-century manuscript, Arabic and Persian Research Institute, Tonk

Chaksu ⑲

Jaipur district. 43 km (27 miles) S of
Jaipur on NH12. **Road map** C4.
🚶 17,000. 🚌 🛕 Shitala Ashtami
(Mar–Apr).

THIS SLEEPY LITTLE village on
the road from Jaipur
towards Sawai Madhopur is
known for its small white
temple dedicated to Shitala
Mata, the goddess who wards
off disease, especially smallpox. A hundred steps lead up
to the shrine, around which
devotees gather for a gossip
after propitiating the deity.
Shitala Mata is much venerated
in parts of rural Rajasthan
where many diseases are still
fatal. Every year in March or
April a fair is held here, which
attracts a large number of
pilgrims. Food is cooked a day
before Ashtami, the eighth and
most auspicious day after the
new moon, and offered cold
to the goddess to ensure
her protection.

Tonk ⑳

Tonk district. 96 km (60 miles) S of
Jaipur on NH12. **Road map** C4.
🚶 1,211,000. 🚌 daily.
🛕 Id (Feb–Mar).

THE SMALL PRINCIPALITY of
Tonk, the only Muslim
kingdom in Rajasthan, was
created by the British in the
early 19th century to appease
the powerful Pathan warlord,
Amir Khan. The legacy of its
nawabs is evident throughout
the old city. They constructed
the imposing Jami Masjid, as
well as a number of fine
painted mansions, of which
the **Sunehri Kothi** ("golden
mansion"), built in 1824 by
Amir Khan in the old palace
complex, is the most
spectacular. Magnificent
enamelled mirrorwork and
gilded stucco cover the walls
and ceilings of its jewel-like
interior, the windows are
fitted with stained-glass and
the floors beautifully painted.

The old city also has many
Raj-style bungalows that were
once the homes of the British
Resident and his entourage.

The nawabs were dedicated
patrons of art and literature.
In the late 19th century, the
third ruler established a grand
centre of Islamic art, now
known as the **Maulana Abul
Kalam Azad Arabic and
Persian Research Institute**.
Its collection of rare Arabic
and Persian manuscripts
includes several illuminated
Korans, such as Aurangzeb's
Alamgiri Koran Sharif and
the *Koran-e-Kamal,* prepared
on the orders of Shah Jahan.
There are also translations of
the epics, the *Ramayana* and
the *Mahabharata* inscribed in
exquisite Persian as well as
Arabic calligraphy.

🏛 **Sunehri Kothi**
Partially operational. Enquire at MAKA
Arabic & Persian Research Institute.
🏛 **MAKA Arabic and
Persian Research Institute**
Near new bus stand. ◷ 10am–5pm.
● Sun. 📞 (01432) 24 7389.

Sawai Madhopur ㉑

Sawai Madhopur district. 172 km
(107 miles) SE of Jaipur. **Road map**
C4. 🚶 97,500. 🚊 🚌 🛫 Mon–Sat.
🛕 Shivaratri (Feb), Ganesha Chaturthi
(Aug–Sep).

AN IMPORTANT railway
junction and entry point
to the Ranthambhore National
Park, Sawai Madhopur is
named after its founder Sawai
Madho Singh I (r.1750–68).
The historic 10th-century

A cart stands outside a village hut on the outskirts of Sawai Madhopur

A rooftop view of the distant Indergarh Fort

Ranthambhore Fort (now in the park), a strategic point on the main route to Central India, was the scene of many terrible battles between its Rajput chieftains and the invading armies from Delhi and Agra. The fort was attacked by Alauddin Khilji *(see pp50–51)* and later by Akbar in 1569. This battle has been glorified in Mughal miniatures and bards have sung about the heroic deeds of its Rajput defenders. The fort was eventually handed over to the Amber kings *(see pp200–203)*. This jungle fort, despite its ruined state, looks daunting. Its massive gateways, ramparts and bastions make entry a tricky affair. Within it is an 8th-century temple dedicated to Ganesha, whose priest receives sacks of letters, sometimes addressed simply to "Shri Ganesha, Ranthambhore", especially during the marriage season, in order to invoke the deity's blessings. Clumps of grass, tied together by newlyweds for luck, are also seen along the way to the fort temple.

ENVIRONS: About 37 km (24 miles) west of Sawai Madhopur is the sprawling **Uniara Palace**. Further towards Tonk, past **Hathi Bhata**, a life-sized elephant carved out of a single rock, is the picturesque **Kakod Fort**. East of Sawai Madhopur, is the vast **Mansarovar Lake**.

Ranthambhore National Park ㉒

See pp224–5.

Indergarh ㉓

Kota district. 52 km (33 miles) S of Sawai Madhopur. **Road map** C4. **Indergarh Fort** ☐ *8am–5pm daily, on request to the caretaker who lives below the fort. Donation optional.*

THIS SMALL TOWN, founded by Raja Indrasal in 1605, lies huddled beneath the ramparts of a picturesque hill fort which is clearly visible from the flat rooftops of houses where, in summer, people sleep at night. Though dilapidated, some fort areas still bear traces of exquisite murals depicting court scenes and legends. Indergarh's two main temples, one dedicated to Bijasan Mata (a form of Durga) and the other to Kuanwalji (Lord Shiva), are popular places of worship for pilgrims.

TALE OF THE TIGER

The tiger plays a major role in Indian myth as a symbol of supreme power, kingship and manhood. In Puranic legend it is Durga, the fearsome goddess with ten arms, who rides a tiger and defeats the invincible buffalo-headed demon, Mahishasura. Yet, for all its aura of strength and power the tiger is a vulnerable creature today.

Durga riding a tiger, detail of a miniature painting

Statistics claim that at the turn of the 20th century India's tiger population was about 40,000, but by 1972, the figure had dropped to roughly 1,800. This was when a special Task Force of the Indian Board for Wildlife constituted Project Tiger to address the alarming issue of dwindling tiger populations across the country. In the first year of Project Tiger, nine wildlife sanctuaries were declared tiger reserves, one of them being Ranthambhore.

There are now 27 Project Tiger Reserves, and the number of tigers has grown substantially, though persistent habitat destruction, illegal poaching and trading of tiger parts for medicinal and other derivatives in many Far Eastern countries continue to threaten the life of this supreme predator.

Ranthambhore National Park ㉒

Park sign

THIS PARK LIES IN the shadow of the Aravalli and Vindhya mountain ranges and covers a core area of 400 sq km (155 sq miles). Its razor-sharp ridges, deep boulder-filled gorges, lakes and jungle are the habitat of carnivores such as the caracal, panther, jackal and hyena, species of deer, and a rich variety of resident and migratory birds. The most famous resident, however, is the endangered tiger, and it is fairly common to catch glimpses of this fascinating animal by day or night. Like other parks in the region, this was originally the Jaipur state's hunting grounds and became a Project Tiger Reserve in 1973.

Rajbagh
Ruined pavilions stand on the banks of Rajbagh Talao, one of the three lakes in the park.

Ranthambhore Fort
The park derives its name from this great Rajput jungle fort that is 1,000 years old and stands at a height of 215 m (705 ft).

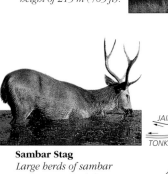

Sambar Stag
Large herds of sambar are seen around the lakes, wallowing in the water, swimming and feeding on aquatic plants, unperturbed by jeeps and visitors.

JAIPUR
TONK
Sawai Madhopur
MUMBAI

Malik Talao
Padam Talao
Rajbagh Talao
Ranthambhore Fort
Jogi Mahal
Laka
Nalghati Valley
Lahapur Val
Man Sarovar

Banyan Tree
India's second-largest banyan tree (Ficus bengalensis) lies in the grounds of Jogi Mahal. Its several spreading branches are all supported by roots.

0 kilometres   5
0 miles   2

Tiger
Sighting the park's main predator is a matter of chance, but traces of its activities are often seen.

VISITORS' CHECKLIST

Sawai Madhopur district. 180 km (112 miles) SE of Jaipur. **Road map** C4. 🚃 Sawai Madhopur. 🛈 RTDC Hotel Vinayak, Sawai Madhopur (07462) 22 1333. ⬜ Oct–Jun: 7–10am & 3–6pm. ⬛ Jul–Sep. 📷 🎫 📷 📷 The Dastkari Kendra, opp Kutalpura village on way to Kundera. 📞 (07462) 25 2049. **No walking** only jeeps hired from Project Tiger, office of the Forest Dept, Sawai Madhopur are allowed inside the park. 📞 (07462) 22 0223.

Indian Roller Bird
This is one of the many bird species found in the park. The others include birds of prey such as the crested serpent eagle and Bonelli's eagle, and many species of pigeons, flycatchers, storks and waterbirds.

Marsh Crocodiles
Muggers, or marsh crocodiles, are commonly seen submerged in water or basking on the shores of the lakes. Ungulates are their main prey, and sometimes one can glimpse a crocodile dragging the carcass of a deer into the water. The monitor lizard and python are some of the other reptiles found in the park.

Sloth Bear
This shaggy bear with short hind legs and a long muzzle emerges at dusk to feed. During the day it shelters in the rocky outcrops and is difficult to sight.

KEY

═ Major road

─ Railway

▬ Park border

☼ Viewpoint

▬ Trails

⌂ Archaeological sight, ruin

🛈 Information centre

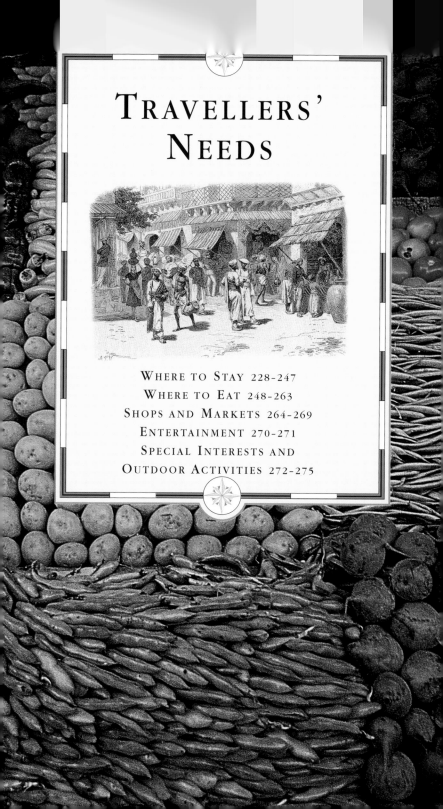

TRAVELLERS' NEEDS

WHERE TO STAY

POPULARLY KNOWN AS the Golden Triangle, the Delhi, Agra and Jaipur region receives the largest number of tourists in India, so this area is well-equipped with places to stay. The choice of accommodation ranges from up-market luxury hotels run by international or leading Indian chains, to small guesthouses and youth hostels. In addition, there are state-run tourist hotels in several towns, with comfortable board and lodging at reasonable rates. On the more exotic

Palace doorman

side are the grand old palaces and *havelis* of the Jaipur region which re-create the lavish lifestyles of former rulers and aristocracy *(see pp232–3)*. For the budget traveller, on the other hand, there is a choice of ashrams and small guesthouses, sometimes with extremely basic facilities. Tented accommodation is as yet rare, as is self-catering. Rooms are usually cheaper during the off-season (Apr–Sep). For more information on places to stay in this region, refer to the detailed listings on pages 234–47.

HOTEL CHAINS, GRADING AND FACILITIES

AT THE TOP END of the range are the five-star deluxe hotels which provide luxurious accommodation for the international visitor. Many of these are part of national chains, such as the **Ashok Group**, or of international groups such as the **Sheraton** and **Radisson** *(see p231)*. Below them are the four- and three-star hotels, guesthouses and tourist lodges, some of which may offer additional facilities, such as a pool or tennis court. International television channels are now shown on most hotel room sets. In Agra and Jaipur, palaces, bungalows and *havelis* have been converted into heritage hotels, which carry the flavour of erstwhile grandeur

and graciousness. Except in some of the lower priced hotels, the bathrooms, even in older properties, are in Western style. Room service, safe deposits and daily laundry are standard in more expensive places. The reception desk can advise on tours, and large hotels have travel agencies on the premises.

Traditional huts, Desert Resort, Mandawa

LUXURY HOTELS

INDIA'S TOP LUXURY hotels match the best in the world in their elegance, professional services, and wide range of facilities. Architecturally, many of them have cleverly combined traditional Indian and modern

Sheraton Towers

Five-star hotel logo

design, while their interiors are sumptuously decorated with the best of Indian crafts and textiles. The hotels run by the large international and national chains are fully air-conditioned and offer a wide range of conveniences such as a resident doctor, shopping arcades and patisseries, banqueting halls, a 24-hour coffee shop, bars and gourmet restaurants. For the business traveller there are business and conference centres equipped with computers for personal use with facilities for access to the Internet. Desk jacks and modems are provided for personal computers and laptops. Additional facilities include beauty parlours and fitness centres, swimming pools and tennis courts. The front desk can often make bookings for golf and other activities. Some hotels even have a regular palmist, tarot card reader or astrologer.

Agra's Mughal Sheraton, renowned for its innovative architecture

◁ **Vegetables temptingly stacked in a roadside stall**

HERITAGE HOTELS

SEVERAL PALACES and stately homes, particularly in Rajasthan, have been restored and converted into hotels. These come under the banner of **Heritage Hotels Association of India**. A private agency, **WelcomHeritage** *(see p231)* specializes in booking accommodation in these hotels which have been classified as Grand, Classic and Ordinary, and are priced accordingly. However, most travel agents can also make bookings at these places.

MIDDLE-RANGE HOTELS

THESE ARE four- and three-star establishments that may lack the stylish decor, slickness and range of facilities of five-star hotels. Though smaller in size they are always comfortable, clean and well-serviced. The rooms are generally air-conditioned with attached baths that have hot and cold running water. Some are surrounded by extensive gardens and may even have cafés and business centres.

BUDGET HOTELS AND TOURIST LODGES

BUDGET HOTELS are usually found in the older sections of cities, near the railway and bus stations. The accommodation is mostly simple and varies from very basic to homely guesthouses. Ceiling fans, mosquito nets and private, Indian- or Western-style bathrooms are generally provided. The rates in Delhi are higher than in the rest of the region.

The wide network of tourist "bungalows" or lodges established by state tourism departments, and the national India Tourism Development Corporation's (ITDC) Ashok Group *(see p297)*, make travelling to lesser-known places easier. The rates are reasonable, and there is a choice of dormitories as well as double rooms with attached bathrooms.

GUESTHOUSES

Logo of the Welcomgroup chain

THE TERM "GUESTHOUSE" can be a misnomer. Both mid-range and budget hotels can have "guesthouse" appended to their name, and so the prices and the services can vary enormously. If you opt for a lower priced one, do make it a point to inspect the room before checking in, especially the bathroom, which may contain an Indian-style toilet. The better guesthouses all have air-conditioning and attached baths with Western toilets. In Jaipur, some families have converted all or part of their large *havelis* into guesthouses, providing meals on order.

A *dharamshala* in Haridwar

PAYING GUESTS

YOU CAN FIND short-term paying guest accommodation in Delhi through the **Government of India Tourist Office** *(see p279)* or your travel agent. In Agra, the tourist information counter at the railway station can supply addresses, and in Jaipur, **Rajasthan Tourism (RTDC)** *(see p231)* has an official and comprehensive list of families under a good Paying Guest Scheme administered by them. **Munjeeta Travel**, based in the United Kingdom *(see p231)* can organize Homestay Tours across India.

DHARAMSHALAS AND ASHRAMS

REST HOUSES for pilgrims known as *dharamshalas* are run by religious trusts, but anyone can stay, as in the **International Rest House** in Brindavan, or **Ramakrishna Mission** and **Sri Aurobindo Ashram** in Delhi *(see p231),* provided the rules of the place are strictly followed. They charge absurdly low rates. In cities, *dharamshalas* in the older sections may have dubious standards of hygiene, and the facilities can amount to a bare room with no bedding, shared with others along with the bathroom. Some temples and ashrams also rent out rooms to guests seeking a religious retreat. The amenities here are basic, though clean, and guests are expected to respect the rules of the community.

A luxurious deluxe room in a five-star hotel

Youth Hostels

There is a network of youth hostels across India, including the YMCA *(see p281)*. They offer unbelievably low rates, although the YMCA's are pricier with better facilities and are found only in selected cities. Though it is not necessary to be a member of Youth Hostel International to gain entry, during the busy season its members do get priority and always get lower rates. Rooms and dormitories are both usually available, and the rules of the hostel must be respected.

National Parks and Camping Sites

The national parks have several places to stay in, but no dedicated camping sites. At the Pushkar fair grounds, Rajasthan Tourism sets up a **Tourist Village** on a large campsite. A few hotels in Rajasthan, such as Samode Bagh or **Sawai Madhopur Lodge** also offer some tent accommodation, and in Uttar Pradesh, apart from private operators, such as **Outdoor Adventures** and **Milestones**, the state government has a river rafting campsite on the River Ganges at Rishikesh.

Prices and Discounts

Rates vary between cities, with Delhi being the most expensive, and the small town hotels being very cheap at times. The five-star luxury

A view of the main swimming pool at the Rajvilas Hotel in Jaipur

and the palace or heritage hotels are at the top end of the scale. Those run by the state tourism develop-ment corporations can vary from state to state with Delhi again being the most expensive. Prices at the so-called guesthouses swing from high to low. Most hotels offer discounts during the low season from April to September. This can bring the original rates down by almost 50 per cent at times.

Every October, hotels raise their rates by a nominal percentage. Various taxes are charged, over and above the listed rates, as notified by the government from time to time. Foreigners have to pay the dollar room rate, plus any additional taxes on the listed price. This is payable in foreign currency or in Indian rupees.

RAJVILĀS

Logo of an Oberoi luxury hotel

Taxes

All hotels with a tariff of Rs 3000 and above are charged a uniform 10% hotel expenditure tax by the government on rooms only. States levy a luxury tax (between 5–25%) on room rents and a sales tax on food and beverages (between 8–20%), both of which vary from state to state. Some hotels levy their own service charge.

Hidden Extras

Services for which you may be charged extra could include bottles of mineral water, breakfast, laundry, extra bedding, telephone calls, e-mails and faxes, the mini bar in your room, and special pay channels on television (you should read the screen or your room service folder before pressing the remote). Hotels usually charge extra for transport to and from the hotel. When telephoning, it is cheaper to use the pay phones in the lobby or at outside STD booths *(see p291)*. At small town hotels with no running hot water, the hotel will give you a bucket of hot water once a day at a nominal cost.

Booking, Checking In and Out

It is a good idea to make your hotel bookings well in advance, especially for the peak October to March tourist

The Glass House on the Ganges in Rishikesh

season when many confer-
ences and cultural festivals
take place. You can fax or
telephone your requirements,
but do insist that you are sent
a written confirmation.

Check out time is usually at
12 noon, though at smaller
establishments they are not so
particular and calculate by the
day. Before checking out, do
study your bills carefully and
retain all the receipts.

TOUTS

At THE AIRPORT or railway
station you may be
besieged by touts *(see p265)*,
many of whom also operate
as taxi and three-wheeler
drivers, who insist on taking
you to hotels where they get
a commission. The best
solution is to have prior
bookings. Failing this, the
tourism counter at the airport
or station will help you find a
place suitable to your needs.
However, if there is no other
option, you should be firm
about how much you are
willing to spend and check
out the tout's commission.
You should also ask for
choices, and when you reach
the hotel, be sure it is
acceptable to you before
dismissing the driver. If touts
continue to pester you, speak
to the nearest policeman.

Samode Bagh's exquisite tents, recreating a royal Mughal ambience

FACILITIES FOR CHILDREN

The STAFF AT HOTELS are
usually very good with
children. Many hotels will
willingly add an extra bed in
your room for a child for a
small extra charge. Very few
provide baby-sitting services,
and you should check at the
front desk, but usually
parents are expected to look
after their children. Most
hotels do not have any
special facilities for children.

DISABLED TRAVELLERS

Only THE NEWER and fancier
hotels make an effort to
provide ramps, special lifts
and wheelchairs for disabled
travellers. However, you can
always seek the help of the
staff. Many of the older
hotels, especially in Rajasthan,
which are converted from
palaces and private mansions,
have several levels within
them, with no ramp or lifts
for easy movement. Do check
out these facilities before
making your bookings.

TIPPING

Tips ARE expected even
though there may be a
service charge on bills. The
amounts are at the discretion
of the guest, starting with
Rs10 for car parking attendants, slightly more for a
porter, and ten per cent of the
total bill for waiters.

Heritage Hotels

THE TITLE "heritage hotel" is given to some palaces and *havelis* that have been discreetly modernized to meet the needs of international travellers and run as high-class hotels. Fitted with modern plumbing and air-conditioning and with facilities such as swimming pools and tennis courts, such hotels take care that their history, architecture and innate elegance are suitably highlighted. The interiors display old sepia photographs, memorabilia and exquisite furniture tended by a caring staff, often old family retainers. The high tariffs of such hotels are compensated for by their special ambience.

Castle Mandawa, Mandawa
This mid-18th century fortress is now a charming heritage hotel and an ideal base to explore the painted havelis of Shekhawati. Live entertainment by Rajasthani folk dancers and musicians, and camel rides are some of its attractions (see p246).

Samode Palace, Samode
All the grandeur of royal Rajasthan is visible in this opulent painted palace. Its magnificent Durbar Hall and Sheesh Mahal are now reception areas where guests can dine (see p247).

JAIPUR AND ENVIRONS

Hotel Pushkar Palace, Pushkar
The lake-side palace, once the property of the Maharaja of Kishangarh, is now a popular hotel in this temple town. Its location is ideal for views of the bathing ghats, the rugged Aravalli Hills and the town's 400 temples (see p247).

Narain Niwas Palace, Jaipur
Surrounded by sprawling gardens and mango orchards, this traditional palace was built in 1928 (see p244).

Neemrana Fort Palace, Neemrana
Built in 1464, this fort was one of India's first heritage hotels. Meticulously restored to re-create the original plan and architecture, its interior is an eclectic blend of traditional design and its modern interpretations (see p246).

```
0 kilometres            100

0 miles         50
```

DELHI

The Hill Fort, Kesroli
This seven-turreted fort is believed to be 600 years old. Built on top of a small hillock, it commands a splendid view from its high ramparts and is a perfect base from which to visit neighbouring sites and sanctuaries (see p243).

AGRA AND AROUND

Laxmi Vilas Palace, Bharatpur
Located near the Keoladeo National Park, the palace was built in 1899 for the women of the royal family. The architecture is a mix of Mughal and Rajput styles. Spacious airy rooms are furnished with period furniture and the courtyards are decorated with colourful frescoes *(see p241).*

Sawai Madhopur Lodge, Sawai Madhopur
A colonial building furnished in the 1930s style, on the outskirts of the Ranthambhore National Park, this was a hunting lodge of the Maharaja of Jaipur *(see p247).*

Usha Kiran Palace, Gwalior
The Maharaja of Gwalior's official guesthouse is now a pleasant hotel with an old-world charm (see p241).

Choosing a Hotel

MOST OF THE HOTELS in this guide, listed according to region, have been included because of their location, the excellence of their service, facilities offered and value for money. Map references refer to the Delhi Street Finder maps on pages 124–131. Colour-coded thumb tabs show the regions covered on each page. For restaurant listings see pages 256–263.

	CREDIT CARDS	SWIMMING POOL	WESTERN BATHROOMS	COFFEE SHOP	GARDEN/TERRACE

DELHI

NEW DELHI: *Indraprastha.* **Map** 5 A1. Rs Rs
19 Ashok Rd. **C** *(011) 2334 4511.* FAX *(011) 2336 8153.*
Basic facilities, good rates, at walking distance from the city centre, this is a popular budget hotel for the intrepid traveller. **11** *Rooms: 540.*
Credit cards: AE DC MC V · Western Bathrooms · Coffee Shop

NEW DELHI: *Prince Polonia.* **Map** 1 B3. Rs Rs
2325/26 Tilak Gali, Paharganj. **C** *(011) 2358 1930.* FAX *(011) 2358 7026.*
@ polinter@del3.vsnl.net.in Friendly, clean and cosy, this hotel provides a cheap option for low-budget travellers. Its convenient location near the railway station is an added advantage. **11 24 TV** *Rooms: 28.* ▤ *21.*
Credit cards: AE DC MC V · Swimming Pool · Western Bathrooms

NEW DELHI: *YMCA Tourist Hostel.* **Map** 1 B5. Rs Rs
Jai Singh Rd. **C** *(011) 2336 1915.* FAX *(011) 2374 6023.* **@** ymcth@ndf.vsnl.net.in
Reasonable rates, plain but comfortable rooms, and good access to the commercial heart of the city. **11 24 TV** *Rooms: 121.* ▤ *80.*
Credit cards: AE MC V · Swimming Pool · Western Bathrooms · Coffee Shop · Garden/Terrace

NEW DELHI: *YWCA of Delhi.* **Map** 1 B5. Rs Rs
Blue Triangle Family Hostel, Ashok Rd. **C** *(011) 2336 0133.* FAX *(011) 2336 0202.*
A homely atmosphere, very popular with budget travellers and students. The hostel has both rooms and dormitories. **11** *Rooms: 46.* ▤ *23.*
Western Bathrooms

NEW DELHI: *Centre Point.* **Map** 1 C5. Rs Rs Rs
Kasturba Gandhi Marg. **C** *(011) 2335 4304.* FAX *(011) 2332 9138.*
@ cpoint@del2.vsnl.net.in A renovated old colonial bungalow, this is a compact hotel close to the city centre. **11 24 TV** *Rooms: 42.* ▤ *42.*
Credit cards: AE DC MC V JCB · Western Bathrooms · Coffee Shop · Garden/Terrace

NEW DELHI: *Janpath.* **Map** 5 A1. Rs Rs Rs
Janpath. **C** *(011) 2334 0070.* FAX *(011) 2336 8618.* **@** janpath@ndf.vsnl.net.in
This well-run hotel is located on a popular shopping avenue and near several travel and car rental agencies. **11 24 TV** *Rooms: 213.* ▤ *213.*
Credit cards: AE DC MC V · Western Bathrooms · Coffee Shop

NEW DELHI: *Jor Bagh "27" Guesthouse.* **Map** 5 A1. Rs Rs Rs
27 Jor Bagh. **C** *(011) 2469 8647.* FAX *(011) 2649 8475.* **@** guesthouse27@hotmail.com
This tranquil and comfortable guesthouse is located in Lutyen's Delhi, opposite the beautiful Lodi Gardens. **11 24 TV** *Rooms: 18.* ▤ *18.*
Credit cards: AE DC MC V · Western Bathrooms · Coffee Shop

NEW DELHI: *Marina.* **Map** 1 C4. Rs Rs Rs
G–59 Connaught Place. **C** *(011) 2332 4658.* FAX *(011) 2332 8609.*
@ marina@nde.vsnl.net.in This unassuming hotel with high-ceilinged, old-fashioned rooms offers basic facilities. **24 TV** *Rooms: 93.* ▤ *93.*
Credit cards: AE DC MC V · Western Bathrooms · Coffee Shop

NEW DELHI: *Nirula's.* **Map** 1 C4. Rs Rs Rs
L Block, Connaught Place. **C** *(011) 2341 7419.* FAX *(011) 2341 8957.*
@ delhihotel@nirula.com A clean and compact hotel, it has an excellent Chinese restaurant *(see p256).* **11 24** *Rooms: 28.* ▤ *28.*
Credit cards: DC MC V · Western Bathrooms · Coffee Shop

NEW DELHI: *Yorks.* **Map** 1 C4. Rs Rs Rs
K–10 Connaught Circus. **C** *(011) 2341 5769.* FAX *(011) 2341 4419.*
Simple rooms and essential services. A reasonably priced city centre hotel with a restaurant. **11 Y TV** *Rooms: 27.* ▤ *27.*
Credit cards: AE DC MC V · Western Bathrooms

NEW DELHI: *Ambassador.* **Map** 5 B3. Rs Rs Rs Rs
Sujan Singh Park, Subramaniam Bharati Marg. **C** *(011) 2463 2600.* FAX *(011) 2463 2252.*
@ ambassador.delhi@tajhotels.com Integrated with an old and gracious residential complex, the hotel has been refurbished and upgraded and is now part of the Taj group. **11 24 TV** *Rooms: 88.* ▤ *88.*
Credit cards: AE DC MC V · Western Bathrooms · Coffee Shop · Garden/Terrace

NEW DELHI: *The Connaught.* **Map** 1 B4. Rs Rs Rs Rs
37 Shahid Bhagat Singh Marg. **C** *(011) 2336 4225.* FAX *(011) 2334 0757.*
@ PROMINENT.HOTELS@gems.vsnl.net.in Unremarkable, but a good place to stay if you need a central location. **11 24 TV** *Rooms: 81.* ▤ *81.*
Credit cards: AE DC MC V · Western Bathrooms · Coffee Shop

Price categories for a standard double room per night including tax and service charges but not including breakfast:

Rs under 550 rupees
Rs Rs 550–1,200 rupees
Rs Rs Rs 1,200–3,000 rupees
Rs Rs Rs Rs 3,000–6,000 rupees
Rs Rs Rs Rs Rs over 6,000 rupees

CREDIT CARDS
Indicates which credit cards are accepted: *AE* American Express; *DC* Diners Club; *MC* Master Card/Access; *V* Visa; *JCB* Japanese Credit Bureau.

WESTERN BATHROOMS
Indicates sit-down, flush toilets; showers and/or baths. Others have squat toilets and bucket-and-mug baths.

COFFEE SHOP
Hotels with coffee shop.

GARDEN/TERRACE
Hotels with a garden, courtyard or terrace.

	CREDIT CARDS	SWIMMING POOL	WESTERN BATHROOMS	COFFEE SHOP	GARDEN/TERRACE
NEW DELHI: *Claridges.* **Map** 5 A3. Rs Rs Rs Rs Aurangzeb Rd. **(** (011) 2301 0211. **FAX** (011) 2301 0625. **@** claridges@del2.vsnl.net.in This large mansion-like hotel with charm and character is located near the historic Lodi Gardens. It also has tennis courts, good restaurants and an irresistible bakery. 11 Y 11 24 TV 5 *Rooms: 162.* 162.	AE DC MC V	●	▦	●	●
NEW DELHI: *Hans Plaza.* **Map** 2 D5. Rs Rs Rs Rs Rs Barakhamba Rd. **(** (011) 2331 6861. **FAX** (011) 2331 4830. **@** hansplaza@hanshotels.com A top-end hotel with modern conference facilities located in an area that has many business offices and banks. A floor here offers extra amenities at a higher charge. 11 Y 24 TV 5 *Rooms: 67.* 67.	AE DC MC V		▦	●	
NEW DELHI: *Imperial Hotel.* **Map** 1 C5. Rs Rs Rs Rs Rs Janpath. **(** (011) 2334 1234. **FAX** (011) 2334 2255. **@** e-mail-luxury@theimperialindia.com One of Delhi's institutions, this colonial-style luxurious hotel located at walking distance from a row of fascinating shops, proudly preserves its Raj ambience. 11 Y 24 TV 5 *Rooms: 230.* 230.	AE DC MC V JCB	●	▦	●	●
NEW DELHI: *Grand Inter-Continental.* **Map** 2 D5. Rs Rs Rs Rs Rs Barakhamba Ave, Connaught Place. **(** (011) 2370 9117. **FAX** (011) 2370 9000. **@** delhi@interconti.com A popular luxury hotel close to the city centre. Adjacent to the World Trade Centre, its location is an advantage for the business traveller. 11 Y 11 24 TV 5 *Rooms: 444.* 444.	AE DC MC V	●	▦	●	●
NEW DELHI: *Le Meridien.* **Map** 5 A1. Rs Rs Rs Rs Rs Windsor Place, Janpath. **(** (011) 2371 0101. **FAX** (011) 2371 4545. W www.lemeridien-hotels.com A magnificent atrium hotel, it includes book shops and boutiques encircling the central space, and excellent restaurants including one cantilevered on the topmost level. 11 Y 11 24 TV 5 *Rooms: 355.* 355.	AE DC MC V	●	▦	●	●
NEW DELHI: *The Metropolitan Hotel Nikko.* **Map** 1 B4. Rs Rs Rs Rs Rs Bangla Sahib Rd. **(** (011) 2334 2000. **FAX** (011) 2334 3839. W www.hotelnikkodelhi.com This centrally located hotel offers state-of-the-art communications facilities for business travellers. 11 Y 11 24 TV 5 *Rooms: 165.* 165.	AE DC MC V JCB	●	▦	●	
NEW DELHI: *The Oberoi.* **Map** 6 D4. Rs Rs Rs Rs Rs Dr Zakir Hussain Rd. **(** (011) 2436 3030. **FAX** (011) 2436 0484. W www.oberoihotels.com Definitely the most exclusive establishment in the city. Speciality restaurants and an enviable executive centre appeal to up-market visitors. 11 Y 11 24 TV 5 *Rooms: 287.* 287.	AE DC MC V JCB	●	▦	●	
NEW DELHI: *The Park.* **Map** 1 C5. Rs Rs Rs Rs Rs Parliament St. **(** (011) 2374 3000. **FAX** (011) 2374 4000. **@** resv.del@theparkhotels.com In the heart of busy Connaught Place, this luxurious hotel has a popular disco with live jazz on fixed days of the week. It also hosts interesting talks and programmes. 11 Y 11 24 TV 5 *Rooms: 224.* 224.	AE DC MC V	●	▦	●	▦
NEW DELHI: *Taj Mahal.* **Map** 5 B3. Rs Rs Rs Rs Rs Mansingh Rd. **(** (011) 2302 6161. **FAX** (011) 2302 7299. **@** tmbc.del@tajhotels.com Situated along a leafy avenue, this beautiful hotel combines traditional decor with modern facilities, superb restaurants and a sumptuous handicrafts and book shop. 11 Y 11 24 TV 5 *Rooms: 300.* 300.	AE DC MC V	●	▦	●	
NIZAMUDDIN: *Jukasso Inn.* **Map** 6 D3. Rs Rs Rs 50 Sundar Nagar. **(** (011) 2435 0308. **FAX** (011) 2435 4402. Located in a peaceful residential area, this is a comfortable up-market guesthouse with a warm, friendly atmosphere. 24 TV *Rooms: 50.* 50.	AE DC MC V		▦		
NIZAMUDDIN: *La Sagrita Tourist Home.* **Map** 6 D3. Rs Rs Rs 14 Sundar Nagar. **(** (011) 2435 1249. **FAX** (011) 2435 6956. Another residence converted into an elegant guesthouse. The staff are extremely courteous and helpful. 24 TV *Rooms: 19.* 19.	AE DC MC V		▦		▦

For key to symbols see back flap

Price categories for a standard double room per night including tax and service charges but not including breakfast:

Rs under 550 rupees
Rs Rs 550–1,200 rupees
Rs Rs Rs 1,200–3,000 rupees
Rs Rs Rs Rs 3,000–6,000 rupees
Rs Rs Rs Rs Rs over 6,000 rupees

CREDIT CARDS
Indicates which credit cards are accepted: *AE* American Express; *DC* Diners Club; *MC* Master Card/Access; *V* Visa; *JCB* Japanese Credit Bureau.

WESTERN BATHROOMS
Indicates sit-down, flush toilets; showers and/or baths. Others have squat toilets and bucket-and-mug baths.

COFFEE SHOP
Hotels with coffee shop.

GARDEN/TERRACE
Hotels with a garden, courtyard or terrace.

	CREDIT CARDS	SWIMMING POOL	WESTERN BATHROOMS	COFFEE SHOP	GARDEN/TERRACE
NIZAMUDDIN: *Maharani Guest House.* **Map** 6 D3. Rs Rs Rs 3 Sundar Nagar. (011) 2435 3128. FAX (011) 2435 4562. Very popular with a business clientele, this converted residence in one of New Delhi's more affluent localities is next door to a market known for its antique shops. 24 TV *Rooms:* 24. 24.	AE DC MC V		■		■
OLD DELHI: *Broadway.* **Map** 2 E3. Rs Rs Rs Asaf Ali Rd. (011) 2327 3821. FAX (011) 2326 9966. This old hotel has easy access to both Old and New Delhi and is upgraded with modern facilities. A restaurant with delectable Kashmiri cuisine is on the premises. 24 TV *Rooms:* 28. 28.	AE DC MC V		■		
FURTHER AFIELD (NORTH): *Oberoi Maidens.* Rs Rs Rs Rs Sham Nath Marg. (011) 2397 5464. FAX (011) 2398 0771. W www.oberoihotels.com Close to Delhi University and the picturesque Ridge, this early 20th-century hotel has the elegant ambience of the Raj days when Edwin Lutyens first stayed here. 24 TV *Rooms:* 56. 56.	AE DC MC V	●	■	●	■
FURTHER AFIELD (WEST): *Diplomat.* Rs Rs Rs Rs Sardar Patel Marg, Diplomatic Enclave. (011) 2301 0204. FAX (011) 2301 8605. @ diplomat@nda.vsnl.net.in The advantage of staying in this stylish, well-managed and friendly hotel is that it is conveniently located near some important embassies. 24 TV *Rooms:* 25. 25.	AE DC MC V		■	●	■
FURTHER AFIELD (WEST): *Ashok Hotel.* Rs Rs Rs Rs Rs Chanakyapuri. (011) 2611 0101. FAX (011) 2687 3216. W www.theashokgroup.com A classic example of early modern Indian design, this majestic government-run hotel has grand suites and a wonderful shopping arcade. 24 TV *Rooms:* 550. 550.	AE DC MC V	●	■	●	■
FURTHER AFIELD (WEST): *Taj Palace.* Rs Rs Rs Rs Rs Sardar Patel Marg, Diplomatic Enclave. (011) 2611 0202. FAX (011) 2611 0808. W www.tajhotels.com Grand and imposing, this is a stylish member of the Taj Group, popular with the rich and famous for its speciality restaurants *(see p258).* 24 TV *Rooms:* 422. 422.	AE DC MC V	●	■	●	■
FURTHER AFIELD (WEST): *Welcomgroup Maurya Sheraton.* Rs Rs Rs Rs Rs Sardar Patel Marg, Diplomatic Enclave. (011) 2611 2233. FAX (011) 2611 3333. W www.welcomgroup.com A plush, top-of-the-market hotel complete with a yoga centre, library, and a superb restaurant by the poolside renowned for its barbequed fare *(see p258).* 24 TV *Rooms:* 515. 515.	AE DC MC V	●	■	●	■
FURTHER AFIELD (SOUTH): *Centaur.* Rs Rs Rs Rs IG International Airport. (011) 2565 2223. FAX (011) 2565 2256. @ centaur@ndf.vsnl.net.in Since it is close to the airport, this modern hotel is popular with transit passengers. 24 TV *Rooms:* 372. 372.	AE DC MC V	●	■	●	■
FURTHER AFIELD (SOUTH): *Qutab Hotel.* Rs Rs Rs Rs Off Aurobindo Marg. (011) 2651 1521. FAX (011) 2696 0828. @ qutab@del3.vsnl.net.in A good base to explore important historic sites as well as some unusual examples of modern Indian architecture. 24 TV *Rooms:* 64. 64.	AE DC MC V	●	■	●	■
FURTHER AFIELD (SOUTH): *Manor Country Hotel.* Rs Rs Rs Rs 77, Friends Colony West. (011) 2692 5151. FAX (011) 2692 2299. @ themanor@rediff.com Perhaps the most elegantly designed boutique hotel in the city, its location in one of the oldest and quietest residential colonies is an added advantage. 24 TV *Rooms:* 13. 13.	AE MC V		■		
FURTHER AFIELD (SOUTH): *Hotel Crowne Plaza Surya.* Rs Rs Rs Rs Rs New Friends Colony. (011) 2683 5070. FAX (011) 2683 7758. @ suryahot@ndf.vsnl.net.in This large, modern hotel has easy access to several boutiques, shops and popular mid-range restaurants in its neighbourhood. 24 TV *Rooms:* 195. 195.	AE DC MC V JCB	●	■	●	

FURTHER AFIELD (SOUTH): *Hyatt Regency.* (Rs)(Rs)(Rs)(Rs)
Bhikaji Cama Place, Ring Rd. **[** (011) 2679 1234. **FAX** (011) 2679 1122.
[W] www.hyatt.com Very much in the five-star tradition, this grand hotel is near a busy commercial complex and is well known for its popular bar and Italian restaurant. **[11] [Y] [TY] [24] [TV] [8]** *Rooms: 508.* **[目]** *508.*

AE DC MC V

FURTHER AFIELD (SOUTH): *Intercontinental Park Royal.* (Rs)(Rs)(Rs)(Rs)(Rs)
Nehru Place. **[** (011) 2622 3344. **FAX** (011) 2622 4288. **[W]** www.parkroyal.com.au
The hotel is in the heart of a buzzing South Delhi business area. Excellent tea and coffee is served in the lobby, while conferences are hosted with professional ease. **[11] [Y] [TY] [24] [TV] [8]** *Rooms: 217.* **[目]** *217.*

AE DC MC V

FURTHER AFIELD (SOUTH): *Radisson Hotel.* (Rs)(Rs)(Rs)(Rs)
National Highway 8, Mahipalpur Rd. **[** (011) 2677 9191. **FAX** (011) 2677 9090.
[W] www.radisson.com Ideal for travellers who want to stay near the airport. Part of an international chain, this hotel has many speciality restaurants *(see p259).* **[11] [Y] [TY] [24] [TV] [8]** *Rooms: 256.* **[目]** *256.*

AE DC MC V

FURTHER AFIELD (SOUTH): *Uppal's Orchid.* (Rs)(Rs)(Rs)(Rs)(Rs)
National Highway 8. IG International Airport. **[** (011) 2506 1515. **FAX** (011) 2506 1516.
[@] info@uppalsorchidhotel.com This eco-friendly, modern five-star deluxe hotel is conveniently located close to the airport. **[11] [Y] [TY] [24] [TV] [8]** *Rooms: 84.* **[目]** *84.*

AE DC MC V JCB

FURTHER AFIELD (SOUTH): *Vasant Continental.* (Rs)(Rs)(Rs)(Rs)(Rs)
Vasant Vihar. **[** (011) 2614 8800. **FAX** (011) 2614 5559. **[@]** skaul@jaypeehotels.com
A luxury hotel close to an up-market residential area, it is also near a modern multiplex cinema and a lively market area that has good eateries and shops. **[11] [TY] [24] [TV] [8]** *Rooms: 118.* **[目]** *118.*

AE DC MC V

FURTHER AFIELD (SOUTH OF DELHI): *Heritage Village.* (Rs)(Rs)(Rs)
Manesar, Gurgaon. **[** (0124) (95124 from Delhi) 229 0711. **FAX** (0124) 229 0345.
[@] sales@sresorts.com Less than a 40-minute drive from the international airport on Jaipur highway, this hotel has an ethnic ambience and is in the vicinity of the new Classic Golf Resort. **[11] [TY] [24] [TV]** *Rooms: 82.* **[目]** *82.*

AE DC MC V

FURTHER AFIELD (SOUTH OF DELHI): *Bristol.* (Rs)(Rs)(Rs)(Rs)
Sikandarpur, Gurgaon. **[** (0124) (95124 from Delhi) 235 6030. **FAX** (0124) 235 7834.
[@] sales@thehotelbristol.com Comfortable and elegant, the hotel is a convenient base for visitors whose interests are focused in this fast expanding part of the region. **[11] [Y] [TY] [24] [TV] [8]** *Rooms: 85.* **[目]** *85.*

AE DC MC V

FURTHER AFIELD (SOUTH OF DELHI): *Ibrahim Kothi.* (Rs)(Rs)(Rs)(Rs)
Distt Pataudi, Haryana. **[** For reservations: (011) 2301 3794. **FAX** (011) 2301 9323.
An elegant palatial establishment belonging to the Pataudi nawabs of cricketing fame, this is an excellent place to take time off for a few days of pampering and self indulgence. *Rooms: 15.*

AE DC MC V

FURTHER AFIELD (SOUTH OF DELHI): *Tikli Bottom.* (Rs)(Rs)(Rs)(Rs)(Rs)
Manender Farm, Gairatpur BBS, Haryana. **[** & **FAX** For reservations: (011) 2335 1272.
[@] honiwala@vsnl.com Surrounded by the Aravalli hills, this Lutyens-style country house, with lovely rooms and deep verandahs, is close to Delhi's airport. It is run by a charming English couple. **[11] [Y]** *Rooms: 3.*

NORTH OF DELHI

HARIDWAR: *Himgiri.* (Rs)(Rs)
Devpura Chowk. **[** (01334) 22 4506. **FAX** (01334) 22 6610.
Specially designed for pilgrims, the rooms offered here are cheap, cool and comfortable. **[TV]** *Rooms: 22.* **[目]** *7.*

HARIDWAR: *Rahi Motel (UPSTDC).* (Rs)(Rs)
Near Bus Stand, Station Rd. **[** (01334) 22 6430. **[W]** www.up-tourism.com
A modern bungalow with a pleasant garden and attentive staff. It also houses the regional office of UP Tourism. **[11]** *Rooms: 20.* **[目]** *3.*

HARIDWAR: *Teerth.* (Rs)(Rs)
Subhash Ghat, Bara Bazaar. **[** (01334) 22 5311.
Though in a crowded area, each room has a balcony with a good view of the river and Har-ki-Pauri, the main ghat. **[11] [24] [TV]** *Rooms: 36.* **[目]** *8.*

HARIDWAR: *Hotel Classic Residency.* (Rs)(Rs)(Rs)
Jwalapur Rd. **[** (01334) 22 8005. **FAX** (01334) 22 0374. **[@]** rclassic@sancharnet.in
A basic but comfortable hotel. The in-house restaurant offers good vegetarian food. **[11] [TY] [24] [TV]** *Rooms: 22.* **[目]** *22.*

AE DC MC V

<table>
<tr><td>

Price categories for a standard double room per night including tax and service charges but not including breakfast:

(Rs) under 550 rupees
(Rs)(Rs) 550–1,200 rupees
(Rs)(Rs)(Rs) 1,200–3,000 rupees
(Rs)(Rs)(Rs)(Rs) 3,000–6,000 rupees
(Rs)(Rs)(Rs)(Rs)(Rs) over 6,000 rupees

</td><td>

CREDIT CARDS
Indicates which credit cards are accepted: *AE* American Express; *DC* Diners Club; *MC* Master Card/Access; *V* Visa; *JCB* Japanese Credit Bureau.
WESTERN BATHROOMS
Indicates sit-down, flush toilets; showers and/or baths. Others have squat toilets and bucket-and-mug baths.
COFFEE SHOP
Hotels with coffee shop.
GARDEN/TERRACE
Hotels with a garden, courtyard or terrace.

</td></tr>
</table>

	CREDIT CARDS	SWIMMING POOL	WESTERN BATHROOMS	COFFEE SHOP	GARDEN/TERRACE
HARIDWAR: *Sagar Ganga Resorts.* (Rs)(Rs)(Rs) Mayapur, Niranjini Akhara Rd. ((01334) 22 8478. This exclusive property once belonged to the Nepal royal family, and has large rooms and an Art Deco ambience. It is situated on the banks of the river with its own private ghat. 11 24 TV **Rooms:** 10. 5.	AE		■	●	■
HARIDWAR: *Suvidha Deluxe.* (Rs)(Rs)(Rs) Subhas Ghat, Sravan Nath Nagar. ((01334) 22 7023. A centrally-located new hotel with an unmistakable small town air, this is essentially a clean, no-frills establishment. 11 24 TV **Rooms:** 28. 11.	AE MC V		■	●	■
KARNAL: *Karna Lake.* (Rs)(Rs)(Rs) Karnal Tourist Complex. ((0184) 226 7759. This hotel is a popular stop-over on the main highway. It offers boating on the nearby lake, and has a small handicrafts bazaar. 11 TV **Rooms:** 19. 19.					■
KURUKSHETRA: *Neelkanthi Krishna Dham Yatri Niwas.* (Rs) Distt Kurukshetra, Haryana. ((01744) 22 1615. This simple and good value tourism department hotel has a central open courtyard with rooms and dormitories around it. For those in search of quiet, there are meditation halls within the complex. 11 **Rooms:** 20. 6.					
MEERUT: *Naveen Deluxe.* (Rs)(Rs)(Rs) Abu Lane. ((0121) 266 0129. FAX (0121) 265 6525. The hotel's main advantage is its proximity to the railway station, bus stand and the main business centre. 11 24 TV 🍴 **Rooms:** 15. 15.	MC V		■		
MEERUT: *Rajmahal.* (Rs)(Rs)(Rs) 187 Abu Lane. ((0121) 266 1779. FAX (0121) 266 6266. Easily accessible, this hotel has clean and comfortable rooms and is popular with business travellers. 11 24 TV 🍴 **Rooms:** 18. 18.	AE DC MC V		■	●	
PANIPAT: *Skylark.* (Rs)(Rs) Skylark Tourist Complex. ((01742) (951742 from Delhi) 26 1051. This pleasant motel is run by Haryana Tourism which has an established reputation for good service and hospitality. 11 24 TV 🍴 **Rooms:** 13. 13.					
RISHIKESH: *Bhandari Swiss Cottage.* (Rs) Tapovan. ((0135) 243 2939. @ bhandariswisscottage@hotmail.com An old and quaint establishment with great charm and character. The accommodation includes tents. **Rooms:** 20. 1.					
RISHIKESH: *GMVN Tourist Bungalow.* (Rs) Muni-ki-Reti. ((0135) 243 0373. FAX (0135) 243 1793. Pleasant and roomy with cottages set in a quiet garden, it is located at a short distance from the city centre. It is advisable to book rooms in advance in this popular hotel. 11 TV **Rooms:** 45. 2.			■		
RISHIKESH: *New Bhandari Swiss Cottage.* (Rs) Tapovan. (No telephone. The main attraction here is the in-house bakery which offers fresh breads, delicious muffins and pies every morning. **Rooms:** 18.			■		
RISHIKESH: *Tourist Rest House (GMVN).* (Rs) Near Natraj Cinema, Haridwar Bypass Rd. ((0135) 243 3002. FAX (0135) 243 0372. The grounds around this hotel are its main draw. A cheap place to stay, the rooms with attached baths are priced higher. 11 TV **Rooms:** 39. 2.			■		■
RISHIKESH: *Yog Niketan and Ashram.* (Rs) Shivanand Nagar, Muni-ki-Reti. ((0135) 243 0227. If you are serious about meditation and *hatha* yoga classes, this is the place to choose. Rates are minimal, but if you plan to stay for more than a week, you will have to pay in advance. 11 **Rooms:** 100.			■		

RISHIKESH: *High Bank Peasants Cottage.* ⓇⓈ ⓇⓈ
Tapovan. 【 *(0135) 243 3478.* FAX *(0135) 243 1654.* @ himalayas@vsnl.com
This cosy little place is attractively located high above the Ganges and
has a pretty flower and vegetable garden. Good discounts are given for
stays extending over a week. **Rooms: 5.**

Credit cards: V

RISHIKESH: *Ganga Kinare.* ⓇⓈ ⓇⓈ ⓇⓈ
16 Veerabhadra Rd. 【 *(0135) 243 1658.* FAX *(0135) 243 5243.*
@ hotelgangakinare@hotmail.com This riverside hotel has a panoramic view of the
hills. It offers free meditation classes, has its own rowing boats, and its in-house
travel desk arranges treks and white-water rafting. 🍽 24 📺 **Rooms: 38.** 38.

Credit cards: AE DC MC V

RISHIKESH: *Ganga View.* ⓇⓈ ⓇⓈ ⓇⓈ
63 Haridwar Rd. 【 *(0135) 243 0781.* FAX *(0135) 243 6146.*
Great views of the Ganges and surrounding mountain ranges come with
this rather modish hotel. The amenities are meant to suit tourists who
want comfort as well as peace. 🍽 24 📺 **Rooms: 28.** 28.

Credit cards: MC V

RISHIKESH: *The Glass House on the Ganges.* ⓇⓈ ⓇⓈ ⓇⓈ
23rd Milestone, Rishikesh-Badrinath Rd. 【 *(01378) 26 9224.* FAX *(011) 2435 1112.*
Ⓦ www.neemrana.com Set in a litchi orchard with a garden of tropical plants and
rare birds, this exclusive resort has a private sand beach. 🍽 **Rooms: 16.**

Credit cards: AE DC MC V

RISHIKESH: *Ananda.* ⓇⓈ ⓇⓈ ⓇⓈ ⓇⓈ ⓇⓈ
The Palace Estate, Narendra Nagar. 【 *(01378) 22 7500.* FAX *(01378) 22 7550.*
Ⓦ www.anandaspa.com Set in a 40-ha (100-acre) estate, this is among India's most
luxurious spa-resorts. It offers meditation, yogic and ayurvedic treatments and
other forms of holistic healing. 🍽 🍷 24 📺 💆 🏊 **Rooms: 75.** 75.

Credit cards: AE DC MC V

SAHARANPUR: *Classic International.* ⓇⓈ ⓇⓈ ⓇⓈ
Dehradun Rd. 【 *(0132) 266 1403.* FAX *(0132) 266 1410.*
A kitsch hotel in the centre of the town, popular with business visitors to
this famous centre of wood-carving because of its location near the
railway station and bus stand. 🍽 24 📺 💆 **Rooms: 24.** 24.

Credit cards: AE MC V

AGRA AND AROUND

AGRA: *Tourist Bungalow (UPSTDC).* ⓇⓈ
Raja ki Mandi, Delhi Gate. 【 *(0562) 215 1720.* FAX *(0562) 215 3472.*
A small, clean and cheerful hotel with a pleasant courtyard. An added
bonus is its thoughtful staff. 🍽 24 📺 **Rooms: 35.** 10.

AGRA: *Ganga Ratna.* ⓇⓈ ⓇⓈ
Fatehbad Rd. 【 *(0562) 233 0329.* FAX *(0562) 233 0193.*
Known for its friendly service and clean rooms, this hotel is conveniently
located near the state emporia. 🍽 📺 **Rooms: 41.** 41.

Credit cards: AE MC V

AGRA: *Lauries Hotel.* ⓇⓈ ⓇⓈ
Mahatma Gandhi Rd. 【 *(0562) 236 4536.* FAX *(0562) 226 8045.*
@ laurieshotel@hotmail.com
One of Agra's oldest hotels, its non-airconditioned rooms keep the rates
low. It also offers camping facilities. **Rooms: 28.**

Credit cards: AE MC V

AGRA: *Taj Khema.* ⓇⓈ ⓇⓈ
Eastern Gate, Taj Mahal. 【 *(0562) 233 0140.* FAX *(0562) 223 0001.*
A small government-run hotel near the Taj with simple, good value
standard rooms. Photographers will appreciate the superb views of the
monument from the raised garden. 🍽 24 **Rooms: 6.** 4.

AGRA: *Agra Ashok Hotel.* ⓇⓈ ⓇⓈ ⓇⓈ
6-B The Mall. 【 *(0562) 236 1223.* FAX *(0562) 236 1620.*
Located close to the railway station, this well-managed hotel offers
traditional hospitality, comfortable rooms and friendly staff.
🍽 🍷 24 📺 💆 **Rooms: 38.** 38.

Credit cards: AE DC MC V

AGRA: *Amar Yatri Niwas.* ⓇⓈ ⓇⓈ ⓇⓈ
Tourist Complex Area, Fatehabad Rd. 【 *(0562) 223 3031.* FAX *(0562) 223 3035.*
Though the decor is slightly garish, the hotel is popular, and has a range
of rooms equipped with essential facilities. 🍽 📺 **Rooms: 32.** 32.

Credit cards: AE DC MC V

AGRA: *Mayur Tourist Complex.* ⓇⓈ ⓇⓈ ⓇⓈ
Fatehabad Rd. 【 *(0562) 233 2302.* FAX *(0562) 233 2907.*
A mid-range, well-managed hotel with cottages set within an extensive
lawn. Very popular and often full, it has a good restaurant with an
efficient and courteous staff. 🍽 📺 💆 🏊 **Rooms: 24.** 24.

Credit cards: AE DC MC V

Price categories / key	CREDIT CARDS	SWIMMING POOL	WESTERN BATHROOMS	COFFEE SHOP	GARDEN/TERRACE

Price categories for a standard double room per night including tax and service charges but not including breakfast:

(Rs) under 550 rupees
(Rs)(Rs) 550–1,200 rupees
(Rs)(Rs)(Rs) 1,200–3,000 rupees
(Rs)(Rs)(Rs)(Rs) 3,000–6,000 rupees
(Rs)(Rs)(Rs)(Rs)(Rs) over 6,000 rupees

CREDIT CARDS
Indicates which credit cards are accepted: *AE* American Express; *DC* Diners Club; *MC* Master Card/Access; *V* Visa; *JCB* Japanese Credit Bureau.
WESTERN BATHROOMS
Indicates sit-down, flush toilets; showers and/or baths. Others have squat toilets and bucket-and-mug baths.
COFFEE SHOP
Hotels with coffee shop.
GARDEN/TERRACE
Hotels with a garden, courtyard or terrace.

AGRA: *Clarks Shiraz.* (Rs)(Rs)(Rs)
Agra Cantt, 54 Taj Rd. (0562) 222 6121. FAX (0562) 222 6128.
@ clarkraz@nde.vsnl.net.in Pleasantly located amidst extensive gardens, this was India's first 5-star hotel and has recently been given an attractive face lift. The rooms have beautiful views of the Taj. **11 Y 24 TV** *Rooms: 237.* 237.
AE DC MC V | ● | ■ | ● | ■

AGRA: *Holiday Inn.* (Rs)(Rs)(Rs)
Sanjay Place Commercial Complex. (0562) 252 3460. FAX (0562) 252 3591.
@ hinnagra@sancharnet.in A new hotel owned by a well-known international chain, it is sensitively designed and serviced in the best traditions of Indian hospitality. **11 Y 24 TV** *Rooms: 148.* 148.
AE DC MC V | ● | ■ | ● | ■

AGRA: *Howard Park Plaza International.* (Rs)(Rs)(Rs)(Rs)
Taj Ganj, Fatehabad Rd. (0562) 233 1870. FAX (0562) 233 0408.
@ hppi@sarovarparkplaza.com A modern and very elegant hotel with a rooftop viewing gallery. The hotel's cuisine is renowned, especially that of the Indian poolside restaurant. **11 Y 24 TV** *Rooms: 76.* 76.
AE DC MC V | ● | ■ | ● | ■

AGRA: *Jaypee Palace Hotels.* (Rs)(Rs)(Rs)(Rs)
Fatehabad Rd. (0562) 233 0800. FAX (0562) 233 0850. @ jaypeeag@nde.vsnl.net.in Comfortable rooms set around a series of impressive terraced courts in 25 acres of lush, landscaped gardens and ponds make this an attractive place for a longer stay. **11 Y 24 TV** *Rooms: 350.* 350.
AE DC MC V | ● | ■ | ● | ■

AGRA: *Mansingh Palace.* (Rs)(Rs)(Rs)(Rs)
Fatehabad Rd. (0562) 233 1771. FAX (0562) 233 0202. w www.mansinghhotels.com This luxurious hotel, named after a famous Rajput king, has a few rooms overlooking the Taj. The bar, jacuzzi, and swimming pool with a water slide are special attractions. **11 Y 24 TV** *Rooms: 97.* 97.
AE DC MC V | ● | ■ | ● | ■

AGRA: *Taj View.* (Rs)(Rs)(Rs)(Rs)
Taj Ganj, Fatehabad Rd. (0562) 223 2400. FAX (0562) 223 2420. w www.tajhotels.com Only 1 km away from the Taj this magnificent hotel nestles amongst acres of landscaped gardens. **11 24 TV** *Rooms: 100.* 100.
AE DC MC V | ● | ■ | ● | ■

AGRA: *The Trident.* (Rs)(Rs)(Rs)(Rs)
Tajnagri Scheme, Fatehabad Rd. (0562) 233 1818. FAX (0562) 233 1812.
@ reservations@tridentag.com This hotel's impressive decor is inspired by the Mughal style. Considered to be one of Agra's best, expect to find the highest standards here. **11 Y 24 TV** *Rooms: 140.* 140.
AE DC MC V | ● | ■ | ● | ■

AGRA: *Amar Vilas.* (Rs)(Rs)(Rs)(Rs)(Rs)
Taj East Gate Rd, Taj Nagari Scheme. (0562) 223 1515. FAX (0562) 223 1516.
w www.oberoihotels.com Set in elegant Mughal gardens with pavilions and pools, every room in this luxurious spa-hotel offers views of the Taj Mahal, which is just 600 m (1,969 ft) away. **11 Y 24 TV** *Rooms: 106.* 106.
AE DC MC V | ● | ■ | ● | ■

AGRA: *Welcomgroup Mughal Sheraton.* (Rs)(Rs)(Rs)(Rs)(Rs)
Taj Ganj. (0562) 233 1701. FAX (0562) 233 1730. w www.welcomgroup.com The architecture of this hotel is a fitting tribute to the great Mughal builders. Gloriously landscaped and lavishly furnished, this is one of India's finest hotels. **11 Y 24 TV** *Rooms: 285.* 285.
AE DC MC V | ● | ■ | ● | ■

BHARATPUR: *Hotel Saras (RTDC).* (Rs)(Rs)
Agra Rd. (05644) 22 3700. FAX (05644) 22 5306. w www.rajasthan-tourism.com A government-run tourist hotel, its main advantage is that it is at walking distance from the Keoladeo National Park. **11 24 TV** *Rooms: 28.* 28.
| | ■ | ● | ■

BHARATPUR: *Eagle's Nest.* (Rs)(Rs)
Agra Rd. (05644) 22 5144. FAX (05644) 22 3170.
This is one of several little guesthouses located in close proximity to the bird sanctuary. Very friendly and welcoming, the hospitality makes up for the lack of sophistication. **11 24 TV** *Rooms: 12.* 3.
| | ■ | ● | ■

BHARATPUR: *Bharatpur Forest Lodge (ITDC).*   (Rs)(Rs)Rs
Keoladeo National Park. **(** *(05644) 22 2760.* **FAX** *(05644) 22 2864.*
This beautifully sited hotel right inside the sanctuary, though
comparitively expensive, is the best place to stay in. Its restaurant is open
to non-residents. **11** **TV** *Rooms: 17.* ▤ *17.*

AE MC V

BHARATPUR: *Chander Mahal Ki Haveli.*   (Rs)(Rs)(Rs)
Peharsar, Naqbai Tehsil, Jaipur-Agra Rd. **(** *(05643) 26 4336.*
A heritage hotel at a short distance from Bharatpur town, it is surrounded
by brilliant yellow mustard fields in winter. **11** *Rooms: 17.* ▤ *17.*

BHARATPUR: *Laxmi Vilas Palace.*   (Rs)(Rs)(Rs)
Kakaji ki Kothi, Agra Rd. **(** *(05644) 22 3523.* **FAX** *(05644) 22 5259.*
An eclectic and lively fusion of Rajput and Mughal architecture. Palatial
rooms, royal hospitality and gourmet cuisine. **11** **TV** ⌂ *Rooms: 25.* ▤ *25.*

AE DC MC V

BRINDAVAN: *Sri Krishna Balaram International Guest House.*   (Rs)
Raman Reti. **(** *(0565) 254 0021.* @ *ramamani@nde.vsnl.net.in*
This guest house offers members of the ISKCON Society and their guests a
discounted fare for rooms. It is also open to non-members. **11** *Rooms: 40.*

BRINDAVAN: *Bhaktivedanta Ashrama & MVT Guest House.*   (Rs)(Rs)
Raman Reti. **(** *(0565) 254 0079.* **FAX** *(0565) 254 0073.* @ *mvte@pamho.net*
Definitely the nicest place to stay in Brindavan. Well designed and
meticulously clean. **11** **24** ⌂ *Rooms: 29.* ▤ *8.*

BRINDAVAN: *Sri Banke Bihari Guest House.*   (Rs)(Rs)
Ahir Pada, Sri Banke Bihari Temple Rd. **(** *(0565) 244 3530.*
An adequate guesthouse, and with a copy of the *Bhagavad Gita* in each
room, appropriate for visitors to this temple town. **24** **TV** *Rooms: 14.*

DEEG: *Midway Hotel.*   (Rs)
Distt Bharatpur. **(** *(05641) 22 1000.*
A tiny guesthouse located close to the bus stand, this government hotel is
at walking distance from Deeg Palace. **11** **24** *Rooms: 4.*

FATEHPUR SIKRI: *The Archaeological Survey Dak Bungalow.*   (Rs)
The Mall. **(** *(05613) 28 2248.*
This spacious old colonial-style resthouse adjoining the historic complex
must be booked through the ASI office, and is usually reserved for
government guests. Meals are cooked on request by the staff. *Rooms: 4.*

FATEHPUR SIKRI: *Gulistan Tourist Complex.*   (Rs)(Rs)
Agra Rd. **(** *(05613) 28 2640.*
Surprisingly attractive for a small town hotel run by the government, it is
close to the local bus stand. **11** **24** **TV** ⌂ *Rooms: 24.* ▤ *8.*

GWALIOR: *Regency Resort.*   (Rs)(Rs)
Malanpur. **(** *(09575) 397 3206. For reservations: (0751) 234 4116.*
If you are agreeable to staying slightly away from the city, you will not
be disappointed by this hotel, located in an open area near a beautiful
lake with boating facilities. **11** **24** **TV** ⌂ *Rooms: 15.* ▤ *15.*

AE DC MC V

GWALIOR: *Shelter.*   (Rs)(Rs)
Padav, Near Indian Airlines Office. **(** *(0751) 232 6209.* **FAX** *(0751) 232 6212.*
@ *hotelshelter@hotmail.com* A newish hotel, typical of many small towns, it is
close to all major tourist sites and the railway station. It also offers assistance
with travel bookings and a 24-hour taxi service. **11** **24** **TV** ⌂ *Rooms: 65.* ▤ *65.*

AE DC MC V

GWALIOR: *Tansen Gwalior (MPSTDC).*   (Rs)(Rs)
6-A Gandhi Rd, Civil Lines. **(** *(0751) 234 0370.* **FAX** *(0751) 234 3520.*
W *www.mptourism.com* Pleasantly located, the hotel is popular with business
travellers. Advance booking is recommended. **11** **Y** **24** **TV** *Rooms: 36.* ▤ *12.*

AE DC MC V

GWALIOR: *Gwalior Regency.*   (Rs)(Rs)(Rs)
Link Rd. **(** *(0751) 234 0670.* **FAX** *(0751) 234 3520.*
A well-appointed hotel in the centre of town with rooms ranging from
good-value "economy" to "super deluxe". It has a discotheque and an
excellent restaurant. **11** **Y** **Y** **24** **TV** ⌂ *Rooms: 51.* ▤ *51.*

AE DC MC V

GWALIOR: *Usha Kiran Palace.*   (Rs)(Rs)(Rs)(Rs)
Jayendraganj, Lashkar. **(** *(0751) 232 3993.* **FAX** *(0751) 232 1103.*
Newly refurbished, this glamorous and luxurious hotel was once the maharaja's
guesthouse. Snooker, croquet and badminton facilities are available on the
premises. **11** **Y** **24** **TV** ⌂ *Rooms: 28.* ▤ *28.*

AE DC MC V

Price categories for a standard double room per night including tax and service charges but not including breakfast:

- ℞ under 550 rupees
- ℞℞ 550–1,200 rupees
- ℞℞℞ 1,200–3,000 rupees
- ℞℞℞℞ 3,000–6,000 rupees
- ℞℞℞℞℞ over 6,000 rupees

CREDIT CARDS
Indicates which credit cards are accepted: *AE* American Express; *DC* Diners Club; *MC* Master Card/Access; *V* Visa; *JCB* Japanese Credit Bureau.

WESTERN BATHROOMS
Indicates sit-down, flush toilets; showers and/or baths. Others have squat toilets and bucket-and-mug baths.

COFFEE SHOP
Hotels with coffee shop.

GARDEN/TERRACE
Hotels with a garden, courtyard or terrace.

Hotel	Price	Credit Cards	Swimming Pool	Western Bathrooms	Coffee Shop	Garden/Terrace
JHANSI: *Sita.* Post Box No 84, Civil Lines, Shivpuri Rd. ☎ *(0517) 244 2956.* FAX *(0517) 244 4691.* Located opposite the railway station, this is probably the most comfortable hotel in town. It also has a good restaurant and offers foreign exchange facilities. 🍴 24 TV 🛏 *Rooms: 29.* ▤ 23.	℞℞	MC V		■	●	■
JHANSI: *Veerangana (UPSTDC).* Civil Lines, Shivpuri Rd. ☎ *(0517) 244 2402.* FAX *(0517) 244 9473.* This spartan, government-run hotel with a pleasant lawn includes dormitories at rock-bottom rates. Beer is available. 🍴 *Rooms: 20.* ▤ 6.	℞℞			■		■
MATHURA: *International Guest House.* Sri Krishna Janm Bhoomi. ☎ *(0565) 242 3888.* Popular and often fully occupied because of its cheap rates. The in-house restaurant serves only vegetarian food. 🍴 *Rooms: 45.*	℞					■
MATHURA: *Mukund Vihar Inn.* Opp Petrol Pump, Masani Rd. ☎ *(0565) 240 4055.* Spacious lawns cradle this homely motel. However, their cafeteria opens only in the evenings. 🍴 *Rooms: 7.* ▤ 2.	℞			■		■
MATHURA: *Agra Hotel.* Bengali Ghat. ☎ *(0565) 240 3318.* Overlooking the river, this small but clean 70-year-old hotel offers all essential facilities. 🍴 *Rooms: 15.* ▤ 5.	℞℞			■		■
MATHURA: *Brijwasi Royal Hotel.* Railway Station Rd. ☎ *(0565) 240 1224.* FAX *(0565) 240 1227.* This large hotel is located close to the Dwarkadhish Temple, and arranges package tours through the Braj district. 🍴 🍸 24 TV *Rooms: 40.* ▤ 40.	℞℞	MC V		■		
MATHURA: *Best Western Radha Ashok.* P O Chhatikara, Masani Bypass Rd. ☎ *(0565) 253 0395.* FAX *(0565) 253 0396.* @ radhaanila@hotmail.com This ritzy hotel, run by a reputable hotel group, is popular with an international clientele. 🍴 🍽 24 TV 🛏 *Rooms: 25.* ▤ 25.	℞℞℞	AE DC MC V	●	■	●	■
MATHURA: *Madhuvan.* Krishna Nagar. ☎ *(0565) 242 0064.* FAX *(0565) 242 0684.* @ bhul@nde.vsnl.net.in One of the fancier hotels in town, visitors are attracted here by its swimming pool, health centre and live performances of Indian classical music in the evenings. 🍴 24 TV 🛏 *Rooms: 27.* ▤ 27.	℞℞℞	AE DC MC V	●	■		
MATHURA: *Mansarovar Palace.* State Bank Crossing. ☎ *(0565) 240 8686.* FAX *(0565) 240 1611.* The façade may be a poor imitation of a traditional gateway, but this is a well-maintained hotel with friendly services. 🍴 24 TV *Rooms: 31.* ▤ 20.	℞℞℞	MC V		■		
MATHURA: *Sheetal Regency.* Deeg Gate, near Sri Krishna Janma Bhoomi. ☎ *(0565) 240 4597.* FAX *(0565) 240 0106.* This friendly hotel is located close to the train and bus stations, and organizes guides and vehicles for sightseeing. 🍴 24 TV *Rooms: 28.* ▤ 17.	℞℞℞	AE DC MC V		■	●	■
ORCHHA: *Betwa Cottages (MPSTDC).* Orchha, Distt Tikamgarh. ☎ *(07680) 25 2618.* W www.mptourism.com Individual cottages are charmingly set in a garden near the banks of the River Betwa. The complex is walking distance from the superb Orchha cenotaphs. Its serene environment is recommended. 🍴 *Rooms: 10.* ▤ 6.	℞℞			■		
ORCHHA: *The Orchha Resort.* Kanchanaghat, Distt Tikamgarh. ☎ *(07680) 252 0678.* @ oswaleep@nde.vsnl.net.in This garish resort is a discordant presence in this serene town, but is popular with tourist groups as it is one of the few options available and offers standard comforts. 🍴 🍽 24 TV *Rooms: 32.* ▤ 32.	℞℞℞		●	■		■

ORCHHA: *Sheesh Mahal (MPSTDC).* (Rs)(Rs) — AE DC MC V JCB
Orchha, Distt Tikamgarh. **(** (07680) 25 2624. **W** www.mptourism.com
A later wing of the historic Jahangiri Mahal (built in 1626) this is now a charming state-run hotel. The rooms, redolent with history, offer visitors a romantic ambience. **11 Y 6** *Rooms: 8.* 1.

JAIPUR AND ENVIRONS

AJMER: *Prithviraj.* (Rs)
Opp Patel Stadium, Jaipur Rd. **(** (0145) 243 2297. **@** hotel.prithviraj@usa.net
Clad in marble, this hotel may have the air of a nouveau riche house, but it offers excellent rates for budget travellers. **24 TV** *Rooms: 22.* 6.

AJMER: *Fort Baghera.* (Rs)(Rs)
P O & Vill Baghera. **(** (01467) 28 1231.
A stopover in this historic 17th-century fort on the Ajmer-Sawai Madhopur bus route offers a chance to savour some folk music and dances. You can also boat on the Varah Sagar Lake. **11 24** *Rooms: 3.*

AJMER: *Khadim (RTDC).* (Rs)(Rs)
Savitri Girls College Rd. **(** (0145) 262 7490. **W** www.rajasthan-tourism.com
A standard state tourism hotel, well kept, with dormitories, air-cooled rooms and facilities to arrange air and rail tickets. **11 24** *Rooms: 51.*

AJMER: *Merwara Estate (Tikam Niwas).* (Rs)(Rs)(Rs)
Daulat Bagh, Mahavir Circle. **(** (0145) 242 0691. **FAX** (0145) 242 0261.
Built on a hillock in 1887 in the colonial style, with painted ceilings, Italian marble floors and Belgian etched glasswork, this is a pleasant hotel overlooking the Anasagar Lake. **11 24 TV 6** *Rooms: 30.*

AJMER: *Mansingh Palace.* (Rs)(Rs)(Rs)(Rs) — AE DC MC V
Near Anasagar, Vaishali Nagar, Circular Rd. **(** (0145) 242 5702. **FAX** (0145) 242 5858.
@ mansingh.jaipur@mailcity.com In spite of its wonderful location near the lake and its good facilities, the services could be more sophisticated to justify the hotel's comparatively high rates. **11 24 TV 6** *Rooms: 95.* 95.

ALWAR: *Alwar Hotel.* (Rs) — MC V
26 Manu Marg. **(** (0144) (95144 from Delhi) 270 0012. **FAX** (0144) 234 8757.
@ ukrustagi@hotmail.com Economical, with basic facilities, the hotel is clean and quiet with comfortable, good-sized rooms. **11 TV** *Rooms: 12.* 7.

ALWAR: *Meenal (RTDC).* (Rs)(Rs)
Near Circuit House, Bhavani Tope. **(** (0144) (95144 from Delhi) 234 7352.
W www.rajasthan-tourism.com This tourism department hotel is located away from the crowded parts of the city, surrounded by trees. It offers reasonable and basic facilities without many frills. **11** *Rooms: 6.* 2.

ALWAR: *Aravalli.* (Rs)(Rs)(Rs) — MC V
1 CEB, Near Railway Station. **(** (0144) (95144 from Delhi) 233 2883. **FAX** (0144) 233 2011.
@ hotelaravalli@rediffmail.com Though small, this is without doubt the best place to stay in Alwar. The hotel is equipped with most facilities and the owners help to organize treks and tours. **11 Y 24 TV 6** *Rooms: 38.* 28.

ALWAR: *Hill Fort Kesroli.* (Rs)(Rs)(Rs)(Rs) — AE MC V
Vill Kesroli, Near M I A. **(** For reservations: (01468) 28 9352.
@ sales@neemranahotels.com For the sheer thrill of dining on its ramparts, a stopover in this 600-year-old, seven-turreted hotel is recommended. *Rooms: 21.*

DUNDLOD: *Dundlod Fort.* (Rs)(Rs)(Rs) — AE DC MC V
Dundlod, Distt Jhunjhunu-Shekhawati. **(** & **FAX** (01594) 425 2519.
@ dundlod@datainfosys.net An 18th-century heritage hotel with lots of atmosphere. A royal welcome with folk music, camels and garlands can be arranged on request, and you could not ask for a more gracious host. **24 6** *Rooms: 45.*

FATEHPUR: *Hotel Haveli (RTDC).* (Rs)(Rs)
1 km S of Fatehpur on NH 11, Distt Sikar. **(** (01571) 23 0293.
W www.rajasthan-tourism.com For those who wish to spend a few days in the Shekhawati area, this clean, reasonably-priced old-fashioned place offers both air-cooled rooms and dormitories. Meals are available. *Rooms: 8.* 1.

JAIPUR: *Bissau Palace Hotel.* (Rs)(Rs) — AE DC MC V
Outside Chand Pol. **(** (0141) 230 4371. **FAX** (0141) 230 4628.
@ sanjai@jpl.dot.net.in A charming heritage hotel, this oasis in the heart of the Pink City has lawn tennis courts, and a fascinating collection of rare books, old silver and armour. **11 24 TV 6** *Rooms: 48.* 48.

For key to symbols see back flap

<table>
<tr><td>

Price categories for a standard double room per night including tax and service charges but not including breakfast:

(Rs) under 550 rupees
(Rs)(Rs) 550–1,200 rupees
(Rs)(Rs)(Rs) 1,200–3,000 rupees
(Rs)(Rs)(Rs)(Rs) 3,000–6,000 rupees
(Rs)(Rs)(Rs)(Rs)(Rs) over 6,000 rupees

</td><td>

CREDIT CARDS
Indicates which credit cards are accepted: *AE* American Express; *DC* Diners Club; *MC* Master Card/Access; *V* Visa; *JCB* Japanese Credit Bureau.

WESTERN BATHROOMS
Indicates sit-down, flush toilets; showers and/or baths. Others have squat toilets and bucket-and-mug baths.

COFFEE SHOP
Hotels with coffee shop.

GARDEN/TERRACE
Hotels with a garden, courtyard or terrace.

</td></tr>
</table>

	CREDIT CARDS	SWIMMING POOL	WESTERN BATHROOMS	COFFEE SHOP	GARDEN/TERRACE
JAIPUR: *Diggi Palace.* (Rs)(Rs) — Sawai Mansigh Rd. (0141) 237 3091. FAX (0141) 237 0359. @ diggihtl@datainfosys.net — This is a small and attractive *haveli*-turned-guesthouse. Unlike some converted family homes, the modest charges here may suit the budget traveller in search of traditional hospitality. Rooms: 43. 11.			■	●	■
JAIPUR: *Gangaur (RTDC).* (Rs)(Rs) — M I Rd. (0141) 237 1641. FAX (0141) 237 1647. — Located in the quiet bylanes of the busy MI road, this popular hotel has a good restaurant serving Indian and Chinese cuisine. On certain days, it also serves a special Rajasthani menu. Rooms: 63.			■	●	■
JAIPUR: *Karauli House.* (Rs)(Rs) — Sodala, New Sanganer Rd. (0141) 229 0763. FAX (0141) 229 2633. — This old family house has been converted to a small guesthouse, and offers a warm and homely atmosphere. Rooms: 3. 3.		●	■	●	■
JAIPUR: *L M B Hotel.* (Rs)(Rs) — Johari Bazaar. (0141) 256 5844. FAX (0141) 256 2176. @ info@lmbsweets.com — With small well-kept rooms, the hotel's main attraction is its location above a famous vegetarian restaurant in the centre of one of Jaipur's most popular bazaars. Rooms: 33. 33.	AE DC MC V		■	●	■
JAIPUR: *Alsisar Haveli.* (Rs)(Rs)(Rs) — Sansar Chandra Rd. (0141) 236 8290. FAX (0141) 236 4652. — This 19th-century *haveli* has retained its medieval look with large courtyards, arched corridors and a huge garden in front. The rooms are well furnished and serviced. Rooms: 35. 35.	MC V	●	■	●	■
JAIPUR: *Jaipur Ashok (ITDC).* (Rs)(Rs)(Rs) — Jai Singh Circle, Bani Park. (0141) 220 4491. FAX (0141) 220 2098. @ reservations@theashokgroup.com The tourism department manages this well-designed hotel located near the railway station. Set in a landscaped garden, it is well-appointed with most modern facilities. Rooms: 50. 50.	AE DC MC V	●	■	●	■
JAIPUR: *Khasa Kothi.* (Rs)(Rs)(Rs) — Mirza Ismail Rd. (0141) 237 5151. FAX (0141) 237 4040. — Literally a "special mansion" built in the colonial style, it was a state guesthouse 100 years ago. Centrally located, it is well-appointed with large rooms surrounded by cool lawns. Rooms: 36.		●	■	●	■
JAIPUR: *Narain Niwas Palace Hotel.* (Rs)(Rs)(Rs) — Kanota Bagh, Narain Singh Rd. (0141) 256 1291. FAX (0141) 256 1045. W www.narainniwas.com Built in 1928, this was the royal Kanota family's country residence. It is surrounded by mango orchards and its traditional interior has been carefully preserved. Rooms: 38. 36.	AE DC MC V	●	■	●	■
JAIPUR: *Royal Castle Kanota.* (Rs)(Rs)(Rs) — Kanota Bagh, Narain Singh Rd. (01429) 23 4033. W www.narainniwas.com Built in 1872, this fortified castle is private and exclusive. Well worth a stay if only to see its unique library and armoury. Rooms: 10.			■		■
JAIPUR: *Chokhi Dhani.* (Rs)(Rs)(Rs)(Rs) — 19 km from Ajmeri Gate on Tonk Rd. (0141) 277 0555. FAX (0141) 277 0558. @ cokidani@datainfosys.net This eye-catching place, designed to look like a village complex, is one of Jaipur's attractions. Equipped with most resort facilities you can easily spend a few lazy days here. Rooms: 73.	AE DC MC V	●	■	●	■
JAIPUR: *Clarks Amer.* (Rs)(Rs)(Rs)(Rs) — Jawaharlal Nehru Marg. (0141) 255 0616. FAX (0141) 255 0013. @ clkamer@jp1.dot.net.in If you want to stay closer to the airport or would like to explore the textile town of Sanganer at leisure, this is a conveniently located hotel, pleasant and well-managed. Rooms: 197. 197.	AE MC V	●	■	●	■

JAIPUR: *Holiday Inn Jaipur.*   ℞℞℞℞
Amber Rd. ☏ *(0141) 267 2000.* FAX *(0141) 267 2335.* @ hijaiin@jp1.dot.net.in
On the town's outskirts en route to Amber, this fine hotel has views of
the beautiful Nahargarh Fort. 🍴 24 TV 🏊 *Rooms: 70.* 🛏 *70.*
AE DC MC V

JAIPUR: *Jai Mahal Palace.*   ℞℞℞℞
Civil Lines, Jacob Rd. ☏ *(0141) 222 3636.* FAX *(0141) 222 0707.* w www.tajhotels.com
Designed by Sir Swinton Jacob, the building is now a luxurious and
elegant hotel. Its attractions include antique furniture and a solar-heated
pool. 🍴 🛎 24 TV 🏊 *Rooms: 100.* 🛏 *100.*
AE DC MC V

JAIPUR: *Mansingh Palace.*   ℞℞℞℞
Sansar Chandra Rd. ☏ *(0141) 237 8771.* FAX *(0141) 237 7582.*
w www.mansinghhotels.com Well-equipped with modern conveniences,
this hotel has a wonderful feeling of space with large windows looking
out of lavishly decorated rooms. 🍴 🛎 24 TV 🏊 *Rooms: 100.* 🛏 *100.*
AE DC MC V

JAIPUR: *Mansingh Towers.*   ℞℞℞
Sansar Chandra Rd. ☏ *(0141) 237 8771.*
w www.mansinghhotels.com This is the elegant and well-appointed new
wing of the Mansingh Palace. 🍴 🛎 24 TV 🏊 *Rooms: 53.* 🛏 *53.*
AE DC MC V

JAIPUR: *Raj Mahal Palace.*   ℞℞℞℞
Sardar Patel Marg, C–Scheme. ☏ *(0141) 238 3260.* FAX *(0141) 238 1887.*
w www.tajhotels.com Among the rich and famous who have stayed here
were Prince Philip and Jacqueline Kennedy. The rooms are standard
sized but luxurious; the restaurant good. 🍴 24 TV 🏊 *Rooms: 23.* 🛏 *20.*
AE DC MC V

JAIPUR: *Ramgarh Lodge.*   ℞℞℞℞
Ramgarh Lake, Ramgarh. ☏ *(01426) 25 2217.* FAX *(01426) 25 2079.* w www.tajhotels.com
Try to stay in a suite overlooking the glorious Ramgarh Lake in this
former royal hunting lodge. Though ideal for polo lovers, there are
facilities for tennis, squash and boating. 🍴 🛎 24 TV 🏊 *Rooms: 18.* 🛏 *18.*
AE DC MC V

JAIPUR: *Samode Haveli.*   ℞℞℞℞
Ganga Pol. ☏ *(0141) 263 2407.* FAX *(0141) 263 1397.* w www.samode.com
Built in phases over 200 years, this gracious mansion offers traditional
Rajasthani folk dances and cuisine. Some rooms, with original wall
paintings and mirrorwork, are stunning. 🍴 🛎 TV 🏊 *Rooms: 22.* 🛏 *20.*
AE DC MC V

JAIPUR: *Trident.*   ℞℞℞℞
Opp Jal Mahal, Amer Rd. ☏ *(0141) 267 0101.* FAX *(0141 267 0303.*
@ reservations@tridentjp.com One of the Trident group of hotels, it has high
standards of service and decor, but without doubt its most attractive quality is its
location directly opposite the Jal Mahal. 🍴 24 TV 🏊 *Rooms: 138.* 🛏 *138.*
AE DC MC V

JAIPUR: *Rajvilas Hotel.*   ℞℞℞℞℞
Goner Rd. ☏ *(0141) 268 0101.* FAX *(0141) 268 0202.* @ reservations@rajvilas.com
A spectacular Oberoi chain boutique hotel with impeccable services. Set
in 32 ha of beautiful gardens, each room, luxury tent, and villa with a
private pool is superbly crafted. 🍴 🛎 24 TV 🏊 *Rooms: 71.* 🛏 *71.*
AE DC MC V

JAIPUR: *Rambagh Palace.*   ℞℞℞℞℞
Bhawani Singh Rd. ☏ *(0141) 238 1919.* FAX *(0141) 238 1098.* w www.tajhotels.com
This sumptuous palace-hotel is an all-time favourite, as its interior still
retains much of the original and splendid decor from the time it was the
home of the Jaipur royal family. 🍴 🛎 24 TV 🏊 *Rooms: 90.* 🛏 *90.*
AE DC MC V

JAIPUR: *Welcomgroup Rajputana Sheraton.*   ℞℞℞℞℞
Palace Rd. ☏ *(0141) 510 0100.* FAX *(0141) 510 2102.* w www.welcomgroup.com
A large, elegantly designed hotel, with consistently high standards of
service. Various cultural programmes held in the evenings add to its
attractions. 🍴 🛎 24 TV 🏊 *Rooms: 216.* 🛏 *216.*
AE DC MC V

JHUNJHUNU: *Hotel Jamuna Resort.*   ℞℞
Distt Shekhawati. ☏ *(01592) 23 2871.*
Run by the owner of Shiv Shekhawati, the swimming pool and outdoor
dining area here is open to non-residents. *Rooms: 4.* 🛏 *1.*

JHUNJHUNU: *Shiv Shekhawati Hotel.*   ℞℞
Distt Shekhawati. ☏ *(01592) 23 2651.*
A well-kept clean, *haveli*-style lodge, whose interesting owner is a fund
of knowledge about the history and architecture of the Shekhawati area,
and is happy to share this information with his guests. *Rooms: 16.* 🛏 *7.*

For key to symbols see back flap

Price categories for a standard double room per night including tax and service charges but not including breakfast:

Rs under 550 rupees
Rs Rs 550–1,200 rupees
Rs Rs Rs 1,200–3,000 rupees
Rs Rs Rs Rs 3,000–6,000 rupees
Rs Rs Rs Rs Rs over 6,000 rupees

CREDIT CARDS
Indicates which credit cards are accepted: *AE* American Express; *DC* Diners Club; *MC* Master Card/Access; *V* Visa; *JCB* Japanese Credit Bureau.

WESTERN BATHROOMS
Indicates sit-down, flush toilets; showers and/or baths. Others have squat toilets and bucket-and-mug baths.

COFFEE SHOP
Hotels with coffee shop.

GARDEN/TERRACE
Hotels with a garden, courtyard or terrace.

	CREDIT CARDS	SWIMMING POOL	WESTERN BATHROOMS	COFFEE SHOP	GARDEN/TERRACE

KISHANGARH: *Phool Mahal Palace.* Rs Rs — AE ● ▦ — ▦
Distt Ajmer. **(** (01463) 24 7405. **FAX** (01463) 24 2001.
Beautifully situated on the banks of the lake, this recently restored heritage property is reason enough to opt for an overnight stay in this otherwise modest town. **11 24 TV** *Rooms:* 16. 9.

KISHANGARH: *Roopangarh Fort.* Rs Rs Rs — ▦ ● ▦
Roopangarh, Distt Ajmer. **(** (01497) 22 0217. **FAX** (01497) 22 0191.
@ tis@giasdl01.vsnl.net.in This captivating fortress-turned-hotel is ideally situated for excursions. It also organizes camel or horse safaris, trips for birdwatching, and tours of craft centres. **11 24 TV** *Rooms:* 22. 4.

MANDAWA: *Castle Mandawa.* Rs Rs Rs Rs — AE DC MC V ● ▦ — ▦
Mandawa, Distt Jhunjhunu. **(** (01597) 22 3124. **FAX** (01597) 22 3171.
One of the oldest and most popular heritage hotels in the region, restored with evocative private and public spaces. Its excellent services try to emulate the famed Rajasthani courtly style. **11 24** *Rooms:* 80. 70.

MANDAWA: *The Desert Resort.* Rs Rs Rs Rs — AE MC V ● ▦ — —
Distt Jhunjhunu. **(** (01597) 22 3515. **FAX** (01597) 22 3151.
A quaint resort designed to look like a traditional village, this is an ideal take-off point from Mandawa into the desert. *Rooms:* 60.

MUKUNDGARH: *Mukundgarh Fort.* Rs Rs — ▦ — ▦
Distt Jhunjhunu. **(** (01594) 25 2395. **FAX** (01594) 25 2598.
Located in the heart of the Shekhawati area, this heritage hotel has an interesting bar, but could do with a face-lift. *Rooms:* 48.

NAWALGARH: *Apni Dhani.* Rs Rs — ▦ — ▦
Jhunjhunu Rd, Nawalgarh, Distt Jhunjhunu. **(** (01594) 22 2239. **FAX** (01594) 22 4061.
@ rcjangid@yahoo.com One of the best guides in the region, the owner of this "eco-conscious" resort offers imaginatively-designed thatched mud huts, equipped with baths and solar panel heating. **11** *Rooms:* 10.

NAWALGARH: *Roop Niwas Palace.* Rs Rs Rs — AE ● ▦ — ▦
P O & Vill Nawalgarh, Distt Jhunjhunu. **(** (01594) 22 2008. **FAX** (01594) 22 3388.
This heritage hotel is a charming blend of European and Rajput style architecture. Well-mannered staff add to its gracious atmosphere. Horse and camel tours are a regular feature. **11 24** *Rooms:* 35. 16.

NEEMRANA: *Neemrana Fort Palace.* Rs Rs Rs Rs — AE MC V — ▦ — ▦
Post Neemrana, Distt Alwar. **(** (01494) 24 6006. **FAX** (01494) 24 6005.
W www.neemrana.com Great hospitality awaits you in this vast, imaginatively restored fort palace. The luxury, personal attention and, in season, the live music, are highly recommended. **11** *Rooms:* 42. 42.

PUSHKAR: *Peacock Holiday Resort.* Rs — MC V ● ▦ — ▦
Panchkund Rd, Distt Ajmer. **(** (0145) 277 2093.
@ peacock@datainfosys.net A large shady courtyard adds to the tranquil atmosphere of this temple town hotel. The rooms have attached baths. Special prices are offered during the Pushkar Mela. **11** *Rooms:* 32. 4.

PUSHKAR: *Tourist Village (RTDC).* Rs — ▦ — ▦
Fair Grounds, Distt Ajmer. **(** For reservations: (0145) 277 2074.
W www.rajasthan-tourism.com During the annual camel fair, the government sets up a tented village with about 300 single and double tents at different price ranges that include meals. A few huts are open all year round. **11** *Rooms:* 30.

PUSHKAR: *Sarovar (RTDC).* Rs Rs — ▦ — ▦
Pushkar, Distt Ajmer. **(** (0145) 277 2040. W www.rajasthan-tourism.com
Located near the Pushkar Palace, this state tourism hotel has both rooms and dormitories. It is one of the few places that can organize camel, horse and jeep safaris. **11** *Rooms:* 38. 2.

PUSHKAR: *Pushkar Palace.* (Rs)(Rs)(Rs) MC V
Pushkar Lake, Distt Ajmer. [(0145) 277 2001. FAX (0145) 277 2226.
Beautifully located on the banks of Pushkar Lake, this 400-year-old
palace hotel commands a panoramic view of the town. During the
annual camel fair, tented lodging is available. **11 24 TV** *Rooms: 53.* 53.

PUSHKAR: *Pushkar Resorts.* (Rs)(Rs) MC V
Vill Ganhera, Motisar Rd. [(0145) 277 2017. FAX (0145) 277 2946.
@ pushres@ndf.vsnl.net.in Clusters of luxury cottages with private lawn
space re-create an oasis. An added attraction is the town's only bar.
11 24 TV *Rooms: 40.* 40.

SAMODE: *Samode Bagh.* (Rs)(Rs)(Rs)(Rs) AE MC V
Vill Fathepura, Bansa, Distt Jaipur. [(01423) 24 235. W www.samode.com
Associated with the Samode Palace hotel, the Bagh has luxury tents with
attached baths situated in an idyllic garden which spreads over 20 ha (50
acre). It offers the ambience of a royal desert camp. *Rooms: 44.* 44.

SAMODE: *Samode Palace.* (Rs)(Rs)(Rs)(Rs) AE DC MC V
Distt Jaipur. [(01423) 24 0013. W www.samode.com
A stay in this 400-year-old palatial heritage hotel with exquisite interiors
and modern facilities offers the chance to savour a royal lifestyle. This is
one of the region's finest heritage hotels. **11 24 TV** *Rooms: 43.* 43.

SARISKA: *Tiger Den (RTDC).* (Rs)(Rs)
Alwar-Jaipur Rd, Distt Alwar. [(0144) (95144 from Delhi) 284 1342. FAX (0144) 284 1344.
W www.rajasthan-tourism.com Adjacent to the Sariska sanctuary, this is the only
cheap option for visitors to the park. The dormitories, rooms and services have
fairly acceptable standards of comfort and efficiency. **11 24** *Rooms: 30.* 10.

SARISKA: *Sariska Palace.* (Rs)(Rs)(Rs)
Sariska, Distt Alwar. [(0144) (95144 from Delhi) 284 1322. @ sariska@del2.vsnl.net.in
After a tiring day out in the sanctuary, the palatial comforts of this former
royal hunting lodge are most welcome. Folk songs, dances and a
campfire are offered in the evenings. **11 24 TV** *Rooms: 80.*

SAWAI MADHOPUR: *Castle Jhoomar Baori (RTDC).* (Rs)(Rs)
Ranthambhore Rd. [& FAX (07462) 22 0495. W www.rajasthan-tourism.com
This charming old royal jungle lodge has superb views of the countryside
and is rich in atmosphere. You can even hear tigers roar at night in the
nearby sanctuary. Very much in demand, so book ahead. *Rooms: 12.* 5.

SAWAI MADHOPUR: *Ranthambhore Regency.* (Rs)(Rs) AE DC MC V
Ranthambhore Rd. [(07462) 22 1176. FAX (07462) 22 1672.
A comparatively new hotel, it offers decent rooms and food for
surprisingly good rates. *Rooms: 31.* 4.

SAWAI MADHOPUR: *Sawai Madhopur Lodge.* (Rs)(Rs)(Rs)(Rs)
Ranthambhore Rd. [(07462) 22 0541. FAX (07462) 22 0718. @ smlodge@jp1.dot.net.in
This 1930's lodge of the Jaipur maharaja is far superior to the rest in
town, combining modern comforts with classic style. Several recreational
facilities are available on the premises. **TV** *Rooms: 33.* 29.

SAWAI MADHOPUR: *Sher Bagh.* (Rs)(Rs)(Rs)(Rs)(Rs)
Sherpur Khiljipur. [For reservations: (011) 2331 6534. W www.sherbagh.com
This enchanting tented camp also organizes interesting forest excursions.
Great food, atmosphere and service. **11 Y 24** *Rooms: 12.*

SAWAI MADHOPUR: *Vanya Vilas.* (Rs)(Rs)(Rs)(Rs)(Rs) AE MC V
Ranthambore Rd. [(07462) 22 3999. FAX (07462) 22 3988. W www.oberoihotels.com
The tents in this forest resort have teak floors and marble bathrooms.
There is also a heated pool, an amphitheatre, and guided tours for
guests. **11 Y 24 TV** *Rooms: 25.* 25.

SILISERH: *Lake Palace (RTDC).* (Rs)(Rs)
Siliserh, Distt Alwar. [(0144) 288 6322. W www.rajasthan-tourism.com
Overlooking the lake, this fairytale palace is best for a quiet retreat, with
the promise of glorious sunsets over the tranquil lake waters. Activities
include boating, long walks and birdwatching. *Rooms: 10.* 2.

UNIARA: *Sardar Fort Uniara.* (Rs)
Tonk-Uniara Highway, Distt Tonk. [For reservations: (01436) 26 0351.
Rooms in the sprawling old Uniara palace en route to Sawai Madhopur
have been made habitable again by sons of the former raja. The fort's
peaceful and evocative atmosphere is recommended. *Rooms: 4.* 2.

For key to symbols see back flap

WHERE TO EAT

THE UNIQUE FLAVOURS of Indian food depend heavily on the imaginative blend of spices and use of fresh ingredients. Once, seasonal fruits and vegetables dictated menus in restaurants, so the standard restaurant offered a choice of Mughlai preparations and a sprinkling of colonial fare, such as roast lamb with mint sauce, fried fish, and vegetables *au gratin*. Today, eating habits, especially in Delhi, have become much more sophisticated, and most Indians, when they dine out, prefer food that is quite different from what is cooked at home. The search for new culinary experiences has led to the proliferation of excellent speciality restaurants, fast food and pizza parlours to satisfy all tastes. These newer, fancier, and more cosmopolitan establishments have added to the eating-out scene, but good Indian food, such as succulent kababs, rich aromatic curries, or even the simple dal and *roti* served at *dhabas* still remain popular. The listings of restaurants on pages 256–63 are organized by area to help you choose where and what kind of food you wish to eat.

Chief chef of a five-star Delhi hotel

The stylish Polo Bar at Rambagh Palace Hotel, Jaipur

RESTAURANTS

THERE IS A WIDE choice of places to eat in Delhi, from snack bars in markets to speciality restaurants in luxury hotels. Every commercial area has a large number of eateries, starting with mobile vans which offer low priced sandwiches, burgers and Indian-style Chinese chowmein and soups. South Indian eating places are widespread and good value for money with a wide choice of dishes. Others specialize in the North Indian barbecued and tandoori meats and fish. Most places, however, offer standard Indian breads and curries. Many of the American fast food giants, such as Pizza Hut, McDonalds and Dominos, have already made their appearance in the bigger cities, and are hot favourites with both children and an older crowd. Agra and Jaipur also have a wide range of restaurants, though good Western food is found mainly in the five-star hotels. Here, too, you will find the tempting lunch buffet where you can feast in luxury.

Most restaurants are open from 11am to midnight. It is a good idea to book in advance for the popular gourmet places. Late hour or early meals are best had at the 24-hour coffee shops at hotels.

Sign of an Indian restaurant

SPECIALITY RESTAURANTS

UP-MARKET restaurants specializing in authentic foods from different parts of the world have become very popular, particularly in Delhi, where you have a choice of cuisines from China and Thailand, Japan, Mexico or Italy, prepared by chefs from these countries. Most of these restaurants tend to be in the luxury hotels, though a few independent ones have been opened in places like the Hauz Khas Village in Delhi. Prices may be a bit steep, but the food and stylish decor are worth it. Afghan and Middle Eastern, Kashmiri as well as Tibetan food are also found in selected places.

For Indian specialities, most of the good hotels in the Jaipur region make it a point to include traditional Rajasthani dishes on the menu, while in Delhi and Agra, almost all places will treat you to a delicious Mughal or Punjabi meal prepared from recipes handed down through generations of cooks.

Barbecued foods, a speciality at Bukhara, Maurya Sheraton

Breakfast on the ramparts of Kesroli Fort

COFFEE SHOPS

A̲LL THE BIGGER HOTELS have 24-hour coffee shops where you can get snacks and even light meals. At busy market places, there are coffee shop-like cafés that are open from 10am to midnight offering a menu of refreshments and simple multi-cuisine dishes that may range from Indian to Indianized Western and Chinese. The quality of food is average. It is safer to stick to the more common dishes, and to avoid fish and prawns here.

ROADSIDE AND MARKET FOOD STALLS

I̲F YOU ARE adventurous, the roadside food stalls or *dhabas* offer a typically Indian meal with a choice of a couple of basic curries, more often than not vegetarian, and *rotis* hot from the fire. However, do remember that the dishes are made to suit an Indian palate that prefers hot spicy food, and when ordering, insist that your meal is made with a minimum of spices. It is also advisable to eat at stalls which appear to have a rapid turnover as the food will be freshly cooked. For health precautions see page 286.

You could also try the Indian-style savoury- and sweet shops. The choice of sweets is overwhelming; syrupy at times, but delicious. The snacks are often deep-fried such as potato and flour fingerlings, or a variety of spiced nuts. Indian-style

Chinese fried chowmein is a great favourite in these places. Indian cities are fast becoming tourist savvy, with market food stalls offering a greater variety of Western-style soups, salads, as well as bakery products, and with the menus almost always in English.

VEGETARIANS

T̲HERE IS A superb tradition of vegetarian cooking in India. Most of the roadside food stalls are strictly vegetarian, and all three cities have good vegetarian restaurants, which include the ubiquitous South Indian eateries that also offer vegetarian *thalis*. Some of them display a sign that says: "Cooked in pure ghee", or "Cooked in ghee made from cow's milk" which is meant to reassure hardcore vegetarians.

A special salad buffet

WINE AND DRINKS

T̲HERE ARE STRICT restrictions on serving alcohol in the Delhi, Agra, Jaipur region, and only some restaurants and hotels with a liquor permit are allowed to serve alcoholic drinks, though there are liquor shops in all cities. A few places are licensed to serve only beer. Most larger hotels have their own bars and serve both "Indian Made Foreign Liquor" (whisky, rum, gin, vodka and beer), as well as many foreign brands, at a price. Indian wines are few, but some excellent foreign wines are available. Drinking your own liquor in a restaurant is not permitted. The 1st and 7th of each month, national holidays and notified election days are "dry days".

PRICES AND TIPPING

P̲RICES ARE fixed everywhere, even at the roadside stalls. At luxury hotels the rates are high and there will be added taxes, but eating at most restaurants and coffee shops in the city is generally affordable, and at the roadside stalls, it is positively cheap. The prices are always listed on the menu and you should check that the figures are right on your bill. Waiters do expect to be tipped, and ten per cent of the bill is appropriate.

A roadside tea stall in Rajasthan

What to Eat

THE FOOD of the Delhi, Agra and Jaipur region is a hybrid cuisine which has grown out of several traditions, techniques and flavours. Its chief influences are the classic Mughal cuisine born in the imperial kitchens, and the vegetarian food of the orthodox Bania (mercantile) community. The British Raj added its own culinary influences, which helped popularize the ubiquitous "Indian curry" in the West. Today, the piquant flavours of cuisine from all over India are on offer together with a range of South Asian and European dishes in top-end restaurants.

Idli *and* dosa, *the popular South Indian steamed rice cakes and crisp pancakes, served with coconut chutney and a spicy lentil curry are a national breakfast favourite.*

Aloo-poori, *a potato curry eaten with puffed deep-fried bread* (poori) *makes a good breakfast or lunch dish.*

***Stuffed* parathas** *are pan-fried breads stuffed with vegetables or mince, eaten with yoghurt and pickles.*

Nihari *is a breakfast stew of shank meat and bone marrow, traditionally slow cooked all night on embers.*

***Soups**, a later addition to Indian cuisine, include the favourite Anglo-Indian Mulligatawny, and* Shorba, *literally the stock of meat or vegetables flavoured with spices.*

Mulligatawny, a dal and meat soup with tamarind

***Shorba*, a meat, tomato or vegetable broth**

TANDOORI PLATTER

The *tandoor*, a clay oven from Central Asia, has generated a kind of barbecued cuisine now popular all over the world. Meats, fish and vegetables are marinated in yoghurt and spices and grilled on skewers.

Cauliflower (*gobbi*)

Leg of lamb (*raan*)

Seekh kabab

Vegetable rings

Cottage cheese (*paneer*)

Vegetarian platter *has a selection of marinated vegetables grilled on a skewer in the* tandoor.

Chicken

Chicken tikkas

Meat and poultry platter *offers a mixed grill served with a twist of lemon and onion rings.*

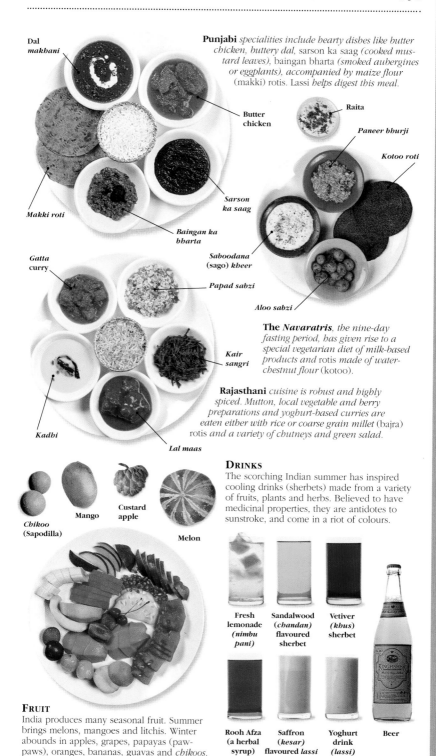

Punjabi *specialities include hearty dishes like butter chicken, buttery dal, sarson ka saag (cooked mustard leaves), baingan bharta (smoked aubergines or eggplants), accompanied by maize flour* (makki) rotis. Lassi *helps digest this meal.*

Dal makhani

Butter chicken

Raita

Paneer bhurji

Kotoo roti

Sarson ka saag

Makki roti

Baingan ka bharta

Saboodana (sago) kheer

Gatta curry

Papad sabzi

Aloo sabzi

The **Navaratris**, *the nine-day fasting period, has given rise to a special vegetarian diet of milk-based products and rotis made of water-chestnut flour (kotoo).*

Kair sangri

Rajasthani *cuisine is robust and highly spiced. Mutton, local vegetable and berry preparations and yoghurt-based curries are eaten either with rice or coarse grain millet (bajra) rotis and a variety of chutneys and green salad.*

Kadhi

Lal maas

Chikoo (Sapodilla)

Mango

Custard apple

Melon

DRINKS
The scorching Indian summer has inspired cooling drinks (sherbets) made from a variety of fruits, plants and herbs. Believed to have medicinal properties, they are antidotes to sunstroke, and come in a riot of colours.

Fresh lemonade (*nimbu pani*)

Sandalwood (*chandan*) flavoured sherbet

Vetiver (*khus*) sherbet

FRUIT
India produces many seasonal fruit. Summer brings melons, mangoes and litchis. Winter abounds in apples, grapes, papayas (pawpaws), oranges, bananas, guavas and *chikoos*.

Rooh Afza (a herbal syrup)

Saffron (*kesar*) flavoured *lassi*

Yoghurt drink (*lassi*)

Beer

The Indian Thali

TRADITIONAL INDIAN MEALS are served on a platter *(thali)* with small bowls *(katoris)* of meat, vegetables and lentils. Pickles, chutneys, a *raita* (whipped yoghurt) and *papads* are typical accompaniments that enhance the flavour of the main dishes. Many types of unleavened bread are served along with rice, either steamed or as an aromatic *pulao*. The meal is best eaten with the fingers of the right hand, and rounded off with a dessert and *paan*.

Curry

This Western brand name for meat or vegetables cooked in an onion and tomato or curd based sauce, hardly describes its spicy variations.

Mutton curry

Kadhai murg

Korma

Dal

Rajma

Yellow dal

Chhola

Dal

A generic name for lentils, India has several variations of this protein-rich dish. Dals are tempered with onions, garlic and ginger or asafoetida and cumin to make them digestible. Rajma (red beans) and chhola (chick peas) are cooked in a similar way.

Roti

Rice

Biryani

Pulao

Rice

Although steamed rice may be eaten every day, the biryani (slow-cooked with meat and spices in clay pots) and the vegetarian pulao, a variation, are served on special occasions.

Paan

The betel leaf and nut (supari), silver-coated cloves and cardamoms are traditional digestives eaten after a heavy meal.

Vegetables

Vegetables (sabzi) *are usually braised in seasoned oil, most popularly in combination with potatoes, but there are other, more exotic offerings such as jackfruit* (kathal) *and okra* (bhindi), *which are cooked with spices and usually with tomatoes.*

Khumb matar

Paneer makhani

Malai kofta

Aloo gobhi

Mixed vegetables

Bhindi

Accompaniments

Raitas, *salads,* chutneys, papads *and pickles are served with every meal as savoury accompaniments to complement the rich and spicy flavours of the main dishes.*

Mint chutney

Pickled onions

Pickled garlic

Raita

Green chilli

Tamarind sauce

Sweets

Indian sweets are commonly made of milk and elaborately decorated with fine sheets of beaten silver. Sprinkled with rose-water and nuts, they round off the perfect festive meal.

Kesari phirni

Kulfi kesari falooda

Gulab jamun

Rasmalai

ROTIS

Breads (*rotis*), leavened or unleavened, made of flour, have different textures and names. They are served along with main dishes and help to scoop the food into the mouth.

Papad

Pudina paratha

Khasta roti

Naan

Bakarkhani

Ajwain paratha

A Glossary of Typical Indian Food

T HE ESSENCE OF TRADITIONAL Indian food
lies in the infinite variations in the
blending and combination of a variety
of spices. Chillies need not be used
and, in fact, are often regarded as the
inputs of a poor cook who uses
them to camouflage the lack of
subtlety in his seasonings. A
typical menu in the region
includes meat, lentils,
vegetables and *tandoori* dishes,
accompanied by rice and *rotis*. Street
food is extremely popular with locals,
and consists of savoury snacks, eaten
through the day.

Jamuns, a
monsoon fruit

SNACKS

Sweet and savoury snacks are
an important part of the
Indian diet.

Aloo tikki
Stuffed potato cutlet
cooked on a griddle.

Chaat
The most popular
items are *papri*, made
of fritters, chickpeas,
potatoes, yoghurt and
spicy sauces; and *gol-
guppas*, puffed flour
crisps filled with
cumin spiced water
and chickpeas.

Jalebi
Crisp golden coils of
flour batter dipped in
a rose-flavoured syrup.

Pakora
Vegetables or cottage cheese
fried in gramflour batter.

*Skewered
tikkas*

The *chaat-wallah's* variety of savouries
served in mouth-watering combinations

Samosa
Deep-fried pastry
triangles filled with
spiced potatoes and peas.

TANDOORI FOOD

The *tandoor* is a clay
oven that looks like an
upturned pot with a
coal fire. Skewered
meats and vegetables
are barbecued in it,
and *rotis* are baked on
its inner walls.

Kababs
Seekh kababs are
flavoured minced lamb
skewered in a long,
tubular shape. Chicken
variations include the
reshmi and *tangri* kababs. For
the vegetarian, a *seekh* kabab
made of spiced vegetables
has been created.

Raan
Leg of lamb cooked in
yoghurt and spices.

Tandoori murg
A whole chicken
(*murg*) marinated in
yoghurt and specially
flavoured spices.

Tandoori salad
Lightly marinated and
grilled vegetables,
such as cauliflower,
potatoes, onions, okra
and capsicum.

Tikkas
Marinated and char-
grilled small chunks of
chicken, mutton, fish
and cottage cheese.
The *burra* kabab is
meat with bone from
the rib, prepared in
the same way.

MAIN NON-VEGETARIAN DISHES

Often spicy and rich, these
are among the most delicious
examples of Indian cuisine.

Bhuna gosht
A dry meat curry, stir-
fried slowly till
tender.

**Butter
chicken**
Tandoori
chicken with
a tomato and
butter sauce.

Kadhai murg
A succulent
chicken curry stir-
fried in a wok.

Rogan josh, a
meat dish

Lal maas
A Rajasthani mutton
dish cooked with red
chillies. A variation is *safed
maas*, a "white" curry with
almonds and cashewnuts.

Mutton or **chicken korma**
Braised meat or chicken
cooked on a slow fire with
yoghurt and spices.

Rogan josh
Cubes of mutton cooked with
red chillies and spices.

Saag gosht
Meat cooked with spinach.

Red chilli

Curry leaves
and *masur* dal

VEGETARIAN DISHES

Traditionally, only seasonal
vegetables (*sabzi*) were used,
limiting the choice of dishes.

Aloo gobhi
Potatoes (*aloo*) cooked with
cauliflower (*gobhi*) and ginger.

Aloo methi
Browned potatoes and
fenugreek (*methi*) leaves.

Baingan ka bharta
Smoked aubergine puréed
with onions and tomatoes.

Bhindi piaz
Okra and onions (seasonal).

Dum aloo
Potatoes with yoghurt and
spices cooked over low heat.

Gatta curry
Gramflour dumplings in a
delicate, aromatic sauce.

A streetside restaurant specializing in *parathas*

SWEETS

Sweets are mainly milk-based.
Gajar ka halwa
Grated carrots cooked in milk and sugar and browned with pistachios and almonds.
Gulab jamun
Deep-fried milk and flour dumplings in a thick syrup.
Kulfi
Hand-churned ice-cream flavoured with pistachios.
Phirni
A Mughlai riceflour pudding, flavoured with saffron (*kesar*).
Rabri
Thickened milk and sugar garnished with nuts.
Rasmalai
A flatter version of the *rasgulla* (*paneer* balls in a thin syrup) in a mildly flavoured creamy sauce.

Gajar ka Halwa

Kadhi
Fried gramflour dumplings cooked in a yoghurt and gramflour-thickened sauce.
Kair sangri
Small local berries cooked with spinach-like leaves.
Khumb-matar curry
A mushroom and pea curry.
Malai kofta
Cottage cheese dumplings in a thick tomato gravy.
Masala baingan
Stuffed aubergines (eggplants) braised in oil.
Paneer
Paneer (cottage cheese), an all time favourite, is cooked in a variety of combinations. *Palak paneer* is with spinach, and *matar paneer* with peas.
Paneer makhani
Cottage cheese in a tomato and butter sauce.
Sarson ka saag
Mustard leaves cooked in milk and served in a puréed form with butter.

LENTILS

Chhola Bhatura

Dal, a lentil curry, is the staple meal. *Masur* and *moong* are two varieties.
Chhola bhatura
Chickpeas thickly coated with a spicy sauce eaten with a puffed, deep-fried bread.
Dal makhani
Unhulled dal cooked in cream and butter.
Rajma curry
A red kidney-bean curry.
Sambhar
A South Indian speciality made with *arhar* dal and a special curry powder.

BREADS

Common breads cooked on a griddle are the *chapati*, paper-thin *roomali roti* and *paratha*. *Pooris* are deep fried, while *tandoori* breads include the *tandoori* and *khastha roti* and *naan*.

RICE

Biryanis and *pulaos* are eaten with *raitas* (whipped yoghurt mixed with onions, tomatoes, coriander and green chillies), and a wide range of pickles and chutneys.
Biryani
Mutton or chicken korma is layered with rice, cooked on a slow charcoal fire, and flavoured with saffron.
Navratan pulao
Rice cooked with nine types of vegetables.
Yakhni pulao
Rice and mutton cooked in stock flavoured with aniseed and whole spices.

DRINKS

Elaichi chai
Flavoured cardamom tea.
Lassi
Whipped yoghurt shake.
Nimbu pani
Fresh, sweetened or salted lime juice with water or soda.
Panna
Peeled raw mango boiled, puréed, and mixed in water with salt, sugar and cumin.
Sherbet
A flavoured sweet drink.

PAAN

Betel leaf packed with areca nut, lime (*catechu*) paste, and other ingredients such as cardamoms and cloves.

***Paan*, a good digestive, can be made to suit individual tastes**

Choosing a Restaurant

THE RESTAURANTS in this guide have been selected to suit a wide price range and many are in recommended hotels. Chosen for their exceptional food, good value, and convenient or interesting location, they are listed region-wise. Map references refer to the Delhi Street Finder maps on pages 124–131. Colour-coded thumb tabs show the areas covered on each page.

	CREDIT CARDS	REGIONAL SPECIALITIES	PURE VEGETARIAN	WESTERN DISHES	OUTDOOR TABLES
DELHI					
NEW DELHI: *Triveni Tea Terrace.* **Map** 2 D5. Triveni Kala Sangam, Tansen Marg. (011) 2371 8833. An ideal place if you wish to enjoy an inexpensive alfresco lunch under flowering creepers in the heart of Delhi's cultural centre. *B, L.*	Rs				■
NEW DELHI: *Bercos.* **Map** 1 C4. E–8 Connaught Place. (011) 2341 8134. Good for a quick and inexpensive Indian or Chinese meal in a busy shopping area, this restaurant is packed to capacity at lunchtime. Crispy honey chicken and double fried pork are a speciality. *L, D.*	Rs Rs	AE DC MC V			
NEW DELHI: *Coconut Grove.* **Map** 5 A1. Indraprastha Hotel, 19 Ashok Rd. (011) 2334 4511. The menu has a varied selection of vegetarian and non-vegetarian South Indian cuisine. The buttermilk is recommended, as is *meen pappas*, a light, mildly spiced fresh fish curry from Kerala. *L, D.*	Rs Rs	MC V	●		
NEW DELHI: *Have More.* **Map** 5 B3. 11–12 Pandara Rd Market. (011) 2338 7070. For those who wish to savour a hearty meal of North Indian food served Punjabi style, this is one of many such Delhi eateries. Located in an unassuming small market that comes alive in the evenings. *L, D.*	Rs Rs	AE DC MC V	●		
NEW DELHI: *Kwality.* **Map** 1 C5. Regal Building, Connaught Place. (011) 2374 2310. The *chhola bhaturas* (spicy chickpeas and deep-fried puffed bread) is an all-time Punjabi favourite in this centrally-located restaurant. *L, D.*	Rs Rs	AE DC MC V	●		
NEW DELHI: *Chinese Room.* **Map** 1 C4. Nirula's Hotel, L Block, Connaught Circus. (011) 5151 7070. Despite the slightly dated Oriental decor, it has kept up with the times with Byte, its new cyber bar. Outpaced since by more accomplished restaurants, it still has a charming ambience. *L, D.*	Rs Rs Rs	DC MC V			
NEW DELHI: *DV8.* **Map** 1 C5. 13 Regal Building, Connaught Place. (011) 2336 3358. Multi-cuisine food along with a lively bar. Happy hours are between 4 and 8pm daily, and there is a "drinks only night" on Wednesdays when you can drink all you want for a fixed price. *L, D.*	Rs Rs Rs	AE DC MC V		●	
NEW DELHI: *Gaylords.* **Map** 1 C5. Regal Building, Connaught Place. (011) 2336 0717. Known for its cold coffee with ice cream, a central location makes this restaurant a popular meeting place at lunchtime. *L, D.*	Rs Rs Rs	AE DC MC V		●	
NEW DELHI: *The Lodi.* **Map** 5 A5. Lodi Rd. (011) 2465 2808. Located in the historic Lodi Gardens, this atmospheric restaurant offers Mediterranean cuisine. Its specialities include lamb Moroccan, Mezze platter and Rainbow trout. Vegetarian food is also available on order. *L, D.*	Rs Rs Rs	AE MC DC V		●	■
NEW DELHI: *The Rampur Kitchen.* **Map** 5 B3. Khan Market. (011) 2463 1222. This cheerful little eatery with speciality food from the princely state of Rampur makes a great place to stop for lunch between shopping and browsing in Khan Market. *L, D.*	Rs Rs Rs	MC V	●		
NEW DELHI: *Dhaba.* **Map** 5 A3. Claridges, 12 Aurangzeb Rd. (011) 2301 0211. Inspired by the popular roadside eateries that line North India's highways, Dhaba offers a range of fresh and spicy food. *L, D.*	Rs Rs Rs Rs	AE MC DC V	●		

Price categories for a meal for one, including tax and service charges but not alcohol:

Rs — under 100 rupees
RsRs — 100–200 rupees
RsRsRs — 200–400 rupees
RsRsRsRs — 400–700 rupees
RsRsRsRsRs — over 700 rupees

CREDIT CARDS
Indicates that major credit cards are accepted.

REGIONAL SPECIALITIES
Specialized cuisine is served from regions of India, such as Rajasthan, Gujarat or South India.

PURE VEGETARIAN
Restaurant serving only vegetarian food.

WESTERN DISHES
French, Italian or other Western fare is on the menu.

OUTDOOR TABLES
Tables for eating outdoors, often with a good view.

	CREDIT CARDS	REGIONAL SPECIALITIES	PURE VEGETARIAN	WESTERN DISHES	OUTDOOR TABLES
NEW DELHI: *Baan Thai*. Map 6 D4. RsRsRsRs The Oberoi, Dr Zakir Hussain Marg. (011) 2436 3030. The authentic Thai food in this top-notch restaurant is served with great style. Guests have an interesting choice of Western or traditional Thai floor-seating arrangements. L, D.	AE DC MC V				
NEW DELHI: *Baluchi*. Map 2 D5. RsRsRsRsRs Grand Intercontinental, Barakhamba Ave. (011) 2341 1001. A fashionable restaurant that specializes in delectable tandoori fare (charcoal grills in a clay oven) from the North-West Frontier region. Live music is played every evening. L, D.	AE DC MC V	●			
NEW DELHI: *Daniells' Tavern*. Map 1 C5. RsRsRsRsRs Imperial Hotel, Janpath. (011) 2334 1234. Original Daniells' lithographs of late 18th-century India create a charming Raj-era ambience in this restaurant, whose specialities include duck and steak, cooked in both Indian and European styles. L, D.	AE DC MC V	●		●	
NEW DELHI: *House of Ming*. Map 5 B3. RsRsRsRsRs Taj Mahal Hotel, Mansingh Rd. (011) 2302 6162. Hailed as the restaurant with the best Chinese cuisine in town. This is now a favourite with those who can afford its expensive cuisine impeccably served in a fashionable setting. L, D.	AE MC DC V				
NEW DELHI: *Kandahar*. Map 5 B3. RsRsRsRsRs The Oberoi, Dr Zakir Hussain Marg. (011) 2436 3030. Famed for its creative and wide selection of traditional Indian and Frontier food, Chef Pankaj prepares delicious meals for both vegetarians and non-vegetarians. Live Indian music in the evenings. D.	AE DC MC V	●			
NEW DELHI: *La Rochelle*. Map 6 D4. RsRsRsRsRs The Oberoi, Dr Zakir Hussain Marg. (011) 2436 3030. Continental food is served here in very elegant surroundings. Excellent value lunch buffet with live jazz on Sundays. Superb seafood, delicious salads and cheeses. L, D.	AE DC MC V			●	
NEW DELHI: *Latino Bar*. Map 1 C5. RsRsRsRsRs The Park, Parliament St. (011) 2374 3000. One of the few restaurants that serves Spanish and Middle-Eastern food. Its lavish meals are accompanied by a selection of fine wines. D.	AE DC MC V			●	
NEW DELHI: *Spice Route*. Map 1 C5. RsRsRsRsRs Imperial Hotel, Janpath. (011) 2334 1234. Its dramatic decor serves as an evocative backdrop to the wide range of spicy cuisine offered here with dishes from Kerala to Indonesia. The jumbo prawns here are scrumptious. Book ahead. L, D.	AE MC DC V	●			
NEW DELHI: *The Blue Elephant*. Map 2 D5. RsRsRsRsRs Grand Inter-Continental, Barakhamba Ave. (011) 2341 1001. Eclectic Thai cooking in an elegant restaurant that offers many speciality cuisines. The atmosphere here is warm and welcoming. L, D.	AE DC MC V				
NIZAMUDDIN: *Karim's*. Map 6 D5. RsRsRs Jha House, Hazrat Nizamuddin West. (011) 2435 8300. A branch of the renowned Old Delhi eatery, Karim's offers authentic Muslim cuisine, delectable kababs and "ishtoo" (stew). ● Mon, Ids and during Ramzan (see p37), only dinner is served. L, D.	AE DC MC V	●			
OLD DELHI: *Chor Bizarre*. Map 2 E3. RsRs Hotel Broadway, Asaf Ali Rd. (011) 2327 3821. This quaint restaurant, decorated with unusual antiques, is famous for its authentic Kashmiri cuisine. *Koftas* and *Haak* (spinach) are perennial favourites. L, D.	AE DC MC V	●			

	CREDIT CARDS	REGIONAL SPECIALITIES	PURE VEGETARIAN	WESTERN DISHES	OUTDOOR TABLES

Price categories for a meal for one, including tax and service charges but not alcohol:

(Rs) under 100 rupees
(Rs)(Rs) 100–200 rupees
(Rs)(Rs)(Rs) 200–400 rupees
(Rs)(Rs)(Rs)(Rs) 400–700 rupees
(Rs)(Rs)(Rs)(Rs)(Rs) over 700 rupees

CREDIT CARDS
Indicates that major credit cards are accepted.
REGIONAL SPECIALITIES
Specialized cuisine is served from regions of India, such as Rajasthan, Gujarat or South India.
PURE VEGETARIAN
Restaurant serving only vegetarian food.
WESTERN DISHES
French, Italian or other Western fare is on the menu.
OUTDOOR TABLES
Tables for eating outdoors, often with a good view.

Restaurant	Price	Credit Cards	Regional Specialities	Pure Vegetarian	Western Dishes	Outdoor Tables
OLD DELHI: *Karim's.* **Map** 2 E2. Opp Jami Masjid. ((011) 2326 4981. Located in the heart of a historic area for close to a century, superlative kababs and "ishtoo" (stew) have been their specialities. ☰ ○ *B, L, D.* ● Mon, Ids and during Ramzan *(see p37),* only dinner is served.	(Rs)(Rs)(Rs)	AE DC MC V	●			
FURTHER AFIELD (WEST): *Sagar Ratna.* Ashok Hotel, Chanakyapuri. ((011) 2611 0101. An up-market branch of a popular restaurant in south Delhi, this serves delicious South Indian food in a more leisurely style. ☰ ○ *L, D.*	(Rs)(Rs)(Rs)	AE DC MC V	●	■		
FURTHER AFIELD (WEST): *Kumgang.* Ashok Hotel, Chanakyapuri. ((011) 2611 0101. This is the only restaurant in the city that serves Korean food, prepared in traditional style. The bar also serves *sake.* ☰ ▼ ○ *L, D.*	(Rs)(Rs)(Rs)(Rs)	AE DC MC V				
FURTHER AFIELD (WEST): *Basil & Thyme.* **Map** 4 E4. Santushti Complex, Chanakyapuri. ((011) 2467 4933. Light Western food, with special daily menus, makes this charmingly located eatery a popular lunching spot. ☰ ○ *L.* ● Sun.	(Rs)(Rs)(Rs)(Rs)	AE DC MC V			●	
FURTHER AFIELD (WEST): *Bukhara.* Maurya Sheraton, Sardar Patel Marg, Diplomatic Enclave. ((011) 2611 2233. Delhi's most famous restaurant for food from the North-West Frontier offers outstanding barbequed chops, skewered chicken, fish or cottage cheese, with a variety of delicious breads. ☰ ▼ ▼ ○ *B, L, D.*	(Rs)(Rs)(Rs)(Rs)(Rs)	AE DC MC V	●			
FURTHER AFIELD (WEST): *China Town.* Ashok Hotel, Chanakyapuri. ((011) 2611 0101. This speciality restaurant offers delicious Chinese food, accompanied by live music on all days of the week except Tuesday. ☰ ▼ ○ *L, D.*	(Rs)(Rs)(Rs)(Rs)(Rs)	AE DC MC V				
FURTHER AFIELD (WEST): *Dum Pukht.* Maurya Sheraton, Sardar Patel Marg, Diplomatic Enclave. ((011) 2611 2233. Master chef Imtiaz Kureishi's *dum* cuisine, lovingly cooked over a slow fire, produces the best biryanis and kakori kababs in town. Also highly recommended are king prawns with pomegranates. ☰ ▼ ▼ ○ *D.*	(Rs)(Rs)(Rs)(Rs)(Rs)	AE DC MC V	●			
FURTHER AFIELD (WEST): *Tea House of the August Moon.* Taj Palace, Sardar Patel Marg, Diplomatic Enclave. ((011) 2611 0202. An eclectic mix of great Japanese and Chinese food with delicious starters is served in a dramatic Oriental setting. ☰ ▼ ▼ ○ *L, D.*	(Rs)(Rs)(Rs)(Rs)(Rs)	AE DC MC V				
FURTHER AFIELD (WEST): *The Orient Express.* Taj Palace, Sardar Patel Marg, Diplomatic Enclave. ((011) 2611 0202. Intimate table settings in a "dining compartment" of the legendary Orient Express, where delectable but expensive Western cuisine and wine are stylishly served by attentive waiters. ☰ ▼ ▼ ○ *L, D. Sun dinner only.*	(Rs)(Rs)(Rs)(Rs)(Rs)	AE DC MC V			●	
FURTHER AFIELD (SOUTH): *Sagar.* Defence Colony Market. ((011) 2462 1451. The fresh and tasty South Indian food served here is so popular that clients often have to queue up for a table. ☰ ○ *B, L, D.*	(Rs)(Rs)			●	■	
FURTHER AFIELD (SOUTH): *Flavours.* Moolchand Flyover, Bank Complex. ((011) 2464 5644. This cheerful eatery is run by an Italian who personally rustles up imaginative pastas, salads and dreamy desserts. ☰ ○ *L, D.*	(Rs)(Rs)(Rs)	AE MC V			●	■
FURTHER AFIELD (SOUTH): *Park Baluchi.* Inside Deer Park, Hauz Khas Village. ((011) 2685 9369. Enchanting sylvan surroundings add to the taste of succulent roasts and chargrills from traditional recipes of the frontier areas. ☰ ▼ ○ *L, D.*	(Rs)(Rs)(Rs)	AE DC MC V	●			■

FURTHER AFIELD (SOUTH): *Swagath.* ⓇⓈⓇⓈⓇⓈ
Defence Colony Market. 🎧 (011) 2465 4537.
This speciality restaurant serves excellent non-vegetarian South Indian food. The fish curries in particular are delicious. ▤ ◖ *L, D.*
AE DC MC V

FURTHER AFIELD (SOUTH): *Dehli Ke Aangan.* ⓇⓈⓇⓈⓇⓈⓇⓈ
Hyatt Regency, Bhikaji Cama Place, Ring Rd. 🎧 (011) 2679 1234.
This restaurant offers Old Delhi's superb Kayastha cuisine in a five-star ambience from a menu devised by the famous Indian chef Jiggs Kalra. A gourmet kabab brunch is offered on weekends. ▤ 🍷 🍴 ◖ *L, D.*
AE DC MC V

FURTHER AFIELD (SOUTH): *Diva.* ⓇⓈⓇⓈⓇⓈⓇⓈ
M-8 Greater Kailash Part II (M-Block Market). 🎧 (011) 2621 5673.
One of Delhi's finest Italian restaurants, Diva's specialities range from pastas and pizzas to grilled lamb chops and seafood. ▤ ◖ *L, D.*
AE MC V

FURTHER AFIELD (SOUTH): *La Piazza.* ⓇⓈⓇⓈⓇⓈⓇⓈ
Hyatt Regency, Bhikaji Cama Place, Ring Rd. 🎧 (011) 2679 1234.
This fancy Italian restaurant uses ingredients that are flown in specially from Italy to be prepared in its open kitchen in full view of its clients. Its Sunday brunches are very popular. Book in advance. ▤ 🍷 🍴 ◖ *L, D.*
AE DC MC V

FURTHER AFIELD (SOUTH): *TK's.* ⓇⓈⓇⓈⓇⓈⓇⓈ
Hyatt Regency, Bhikaji Cama Place, Ring Rd. 🎧 (011) 2679 1234.
Famed for its Japanese barbequed delicacies, the special brunch each Sunday with free champagne is a treat. ▤ 🍷 ◖ *L, D.*
AE DC MC V

FURTHER AFIELD (SOUTH): *Village Bistro.* ⓇⓈⓇⓈⓇⓈⓇⓈ
Hauz Khas Village, Near Deer Park. 🎧 (011) 2685 2227.
This is a part of a restaurant complex overlooking the Hauz Khas Deer Park. *Tawa*, its rooftop section, serves barbequed fare. ▤ ◖ *L, D.*
AE DC MC V

FURTHER AFIELD (SOUTH): *Great Kebab Factory.* ⓇⓈⓇⓈⓇⓈⓇⓈⓇⓈ
Hotel Radisson, National Highway 8, Mahipalpur. 🎧 (011) 2677 9191.
Nearly 150 types of delicious kababs to please both meat eaters and vegetarians are served here by attentive waiters. One can eat as much as one wants at a fixed price. ▤ 🍷 ◖ *D.*
AE DC MC V

FURTHER AFIELD (SOUTH): *Seventy Seven.* ⓇⓈⓇⓈⓇⓈⓇⓈⓇⓈ
The Manor, Friends Colony West. 🎧 (011) 2692 5151.
This elegant and understated restaurant in a small exclusive hotel specializes in nouvelle cuisine and such delicacies as Norwegian salmon. The decor is minimalist chic. ▤ 🍷 ◖ *D.*
AE DC MC V

FURTHER AFIELD (SOUTH OF DELHI): *Zafran.* ⓇⓈⓇⓈⓇⓈ
The Bristol Hotel, Gurgaon–Faridabad Rd. 🎧 (0124) (95124 from Delhi) 235 6030.
The restaurant serves an exotic *samudri badshah* (tandoori lobster) and tandoori duck to a background of live music. ▤ 🍷 ◖ *L, D.*
AE DC MC V

NORTH OF DELHI

HARIDWAR: *Ahaar.* ⓇⓈ
Upper Rd. 🎧 No telephone.
A variety of cuisines, such as Punjabi, South Indian and Chinese, are offered here. The ice-cream parlour also has a variety of flavours. ◖ *L, D.*

HARIDWAR: *Bestee.* ⓇⓈ
Shiv Murti Chowk, Jassa Ram Rd. 🎧 (01334) 22 7210.
Good breakfasts may be had here, although the restaurant is more famous for its tasty snacks, milk shakes and seasonal fruit *lassis*. ◖ *L, D.*

HARIDWAR: *Chinkara Hills.* ⓇⓈ
Haridwar Rishikesh Rd, Raiwala, Distt Dehradun. 🎧 (0135) 248 4361.
This mid-way halt offers quick snacks to tourists en-route to Haridwar. The attraction is the promise of non-vegetarian food and liquor, both banned in Haridwar, that are available here. ◖ *B, L, D.*

HARIDWAR: *Mid-way Resorts.* ⓇⓈ
Near Raiwala Railway Bridge, Rishikesh-Haridwar Rd. 🎧 (0135) 248 4208.
Essentially a tourist stop, good for a quick drink and snack. 🍷 ◖ *B, L, D.*

HARIDWAR: *Shivalik.* ⓇⓈ
Station Rd. 🎧 No telephone.
Specialising in Gujarati food from West India, Indian, Western and the ubiquitous "Chinese" dishes are also available here. ◖ *B, L, D.*

For key to symbols see back flap

	CREDIT CARDS	REGIONAL SPECIALITIES	PURE VEGETARIAN	WESTERN DISHES	OUTDOOR TABLES

Price categories for a meal for one, including tax and service charges but not alcohol:

Rs under 100 rupees
Rs Rs 100–200 rupees
Rs Rs Rs 200–400 rupees
Rs Rs Rs Rs 400–700 rupees
Rs Rs Rs Rs Rs over 700 rupees

CREDIT CARDS
Indicates that major credit cards are accepted.
REGIONAL SPECIALITIES
Specialized cuisine is served from regions of India, such as Rajasthan, Gujarat or South India.
PURE VEGETARIAN
Restaurant serving only vegetarian food.
WESTERN DISHES
French, Italian or other Western fare is on the menu.
OUTDOOR TABLES
Tables for eating outdoors, often with a good view.

Restaurant	Rs	Credit	Regional	Pure Veg	Western	Outdoor
RISHIKESH: *Anjali.* Railway Rd. ((0135) 243 1779. This down-to-earth eatery provides standard Indian fare at very reasonable prices. ▤ ◐ *B, L, D.*	Rs		●	■		
RISHIKESH: *Chotiwala.* Swarg Ashram, Across Shivanand Jhula. ((0135) 243 0070. A rooftop restaurant that is part of a popular chain in the region, it prepares delicious *thali* meals for orthodox Hindu pilgrims. ◐ *B, L, D.*	Rs	MC		■		
RISHIKESH: *Neelam.* Laxman Jhula Rd. (No telephone. Bland Western food, such as soups, macaroni and rice pudding offered here, makes this eatery a change from the usual "pilgrim fare". ◐ *B, L, D.*	Rs			■	●	
ROORKEE: *Cheetal Grand.* Delhi-Mussoorie Rd, Khatauli. ((01396) 27 2468. This pleasantly landscaped restaurant-cum-hotel, midway between Meerut and Roorkee, serves quick, hot meals courteously. ▤ ◐ *B, L, D.*	Rs				●	■
AROUND AGRA						
AGRA: *Only Restaurant.* 45 Taj Ganj Rd. ((0562) 222 6834. The reliable if pedestrian Indian, Western and Chinese food served here is accompanied by live Indian music in the evenings. ▤ ◐ *L, D.*	Rs	AE DC MC V	●		●	
AGRA: *Dasaprakash.* Meher Theatre Complex, Balu Ganj, Gwalior Rd. ((0562) 236 3535. The restaurant, run by a reputed chain, specializes in hygienically cooked, reasonably priced vegetarian South Indian food. ▤ ◐ *B, L, D.*	Rs Rs	MC V	●	■	●	
AGRA: *Pizza Hut.* 8 Handicrafts Nagar, Fatehbad Rd. ((0562) 233 3051. For those who cannot stay away too long from American fast food, this familiar and popular restaurant is a comforting sight. ▤ ◐ *L, D.*	Rs Rs	AE DC MC V			●	
AGRA: *The Park.* 183 Taj Rd, Sadar Bazaar. ((0562) 222 5849. This new restaurant serves Indian, Chinese and Continental cuisine. Be sure to try their speciality *tikka labadar*. Outdoor seating can be arranged for guests on request. ▤ ◐ *B, L, D.*	Rs Rs				●	■
AGRA: *Bagh-E-Bahar.* Welcomgroup Mughal Sheraton, Taj Ganj. ((0562) 233 1722. An attractive restaurant with Continental fare, good and lively Western music at night. ▤ ▮ ◐ *B, L, D.*	Rs Rs Rs	AE MC DC V	●		●	■
AGRA: *Olive Garden.* Holiday Inn. ((0562) 252 3460. This multi-cuisine restaurant's speciality is the buffet served for breakfast, lunch and dinner, although it does have an à la carte option as well. It also offers a wonderful garden view. ▤ ◐ *B, L, D.*	Rs Rs Rs	AE MC V			●	
AGRA: *Taj Bano.* Welcomgroup Mughal Sheraton, Taj Ganj. ((0562) 233 1722. No snacks here, but complete meals from a wide choice of cuisines are accompanied by a live sitar recital at lunch and dinner. ▤ ▮ ◐ *B, L, D.*	Rs Rs Rs	AE MC DC V	●		●	
BHARATPUR: *Hotel Pelican.* Near National Park entrance. ((05644) 2242 4221. The restaurant in this hotel serves Indian and Western food, and there is a surprising, but modest selection of Israeli dishes. ◐ *B, L, D.*	Rs				●	■

BHARATPUR: *Spoonbill.* (Rs)(Rs)
Behind RTDC Hotel Saras. ((05644) 22 3571.
This popular, thatched garden eatery offers Indian and Chinese food, and
on winter evenings there is a welcoming campfire. ○ *B, L, D.*

BHARATPUR: *Bharatpur Forest Lodge.* (Rs)(Rs)(Rs) | MC V
Inside the National Park. ((05644) 22 2722.
Attached to the pleasant hotel inside the park, this state-run restaurant
has sumptuous buffets laid on for hungry birdwatchers. ▤ ○ *B, L, D.*

BRINDAVAN: *ISKCON Bhojanalaya.* (Rs)
Bhakti Vedanta Swami Marg, Raman Reti. ((0565) 254 0021.
A part of the clean and hygienic ISKCON guesthouse, wholesome
vegetarian food at good prices is served here. ▤ ○ *B, L, D.*

FATEHPUR SIKRI: *Kallu Hotel.* (Rs)
Below Buland Darwaza. (No telephone.
The colourful owner, Kallu, is a local institution and amiably presides
over hearty *paranthas* and omelettes, or a spicy meat curry. ○ *B, L, D.*

FATEHPUR SIKRI: *Shere Punjab.* (Rs)
Bypass Rd. ((05613) 28 2238.
A little way from the famous archaeological site, this roadside eatery is
the place for a satisfying Punjabi *dhaba*-style meal. ○ *B, L, D.*

FATEHPUR SIKRI: *Gulistan Tourist Complex.* (Rs)(Rs) | AE DC
Fatehpur Sikri Complex. ((05613) 28 2490.
The cheery environs of this garden restaurant enhance its varied menu. It is
popular with tourists looking for a suitable stopover point. ▤ ▾ ○ *L, D.*

GWALIOR: *Volga.* (Rs)
Jayendraganj, Lashkar. ((0751) 232 1092.
This old Gwalior restaurant lives up to its reputation as one of the best
Indian food places in the city. ▤ ▾ ○ *L, D.* ● Diwali & Holi.

GWALIOR: *Kwality.* (Rs)(Rs) | AE MC V
M L B Rd, Deen Dayal Market. ((0751) 242 3243.
One of Gwalior's most popular restaurants, Kwality specializes in Indian
cuisine - their *kakori* chicken is a particular favourite. ▤ ○ *L, D.*

MEERUT: *Alfa.* (Rs)(Rs)
Bombay Bazaar, Meerut Cantt. ((0121) 266 0532.
The garlic and mustard flavoured *tikkas* are recommended. ▤ ○ *L, D.*

ORCHHA: *Kaleva.* (Rs)(Rs)(Rs) | AE MC V
The Orchha Resort, Kanchana Ghat, Tikamgarh. ((07680) 52 677.
Imaginatively designed and conveniently located, this restaurant offers a
choice of both buffet and à la carte meals. ▤ ○ *B, L, D.*

ORCHHA: *Sheesh Mahal.* (Rs)(Rs)(Rs) | AE MC V
Orchha, Distt Tikamgarh. ((07680) 25 2624.
Located within the Jahangiri Mahal, the fortifying breakfasts and buffet
dinners here are served romantically on the terrace. ▤ ▾ ○ *B, L, D.*

AROUND JAIPUR

AJMER: *Bhola Hotel.* (Rs)
Agra Gate, Subzi Mandi. ((0145) 243 2844.
The restaurant section of a hotel, this is a good place for vegetarian food,
especially the *thali* which constitutes a complete meal. ○ *B, L, D.*

AJMER: *Honeydew.* (Rs)
Near KEM Resthouse, Station Rd. ((0145) 262 2498.
Popular with tourists, this fast-food restaurant serves Indian-style burgers
and pizzas and a deliciously cooling banana *lassi.* ▤ ▾ ○ *B, L, D.*

ALWAR: *Hotel Aravalli.* (Rs)(Rs)
Near Railway Station. ((0144) (95144 from Delhi) 233 2883.
This restaurant with an attached bar serves standard Indian and Indian-
style Chinese dishes. ▤ ▾ ○ *B, L, D.*

ALWAR: *Prem Hotel.* (Rs)(Rs)
Off Hope Circle. ((0144) (95144 from Delhi) 233 5284.
An unpretentious vegetarian eatery with reasonably priced snacks, the
speciality here is their inexpensive *thali* meal. ○ *B, L, D.*

Price categories for a meal for one, including tax and service charges but not alcohol:

(Rs) under 100 rupees
(Rs)(Rs) 100–200 rupees
(Rs)(Rs)(Rs) 200–400 rupees
(Rs)(Rs)(Rs)(Rs) 400–700 rupees
(Rs)(Rs)(Rs)(Rs)(Rs) over 700 rupees

CREDIT CARDS
Indicates that major credit cards are accepted.

REGIONAL SPECIALITIES
Specialized cuisine is served from regions of India, such as Rajasthan, Gujarat or South India.

PURE VEGETARIAN
Restaurant serving only vegetarian food.

WESTERN DISHES
French, Italian or other Western fare is on the menu.

OUTDOOR TABLES
Tables for eating outdoors, often with a good view.

Restaurant	Price	Credit Cards	Regional Specialities	Pure Vegetarian	Western Dishes	Outdoor Tables
JAIPUR: *Bake Hut.* Near Niros, Mirza Ismail Rd. (0141) 237 7136. The name says it all: you will find oven-fresh take-away breads, croissants, pastries, doughnuts and other such treats here. L, D.	(Rs)			■	●	
JAIPUR: *Chaitanya Restaurant.* City Centre, Sansar Chandra Rd. (0141) 237 5584. Chinese and Western-style vegetarian dishes with innovative touches are offered here. The restaurant also serves various fast foods and has an attached ice-cream parlour. Holi & Diwali. L, D.	(Rs)	AE MC V	●	■	●	
JAIPUR: *Indian Coffee House.* Mirza Ismail Rd. (0141) 236 2024. The aroma of freshly ground coffee will lead you straight here for the best cup in town. Run by a well-known chain, a modest range of snacks and decent breakfast options are also available. B, L, D.	(Rs)			■		
JAIPUR: *Lassiwala.* Opp Niros, Mirza Ismail Rd. No telephone. You will have to queue up here for the irresistible North Indian *lassi*, a thick, creamy, sweet or salty drink made of curds, variously flavoured and served in terracotta tumblers. L, D.	(Rs)					
JAIPUR: *Rajasthan Motel.* Jaipur-Agra Highway, Mahuwa. (07461) 23 3210. A highly recommended mid-way stop for the hungry bus or car traveller on the Jaipur-Agra road. B, L, D.	(Rs)	AE MC V	●		●	■
JAIPUR: *Motel Behror (RTDC).* Jaipur-Delhi Highway, Behror. (01494) 22 0049. This pure vegetarian restaurant is run by the state's tourism department. Its speciality is the Rajasthani *thali*. B, L, D.	(Rs)			●	■	
JAIPUR: *Bhuwaneshwari.* Bissau Palace Hotel, Outside Chand Pol. (0141) 230 4371. Located in a grand palace setting, this restaurant offers authentic Rajasthani delicacies served with style. B, L, D.	(Rs)(Rs)	AE DC MC V	●		●	■
JAIPUR: *Copper Chimney.* Opp GPO, Mirza Ismail Rd. (0141) 237 2275. High standards of hygiene and service distinguish this Kwality chain restaurant which has a good selection of traditional and local dishes, such as the spicy *lal maas*, a Rajasthani mutton dish. B, L, D.	(Rs)(Rs)	AE DC MC V	●		●	
JAIPUR: *Golden Dragon.* Hotel Imperial Building, Mirza Ismail Rd. (0141) 237 8651. A pleasant garden restaurant that mainly offers Chinese food, though there is also a selection of Indian and Western dishes. L, D.	(Rs)(Rs)	AE DC MC V	●		●	■
JAIPUR: *Gulab Mahal.* Jai Mahal Palace Hotel, Civil Lines. (0141) 222 3636. Elegant service and surroundings. The restaurant is reputed for its Rajasthani *thali* and juicy, garlic flavoured chicken *tikkas*. B, L, D.	(Rs)(Rs)	AE DC MC V	●		●	
JAIPUR: *Handi Restaurant.* Mirza Ismail Rd. (0141) 236 4839. A tandoori food establishment with stylish variations of barbequed dishes. Their chicken and *tikkas* are worth trying. L, D.	(Rs)(Rs)		●		●	■
JAIPUR: *Niros.* Mirza Ismail Rd. (0141) 237 4493. This hugely popular eating place offers Indian, Continental and Chinese food. A favourite is the refreshing American ice-cream soda. L, D.	(Rs)(Rs)	AE DC MC V	●		●	

JAIPUR: *Shiva Oasis.* ⓇⓈⓇⓈ AE
Delhi-Jaipur National Highway 8, Behror. **(** *(01494) 22 2102.*
A limited selection of basic dishes are offered at this mid-way roadside
stop on the busy Delhi-Jaipur highway. 🍽 🌙 *B, L, D.*

JAIPUR: *Surya Mahal.* ⓇⓈⓇⓈ MC
Near Niros, Mirza Ismail Rd. **(** *(0141) 511 2412.* V
This multi-cuisine restaurant specializes in Rajasthani food, and serves a
delicious *kulcha* and *paneer.* 🍽 🌙 *B, L, D.*

JAIPUR: *Laxmi Misthan Bhandar (LMB).* ⓇⓈⓇⓈⓇⓈ AE
Johari Bazaar. **(** *(0141) 256 5844.* MC
Jaipur's most famous vegetarian restaurant, it also has the largest V
selection of Indian sweets made by its traditional *halwais.* 🍽 🌙 *B, L, D.*

JAIPUR: *Nahargarh Fort.* ⓇⓈⓇⓈⓇⓈ
Nahargarh. **(** *(0141) 510 4844.*
A good place to enjoy a stunning sunset view of Jaipur city over a
steaming cup of coffee or a cool sundowner. This little restaurant
overlooks the magnificent fort of Nahargarh. 🌙 *L, D.*

JAIPUR: *Dhola Maro.* ⓇⓈⓇⓈⓇⓈ AE
Hotel Clarks Amer, Jawaharlal Nehru Marg. **(** *(0141) 255 0616.* DC
This restaurant is popular for its *ghazals* held every day except Thursday. MC
The grilled chicken is delicious. 🍽 🍸 🌙 *D.* V

JAIPUR: *Shivir.* ⓇⓈⓇⓈⓇⓈ AE
Hotel Mansingh, Sansar Chandra Rd. **(** *(0141) 238 7771.* DC
A wonderful view of the city is available from this rooftop restaurant of MC
the centrally located Mansingh Hotel. There is an excellent range of *thali* V
meals along with traditional Rajasthani dishes. 🍽 🌙 *L, D.*

NAWALGARH: *Apani Dhani.* ⓇⓈⓇⓈ
Jhunjhunu Rd, Nawalgarh, Shekhawati. **(** *(01594) 22 2239.*
In this exceptionally designed Eco Farm you will be served wholesome
vegetarian food made from garden-fresh vegetables organically grown on
the premises, to be eaten in a traditional Indian style. 🌙 *L, D.*

NAWALGARH: *Roop Niwas Palace.* ⓇⓈⓇⓈⓇⓈ
1 km from Nawalgarh Fort. **(** *(01594) 22 2008.*
Vegetarian, non-vegetarian and special Rajasthani meals from a fixed
menu are served here. This is a good place to refresh yourself after an
expedition to the Nawalgarh Fort. 🌙 *L, D.*

NEEMRANA: *Amaltasse.* ⓇⓈⓇⓈⓇⓈⓇⓈ
Neemrana Fort, Neemrana. **(** *(01494) 24 6007.*
In the enchanting environs of the magnificent Neemrana Heritage Hotel,
this unusual French restaurant offers a gourmet four-course candle-lit
dinner that is worth the drive from Delhi. Book ahead. 🍽 🍸 🌙 *L, D.*

PUSHKAR: *Om Shiva.* ⓇⓈ
Opp State Bank of Bikaner & Jaipur, Mahadev Chowk. **(** *(0145) 277 2647.*
One of the few places in Pushkar that offers an excellent breakfast, a
good buffet meal, and a great view of the temple town. 🌙 *B, L, D.*

PUSHKAR: *Sun-n-Moon.* ⓇⓈ
Near Brahma Temple. **(** *(0145) 277 2883.*
This open-air restaurant caters to the foreign traveller with a selected
menu of Western dishes that includes a delicious apple pie. 🌙 *B, L, D.*

PUSHKAR: *Sunset Café.* ⓇⓈ
Hotel Pushkar Inns, Sunset Point. **(** *(0145) 277 2725.*
Its scenic position near the lake makes it a good place to enjoy a light
Indian or Western snack, especially at sunset, when crowds gather here.
Try the selection of pancakes on offer. 🌙 *L, D.*

PUSHKAR: *Raja Garden Restaurant.* ⓇⓈⓇⓈ AE
Near Main Bazaar. **(** *(0145) 277 2722.* MC
Located near the bazaar, this restaurant specializes in Western fare and an V
inexplicable supply of Marmite! Do try their cheese *naan.* 🌙 *B, L, D.*

PUSHKAR: *Pushkar Palace.* ⓇⓈⓇⓈⓇⓈ AE
Eastern side of Pushkar Lake. **(** *(0145) 277 2001.* MC
Prices here are relatively high for Pushkar, but the ambience, the buffet V
and other meals justify the rates. 🍽 🌙 *L, D.*

SHOPS AND MARKETS

THE COLOURFUL MARKETS of the region carry a vast and exciting range of handicrafts. The government-run state emporia are well stocked with merchandise at fixed and reasonable rates. Shopping arcades of larger hotels cater to travellers who are hard-pressed for time, though their more sophisticated boutiques are usually pricier. For the more adventurous, there are the street

Puppet

stalls and bazaars that offer glimpses of local colour, and where bargaining is a way of life. Delhi has some of the region's most elegant shops (see pp118–19), but the charming bazaars of Jaipur and Agra offer visitors a chance to actually observe skilful craftsmen at work. In the smaller towns beyond the main cities, local crafts are often sold in quaint village stores or on the roadside.

Pavement hawkers in Jaipur

OPENING HOURS

MOST SHOPS usually open at 10am and shut down by 7:30pm, though the smaller markets keep longer hours. The government-run emporia close an hour earlier. Markets for fresh produce open at dawn and stay open until late evening, while the temporary bazaars that spring up at different localities on festivals or particular week days gather the crowds until late at night. In Jaipur and Agra, the closing day is Sunday, but in

Delhi, each locality has its own weekly holiday. Shopping centres in the New Delhi area are closed on Sundays, but in South Delhi and Karol Bagh, the closing days are Monday or Tuesday. By law all shops are required to remain closed on the three main national holidays, that is, Republic Day (26 Jan), Independence Day (15 Aug) and Mahatma Gandhi's birthday (Martyr's Day, 2 Oct).

HOW TO PAY

THE RUPEE is accepted everywhere. The bigger stores accept international credit cards such as VISA, MasterCard, American Express and Diners, and usually display signs prominently inside the shops. But they are still not very common in the smaller shops and towns, and it is always sensible to keep some cash handy when travelling. Traveller's cheques can be encashed at local branches of the State Bank of India (see p288), but again, this facility may not be available in the smaller towns.

Bright glass and plastic bangles

BARGAINING

BARGAINING is an essential part of the shopping experience in India, and at the smaller markets, prices are quoted with the expectation that customers will haggle. Some of the most familiar scenes at all bazaars are those of local shoppers indulging in long and often acrimonious discussions with shopkeepers about price and quality. Most shopkeepers are tourist savvy today and will usually quote a higher price to foreigners. The best way to check out prices is to browse through a fixed-price shop like a government emporium. This will also give you an idea of quality. However, the price you offer to pay should be realistic and not so low that you miss out on a good purchase altogether. If this price is still unacceptable to the shopkeeper, an old and usually very effective bargaining tactic is to walk away feigning indifference.

All the bigger and fancier shops and boutiques, retail outlets of manufacturers and the government emporia have fixed prices with no scope for bargaining. Increasingly, in fact, more shops are tagging their goods with labels that clearly indicate item prices.

Attractive terracotta pots, which are incredibly cheap yet durable

Paper kite stall in Jaipur

RIGHTS AND REFUNDS

BY LAW ALL SHOPS are obliged to give you a receipt or cash memo for all purchases. When buying insist on getting one to which sales tax, generally seven or ten per cent of the total cost, has been added. Often the shopkeeper will say that you can save on the tax if you do not take a receipt, but do insist on one nevertheless. Refunds or the exchange of damaged goods are impossible without one and it is absolutely essential for the more expensive purchases. Bigger shops can be fussy about taking back goods but you can talk to the manager if absolutely necessary.

Delicately inlaid marble

If the shop is going to ship your purchases, make sure that you know all the costs involved, including taxes. Also, insist that all the paperwork is done correctly and you have copies of it all. If you wish you can also ship the larger purchases yourself through the international courier services *(see p291)*.

ANTIQUES

ANTIQUES and art objects that are more than a hundred years old cannot be taken out of the country. If in doubt about your purchases, consult the office of the Archaeological Survey of India *(see p279)*. You should also get a certificate from the shop stating the age of the artifact.

TOUTS

IN THE LARGER MARKETS that are frequented by tourists, persistent touts can be a problem. Ignore the offers of fantastic bargains because the prices you pay are often suspect. Also beware of polite young men inviting you home for a cup of tea because "home" will be a shop down the lane. Tourist buses will of course stop at their selected shops but you don't have to buy anything from them. Try to shop for expensive things at big shops with price tags on their goods and beware of of shops with "government-approved" boards as these are usually private enterprises.

BAZAARS

A VISIT to a traditional Indian bazaar is worth the experience rather than the actual shopping. These lively places offer fantastic bargains and a colourful atmosphere. Most bazaars are located in the heart of the old cities, where narrow lanes are lined with rows of shops selling a variety of merchandise from car spare-parts, machinery, cooking utensils and provisions to textiles and jewellery. Vegetables and other fresh produce are sold on the roadside. Most cities also have the weekly bazaars, and rural India has seasonal *haats* that travel from village to village for the local people to shop for everything from

agricultural equipment to clothes to pots and pans. The bazaars in Agra and Jaipur were originally craft guilds and some still specialize in specific local crafts such as textiles, jewellery, marble inlay and leatherwork, where you can watch the craftsmen at work, admire their skills and buy directly from them.

A streetside stall where bargaining skills are essential

GOVERNMENT EMPORIA

THE CENTRAL GOVERNMENT and the state governments all run shops selling handicrafts and handloom textiles that are special to their region or state. The prices are fixed and the products genuine. Rajasthali, the Rajasthan emporium, concentrates on handicrafts from Jaipur. While Delhi is a centre for emporia from all the states, neither Agra nor Jaipur offer the same range of regional products. October is a good time for bargains and discounts.

Roadsides flooded with colourful, seasonal fruit

Anokhi, Jaipur, combining traditional designs with modern-day use

SHOPPING IN AGRA

THE EXQUISITE *pietra dura* work on the Taj Mahal is still practised in Agra by descendants of craftsmen who worked on the historic monument. Replicas of the delicate semi-precious stone inlay designs are found on marble and alabaster boxes and bowls, tabletops, chess-boards and trays readily available in Agra's bazaars. Large wall panels and ornate sofa backs can be made to order and shipped directly abroad. Plain marble, red sandstone and soapstone items are also popular. Another beautiful craft is *zardozi* embroidery done on silk or velvet with gold and silver thread and sequins to create dress material, bags, jackets and shoes.

Agra is renowned for its shoe industry. The designs are somewhat basic, but the shoes are sturdy and certainly worth their price.

You can also shop for cotton *dhurries* woven in modern or traditional designs.

NORTH OF DELHI

SMALLER TOWNS near Delhi have their own craft specialities. There are several weaving centres producing pile carpets which are sent to Delhi and other cities to be sold. **Panipat** is famous for its attractive cotton floor coverings and woven home furnishings. In **Saharanpur**, you will find all kinds of woodcarved items in intricate designs and brass inlay work ranging from tables and screens to boxes and ashtrays.

SHOPPING IN JAIPUR

JAIPUR IS TRULY a shopper's paradise. The range of textiles and handicrafts available here includes an irresistible selection of fabrics (embroidered, block-printed, tie-and-dyed), as well as ready-made garments. Rolls of colourful quilts in light layered cotton, but surprisingly warm, are piled high on streetside shops, and government emporia and larger shops stock the beautiful Mughal designed woollen carpets that are made in Jaipur. The city is known for its jewellery which ranges from folk designs in silver to the elegant and more pricey gold jewellery in *meenakari* and *kundan* work *(see p187)*.

Jaipur blue pottery

There is also a wide variety of handmade leather goods from *jootis* and bags to saddles and wallets, while in furniture, there is a dazzling choice of carved and painted tables, chairs, screens, wall brackets, candle and lamp stands.

Jaipur was a centre of miniature painting, and artists now sell perfect reproductions at a fraction of the price of originals. Both the religious *pichhwai* and the narrative *phad* cloth paintings make wonderful wall hangings. Blue pottery is another of Jaipur's traditional crafts, using delicate Persian, Turkish and Indian designs on vases, door-knobs and tiles.

AROUND JAIPUR

BOTH SANGANER and Bagru *(see p204)* are famous for their blockprinted textiles dyed in vegetable colours. In Rajasthan every village has its own artisans. The cobblers produce brightly decorated sandals and bags, potters mould clay into delightful terracotta bowls and plates, and the wood-carver will have wide-eyed puppets hanging on the walls of his workshop. The village markets teem with brightly dressed men and women responding to the cajoling and loud calls of hawkers. Among the traditional metal cooking pots and modern clothes made of synthetic fabric, there are toys and trinkets, lacquer bangles and silver jewellery.

Weaving a carpet on a traditional pit-loom

DIRECTORY

GOVERNMENT EMPORIA

Oswal Emporium
30 Munoro Rd, Sadar Bazaar, Agra.
(0562) 222 5710.

Handloom House
MI Rd, Jaipur.
(0141) 236 5331.

Khadi Ghar
MI Rd, Jaipur.
(0141) 237 3745.

Rajasthali
Govt Hostel, MI Rd, Jaipur.
(0141) 236 7176.

Rajasthan State Handloom Dev. Corp. Ltd.
Chomu House, Jaipur.
(0141) 236 5559.

JEWELLERY

Koh-i-Noor
41 MG Rd, Agra.
(0562) 236 4156.

Munshi Ganeshi Lal & Son
9 MG Rd, Agra.
(0562) 233 0168.

Amrapali
Tholia Building, MI Rd, Jaipur.
(0141) 237 5802.

Bhuramal Rajmal Surana
Johari Bazaar, Jaipur.
(0141) 256 0628.

Dwarka's
H 20 Bhagat Singh Marg, C Scheme, Jaipur.
(0141) 236 0301.

Gem Palace
MI Rd, Jaipur.
(0141) 237 4175.

Surana Jewellers
B 73, Surana Encl, Jaipur.
(0141) 237 2544.

Silver Mountain
Chameli Mkt, Jaipur.
(0141) 237 7399.

TEXTILES

Anokhi
2 Tilak Marg, Jaipur.
(0141) 275 0860.

Naika
Tholia Building, MI Rd, Jaipur.
(0141) 236 2664.

Rashid
Shri Govind Dev Colony, Tal Katora Rd, Jaipur.
(0141) 231 3237.

Shilpi Handicrafts
Near Siliberi, Sanganer.
(0141) 273 1106.

Soma Shop
5 Jacob Rd, Civil Lines, Jaipur.
(0141) 222 2778.

EMBROIDERED TEXTILES

Indian Crafts Gallery
Fatehabad Rd, Agra.
(0562) 223 0336.

Thar Inc.
65, Mathur Vaishya Nagar, Tonk Rd, Jaipur.
(0141) 255 4617.

CARPETS AND DHURRIES

Kanu Carpet Factory
18/160/1-A, Purani Mandi Taj Ganj, Agra.
(0562) 233 0167.

Ambika Exports
Moti Doongri Rd, Jaipur.
(0141) 260 9821.

Ankur Exports
Opp Rambagh Palace, BS Rd, Jaipur.
(0141) 274 1853.

Shyam Ahuja
Rambagh Palace, Jaipur.
(0141) 226 4691.

Siddharth Carpet Mfg Co
Barwara House, Jacob Rd, Jaipur.
(0141) 238 4981.

PAINTINGS AND OBJETS D'ART

Shree Ganpati Arts
S-17 Golimar Garden, Amer Rd, Jaipur.
(0141) 267 2212.

Expo Plus
Prithviraj Rd, Jaipur.
(0141) 238 3044.

Juneja Art Gallery
Lakshmi Complex, MI Rd, Jaipur.
(0141) 236 7448.

Ved Pal Sharma Banno
Chanakya Marg, Subhas Chowk, Jaipur.
(0141) 260 3450.

BLUE POTTERY

Kripal Singh Shekhawat
B 18a Siva Marg, Bani Park, Jaipur.
(0141) 220 1127 (by prior appointment).

HANDMADE PAPER

Salim's Paper
Gramodyog Rd, Sanganer.
(0141) 273 0076.

BOOKS, TEA AND SPICES

Saroj Handicrafts and Arts
A-2 Tilak Marg, C-Scheme, Nandanam Apts, Jaipur.
(0141) 511 0927.

Maharaja Exports
Fatehabad Rd, Agra.
(0562) 233 4117.

Anukamba Mansion
MI Road, Jaipur.
(0141) 236 4682.

Books Corner
MI Road, Jaipur.
(0141) 236 6323.

The Book Shop
Rambagh Palace, Bhawani Singh Rd, Jaipur.
(0141) 238 1430.

SHOES

Yogi Shoes & Leather Crafts
Fatehabad Rd, Agra.
(0562) 233 0029.

Bharat Boot House
Johari Bazaar, Jaipur.
(0141) 256 4914.

Fancy Nagara Shoe Store
Ramganj Bazaar, Jaipur.
(0141) 261 3291.

MARBLE INLAY

Ganesi Lal International
Clarks Shiraz, Agra.
(0562) 226 4691.

Indo Cottage Industres
6 Fatehabad Rd, Agra.
(0562) 233 0232.

UP Handicrafts Complex
Fatehabad Road, Agra.
(0562) 233 1666.

BAZAARS

Agra
Johari Bazaar
Cotton *dhurries.*

Kinari Bazaar
Jewellery and *zari* work.

Taj Ganj
Marble inlay.

Jaipur
Johari Bazaar, Gopalji ka Rasta, Haldiyon ka Rasta
Jewellery and tie-and-dye textiles.

Khajanewalon ka Rasta
Marble carving.

Kishanpol Bazaar
Tie-and-dye textiles.

Maniharon ka Rasta
Lac bangles.

Nehru Bazaar
Embroidered *jootis.*

Ramganj Bazaar
Shoes.

What to Buy

THE BAZAARS, MARKETS and boutiques of Delhi, Agra and Jaipur showcase the wide range of the region's arts and crafts. In many places there is the joy of watching artisans at work and buying directly from them. The quality can vary, but the range is unbelievable, from exotic, aromatic spices, to ceramics and handicrafts, carpets, textiles and jewellery. There are also elegant contemporary interpretations of traditional design.

A bronze monkey

Jewelled and enamelled armband

Jewellery

Antique and jewellery shops stock exquisite pieces of gem-encrusted kundan *and enamelled* meenakari *jewellery. Also available are the silver ornaments worn by local men and women.*

Silver anklets, bracelet and armband

Hand-crafted cutlery

A pencil holder

Metal

Bronze and brass objects of everyday use, such as pots, lamps or boxes, are widely available along with an exciting range of artifacts in silver and other metals created by contemporary designers.

A goblet in mixed metal

Brass pots (lotas)

Silver fan (pankha)

Pottery

Abundant earthenware vessels and toys made by local potters can be seen stacked along the roadside. Commonly found are a sophisticated range of patterned tableware from Khurja, and Jaipur's famous blue pottery.

Door-knobs

Terracotta votive figure

Tiles with floral motifs

Jaipur blue pottery jar with lid

A folk animal in terracotta

Textiles

Blockprints and silk and cotton woven textiles in a dazzling choice of colours and designs can be bought as yardage or ready-made garments, scarves and saris. Floor coverings are either the thick pile carpets or the colourful cotton dhurries *used in Indian homes.*

Pile carpet with floral design

Window blinds

Scarves by Abraham & Thakore

Light-weight cotton quilts

Joss sticks (agarbatti)

Herbal Products

Traditional natural remedies have been re-invented to suit the contemporary need for eco-friendly cosmetics, soothing oils and lotions, tea and joss sticks.

Neem oil

Traditional perfumes (attar)

Soap

Lemon hairwash

Herbal tea

Handicrafts

Materials such as handmade paper, leather, stone and wood are used to make decorative and functional objects such as shoes, plates, boxes and puppets.

Handmade paper box

Embroidered slippers

ENTERTAINMENT

EXCEPT FOR DELHI, which offers a wide range of cultural entertainment round the year *(see pp120-21)*, options in most other cities are often restricted to the cultural fare offered by the hotels. Although both Agra and Jaipur have a strong tradition of folk and classical performing arts, these can

Folk entertainer

only be seen during the peak season. One reason for this is that most Indians prefer to spend their evenings or holidays with the family. As outings invariably include children, the cinema is a favourite, while religious festivals, which offer free entertainment, are also popular. However, dining out is a rising fad among the urban elite.

INFORMATION SOURCES

YOUR TRAVEL AGENT is the best source of information on what is happening, where and when. Otherwise, calendars of cultural events are available from the tourist offices and also at hotels. Local newspapers also list daily events and advertise major cultural festivals, such as the Taj Mahotsav *(see p40)*. Small tourist oriented local publications, such as *Jaipur Vision*, available at book shops and hotel receptions, also carry listings of cinemas, restaurants and bars, swimming pools and shops.

BOOKING TICKETS

ALL THE LARGER HOTELS in the region have regular evening performances of classical music and dance in their main restaurants. The dinner cover charge usually includes the performance. But if a show at a theatre or hall is

announced, the tickets are available at the venue and your hotel or travel agent will be able to book them for you.

CLASSICAL MUSIC AND DANCE

KATHAK and Hindustani music *(see p28)* flourished in this region, patronized first by the Mughal, and later by the regional courts. In an attempt to revive these traditional art forms, classical dance and music festivals are now held regularly in the cities during the peak tourist season sponsored by various cultural organizations. Among auditoria, the **Sur Sadan** in Agra, and in Jaipur, **Ravindra Manch** and **Panghat** are the most popular venues, while on special occasions, well-known dancers also perform before the main deity of the Govind Dev Temple in Jaipur. In Mathura and Brindavan the religious festivals of Holi and Janmashtami also attract classical dancers and singers.

A Rajasthani folk dancer

The devotional Sufi qawwali, originally based on the classical *raga* idiom *(see p28)*, is now a popular concert form. However, the best places to hear authentic qawwalis are at the Sufi shrines at Ajmer and Fatehpur Sikri where they are a daily ritual, while during the Urs festivities, special all-night soirées are held.

FOLK THEATRE, MUSIC AND DANCE

FEW AREAS in this region can match the colour and vibrancy of Rajasthan's indigenous folk forms. Sadly, folk theatre and itinerant storytellers like the *phad* bards are fast losing their audiences and can often only be seen in smaller places. Yet, since Jaipur is the capital of the state, some of the best bards and dancers come here to perform at urban centres such as the **Jawahar Kala Kendra**. The *ghumar* dance, performed by women during religious festivals and

The *bhopa* musicians performing round a campfire

weddings, and the *kalbelia* or snake dance of a nomadic tribe can be seen at hotel shows. Folk singers, such as the *bhopas*, the Manganiyars or Langas, come regularly to the Pushkar Fair and smaller towns, attracting people with their rich and expressive repertoire of folk ballads.

During the Janmashtami festival (Aug–Sep) the Raslila, an enactment of the story of Lord Krishna, is held in the Brajbhumi area of Brindavan and Mathura *(see p162)*. Local Ramlilas *(see p37)*, are staged all over North India during Dussehra (Oct–Nov). These folk productions, often loud and melodramatic, have a unique vivacity and charm.

PUPPET SHOWS

PUPPETRY IS a strong folk tradition practised by the Bhatt pastoral community in Rajasthan. String puppets, called *kathputlis,* play out heroic stories of popular folk and legendary characters. The romance of Dhola and Maru, royal lovers who were separated only a few weeks after they were betrothed but finally united, is one of the most popular puppet shows. The riveting performances of these travelling puppeteers is seen at every fair and festival.

CINEMAS

CINEMA IS still the country's most popular form of entertainment, and even the smallest town has a theatre screening the latest Hindi blockbuster. Jaipur's cinema halls are famous, and the **Raj Mandir**, actually a theatre hall with a flamboyantly kitschy interior, even screens World Cup cricket matches! Indian films are a fantastic mix of action and romance, song and dance, shot in fabulous sets and locales. The films range from the crass to the brilliant.

Dubbing in Hindi of Western mega-hits is the new rage, with films like *Star Wars* and *The World is Not Enough* taking the lead. Though art films have won many international awards, and directors such as Satyajit Ray are considered among the world's best, their films are rarely shown commercially. Nevertheless, a visit to the local cinema will give you an insight into the Indian people's most frequented form of popular entertainment.

Crowds jostling for tickets to a Hollywood mega-hit dubbed in Hindi

NIGHTLIFE AND BARS

EXCEPT FOR THE five-star hotels, options for nightlife in Agra and Jaipur are limited. The luxury hotels all have their own bars where there is a good choice of both local and foreign liquors and the atmosphere is pleasant. A few other places in both the cities are licensed to have bars. The choice of spirits is limited but the atmosphere is lively.

DIRECTORY

PERFORMING ART CENTRES

Sur Sadan
Mahatma Gandhi Rd, Agra.
(0562) 215 4498.

Birla Auditorium
Statue Circle, Jaipur.
(0141) 236 4051.

Jawahar Kala Kendra
Jawaharlal Nehru Marg, Jaipur.
(0141) 270 6501.

Panghat
Rambagh Palace,
Bhawani Singh Rd, Jaipur.
(0141) 238 1919.

Ram Niwas Bagh
Behind Central Museum, Jaipur.
(0141) 256 5244.

Ravindra Manch
JN Marg, Jaipur.
(0141) 238 2343.

Welcomgroup Rajputana Palace Sheraton
Palace Rd, Jaipur.
(0141) 2510 0100.

CINEMAS

Anjana
MG Rd, Agra.
(0562) 215 0371.

Sanjay Talkies
Sanjay Place, Agra.
(0562) 215 0384.

Shree
MG Road, Agra.
(0562) 252 4685.

Ankur
Jaipur.
(0141) 260 0531.

Laxmi Mandir
Jaipur.
(0141) 274 1504.

Man Prakash
Jaipur.
(0141) 256 3123.

Moti Mahal
Jaipur.
(0141) 220 1723.

Prem Prakash Talkies
Jaipur.
(0141) 256 5083.

Raj Mandir
Jaipur.
(0141) 237 9372.

BARS

Cheeta
Hotel Jaipur Ashok, Jaipur.
(0141) 220 4491.

Polo Bar
Rambagh Palace,
Bhawani Singh Rd, Jaipur.
(0141) 238 1919.

Rajwada Library Bar
Rajvilas, Jaipur.
(0141) 264 0101.

Rana Sanga Roof Top Bar
Mansingh Palace, Jaipur.
(0141) 237 8771.

SPORTS AND OUTDOOR ACTIVITIES

Previously, only the traditional sports such as cricket and polo provided visitors with opportunities for participating in outdoor activities. But today, the tourism industry offers a vast diversity of choices for specialist holidays. For sports lovers, the main cities, especially Delhi and Jaipur, offer clubs and grounds for golf, tennis, swimming and riding. Those in search of adventure can explore the foothills of the Himalayas and

After a polo match

the Aravallis by trekking or rock climbing, while the tumultous mountain streams above Rishikesh are ideal for white-water rafting and kayaking.

A camel or horse safari is a good way to experience the haunting beauty of the Rajasthan desert, and wildlife enthusiasts can visit the national parks for tiger-spotting and birdwatching. For those wishing to delve deeper into the mystique of the region, there are centres for yoga and meditation, naturopathy and spiritual studies.

SPECTATOR SPORTS

Cricket has emerged as the main national sport and, no matter where you travel you will see men and boys batting, bowling and fielding. India hosted the 1996 World Cup, an event that further fuelled the passion for the game and its players, who enjoy a celebrity status equal to film stars. Each year, especially in winter, several international cricket teams come to India, and test matches are played at various cities. The scenic Feroze Shah Kotla ground in Delhi is a major venue. All-night matches are played at the Jawaharlal Nehru Stadium, lit up especially for the occasion. In Jaipur, the Man-singh Stadium is the main cricket playing ground.

Advertisements for national and international matches appear well in advance in all the newspapers, and tickets (usually on sale ten days earlier), are in great demand

even though the more important matches are broadcast on the national network and sports channels.

Indian football is yet to reach international standards, and world-class matches are rarely held in the country. However, passions run high at the Ambedkar Stadium in Delhi where national tournaments are held, and a view from the stands can be a very enjoyable experience on a sunny winter afternoon.

TENNIS AND SWIMMING

In Delhi, the Lawn Tennis Association maintains some excellent tennis courts. So do some of the city's clubs and sports complexes. In Jaipur, the main tennis courts are at the **Jai Club**, just off Mirza Ismail (MI) Road. Both these cities are venues for the Davis Cup matches, and with India winning the 1999 Wimbledon doubles championship, there is a rapidly growing interest in this international sport.

A tennis match

However, because of the scarcity of public tennis courts they are often booked in advance and the best option for a quick game is at your own hotel's tennis court.

Come summer and all clubs, sports centres and five-star hotels in the region open their swimming pools. The most easily accessible to visitors are in the five-star hotels, usually with attached saunas and fitness centres. Non-residents can take temporary membership or pay a fee to use hotel pools.

GOLF

All major cities have well-maintained golf courses. In Delhi, the oldest and most prestigious course is at the **Delhi Golf Club**, located next to The Oberoi Hotel. This 27-hole course, creatively developed around a cluster of beautiful medieval pavilions, hosts many international

The Jawaharlal Nehru open air Stadium in New Delhi

tournaments in the winter season. Military cantonments, both here and at Agra, have their own golf courses. Just outside Delhi, the **Classic Golf Resort** is publicized as a weekend getaway, but is open to golfers through the week. In Jaipur, the Rambagh Palace Hotel has its own golf course and offers golf sets on hire for residents to play on the premises. Most golf clubs offer temporary membership to visitors for a fee.

RIDING

BOTH DELHI and the Jaipur area have excellent riding clubs which non-members may use for a nominal fee. The **Delhi Riding Club** has a stable full of well-groomed horses for hire. In Shekhawati, the heritage Dunlod Fort (*see p243*) has a polo ground, organizes horse safaris and teaches equestrian skills.

Visitors on a horse safari in Rajasthan

POLO

POLO WAS ONCE the preserve of royalty and the army, and the Jaipur maharajas used to personally lead their teams to tournaments abroad. Corporate sponsorship has now revived interest in the game, and a major attraction is the gaiety, pomp and glamour attached to it. Winter is the main polo season in Delhi and Jaipur. Most tournaments in Delhi are played at the polo grounds adjacent to the Race Course on Kamal Ataturk Road, and in Jaipur, matches are played at the **Rajasthan Polo Club** near the Rambagh Palace Hotel.

A golfer teeing off beneath the ramparts of Jaipur's Moti Doongri Fort

Ramgarh and Dundlod are major polo centres, where the game is also taught. In March, visitors may see some traditional elephant polo at Jaipur's Chaugan Stadium.

HELI-TOURISM

HELICOPTER PACKAGE trips are a new departure for the tourism industry in India. Apart from the transport by helicopter, they include lodging, meals and sightseeing. Heli-getaways in the region, organized by **Deccan Aviation** for those who can afford it and are strapped for time, so far include Agra, Jaipur-Sariska, and Jaipur-Ranthambhore. From Delhi, **World Expeditions India** organizes heli-skiing in winter, and also cycling tours.

JEEP AND DESERT SAFARI

AN ADVENTUROUS WAY to see the countryside is by safari. For wildlife sanctuaries, jeep safaris are common with camping along the way. Camel safaris, organized by travel agents from Jaipur, and by

most heritage hotels especially in Kishangarh (*see p215*), Mandawa and Nawalgarh (*see p246*), promise unexpected glimpses of desert life and a first-hand acquaintance with the ship of the desert. Prices vary, depending on the duration of the safari. Camping out in the desert is a romantic experience, especially at night around a campfire with your camel driver relating thrilling stories of desert lovers and villains. Elephant and horse safaris can also be organized for groups through private travel agents.

CHILDREN'S ACTIVITIES

DELHI OFFERS MUCH to amuse children, beginning with a sprawling Zoo. The Appu Ghar Amusement Park has several roller coasters, water rides and other thrilling games. The **National Science Centre** and the **Nehru Planetarium** organize special shows for children on certain events, such as eclipses. The Rail Museum is also a great hit with children, and offers rides on a special toy train.

Experiencing desert life on a camel safari in Rajasthan

Rock climbing

CAMPING, TREKKING AND ROCK CLIMBING

THE HIMALAYAN foothills above Rishikesh have ideal locations for camping, trekking and rock climbing. As most of Rajasthan's forts nestle in the craggy slopes of hillsides, they also offer excellent opportunities for rock climbing and exploring the neighbouring countryside. Just beyond South Delhi, near Sohna in Gurgaon, there are many attractive hiking trails. The best source of information on these activities is the **Indian Mountaineering Federation**, and private operators, such as Milestones and Outdoor Adventures *(see p231),* who specialize in organizing treks. Most organizers can provide reliable guides, as well as campsite equipment such as tents and sleeping bags, though you may feel more comfortable carrying your own things. The best time for this activity is in the summer months from April to June, and after the monsoon from October to early December, before the weather gets too cold.

ECOTOURISM

THIS RELATIVELY new concept in tourism, which combines various aspects of nature study along with participation in conservation activities, is steadily gaining ground in India. There are three main national parks in Rajasthan. Ranthambhore *(see pp224–5)* and Sariska *(see pp210–11)* are known for their tiger populations, while birdwatchers will find many exotic inhabitants at Bharatpur's Keoladeo Ghana *(see pp168–9).* Tours can be arranged through Rajasthan Tourism. Near Delhi are smaller sanctuaries such as the Sultanpur Sanctuary *(see p116).* The **World Wide Fund for Nature, India (WWF)**, with its headquarters in Delhi, has an active programme of activities, such as camps, film shows and seminars.

CULTURAL STUDIES

YOGA AND MEDITATION are taught at ashrams found in most cities. In Delhi, at the **Shivanand Yoga Vedanta Nataraja Centre** there is a good programme all year round. The best centres are, however, found in Rishikesh, where some of the best gurus conduct courses of yoga and Hindu philosophy all year round, and an International Yoga Festival is held here every year *(see p41).* Naturopathy and ayurveda, two Indian systems that rely on the healing powers of

Logo of a yoga centre in Rishikesh

natural foods and herbs, are also practised and taught at many centres, such as the **Ayurveda Kendra Clinic**. In Delhi, the **Kairali Health Resort** specializes in ayurvedic oil massages. Pranic healing, a method that channels positive forces through the *chakras* or energy centres in the body, is taught at the **Aurobindo Centre**. Those who are interested in Buddhist philosophy will find information on this area of study in Tibet House and at the **Toshita Mahayana Meditation Centre**. The **Sadhan Sansthan** can provide details of courses in *vipassana*, an old and efficacious form of meditation, while astrology and palmistry are taught at the Bharatiya Vidya Bhavan. Triveni Kala Sangam *(see p76)* holds short courses in classical singing, dance and in painting. Crafts skills can be studied at the Crafts Museum. Some travel agencies have devised special interest tours on subjects such as architecture, traditional crafts and spiritualism, and can draw up itineraries and organize tours to suit individual choices. These agencies have government recognition and are members of international organizations. A "Gourmet Journey through India" is one such tour on the agenda of **Indo Asia Tours** who engage specialists as their consultants.

A yoga *asana*

Trekking in the Himalayan foothills

River rafters relaxing on the banks of the Ganges

KAYAKING AND RIVER RAFTING

JUST NORTH OF RISHIKESH, a series of rapids on the Ganges as it rushes down the mountains make for excellent kayaking and river rafting *(see p145)* opportunities. A normal trip stretches over three days as participants are carefully introduced to the intensity of the rapids. The best time for rafting and kayaking is from September to April, when campsites are set up on the pristine beaches along the river both by the Uttar Pradesh State Government

(see p279), and professionally trained private groups, such as Outdoor Adventures *(see p231)* and **Himalayan River Runners**. The complete equipment – tents, rafts, life-saving jackets and helmets – is supplied, and all meals.

FISHING

FISHING is permitted in many of the region's rivers and lakes. But you must obtain a licence to do so from the designated local authority on site. In Delhi, the Okhla Barrage, as well as the nearby Suraj-kund and Badkhal lakes are popular with amateur anglers. Further north, where hill streams join the Chandrabhaga and the Ganges, particularly above Haridwar and Rishikesh, the rivers yield a good catch of the local variety of carp and other fish, though rarely trout.

WATER SPORTS

RAMGARH LAKE *(see p197)* near Jaipur, where some events of the 1984 Asian Games were held, is being developed by Rajasthan Tourism as a venue for water sports with facilities for parasailing, water-skiing and wind surfing. Currently, you can hire rowing, pedal and motor boats for a ride on the lake. Also, in and around Delhi a number of man-made lakes have facilities for boating and water sports.

White-water rafting on the River Ganges

DIRECTORY

SPORTS

Classic Golf Resort
NH8 (to Gurgaon), Distt Gurgaon.
(011) 2614 7417.

Delhi Golf Club
Zakir Hussain Marg, Delhi. Map 5 C4.
(011) 2436 2768.

Delhi Riding Club
Safdarjung Rd, Delhi. Map 4 F5.
(011) 2301 1891.

Jai Club
Mahaveer Marg, C Scheme, Jaipur.
(0141) 237 2321.

Rajasthan Polo Club
Ambedkar Circle, Near Rambagh Palace, Jaipur.
(0141) 238 3580.

HELI-TOURISM

Deccan Aviation
54 Block E, Anand Niketan, Delhi.
(011) 2410 3520.

CHILDREN'S ACTIVITIES

National Science Centre
Bhairon Marg, Delhi. Map 6 D1.
(011) 2337 1297.

Nehru Planetarium
Teen Murti House, Delhi. Map 4 E3.
(011) 2301 4504.

CAMPING AND TREKKING

Indian Mountaineering Federation
Benito Juarez Road, Delhi.
(011) 2467 1211.
www.indmount.com

ECOTOURISM

WWF India
Max Mueller Marg, Delhi. Map 5 A4.
(011) 2461 6532.

CULTURAL STUDIES

Aurobindo Centre
Off Aurobindo Marg, Delhi.
(011) 2651 2491.

Ayurveda Kendra Clinic
Rishikesh.
(0135) 243 0626.

Indo Asia Tours
C–28 Housing Society, South Extn I, Delhi.
(011) 2469 3574.

Kairali Health Resort
120 Andheria More, Mehrauli, Delhi.
(011) 2680 2106.
www.kairali.com

Sadhan Sansthan
16 Hemkund Towers, Nehru Place, Delhi.
(011) 2645 2772.

Shivanand Yoga Vedanta Nataraja Centre
52 Community Centre, East of Kailash, Delhi.
(011) 2648 0869.

Toshita Mahayana Meditation Centre
9 Padmini Enclave, Delhi.
(011) 2651 3400.

RIVER RAFTING

Himalayan River Runners
F 5 Hauz Khas Enclave, Delhi. (011) 2685 2602.
www.hrrindia.com

World Expeditions India
G-1 MG Bhavan, Madangir, Delhi.
(011) 2608 3358.

SURVIVAL
GUIDE

PRACTICAL INFORMATION

THE COUNTRY'S most popular travel circuit, the three cities of Delhi, Agra and Jaipur, receives the majority of the 2.5 million tourists who visit India annually. Because of this, the range of transport, accommodation and information offered here is among the best in India. The more remote areas are still not equipped to cater to the international traveller who may seek better banking facilities or prefer to pay by credit card. The government-run Department of Tourism (DOT) has

Logo of the Department of Tourism

a centrally located office in Delhi and many overseas branches. You can also get the latest and most relevant information at the local state tourist departments of Delhi, Rajasthan and Uttar Pradesh. There are innumerable travel agencies, but it is wise to approach a reputable one when booking accommodation, travel tickets and sightseeing tours. It is also wise to plan and book ahead if you wish to make a visit in the winter months, since this is the peak tourist season.

WHEN TO GO

THE FINEST WEATHER for travelling in North India is from October to March. This season also coincides with an abundance of festivals and cultural events, especially from October to December *(see pp40–41)*. Though it can get quite cold at night in winter (Dec–Jan), the days are crisp and sunny, and the brief spring of February and March is beautiful, with the flowers in full bloom. Try to avoid the summer (Apr–Jun), and rainy season (Jul–Sep) if possible. Summer in North India is unbearably hot, dry and dusty, compounded by power cuts, and during the monsoon, the humidity accentuates the heat, making travelling very uncomfortable. Climate and rainfall charts can be found on pages 38–41.

Brightly coloured blossoms adorning a Delhi roundabout

WHAT TO TAKE

THE CLOTHES you need will depend on the time of year that you visit. At the height of the winter you will need warm clothes – a jacket or a thick pullover, socks and warm trousers, especially during the early mornings and nights, although the days can be much warmer. For autumn and spring, pack light woollens and clothes in natural fibres that are easy to wash. In summer only loose cotton clothes are comfortable. Indian-made ready-to-wear cotton shirts and women's outfits are available everywhere. Choose easy-to-remove footwear as you will have to take off your shoes in places of worship. A first-aid kit is a must *(see p286)*. An umbrella or light raincoat is a good idea, and a powerful torch could be packed for unexpected power cuts.

ADVANCE BOOKING

SINCE ALL THREE CITIES are both tourist and commercial centres, it is advisable to have confirmed advance bookings for your accommodation and travel, especially during the peak tourist season. Airline tickets are easier to obtain at short notice, but as you can get confirmed train bookings at least two months in advance, it is wise to book ahead for train travel. Hotels and travel agents also book coach tours within Delhi, as well as to Agra and Jaipur as they are within a comfortable distance of each other.

VISAS AND PASSPORTS

EVERYONE NEEDS A visa to enter India. There are three types of visa for tourists, available from Indian Consular Offices around the

Visitors in local attire enjoying a rural festival

◁ **The annual Pushkar camel fair, a riot of colour**

world: the 15-day single/
double entry visa, the 90-day,
or the longer multiple entry
visa for six months.

Getting a visa extension
beyond 15 days is a complicated procedure. First, you
must collect an extension form
from the **Ministry of Home
Affairs** office, then ill and
submit it to the **Foreigners'
Regional Registration Office
(FRRO)**, who will stamp it.
Finally, you must go back to
the Ministry of Home Affairs
for the actual visa extension.

There are certain places in
India that are "Restricted
Areas" and for which special
permits are required. These
include Sikkim, all the
Northeastern states, Andaman
and Nicobar Islands and
Lakshwadweep.

EMBASSIES AND CONSULATES

Most countries have
diplomatic missions in
Delhi, but no representation
in the other two cities. Consular officials can re-issue
passports and help in case of
theft, imprisonment, hospital-
ization or other emergencies.
Some embassies have been
shortlisted on page 281.

CUSTOMS INFORMATION

When entering India,
visitors are allowed the
usual duty-free 950 ml of
alcohol and 200 cigarettes. For
expensive articles, such as
video cameras, jewellery,
music systems or laptop
computers, you will have to
fill in the tourist baggage
re-export form,
undertaking to
take these
items back or
else pay a fairly
heavy duty on
them when you
leave. Regarding
currency, if you are
carrying more than $10,000 in
cash or traveller's cheques,
you are expected to fill in the
Currency Declaration Form at
the airport, to be attested by a
customs official.

Antiques over a hundred
years old cannot be taken out
of the country. Neither can

Tourist bargaining with a vendor

wildlife products, such as
animal pelts, shahtoosh
shawls or ivory. Consult the
**Archaeological Survey of
India (ASI)**, or the **Ministry
of Environment & Forests**
for details of these rules.

IMMUNIZATION

There are no official
immunization require-
ments unless you travel from
designated countries in Africa,
South America and Papua
New Guinea, in which case
you will need a valid
vaccination certificate for
yellow fever. Vaccination
against tetanus, typhoid and
hepatitis A and B is a good
idea. You can also start a
course of anti-malarial tablets
before you arrive in India,
after consulting a reliable
physician about the course.

INSURANCE AND DRIVING LICENCE

Before arriving in India do
take out an insurance
policy for medical emer-
gencies and theft.
In fact, if you
are planning
to take part in
any adventure
activities or
sports, medical
insurance is a necess-
ity. To drive in India
an International Driving
Licence is required, which
you should get before leaving
for India. **The Automobile
Association of Upper India
(AAUI)** *(see p299)* can help
with a temporary driving
licence, but you will have to
take a driving test for one.

Visa stamp

(see p299)

DIRECTORY

TOURIST OFFICES

Government of India Tourist Offices
88 Janpath, Delhi.
Map I C5.
☏ *(011) 2332 0008.*
191, The Mall, Agra.
☏ *(0562) 222 6378.*
State Hotel, Khasa Kothi, Jaipur.
☏ *(0141) 237 2200.*
Ⓦ www.tourismindia.com

Delhi Tourism
N-36, Middle Circle, Connaught
Place, Delhi. **Map** I C5.
☏ *(011) 2331 5322.*
@ delhitourism@vsnl.com

Rajasthan Tourism
Bikaner House, Shahjahan Rd,
Delhi. **Map** 5 B2.
☏ *(011) 2338 9525.*
Paryatan Bhavan, Govt Hostel
Campus, MI Rd, Jaipur.
☏ *(0141) 511 0595.*
Ⓦ www.rajasthan-tourism.com

Uttar Pradesh Tourism
Chandralok Building, 36 Janpath,
Delhi. **Map** I C5.
☏ *(011) 2371 1296.*
64 Taj Rd, Agra.
☏ *(0562) 222 6431.*
Ⓦ www.up-tourism.com

USEFUL ADDRESSES

Archaeological Survey of India
Janpath, Delhi. **Map** 5 A2.
☏ *(011) 2301 5273.*

Foreigners' Regional Registration Offices
8, East Block, RK Puram
Sector I, Delhi.
☏ *(011) 2671 1443.*
16 Idgah Colony, Agra.
☏ *(0562) 221 7629.*
Police Headquarters, Behind
Hawa Mahal, Jaipur.
☏ *(0141) 261 9391.*

Ministry of Environment & Forests
Bikaner House, Delhi. **Map** 5 B2.
☏ *(011) 2436 0605.*

Ministry of Home Affairs
Lok Nayak Bhavan, Khan Market,
Delhi. **Map** 5 B3.
☏ *(011) 246 93334.*

TOURIST INFORMATION

THE DEPARTMENT of Tourism offices have information on travel throughout India, and its tourism counter in the arrival hall of Delhi's international airport also gives essential information. However, the state tourism departments *(see p279)* will provide more reliable and detailed advice on the three cities. The staff are helpful, with plenty of practical information on sight-seeing, travel and accommodation. Tourist brochures and maps are usually distributed free of charge.

Tourist brochures

ADMISSION CHARGES

MOST MUSEUMS, historical monuments and wildlife parks charge an entry fee. This is often a modest amount, though admission to World Heritage Sites costs more. There are often additional fees for cameras and video cameras. Most places of worship do not have any admission fee, but often have a donation box.

HOLIDAYS AND OPENING HOURS

ALL BANKS and government offices remain closed on the three national holidays of Republic Day (26 Jan), Indep-

endence Day (15 Aug) and Martyr's Day (2 Oct) *(see p39)*, when markets too are closed. Each year a new holiday list is issued by the Indian government, which includes all major religious festivals whose dates change according to the lunar calendar. Certain religious holidays are termed "restricted", so while the office may be open, the required official may be on leave. Monuments and museums normally open from 10am to 6pm, and generally close on Mondays and on government holidays. Shop timings are usually from 10am to 7:30pm. In Delhi, the markets are shut on different days of the week, but in Agra and Jaipur, they are closed on Sundays. Government offices work from Monday to Friday from 9:30am to 6pm, with a half hour lunch break. Senior officials often work overtime.

GUIDES

ALL TOURIST OFFICES, travel agents and hotels can arrange a certified expert for you at fixed hourly rates. At popular sights amateur guides swarm around tourists hoping to be hired. You should ignore them and look instead for English-speaking guides wearing a metal badge that certifies government tourist department approval.

BACKPACKERS

FOR STUDENTS and young travellers, each of the three cities has branches of the **Youth Hostels Association of India (YHAI)**. In Delhi, check with the **Vishwa Yuvak Kendra**. There is also a comfortable **YMCA** in Delhi. If you plan to travel by bus and train, you should bring a sturdy backpack that can take rough handling. The safest way to carry money is in a pouch fixed to your belt.

FACILITIES FOR THE DISABLED

FACILITIES FOR THE disabled are still not well developed in public buildings and places of interest, as ramps or rails are seldom provided. However, airports and all main railway stations do have wheelchairs, ramps and escalators, and porters to carry your luggage. Pavements are difficult to negotiate in a wheelchair as they are often bumpy. Few hotels are equipped for the needs of the disabled traveller. The staff, however, are always helpful.

TRAVELLING WITH CHILDREN

CHILD-MINDING SERVICES for tourists are rare, but Indians love children so they can accompany parents to most places. However, they must be protected against the fierce sun, and drink only mineral water. Most well-known restaurants have food that children may safely eat.

PLACES OF WORSHIP

THE THREE CITIES have a number of temples, *gurudwaras*, churches, mosques and, in Delhi, a synagogue, holding regular services. Since many are also places of historical or archaeological interest, they are open to foreign tourists. However, certain rules of etiquette *(see pp282–3)* must be observed. Most of these places are open till late in the night, but it is safer, and preferable, to visit them during the day.

Visitors enjoying a camel ride at the Pushkar fair

INDIAN STANDARD TIME AND CALENDAR

IN SPITE OF ITS SIZE, India has only one standard time. India is 5.5 hours ahead of Greenwich Mean Time (GMT), 4.5 hours behind Australian Eastern Standard Time, and 10.5 hours ahead of US Eastern Standard Time.

For all official work, the Western Gregorian calendar is used in India. This avoids the confusion of traditional calendars, which vary between religions and regions. For example, at the Millennium, the official Indian calendar (Saka era), had reached only 1922, whereas the old Hindu calendar, which follows the Samvat era, reads as 2057.

MEASUREMENTS AND CONVERSION CHART

THE METRIC SYSTEM is most commonly used all over the country.

Imperial to Metric
1 inch = 2.5 centimetres
1 foot = 30 centimetres
1 mile = 1.6 kilometres
1 ounce = 28 grams
1 pound = 454 grams
1 pint = 0.6 litres
1 gallon = 4.5 litres

Metric to Imperial
1 centimetre = 0.4 inches
1 metre = 3 feet 3 inches
1 kilometre = 0.6 miles
1 gram = 0.04 ounces
1 kilogram = 2.2 pounds
1 litre = 1.8 pints

Little photo shops in a tourist area, offering quick photo services

LANGUAGE

THERE ARE MANY regional languages spoken in India, and in the northern region, both Hindi and English are used as official languages. In the cities, some English is spoken by a wide range of people, especially by those who deal with tourists – taxi drivers, guides – and in hotels, shops and offices. However, it is useful to know a few basic phrases in Hindustani, the colloquial language of the region *(see p320)*. Road signs and numbers are both in English and Hindi.

A range of plugs

ELECTRICITY

THE ELECTRICAL CURRENT is 220-240 volts, 50 Hz. Supply is erratic in summer when power cuts can last for hours, but more reliable in winter. Triple round-pin sockets are the norm, but adaptors for other varieties are available at large markets, as are transformers, needed for some appliances. Do bring along a power surge cable to protect your laptop computer againt voltage fluctuations.

PHOTOGRAPHY

COLOUR CAMERA FILM, easily available at most photo shops, is best bought at large shops. Such shops also have excellent developing and printing facilities and offer quick services. It is courteous to ask permission before photographing people or places of worship. Photographing security sensitive areas is strictly prohibited. Notice boards indicate where photography is not allowed.

USEFUL ADDRESSES

Youth Hostels/Vishwa Yuvak Kendra
5 Nyaya Marg, Chanakyapuri, Delhi. **Map** 4 D3.
C (011) 2611 6285.
Sanjay Place, MG Rd, Agra.
C (0562) 235 4462.
Bhagwan Das Rd, Jaipur.
C (0141) 274 0515.

YMCA
Jai Singh Rd, Delhi. **Map** 1B5.
C (011) 2374 6063.

EMBASSIES IN DELHI

Australia
C (011) 2688 8223.

Ireland
C (011) 2462 6733.
@ ireland@ndf.vsnl.net.in

New Zealand
C (011) 2688 3170.
W www.immigration.govt.nz

South Africa
C (011) 2614 9411.

United Kingdom
C (011) 2687 2161.
W www.ukindia.org

USA
C (011) 2419 8000.

PLACES OF WORSHIP

Baha'i House of Worship
Kalkaji, Delhi.
C (011) 2644 4029.

Cathedral of the Immaculate Conception
Wazirpura Rd, Agra.
C (0562) 215 1318.

Cathedral Church of the Redemption
Church Rd, Delhi. **Map** 4 E1.
C (011) 2309 4229.

Judah Hyam Synagogue
2, Humayun Rd, Delhi. **Map** 5 B3.
C (011) 2463 5500.

Sacred Heart Cathedral
Bangla Sahib Rd, Delhi.
Map 1 B5.
C (011) 2336 3593.

Etiquette

FRIENDLY AND EASY-GOING by nature, Indians consider hospitality intrinsic to their culture and religion. Guests are treated with immense courtesy, and people on the street will go out of their way to help you. If you have any doubts on issues regarding fares, rates or directions, it is better to be patient but firm, rather than arguing or becoming aggressive. As there are diverse religions, castes and social hierarchies in the region, it is safest to address everyone with respect without making allusions to their religious, ethnic or regional group. Public demonstrations of love, such as kissing, are frowned upon. Customs and rules of etiquette still follow traditional Indian norms, except in very Westernized sections of urban society.

Devotees with heads covered in a place of worship

GREETING PEOPLE

THE MOST COMMON form of Indian greeting is the *namaskar* or *namaste* (pronounced "namastey") when meeting or parting. The palms are pressed together, raised towards the face, and the head is bent slightly forward. Greetings and gestures may vary with religion or regional group. Muslims raise their right hand towards the forehead with the words *adaab* or *salaam aleikum*.

Namaskar, the traditional greeting

In North India, *"ji"* usually follows the name as a term of respect. On the first meeting, however, it is best to address someone formally with a Mr or Mrs or even Madam before their name. The use of first names is a sign of familiarity. However, the Western handshake is also commonly used, though Indian women still prefer to greet visitors with a *namaskar*.

In many traditional families, it is a polite gesture to touch the feet of elders when greeting them. As a rule, elders are never addressed by their first names. However, a courteous greeting in any form will be acknowledged. Personal questions about subjects which a foreigner may find intrusive, such as one's salary or relationship with one's mother-in-law, are not really considered offensive in Indian society. Seldom seen as an intrusion, they reflect a friendly interest in a new acquaintance.

BODY LANGUAGE

INDIANS TEND TO shake their heads a lot while talking, and it can be very confusing because sometimes what seems to be a negative shake is actually a sign of agreement. Indians also tend to talk loudly and gesticulate with their hands, giving the impression of being very agitated when they are actually having a perfectly normal conversation.

The head is considered to be the spiritual centre, and an elder will touch the head of a younger person in blessing. The feet are considered the lowliest part of the body, and shoes are treated as unclean. In many traditional Indian homes, you may have to slip them off at the door or before you enter the kitchen. At gatherings where the seating is on the floor, try to sit with your feet crossed or tucked away and not stretched out before you. When food is offered to you, it should be accepted with the right hand.

PLACES OF WORSHIP

EVERY MAJOR RELIGION of the world is practised in India. The etiquette differs in the places of worship of each religion, but everywhere a simple decorum is expected. If in doubt about what you should do, it is best to observe those around you. Do not disturb people at their prayers by taking photographs or talking loudly. In any case, you should ask permission to take photographs. Clothes should be clean and unrevealing, and the head covered. Women should wear dresses that cover the upper arms and are

A devotee bathing a linga in milk in a Shiva temple

at least mid-calf length, and men should avoid shorts. At most places of worship, shoes are taken off at the door, and you should sit with your feet turned away from the image or the central holy book.

In Hindu temples, it is permissible to offer flowers and incense for worship. Apart from the central deity, the temples often have subsidiary shrines in other parts of the temple precincts. Do not sit or lean against them. Even those in ruins are considered holy. Some Hindu temples do not welcome non-Hindus, but this is rarely the case. However, if stopped at the door, please do not take offence. In mosques and in *gurudwaras*, the head should be covered with a scarf or large handkerchief when you enter, but not with a hat. You should avoid entering a mosque during prayers, and men should stay away from the women's enclosure.

SUITABLE DRESS

THE INDIAN STYLE of clothing is relatively modest and covers the body well. In small towns, women still prefer the traditional sari or the *salwar-kameez* and seldom wear Western outfits, though very small girls can be seen in skirts or dresses. Delhi has a more cosmopolitan attitude, and in the trendier parts of the city, jeans, short skirts and shorts are common. However, Indian men tend to stare a lot at women, so be prepared for this, whatever you wear. Agra

Traditional village women in *ghunghat*, veiling their faces

and Jaipur are much more conservative cities where short skirts and shorts might well attract unwanted attention.

Do dress a little formally when visiting Indian homes, as Indians like to dress up for occasions. In fact, owning a couple of Indian outfits makes great sense. Ready-made clothes for both men and women are available in most markets at reasonable rates, and are easy and comfortable to wear.

BARGAINING

BARGAINING is a part of life in India, but do not get aggressive about it. Firmly state what you would like to pay and walk away if the shopkeeper does not agree. Larger shops usually have fixed price tags and do not readily discount.

Shoes left at the entrance to a religious place

EATING INDIAN STYLE

MOST INDIAN MEALS are eaten with the fingers to tear the chapati or bread, and to scoop up rice and curry. At best, a spoon may be given to you. It is considered impolite to use your left hand. Most restaurants provide finger bowls at the end of the meal.

TIPPING

THERE ARE NO FIXED norms for tipping, or *baksheesh*, as it is called. Most restaurants add a service charge to the bill; a ten per cent tip over that is quite adequate. In smaller eateries, the waiter would be happy with less. Hotel staff, porters and most taxi drivers expect to be tipped. So do hairdressers. A small tip given to the person who minds your shoes outside a place of worship will be happily accepted.

The traditional Indian *thali* meal, eaten with the right hand, seated on the floor

SMOKING AND ALCOHOL

THOUGH CIGARETTE kiosks abound, and pavement sellers even sell one cigarette at a time, in Delhi smoking is officially banned in public places like airports, railway stations and offices (though in practice the ban is often ignored). Only certain restaurants are licensed to serve alcohol, and you are not allowed to drink in parks, buses or trains. Drinking near a place of worship can lead to arrest. It is also considered very offensive.

BEGGARS

TRAVELLERS CAN FIND beggars difficult to handle as they target foreigners and can be extremely persistent. Tourists who give money to one soon find themselves surrounded by a raucous throng demanding *baksheesh*. Be careful of being pickpocketed in the confusion. Beggars are found in the largest numbers around places of worship as people always give them alms or even food there. But it is best not to encourage them and to walk on till they leave you alone. If necessary, complain to a nearby policeman.

If you do want to help monetarily, your hotel may have a donation box and the staff will be able to suggest a few charitable institutions.

Personal Security and Health

Police officer's badge

THE THREE CITIES of Delhi, Agra and Jaipur are well equipped with an efficient police force and a number of good hospitals. As long as you take a few simple precautions, there is little need to worry. For instance, do not get too friendly with strangers, protect your valuables and do stay and eat only in places that look clean. If you face a difficult situation, take the help of a policeman or file a report at the closest police station.

Policemen in uniform

IN AN EMERGENCY

THE NATIONAL emergency number for police is 100, the fire brigade is 101, and for an ambulance it is 102. Your embassy can also advise you in an emergency. If in need of immediate medical attention, your hotel's doctor-on-call can refer you to a private clinic. Otherwise, all public and most privately owned hospitals and clinics run a 24-hour service for casualty and emergency cases.

GENERAL PRECAUTIONS

TRAVELLING IN THE region is relatively safe for tourists. Since Delhi, Agra and Jaipur are major tourist centres, there are bound to be touts, beggars and pickpockets who target the tourist. Take simple safety measures, such as wearing a money belt under your shirt in which to keep important documents, such as your passport. Protect your camera and avoid wearing jewellery or carrying large amounts of cash in crowded areas. You can leave your valuables in the hotel safe but insist on a receipt. While shopping, make sure that the shopkeepers make out a bill and process your credit card in front of you. It is also advisable to use a padlock, available at railway stations, during train journeys.

Some shopkeepers lead tourists into believing that goods bought in India can be sold back home at great profit. Unless you can judge a product's authenticity, it is best not to invest your money on such dubious purchases.

A word of caution about dealing with the police. If you find yourself in any trouble, for instance, if you have lost your passport or valuables, you must inform the nearest police station and file an FIR (first information report), but it is also advisable to contact your embassy for advice about the correct procedure.

NARCOTICS

THE IMAGE OF INDIA as a country that is tolerant of drug use is not true. Possession of all drugs, from hashish to heroin, is banned by law, and penalties for possession, use and trafficking in illegal drugs are strictly enforced. Drug convictions lead to a minimum sentence of ten years without parole or remission. As a precaution, do not leave your luggage unattended or unlocked at public places, and by no means carry anything for strangers or check in their luggage at airports.

WOMEN TRAVELLERS

WOMEN, both Indian and foreign, face a certain amount of unwanted attention from men in North India, even though "eve-teasing" is a punishable offence. When travelling alone, women can face problems – from being stared at, to more active harassment such as suggestive comments and unwanted body contact on buses and in other crowded places.

Take your cue from Indian women who continue with their independent lifestyles despite such hazards. Avoid wearing clothes that can be thought of as provocative, such as shorts, skimpy dresses and mini skirts at public places, though they can be safely worn inside the hotel. Ignore men lounging at street corners, and if their attention gets offensive, walk towards a policeman. Beware of men who try to draw you into a conversation, and threaten to call the police if they continue to do so.

Avoid moving about alone in quiet places and in the rougher parts of the city. When hiring a car or a taxi, get the hotel to make the booking for you. Hitchhiking is not advisable under any circumstances. A confident attitude, common sense and wariness can help women travellers tackle problems that arise from travelling alone.

A Delhi police jeep

A hospital ambulance

LEGAL ASSISTANCE

LEGAL PROBLEMS are very rare for travellers, but if you do find yourself in a legal tangle, immediately contact your embassy (see p281). Always carry your passport and keep a photocopy handy. Do not hand your travel papers over to anyone until your embassy has been informed. Some insurance policies also cover legal costs for certain emergencies such as accidents.

PUBLIC TOILETS

WAYSIDE PUBLIC TOILETS have poor hygiene. However, though still few in number, those public toilets, known as Sulabh Shauchalayas, located on main city roads are a great civic invention. Attractively designed, they are easy to spot, extremely clean, and charge a very nominal amount for use. They are, however, of the Asian-squat kind and can be difficult to handle. Some restaurants and hotels allow you to use their toilets, but it is best to carry some spare toilet paper as not all public toilets are equipped with it.

A pharmacy situated in a local market

PHARMACIES

MOST BIG MARKETS in the three cities have well-stocked pharmacies (or chemist shops, as they are known in India). The pharmacists are often able to advise you on simple remedies. They also stock toiletries, sanitary napkins and tampons, cosmetics, infant food and disposable diapers. If you are taking any special medication, it is advisable to carry the prescriptions, or show the packaging with the generic name if the brand is unfamiliar to the pharmacist. Most pharmacies are open between 9am and 7:30pm. Public hospitals such as AIIMS usually have round-the-clock pharmacies which are also open to non-patients.

Sign identifying a toilet

HOSPITALS AND MEDICAL FACILITIES

DO TAKE comprehensive medical insurance before arriving in India. **MASTA** (Medical Advisory Service for Travellers Abroad) in the UK can give a health update for travellers to India.

In Delhi, there are excellent private hospitals and medical specialists, and though it is crowded like other government hospitals, the renowned **All India Institute of Medical Sciences (AIIMS)**, is a highly advanced hospital and centre of research. Most of the embassies have a list of approved hospitals and clinics as well as the names of the best medical specialists and dental practititioners in town. The local **Indian Red Cross Society** is the safest option for blood transfusions.

DIRECTORY

EMERGENCY NUMBERS

- Ambulance/Emergency 102.
- Fire Brigade 101.
- Police 100.

HOSPITALS AND MEDICAL FACILITIES

Delhi
All India Institute of Medical Sciences (AIIMS),
Aurobindo Marg.
(011) 2656 1123.

East West Rescue,
B-28 Greater Kailash I.
(011) 2629 3701.

Escorts Heart Institute,
Maulana Muhammad Ali Rd.
(011) 2682 5000.

Indraprastha Apollo,
Mathura Rd, NH2.
(011) 2692 5858.

Agra
Parikh Nursing Home, MG Rd.
(0562) 26 0444.

Jaipur
Sawai Man Singh Medical College.
(0141) 256 6251.

MASTA, London
(020) 7291 9333.
www.masta.org

Indian Red Cross Society
1 Red Cross Rd, Opp Parliament House, Delhi. **Map** 4 F1.
(011) 2371 6441.

Pavement quacks peddling concoctions of a dubious nature

HEAT AND SMOG

SUMMER IN NORTH INDIA is dry and very hot, and the monsoon months that follow are oppressively humid. It takes time to get acclimatized to this weather, so take things at a relaxed pace in the first few days. The best way to beat the heat is to drink lots of fluids at regular intervals, and add a little salt to your food to prevent dehydration. Bathe often and avoid going out in the hottest part of the day, between noon and four o'clock. While walking, try to rest in the shade at regular intervals, for continuous exposure to high temperature can cause heat stroke.

It is advisable to wear light shoes and loose-fitting cottons that cover your arms and legs, as exposed skin can get badly sunburnt. Polyester clothing and covered shoes and socks trap perspiration and can lead to annoying prickly heat and fungal infections. Prickly heat powder is available at most pharmacies. Wear a wide-brimmed hat and sunglasses and use sun-screen to protect your skin.

In the winter, the city air can get quite smoggy. Asthmatic travellers should carry their medication at all times.

FIRST-AID KIT

MOST FIRST-AID ITEMS are readily available at the pharmacies in the cities, and while going on excursions or day-long trips, it is advisable to carry a basic first-aid kit. This should include any personal medication, aspirin or painkillers for fevers and minor aches and pains, and antiseptic and calamine lotion for cuts and bites, an anti-fungal ointment, plaster and crêpe bandages, scissors, insect repellent and tweezers; antihistamines for allergies, anti-diarrhoea tablets and, water purification tablets; lip

Sugarcane and other juices sold on the street, tempting but best avoided

balm, a couple of disposable syringes and a thermometer.

There are some effective herbal remedies, but you should buy only brands recommended by a reliable practitioner or pharmacist.

MINOR STOMACH UPSETS

DIARRHOEA IS a common stomach disorder among travellers, usually caused by a change of diet, water and climate. Since Indian food is mostly hot and spicy, it can lead to digestive disorders. In such cases, it is best to eat plain boiled food without spices until the attack subsides. Most important-antly, make sure you drink plenty of liquids to replace your body fluids. Avoid tap water and opt for sealed bottles of mineral water, such as Evian or Bisleri, if available. Most known international brands of carbonated drinks are widely available, and are clean and safe, as is fresh coconut water. No matter how tempting the food looks, it is advisable not to eat from streetside food carts. If you do want to eat in a *dhaba*, it is best to go to one that seems popular with the local people. The food there is more likely to be fresh and

A hand fan

of a reliable quality. However, it is best to avoid raw salads, cut fruit, cold cuts and fresh juices at wayside eateries.

A good pharmacist will suggest standard diarrhoea medication. In the case of a severe attack, with nausea, cramps and exhaustion, it is best to consult a doctor. You must immediately take oral rehydrating salts (ORS), which are commercially available under the popular Indian brand names of Electral or Electrobion. An effective homemade remedy of half a teaspoon of salt and three teaspoons of sugar mixed in boiled water which has been cooled also helps to keep the body fluids in balance.

INSECT-BORNE DISEASES

THE SUMMER and monsoon months are the seasons for malaria, though it can occur at any time of the year. Its symptoms include violent shivering followed by high fever and sweating. Caused by a parasite carried in the saliva of the female *Anopheles* mosquito, the incubation period can vary from a few days to several weeks. Another serious mosquito-borne disease is dengue fever, carried by the *Aëdes egypti* mosquito. The symptoms are similar to malaria and include severe pain in the joints and muscles, and often, rashes. The dengue

Vicks Vaporub, a decongestant

mosquito is more active at daytime, unlike others that are active in the dark, between sunset and dawn.

If you are sleeping in a room without air-conditioning, keep the screened windows closed at all times. You can also ask the hotel for a mosquito repellent gadget, as well as a net over your bed. Avoid wearing dark clothing and strong perfumes as these attract mosquitoes. If going outdoors in the evenings, you should wear shoes and clothes that completely cover your arms and legs, and rub mosquito repellent cream on any part of the skin that is exposed.

Mosquito repellent coil and cream

If you do experience symptoms of malaria, it is best to seek medical help immediately. You must take courses of preventive anti-malarial drugs before, during and after your trip. For the latest information on malaria medication, call a travel clinic or MASTA *(see p285)* who post details free of charge.

CUTS AND BITES

INSECT BITES ARE A common problem in the rainy season. Many monuments have huge beehives, so you should carry a good antiseptic ointment and antihistamine that would help in case of wasp and bee stings. Snake bites are rare, but if bitten, tie on a tight crêpe bandage, keep the limb immobile and seek immediate medical help. Clean all cuts with an antiseptic solution and cover with sticky plaster or a light bandage.

FOOD- AND WATER-BORNE DISEASES

TRAVELLERS must guard against two types of severe intestinal infection, known as dysentery. The first,

bacillary dysentery, is accompanied by severe stomach pains, vomiting and fever, but rarely lasts longer than a week. Amoebic dysentery has similar symptoms but takes longer to manifest itself. If not treated with a course of prescription drugs, this can later become a recurring, chronic ailment. The same is true of Giardiasis, a type of chronic diarrhoea, caused by contaminated water.

Some forms of hepatitis, a serious liver ailment, such as Hepatitis A and B, can be prevented with a vaccine. Its symptoms include extreme fatigue, body aches, fever, severe chills and jaundice. The only treatment is plenty of boiled water, rest and a strictly controlled diet.

If you are visiting a site ravaged by floods you must get yourself vaccinated early enough against cholera, a serious disease that can be fatal unless the patient is rushed to hospital for rehydration and medication.

Typhoid, which has a vaccine, is another gastro-intestinal disease transmitted through contaminated water or food. Early symptoms may seem like flu, but develop into high fever, leading to acute dehydration and weight loss. A doctor should be immediately consulted for the right antibiotics.

Since they are the most common ailments faced by travellers to India, certain common-sense precautions, such as eating only at clean places and drinking mineral water, are the best prevention against gastric infections.

Bottled mineral water

PEOPLE- AND ANIMAL-BORNE DISEASES

AWARENESS OF sexually transmitted diseases such as HIV, which causes Acquired Immune Deficiency Syndrome

(AIDS), is still low, and screening at blood banks unreliable. In case blood transfusion is required, do contact the **Indian Red Cross Society** *(see p285)*.

Meningitis, a severe inflammation of the membranes surrounding the spinal cord and brain, is accompanied by high fever and occasional seizures. Penicillin drugs are effective in combating it, but patients must be rushed to a hospital straight away.

To avoid getting rabies if you are bitten by an animal, clean the wound immediately with an antiseptic solution and seek medical help at once, for treatment involves a course of injections. There is also a vaccination against rabies. Vaccination against tetanus is also essential while travelling. This potentially fatal infection is transmitted through open wounds, and its symptoms include lock-jaw, stiff muscles and fatal convulsions. You should clean the wound and go to a good doctor without delay.

Tuberculosis, commonly transmitted through coughing and close household contact with an infected person, is not a great risk for travellers.

Before an inoculation, buy your own disposable syringe, or insist that a new syringe and needle is unwrapped in front of you. Avoid shaves at dubious barber shops, and insist on a new razor blade. Any procedure using needles, such as tattooing and ear-piercing, is best avoided.

Delicious streetside food, often difficult to stomach

Banking and Local Currency

Logo of the State Bank of India

THE THREE CITIES provide accessible banking facilities and also money exchange services, with English speaking staff at all the counters. Delhi has a good selection of international banks with a range of services. Exchange facilities are available at major banks and hotels, travel agencies, the international airport, and registered money changers. Unauthorized dealers and touts might offer enticing rates, but they are illegal operators. Some shops will also give better value for money against purchases in major foreign currencies. Traveller's cheques are the safest way to carry money, but always keep some small change and notes for telephones, transport, tips and purchases.

BANKS AND BANKING HOURS

THERE ARE MANY BANKS with branches across the country offering services, including international money transfers. Most national banks, such as the **State Bank of India**, have their head offices

American Express, offering money changing and banking facilities

and several branches in Delhi, as well as in the other cities. The State Bank's counter at the international airport, Central Bank of India at the **Ashok Hotel** *(see p231)* and select branches of **Standard Chartered** in Delhi offer 24-hour banking services. The Ashok also offers 24-hour money exchange facilities. Foreign banks have offices in Delhi, though not always in the other two cities. Indian banks with branches abroad and foreign banks with branches in India can also wire money by telex from their various offices.

Banking hours are between 9:30/10am–2pm (Mon–Fri), and 9:30/10am–12 noon (Sat). Banks can be closed on regional and national holidays *(see p39)*, and occasionally they shut down without any notice at all in response to public protests or strikes.

CHANGING MONEY

MOST HOTELS change money for resident guests, but banks offer the best rates. Visitors staying at government hotels require a receipt to show that they have changed their money in a bank. The State Bank of India, in Agra the **Allahabad Bank**, and the **Rajasthan Bank** in Jaipur are the best places in the region. Agents such as **Thomas Cook** *(see p297)* and **LKP Forex Ltd** also change money at the official rates, but with higher service charges. Newspapers publish exchange rates for major international currencies. The "black market" in India offers better rates than the official ones, but it is safer to go to authorized dealers.

CREDIT CARDS

INTERNATIONAL CREDIT cards such as VISA, Master Card, Amex and Diners Club are accepted in the larger shops, hotels and restaurants. Look out for the credit card sticker on shop windows. Cards can also be used to book rail and air tickets. American Express in Delhi gives traveller's cheques in US dollars or pounds sterling. Against some cards you can get a cash advance in rupees at many international banks. But credit card related fraud is on the increase, so keep your cards safely, and insist that receipt vouchers at shops are made out in front of you.

Currency

THE UNIT OF CURRENCY is the rupee (Rs), divided into 100 paisas. Among the coins the most commonly used are the 50 paisa and the one, two and five rupee ones. Currency notes range from Rs10 to the newly minted Rs1,000.

Be careful with the 100 and the 500 rupee notes which are quite similar in colour. Also, be wary of accepting torn or taped notes, as banks and shops are very often reluctant to accept or even change them for you.

Traveller's Cheques

THE WELL-KNOWN NAMES in traveller's cheques in US dollars or pounds sterling are easy to cash, and can be

The ATM at Citibank, Connaught Place, New Delhi

exchanged at all banks and exchange counters. Banks have the lowest surcharge so they give the best value. They always charge a small fee per cheque, so using large denomination cheques at a time is much more economical. Traveller's cheques give better exchange rates than cash.

ATM Services

ALL THE FOREIGN and some Indian banks have ATM (automatic teller machine) counters accepting VISA, Master Card, Amex or Diners Club cards. Instructions are displayed in English, and the cash dispensed is in rupees.

Bank Notes
All currency is minted by the Reserve Bank of India. The notes have either Mahatma Gandhi or the Ashoka lions on one side.

10-rupee note

20-rupee note

50-rupee note

100-rupee note

500-rupee note

Coins
The following silver coins are in circulation, with variations of the Rs1 coin. All bear the national insignia.

50 paisa

1 rupee

Rs 2

Rs 5

Communications

Telephone booth sign

THE POST and telecommunications systems in India are now fairly sophisticated. In addition to the government network, several reputable international courier agencies have offices here. All the main hotels have business centres, and most markets have shops from which international calls can be made, e-mail and faxes sent and the Internet accessed. A wide range of newspapers and magazines is sold in the three cities and, particularly in Delhi, most international newspapers and magazines are available in bookshops.

Stamps in five-rupee denomination

POSTAL SERVICES

THE INDIAN postal service is efficient and reliable. It offers general or registered mail, parcel, *poste restante,* speed post and courier services. Most post offices are open from Monday to Friday between 10am and 5pm, and on Saturdays, only until 12 noon. The closing time for certain services, such as registered mailing, is usually earlier.

Letters sent *poste restante* are held at the post office for up to a month. In Delhi, the **Foreign Post Office**, and in Agra and Jaipur, the **General Post Office (GPO)** will hold your letters for you, but accessing them may take some time. Letters should be addressed with the surname underlined and in capital letters c/o Poste Restante, followed by the name and place of the post office. American Express also provides this service to its clients, and so does the India Tourist Office at Janpath in Delhi *(see p279).* The procedure for sending parcels is not very simple, so check the details before trying to do so on your own.

In some places your hotel sells stamps and may offer to post letters and smaller parcels for you. Indian letter boxes are colour coded: local letters, green; metropolitan and other cities, red; Quick Mail Service (QMS), yellow.

A regular post box

FAX AND TELEGRAPH SERVICES

FAX SERVICES are available at main post offices and also at market ISD/STD booths which, though often easier to access, charge more. The business centres of all large hotels have centralized telecommunication services, but these are open for use only to those who are staying there.

INTERNET AND E-MAIL

THE INTERNET is widely used in Indian cities and most larger hotels offer net access to guests. Privately operated cyber cafés with the latest facilities are more common in Delhi than in the other two cities. Libraries, such as the British Council and United States Information Centre in Delhi, have Internet facilities which can be used for a small payment to browse the web and to use for e-mailing.

COURIER SERVICES

WHILE IT IS BETTER to ship larger items such as furniture by regular land, sea or air cargo, letters, documents or smaller parcels are better sent through a courier agency, even though it may be more expensive. **United Parcel Service (UPS)**, an international courier agency, has a widespread network of branches all over the world. Many shops offer to send purchases by courier, but except for the government emporia and well-known shops, you will be doing so at your own risk. If necessary, send the parcel yourself, even though it may be bothersome.

TELEVISION AND RADIO

THE STATE-RUN Doordarshan television network has programmes in English and the major regional languages. With the arrival of satellite TV, the choice has become much wider. Cable TV is available almost everywhere, including most hotel rooms. Through it you can watch international channels, such as the BBC World Service, CNN, Discovery, National Geographic and the Hong

General Post Office or Gole Dak Khana, New Delhi

Kong-based Star TV network. Star Sports and ESPN are exclusive sports channels whereas Channel V and MTV are the music channels.

India also has a wide radio network, with programmes in English and local languages. It is still the best form of information, especially in the rural areas. FM channels are now available in many cities. You should check the daily papers for interesting television and radio programmes.

Some of the major English-language newspapers

NEWSPAPERS AND MAGAZINES

INDIA HAS A WIDE VARIETY of national English language newspapers. Leading papers like *The Times of India* and *The Hindustan Times* make for lively reading with fierce debates, cartoons and good sports coverage. Weekly magazines, such as *India Today* and *Outlook*, provide excellent coverage of local and international news. Readily available monthly

magazines, such as *Delhi Diary* and *First City* list restaurants, films, exhibitions and other events in Delhi. Agra and Jaipur also have local newspapers in English and Hindi which give details of current cultural programmes.

INTERNATIONAL AND LOCAL CALLS

ALL MAJOR HOTELS offer international subscriber dialling (ISD) services. You can also book a trunk call from a private telephone. Most markets also have ISD/STD (subscriber trunk dialling) booths from which local and international calls can be made at cheaper rates than the hotels. Look for the yellow ISD/STD sign above the shop. To make an international call you will need to dial: the international access code, followed by the country code, the area code and the local number. Domestic long-distance calls are made on the STD lines, and the service covers a large part of the country, including villages. STD rates depend on the distance and time of the call. These calls are cheapest between 11pm and 6am Indian time. Local calls can also be made from public STD telephone booths. The latter take new one rupee coins, renewable for every additional three minutes.

Easy-to-operate public telephone

ADDRESSES

THE OLDER SECTIONS of Indian cities are often a maze of lanes and alleyways. Some road signs can be confusing and hard to decipher, and sometimes there may not even be a road sign. If you are lost, a passerby will always help, but the best bet is to get directions from a taxi or auto-rickshaw driver. The newer residential localities are divided into blocks, and the block number usually appears with the house number. So B4/88 Safdarjung Enclave would be: house number 88 in the B4 block of Safdarjung Enclave colony.

Various services, advertised through large signboards

USEFUL DIALLING CODES AND NUMBERS

- To make an inter-city call, dial the STD code of that city and the local number. For Delhi, dial 011; Agra, dial 0562; and for Jaipur, dial 0141.
- To make an international call (ISD), dial 00, the country code, area code and the local number.
- Country codes are: UK 44; France 33; USA & Canada 1; Australia 61; Ireland 353; New Zealand 64; South Africa 27; Japan 81.
- Dial 180 to book a Trunk call in the country, and 186 for international calls.
- For directory assistance dial 197 in Delhi, Agra and Jaipur.
- For the morning alarm, dial 116 in Delhi, Jaipur and Agra.

TRAVEL INFORMATION

MOST INTERNATIONAL VISITORS to India arrive by air, and though road and ferry links are used between India and her neighbours, such as Pakistan, Bangladesh and Sri Lanka, this method of travel can be a complicated one. Travelling within the country, and especially between the three cities of the Golden Triangle is possible by air, train and road. Whatever your mode of transport, you should be prepared for delays and unexpected detours that

The Maharaja, mascot of Air India

may test your patience. The distance between the three cities is less than 250 km (155 miles) and only takes a few hours by road or rail. The state-run Indian Airlines has the widest network of air routes. Private airlines like Sahara and Jet Airways also cover many cities in this region. Indian Railways is one of the world's largest networks, and travelling first class is a good way to see the country. The long-distance luxury coach is another easy option.

Aeroplanes lined up on the international airport tarmac

ARRIVING BY AIR

ALL THE MAJOR international airlines land in India, normally as stopovers on air routes between East and West. The international airports are at Delhi, Bombay (Mumbai), Calcutta (Kolkota), Madras (Chennai), Trivandrum (Thiruvananthapuram) and Goa, from where connecting domestic flights cover the rest of India. A direct flight from London to Delhi takes approximately nine hours. From Delhi there are several connecting flights onwards to Agra and Jaipur.

AIR FARES

AIR FARES can vary according to the airline and the season. Before buying your ticket, do find out from a few travel agents about special offers or discounted fares. Cheaper fares are offered during the off-peak season, but usually stipulate the route and duration of the journey.

CUSTOMS

THE GREEN CHANNEL is for those who do not have dutiable goods as listed in the Immigration Certificate. The Red Channel is for passengers with goods that attract customs duty, including money in excess of US$2,500.

INTERNATIONAL AND DOMESTIC AIRPORTS

THE MAIN AIRPORT in Delhi is called Indira Gandhi (IG) International Airport. It has two terminals: Terminal I for domestic flights, and Terminal II for those coming from abroad. The latter has more facilities, with 24-hour currency exchange counters, left luggage services and an air-conditioned visitors' lounge. Travel agencies located in the arrivals area can help you organize your tour itinerary and onward

DL1Y 1164
ALL INDIA TOURIST PERMIT

Licence plate of a taxi

bookings, while the hotel counters, also located here, can arrange accommodation in a reliable hotel. Terminal I (domestic) is at Palam, 7 km (4 miles) from Terminal II. If transferring to a domestic flight from an international one (or vice versa), do allow enough time to get between the two terminals (approximately 15 minutes driving time). Airport coaches run hourly between the two during peak hours when most international flights arrive, and offer free transfers.

GETTING TO AND FROM THE AIRPORT

THE DOMESTIC TERMINAL is 12 km (7 miles), and the international terminal, 19 km (12 miles) southwest of the city centre (Connaught Place). Coaches run regularly between these destinations free of charge. You can also book a pre-paid taxi from a counter outside the arrivals area. The rates of these are fixed – about Rs 200 from Terminal II and Rs 150 from Terminal I to the city centre. If you are booking your accommodation in advance, do check if your hotel is offering a free pick-up service. The trip from the airports to the city centre can take up to 50 minutes, but if your flight arrives or departs in the early hours of the day, it should certainly take less.

Passengers in the airport lounge

TRAVEL PACKAGES

INDIAN AIRLINES offers two travel packages if paid in US dollars. The "Discover India Fare" for 15 or 21 days is about $500–750, and allows unlimited travel with certain route restrictions. "India Wonder Fare" for about $300 is for seven days of travel in one region. It does not include the Andaman Islands.

DOMESTIC FLIGHTS

WHILE Indian Airlines offers the largest choice of routes and the most frequent services, the two major private-run airlines, Jet Airways and Sahara Airlines, also connect a wide network of cities. Delhi is connected to all Indian airports, while Agra and Jaipur, an hour's flight from Delhi, offer fewer connections. While all domestic airlines have their own booking offices, tickets can also be booked through travel agents (see p297).

Air tickets

CHECK-IN

INTERNATIONAL FLIGHTS usually ask you to check-in three hours ahead of the flight departure time. For most domestic flights, it is normally one hour, except when security checks are more stringent, for places such as Kashmir. There is a restriction on the amount of baggage you can carry with you. Most airlines allow 20 kg per person in the hold and one item of hand baggage, though some international airlines allow two full suitcases plus one item of hand baggage. Excess baggage charges can be high.

TAX CLEARANCE CERTIFICATE

IF YOU STAY in India for more than 120 days from the date of issue of the visa, you need a tax clearance certificate to leave the country. You should apply for the certificate to the **Income Tax Department** Foreign Section. This is to prove that you have financed your trip with your own foreign exchange and not by working in India. Do keep all documents about travel finance in case they are needed later.

DEPARTURE TAX

WHEN LEAVING INDIA, you have to pay a Foreign Travel Tax of Rs 500, unless already included with your ticket. But if travelling to Pakistan, Nepal, Sri Lanka, Bhutan, Burma (Myanmar), the Maldives or Afghanistan, only Rs 150 has to be paid.

AIRPORT	📞 INFORMATION	DISTANCE TO CITY CENTRE	AVERAGE JOURNEY TIME
Delhi (IG Domestic) Terminal I	(011) 2565 2993	12 km (7 miles)	Road: 30 minutes
Delhi (IG International) Terminal II	(011) 2565 2011	19 km (12 miles)	Road: 50 minutes
Agra	(0562) 222 6121	16 km (10 miles)	Road: 45 minutes
Jaipur (Sanganer)	(0141) 272 2638	13 km (7 miles)	Road: 30 minutes

Travelling by Train

Indian Railways logo

Travelling through India by train is a truly unforgettable experience. It can be extremely relaxing or uncomfortable, a lot of fun, or frustrating. But if you can spare the time, it is the best way of getting to know the Indian people and seeing the countryside. India has a well organized railway network but it is also extremely busy, so plan your train journey carefully and do book your tickets well in advance. There are computerized ticket counters at railway stations, and most travel agents can buy tickets for you. The journey between Agra, Delhi and Jaipur takes only a few hours.

A modern diesel engine train

THE RAILWAY NETWORK

The Indian railway network is divided by region and the three cities of Agra, Delhi and Jaipur are served by Northern Railways. Delhi has three major railway stations: Delhi Main, New Delhi and Nizamuddin, so check from which station your train will be leaving. Most fast trains for Agra, such as the Shatabdi Express, (New Delhi) and the Taj Express (Nizamuddin) take less than three hours. This makes a day trip to Agra possible. Another Shatabdi Express runs between Delhi and Jaipur and takes about five hours after an early start from New Delhi. The Gangaur Express runs between Agra and Jaipur.

Train timetable

TRAINS AND TIMETABLES

There are three kinds of trains: passenger, express and mail. It is best to take the express trains as they have

fewer stops and offer better facilities and services. Avoid passenger trains as they stop at all the small stations, sometimes for long periods, and are always very crowded. The major cities are connected by air-conditioned super-fast trains, such as the Rajdhani and Shatabdi Express, which make minimal stops.

Their fares include meals, and the Rajdhani also provides its overnight passengers with bedding. Trains have a first and second class, chair-cars, and two- and three-tiered sleeper coaches. Where these are air-conditioned, the fares will increase. Sleeper coaches are a comfortable option on longer journeys, and save useful daytime hours. Train timings are subject to change; these are listed in the updated railway timetable, *Trains at a Glance,* a handy 100-page guide is available at all major railway stations, and even at some bookshops.

TRAIN TICKETS AND FARES

Be sure to buy your tickets in advance with reserved seat numbers noted on them. Your hotel travel counter or your agent can arrange this for you. Avoid buying tickets from touts, as this is both illegal and unreliable. Reservation fees are nominal and tickets can be booked six months in advance. An **International Tourist Bureau**, on the first floor of New Delhi Railway Station, meant only for foreigners, is open Mon–Sat, from 7:30am to 5pm. The tickets, payable in US dollars or pounds sterling, get priority reservation and are exempted from reservation fees. Though refundable, the tickets are still subject to any cancellation charges. Other railway booking centres are located at **Nizamuddin** and **Sarojini Nagar**.

INDRAIL PASS

If you are planning to travel extensively around India, the Indrail Pass is a convenient option, saving on hours of queueing time and also on reservation charges. It offers unlimited travel across the country, either first or second class, from 7 to 90 days. It can be bought in India or abroad, but must be paid for in foreign currency. The pass, however, may work out more expensive than buying tickets for individual trips. Ensure that you have a confirmed seat number for each journey.

A crowded railway platform

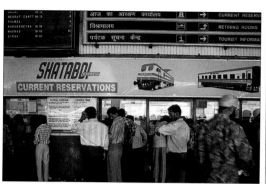
Railway ticket booking centre at New Delhi Railway Station

SERVICES

AT THE STATION look for the licensed porters or *coolies* who wear a red shirt and an armband with a metal tag bearing a licence number on it. Note the porter's number because you could lose sight of him in the chaos. The tariff varies according to weight, although Rs10–20 per item is an acceptable rate. You would be wise to settle on a fee at the time of hiring your porter.

Railway waiting rooms are the best place to spend the night if you are unable to go elsewhere. Go to the Upper Class Waiting Rooms. The Rail Yatri Niwas, at New Delhi station, offers

Porters in red, easy to recognize

very basic facilities, but is a convenient and safe night halt. Left luggage facilities, called cloakrooms, are offered at most stations. On a day trip to a city, you can leave heavy bags here for a small charge. Avoid stalls with uncovered food and use the station canteens that are reasonably clean and provide reliable mineral water and hygenically-packed meals.

ON BOARD

INDIANS TRAVEL with a lot of luggage and like making friends on a train, so unless you bury yourself in a book, be prepared to spend time talking about yourself! Try to get a window seat or the uppermost sleeper. Toilets are of the Indian and Western kind. Carry your own toilet paper, soap and towel.

DIRECTORY

RAILWAY ENQUIRIES

Delhi
General Enquiries:
(011) 131.
Arrivals
North 1331. East 1332. West 1333. South 1334.
Departure
North 1336 . East 1337. West 1338. South 1339.

Agra
(0562) 131-35 Cant.
(0562) 36 4612 City.

Jaipur
(0141) 131.

RAILWAY BOOKING CENTRES IN DELHI

International Tourist Bureau
Map 1 C3.
(011) 2375 0207.

Nizamuddin
Map 6 E5.
(011) 2435 8753.

Delhi Main Rly Stn
Map 2 D1.
(011) 239 7357.

Palace on Wheels
Bikaner House, Shahjahan Rd.
Map 5 B2.
(011) 2338 1884.

Royal Orient
Tourism Corporation of Gujarat Limited, Baba Kharak Singh Marg. Map 1 B5.
(011) 2336 3802.

THE ROYAL TRAINS

Insignia of the Jaipur State Railway

Travel like the maharajas in the most luxurious trains in India – the **Palace on Wheels** and the **Royal Orient**. From September to April, the Palace on Wheels operates week-long tours through the finest sights of Rajasthan, covering Jaipur, Udaipur, Jaisalmer, Jodhpur, Bharatpur and Agra. The Royal Orient goes through Rajasthan to Ahmedabad, Gujarat. In opulently furnished coaches re-created to look like the saloons of erstwhile royalty, you will be impeccably served and royally pampered as you travel through former glorious kingdoms.

Royal service in the Palace on Wheels

Travelling Around by Coach

Boarding a luxury coach

A LL THE MAJOR Indian cities are well connected by a network of roads, and the highways linking Delhi, Agra and Jaipur are among the busiest in North India. The advantage of travelling by long-distance coaches over trains is that you have a wider choice of timings and stops. Deluxe coaches run by the state tourist departments are comfortable and run on time. The Transport Ministry-owned buses running throughout the day from city bus depots, though cheaper, can be crowded. Travel agencies and private tour operators have a wide choice of itineraries between the three cities and their surrounding areas.

Logo of the India Tourism Development Corporation (ITDC)

Buses for various destinations at the ISBT, Delhi

in advance though they can also be bought on the spot for all buses. The five-hour journey breaks midway for refreshments. From Jaipur, state tourism buses leave from a stand outside Hotel Sheetal.

STATE GOVERNMENT-RUN COACHES

T HE TRANSPORT DEPARTMENT of the three states also run buses to these three and other cities of India. The main bus station in Delhi is the **Inter-State Bus Terminus (ISBT)** at Kashmiri Gate. It is a chaotic place, so do arrive early to book your ticket. Then check at the enquiry counter to find the stand where your bus will arrive. Finally, be prepared for a lot of jostling as the passengers push to get the best seats. Rajasthan state buses leave from Bikaner House. Buses for Agra leave from another bus station at **Sarai Kale Khan (SKK)**, a comparatively less crowded bus stop near Nizamuddin railway station. The trip takes about four hours to Agra and almost five to Jaipur. From Agra and Jaipur, buses leave hourly for the other two cities, at Agra from the **Idgah** bus stand, and at Jaipur, from **Sindhi Camp**.

DEPARTMENT OF TOURISM-RUN BUSES

G UIDED TOURS around the three cities are organized by the state tourism departments as well as the Indian government's **Ashok Tours & Travels**. Addresses of state tourism offices are given on page 279. The Government of India Tourist Office in each

city offers the latest information on timings and pick-up points. Buses run by the tourism department are by far the best option; they are clean, uncrowded and comfortable, and make less frequent midway stops than ordinary buses which may be much cheaper. Delivery and pick-up points are usually in the city centres.

The Uttar Pradesh Tourism Department (UPTDC) buses also pick up tourists coming from Delhi to Agra by the Taj Express at the railway station. After the day's city tour, the passengers are dropped back at the station in time to catch the evening train to Delhi.

The best option to go to Jaipur from Delhi is by the Rajasthan Tourism Pink Line which leaves at 1:30pm from Bikaner House *(see p279)*. It is a good idea to buy tickets

RTDC coach ticket

PRIVATE TOUR OPERATORS

T OUR BUSES run by private operators and travel agencies leave regularly from Delhi for places in the region during the tourist season. To Agra it is a day's trip, unless

Delhi Tourism organizes a variety of innovative package tours

An overcrowded bus – a common sight

you take in Fatehpur Sikri and all the Agra sites and also want to shop, in which case it involves at least a night's stopover, as it does for Jaipur. Most hotels and travel agents also organize the night's accommodation at a reasonable place. If you are on a travel agent's tour bus, then a guided tour is usually part of the package and the fare includes a guide as well as the overnight stay at a hotel. Most travel agents have a tie-up with luxury buses that pick up tourists from designated hotels. You can make reservations through your hotel's reception desk or through any of the travel agencies who operate in the region.

Logo of the Rajasthan Transport Corporation

COACH TICKETS AND FARES

Bus or coach fares are much less than train fares and depend on the kind of transport you are taking. There is a good choice – from ordinary to deluxe and deluxe air-conditioned coaches. Ordinary buses are slow,

uncomfortable and usually very crowded. A deluxe bus is good for a trip in winter, but in the hot weather, air-conditioning is the only way to survive long-distance travel. If opting for a deluxe bus, you can book your ticket in advance and can also reserve your seat.

PACKAGE TOURS

There are places in and around the three cities within easy travelling distance that should be seen. These include religious sites, places of historical interest and wildlife sanctuaries. State tourism departments have a wide range of itineraries and package tours. These are also offered by private tour operators and agencies who can arrange tours to suit your individual interests. Tourism offices and travel agents who specialize in adventure tours (*see p275*) offer excursion packages that include transport, guides and a few days' stay in these places.

A clean and comfortable luxury bus run by Rajasthan Tourism

Travel by Road

Milestone with distances in kilometres

D RIVING is a comfortable and leisurely way to travel between the three cities. It gives you the opportunity to do the trip at your own pace and visit places along the way. Hiring a chauffeur-driven car makes sightseeing or shopping within the cities much easier as one is relieved of the stress of negotiating traffic and locating destinations. Cars can be hired from car rental companies, hotel and other taxistands.

An international company offering car rental services in India

RENTING A CAR

I F YOU PLAN to bring your own vehicle into India, it will have to be done under a carnet. This means you take it out after your visit or else must pay exorbitant taxes. Alternatively, there is a good choice of inter-national and local car rental companies in Delhi. Among them, **Hertz, International Travel House** and **Budget** offer both self-driven and chauffeur-driven cars which can be hired through travel counters at larger hotels or from tourist offices. Rates are fixed on a daily rental and minimum mileage basis, with each extra mile carrying an extra cost. Fuel and other running costs are extra and a security deposit is taken in advance to be refunded only if there is no damage to the car when you return it. If you plan to drive yourself, make sure you are carrying your international driving licence. If you fail to do so, you might be able to get a temporary one from the

Automobile Association of Upper India (AAUI), Delhi, provided you have a passport or a valid driving licence from your own country. You may also be required to take a driving test, though this may not always be the case.

A wiser and more common

Logo of the Automobile Association

option is to hire a chauffeur-driven car. It is usually cheaper than hiring a self-drive car and fairly hassle-free. If lucky, you may find a driver who could double up as a guide and an interpreter.

HIRING A CHAUFFEUR-DRIVEN CAR

U NLESS YOU ARE mentally geared to cope with the not-so-well-maintained Indian roads and driving conditions, you should rent a chauffeur-driven car. The drivers are familiar with Indian traffic rules and you won't have to worry about parking either. Taxis with DLY or DLZ number plates can be hired through travel agents, hotels and some taxistands. They have permits to travel beyond

city limits, and you can insist on getting a driver who is familiar with the city you plan to visit. Certain companies require foreign nationals to pay rentals in foreign curr-ency. But some are willing to accept payment in rupees after negotiating a per kilometre rate payable in cash. Car companies in these cities normally charge a fixed rate for

Logo of a car rental company

a minimum of four hours or 40 km (25 miles), or up to 80 km (50 miles) for eight hours. Rates differ according to the type of car and from where you rent it.

FUEL AND FUEL STATIONS

H IGHWAYS AND main roads have petrol (gasoline) pumps at regular intervals, usually closer to a town. Most fuel stations now carry un-leaded petrol. All three cities have some fuel stations that are open 24 hours; some on the highways are also open round-the-clock. Most cars run on petrol, though some newer ones are being made with diesel engines. Taxis usually run on diesel, which is about half the price of petrol. It is a good idea to use the fuel station's toilet facilities before the next leg of the journey. City stations often have a telephone booth, but only for local calls.

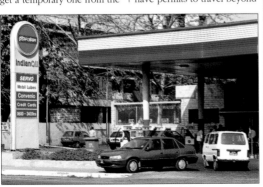

Fuel stations, found at regular intervals along the highways

ROAD SIGNS AND ROAD MAPS

GOOD MAPS ARE available for the three major cities as well as some of the smaller ones. The placement of road signs is erratic and at times these are not in English. Road names have also changed, particularly in Delhi, from the old English names, to names of well-known Indian or international figures. For Delhi there is the excellent *Eicher City Map*. Agra and Jaipur also have fairly clear state tourism city maps which display the major roads and sights. All are in English.

If you are travelling by road between the three cities, you should acquire a road map of North India from the **AAUI (Automobile Association of Upper India)**. The government **Survey of India** also has a good collection of detailed maps available at their office. Maps also indicate lesser known places and road categories. Road signs will also inform you of approaching motels and eateries on the highway.

DLY and DLZ taxis which travel beyond the city limits

RULES OF THE ROAD

THOUGH THERE ARE established traffic rules, such as lane driving and the discreet use of high-beam lights, traffic can be chaotic on Indian roads. All too frequently, traffic lights do not function, and though major crossings have policemen to guide you, this is more often the exception than the rule. Bear in mind that there are numerous types of road users, from pedestrians to cyclists, bullock carts and containers. On the highways, be wary of trucks which muscle in whenever possible. There are also some unwritten rules which should be kept in mind. Few adhere to lane driving, and overtaking, meant to be from the right, is often from the opposite side, with no warning. Crossing red lights is one of the biggest hazards, the cause of most accidents, and horns are used even in "No Horn" areas.

DL·8C·D·0746

Licence plates with bold and clear lettering

PARKING

PARKING CAN BE a serious problem in busy shopping centres and in the commercial complexes of the three cities. With the boom in car production in recent years, parking lots are unable to cope with the number of cars driving in. Private parties are contracted by the state to ensure car safety and facilitate parking for a fee ranging from Rs5 to Rs10. You should keep your key but will have to leave your car in neutral gear so that it can be moved back and forth. Make sure the attendant gives you a receipt and check that you pay no more than the amount that is written on it. In New Delhi, Connaught Place is one of the few places which has a tiered and neatly planned and protected car parking lot.

Hand-cart prohibited

Bullock-cart prohibited

No horn please

Bicycle crossing

DIRECTORY

24-HOUR CAR RENTALS

Budget Rent-a-Car
78/3 Janpath, Delhi.
(011) 2331 8600. **Map** 1 C5.
@ bunor@vsnl.net.in
Mumtaz Hotel, Agra.
(0562) 233 1771.

International Travel House
14 A&B, Basant Lok, Vasant Vihar, Delhi. (011) 2619 1348.
Mughal Sheraton, Agra.
(0562) 233 0350.
Shri Gopal Tower, Krishna Marg, C–Scheme, Jaipur.
(0141) 236 1268.
W www.travelhouseindia.com

Hertz
GF 29, Ansal Chamber, Part 1, Bhikaji Cama Place; Delhi.
(011) 2678 6681.

AAUI

14F, Middle Circle, Connaught Place, Delhi. **Map** 1 C5.
(011) 2331 2323.
@ aauindia@del3.vsnl.net.in

ROAD MAPS

Survey of India
24 Janpath Barracks, Delhi.
(011) 2332 2288.

24-HOUR PETROL STATIONS

Queens Rd Service Stn
Vasant Vihar, Delhi.
(011) 2614 7843.

Inter Club
67 Anand Lok, New Delhi.
(011) 2626 3845.

Local Transport in the Cities

Logo of the Delhi Transport Corporation

THE CHOICE OF LOCAL transport in the three cities is immensely varied. It ranges from buses and taxis to horse-drawn *tongas* and sputtering auto-rickshaws. All three cities are notorious for their traffic jams, and the narrow lanes of the older sections are best negotiated by the smallest vehicle possible. Here, a cycle-rickshaw is often the smartest option. Parking is a real problem, and in some of the extremely crowded areas, there are stringent car parking rules. Though there is a wide choice of local transport, a taxi or hired car is usually the most comfortable and stress-free way to travel. The drivers often speak some English.

Taxistands, found in all areas

GETTING AROUND

DELHI, AGRA AND JAIPUR are all old cities with historic areas that can be congested. The roads carry vehicles that range from ambling bullock carts to expensive Mercedes Benzes. In between there are others such as bicycles, rickety cycle-rickshaws, horse carriages, three-wheelers, taxis, tempos, buses, trucks and, in Jaipur, carts pulled by benign but doleful looking camels.

Taxi meter

Perhaps the best way to move around in these three cities is to hire an auto-rickshaw (also known as scooters or autos), or a taxi. In the crowded older city areas, a cycle-rickshaw is the best option. Almost all deluxe hotels have a travel desk to help you with car or taxi hire. It is advisable to avoid public buses which, though cheap, are crowded, especially during peak traffic hours.

TAXIS

THE BLACK-AND-YELLOW taxis in Delhi move within the city limits. Unlike in other cities, they do cruise the streets, though it is safer to hire one from a taxistand. Large hotels have taxis on their premises, and these are always well-maintained with the meters in good working order. There is usually more than one stand in a locality, and taxis can be summoned by telephone provided you have the name and number of the stand. Another type of taxi, which is licensed to run inter-state, is usually white in colour and has a DLY or DLZ on its number-plate. These can be hired through car rental companies, travel agencies and a few taxistands.

In Agra and Jaipur, the only option is the tourist taxi which does not run by the meter, but charges according to distance or by the day, or a pre-fixed rate. Your hotel or travel agent will tell you what the latest rules are for hiring these taxis. Many drivers have a tie-up with certain shops which give them a commission on sales, so you must be firm about where you want to go.

AUTO-RICKSHAWS

YOU CAN'T MISS THEM on the roads. The three-wheeled, black-and-yellow or green-and-yellow auto-rickshaws zigzag through the traffic like buzzing bees. They offer a noisy, bumpy ride but are still a better option than buses and cheaper than taxis. In Delhi, they can carry up to three passengers, but in smaller towns, where they look a little different, they are often jammed with people and baggage. Auto-rickshaws are useful for travelling short distances or through crowded localities.

Auto-rickshaw, a cheaper travelling option

FARES AND METERS

ALL AUTO-RICKSHAWS and taxis in Delhi have meters, but this is not so in Agra and Jaipur where fares should be negotiated in advance. You should insist on paying by the meter in Delhi. Starting at Rs 13 for taxis and Rs 8 for auto-rickshaws, the meters register a fare increase proportionate to the number of kilometres travelled. As rates keep changing according to the

Different modes of transport jostling in the streets of Jaipur

Cycle-rickshaws, convenient for covering short distances in inner city areas

increase in fuel prices and meters are not always simultaneously calibrated, the drivers of taxis and auto-rickshaws always carry an updated fare chart to enable you to calculate the exact amount from the meter reading. Both day and night fares are given separately on either side of the fare chart. Be sure to check the correct column before you pay. Night fares, from 10pm to 6am, are up to 20 per cent extra.You also have to pay an extra charge for luggage.

At railway stations and the airport, you should look for the pre-paid taxi and auto-rickshaw booths where you will be asked to pay a fixed amount in advance according to the distance you travel. You will be given a receipt, to be handed over to the driver at the end of the journey. Also, do carry smaller notes and small change, as very often, the drivers do not have the correct amount to return. It is not necessary in India to tip the drivers, but if you do, they will gladly accept it.

RICKSHAWS, TONGAS AND TEMPOS

T HE CYCLE-RICKSHAW is the most common mode of transport in the small towns and congested older sections of Indian cities. A convenient means of covering short distances, these are most commonly seen in the walled city of Old Delhi. In Agra and Jaipur, these are the most popular means of local transport. Always fix the fare beforehand. In small towns, the creaky horse-drawn carriages called *tongas* and *ikkas* offer a leisurely ride. Tempos are wagons with the rear half fitted with seats. They are not very comfortable, and start a trip only when all seats are occupied.

BUSES

T HE BUS SERVICE in most Indian cities is never adequate for the large numbers who can only afford this means of travel, and so buses are always crowded. You buy the bus ticket from a conductor once you have boarded the bus. However, if a bus is full, it will not stop, and bus stops are usually seen full of waiting commuters. Delhi's bus drivers are notorious for their reckless driving. Even the so-called luxury buses drive at great speed. Avoid the experience even though it is the cheapest way to travel.

DELHI METRO RAILWAY

D ELHI HAS a ring railway, encircling a core area of the city and facilitating connections between some of the outer localities to central parts of the city. The recently launched Metro Rail is now operational between Shahdra and Tis Hazari. The Delhi Metro will be functional by 2005. It has been planned with underground and overhead railway lines, well integrated with other modes of transport and availability of parking areas.

Auto-rickshaws like this, called Vikram, which ply in smaller cities to the north of Delhi

The "new look" Maruti Omni which is quickly replacing the old Ambassador taxis in Delhi

General Index

Acknowledgments

DORLING KINDERSLEY would like to thank the following people whose contributions and assistance have made the preparation of this book possible.

CONTRIBUTORS

ANURADHA CHATURVEDI is a consultant on architectural conservation with the Indian National Trust for Art and Cultural Heritage (INTACH).

DHARMENDAR KANWAR is a well-known travel writer based in Jaipur. She has published several books on the architecture and culture of the region.

PARTHO DATTA teaches Indian history at a college in Delhi University. He is interested in modern urban studies on which he has written several papers.

PREMOLA GHOSE is a gifted writer and illustrator of children's books. She is the Programme Officer at the India International Centre, New Delhi.

RANJANA SENGUPTA is a journalist and author of books on Ajanta and contemporary Indian society. She is currently writing a book on Delhi after 1947.

SUBHADRA SENGUPTA is a freelance journalist based in Delhi who writes on travel and tourism for several Indian newspapers and magazines.

CONSULTANTS

AJAI SHANKAR is a senior civil servant with the Government of India and is the Director-General of the Archaeological Survey of India (ASI).

AMAN NATH has written extensively on the crafts and architecture of Rajasthan. He is involved in the restoration of heritage properties in this region.

DALJEET KAUR is the curator of the Indian miniature paintings section in the National Museum, New Delhi and has written several books and articles on this subject.

EBBA KOCH has travelled extensively in the subcontinent and is an internationally acknowledged expert on the art and architecture of the Indo-Islamic and Mughal periods.

GILES TILLOTSON is Senior Lecturer in South Asian Art at SOAS (University of London), and the author of books on architecture in India during the Mughal, Rajput and British periods.

JYOTINDRA JAIN is the founder-director of the Crafts Museum, New Delhi, and has authored several books on Indian crafts.

KISHORE SINGH is one of India's leading travel writers and is with the *Business Standard* in Delhi. He has written several books on Rajasthan.

KUMKUM ROY is an Associate Professor of Ancient History at the Jawaharlal Nehru University, New Delhi. She writes for several prestigious academic journals.

MARTAND SINGH is one of the country's best-known experts on textiles. He is based in Delhi and is a founding member of the Indian National Trust for Art and Cultural Heritage (INTACH).

NARAYANI GUPTA is a Professor of Modern Indian History at Jamia Millia Islamia in New Delhi. Her book on the history of Delhi is widely regarded as an authoritative text.

RV SMITH is a journalist who writes on the history and legends of Delhi. His column, "Quaint Corner", has been a regular feature in *The Statesman* for over 25 years.

SATISH GROVER heads the Department of Architecture at the School of Planning and Architecture, Delhi. He has written three seminal books on the history of Indian architecture.

SUNIL KUMAR is an Associate Professor in Medieval Indian History at Delhi University. He has a special interest in the Sultanate period and is currently writing a book on the subject.

VIJAYAN KANNAMPILLY is a journalist and painter based in Delhi and has a special interest in Indian design and contemporary art.

EDITORIAL AND DESIGN
PUBLISHER Douglas Amrine
EDITORIAL DIRECTOR Vivien Crump
ART DIRECTOR Gillian Allan
SENIOR MANAGING EDITOR Louise Bostock Lang
PRODUCTION Marie Ingledew

MAP COORDINATOR
David Pugh.

DESIGN AND EDITORIAL ASSISTANCE
Ipshita Barua, Kiran Mohan, Nandini Mehta, Priyanka Thakur, Tara Sharma, Vandana Mohindra.

CARTOGRAPHY ASSISTANCE
Kishorchand Naorem, Shivanand.

PROOF READER
Abha Kapoor.

INDEXER
Bibhu Mohapatra.

ADDITIONAL ILLUSTRATIONS
Aniket Vardhan, Arun P, Mugdha Sethi.

ADDITIONAL PHOTOGRAPHY
Anal Shah, Anand Naorem, Benu Joshi, Ipshita Barua, Mugdha Sethi.

DTP DESIGNERS
Jessica Subramanian, Shailesh Sharma.

SPECIAL ASSISTANCE
Dorling Kindersley would like to thank all the regional and local tourist offices in Delhi, Agra and Jaipur for their valuable help. Particular thanks also to: Ajai Shankar, ASI, New Delhi; Dr Daljeet, National Museum, New Delhi; Malaynil Singh, TCI; Delhi School of Planning and Architecture; Siraj Qureshi and RVI Singh in Agra.

FOOD PHOTOGRAPHY
Dorling Kindersley would like to thank Chef Pankaj Mehra of the Kandahar Restaurant (The Oberoi Hotel, New Delhi) for personally supervising the presentation of the food layouts for the book.

PHOTOGRAPHY PERMISSIONS

Dorling Kindersley would like to thank the following for their kind permission to photograph their products: Abraham & Thakore, Preeti Paul. The publishers would also like to thank the following for permission to photograph at their establishments: Biotique, New Delhi; City Palace Museum, Jaipur; Crafts Museum, New Delhi; Gem Palace, Jaipur; Mathura Museum, Mathura; Maulana Abul Kalam Azad Arabic & Persian Research Institute, Tonk; The Next Shop, New Delhi; Ogaan, New Delhi.

PICTURE CREDITS

t = top; tl = top left; tlc = top left centre; tc = top centre; tr = top right; cla = centre left above; ca = centre above; cra = centre right above; cl = centre left; c = centre; cr = centre right; clb = centre left below; cb = centre below; crb = centre right below; bl = bottom left; b = bottom; bc = bottom centre; bcl = bottom centre left; br = bottom right; d = detail.

The publishers are grateful to the following individuals, picture libraries and companies, for permission to reproduce their photographs:

ABRAHAM & THAKORE: 118b; AVINASH PASRICHA: 28cla/clb, 28 & 29c, 29bl, 120b, 292c, 293t; BOBBY KOHLI: 54 & 55c, 55b, 56 & 57c, 57tr; B. R. CHOPRA FILMS: 209b; BRITISH LIBRARY, London: 43b; CRAFTS MUSEUM, New Delhi, Pankaj Shah: 86tr/ca/cb, 87tl/tc/cb; DEAN K BROWN: 78t; DK CLASSIC ASIAN COOK BOOK: 254tc/crb; DN DUBE: 52bl/b, 53cr, 75bc, 170tr, 171t, 172tr/c.

FOTOMEDIA PICTURE LIBRARY: 9 (inset), 29tr, 52tc, 54clb, 55tr, 56cb, 105b, 120c (4 pics), 133 (inset), 295bl; Aditya Arya: 295br; Akhil Bakshi: 21t, 22bcr, 28br/b, 29b, 32clb, 195b, 272t, 289t, 294t/b/bl; Amar Talwar: 60cl, 172b, 251clb, 269b, 296t; Amita Prashar Gupta: 266b; Ashim Ghosh: 21bl, 22bcl, 50b, 58cb, 173b, 271t, 278b, 280b, 281b, 283t, 301t; Ashish Chandola: 168b; Ashish Khokar: 283c, 297t; Ashok Dilwali: 150b, 170tl, 172tl; Ashok Kaul: 61tl, 215b; Bimla Verma: 20tl, 22t, 23cr, 34tr, 49bl, 93b, 141bl, 163b, 268br/bcr; BN Khazanchi: 36c, 37br, 169bc, 272c; BPS Walia: 143br, 270c; Christine Pemberton: 15c, 40cl; Deepak Budhraja: 40b; Dharmendar Kanwar: 266t; E Hanumantha Rao: 18tl/clb/bc, 211trc, 225cb/b; François Gautier: 21b; J Saha: 20b; Jatinder Singh: 20tr; Jitendra Singh: 22bc; Joanna van Gruisen: 18cra/b/bl,19cra/bl, 48cb, 61ca, 210b, 224cl; M Balan: 33bcl, 169b; Manu Bahuguna: 39b, 71b, 91b, 232b/bl, 273t; Marie D' Souza: 33cr, 60t, 180t, 269br; Mathew Titus: 23br; Mohit Satyanand: 274b; MS Oberoi: 22br, 254t; Nagaraja: 211t; Neeraj Mishra: 18cla; Nihal Mathur: 224tr; NP Singh: 32b, 184bl; NPS Jhalla: 268bc; NS Chawla: 27c; Pallava Bagla: 18tr, 19tl/tr/tc/trc, 35cr, 38t, 210tl; Pankaj Sekhsaria: 169trc; Pradeep Das Gupta: 255tc; Pradeep Mandhani: 40cl, 61t, 272b; Prakash Israni: 17tl, 22cl, 35cla, 37b, 163tlc, 173bl, 274t; Prem Kapoor: 37c, 38b, 46t, 60b, 60 & 61c, 61br/b; Raj Salhotra: 32cla; Ravi Kaimal: 17c; RK Wadhwa: 23cra; RS Chundawat: 18crb, 116b, 210tr, 211b; S Nayak: 168c; S Venugopal: 141c; Sanjay Saxena: 32cl, 145c, 185b; Sanjeev Saith: 16b,137b, 275t/b;

Sanjiv Misra: 41t; Shalini Saran: 20c, 28tr, 30cl, 32 & 33c, 37t, 38c, 46br, 49tl, 50 & 51c, 52br, 53br, 54br, 57tl, 63 (inset), 73t/b, 88, 107b, 114t, 147b, 150tr, 152tl, 153b, 173tl, 174b, 216tl, 249b; SK Panda: 19cla; Subhash Bhargava: 17b, 23ca, 36t/b, 39c/bl, 50cb, 54cla, 58t, 144b, 164t/cl/b, 165ca/b, 184t, 192c/bl, 200b, 225t, 228c, 254c, 268cr, 273c/b, 274tr; Sudhir Kasliwal: 48c, 187t/b/bl/cl, 195t, 268tr/trc, 276 & 277; Tarun Chopra: 49br; Thakur Dalip Singh: 33bc; Toby Sinclair: 18br, 19crb/clb, 33bl, 122, 210cb, 224tl/c/b, 225ca, 270b; TS Satyan: 19br, 76c, 141t, 197b, 228t, 252b (2pics), 255b; V Muthuraman: 226 & 227, 251cb.

FRAZER & HAWS, New Delhi: 118c; FREDRIK & LAURENCE ARVIDSSON: 2 & 3, 14, 66, 89t, 98, 132 & 133, 136, 146, 178, 179b; GANESH SAILI: 101b; HENRY WILSON: 212t, 231t, 232c; ITC HOTEL LTD. WELCOMGROUP: 121t, 228b, 248b, 249c; KAMAL SAHAI: 45tr/cla, 47tl; NATIONAL MUSEUM, New Delhi: 44t/cl/bl, 45b, 46c, 46cb, 46 & 47c, 47b, 50t, 51t/bl, 53tr, 72tl/tr/ca/cl/bl/br, 141br, 167b; JC Arora: 43t, 54bl, 55bl, 64b, 74tl/tr, 75t; RC Dutta Gupta: 29t, 44cla/clb/br, 44 & 45c, 45tlc/cl/cr, 46b, 47tr/cl, 48t/b, 52t, 54t, 74b, 75c/br; NEEMRANA PALACE HOTELS: 48ca, 49tr, 230b, 233c, 249t; THE OBEROI GROUP OF HOTELS: 229b, 230t; OTTO PFISTER: 168t/bl, 169t/c, 211c, 270t; P ROY 187cr/cb.

PRESS INFORMATION BUREAU: 58 & 59 c, 59cr; SATISH SHARMA: 22 & 23c, 23tl/tc/b, 34bl, 35tl; SYNDICATIONS TODAY: 61cb; TEEN MURTI MEMORIAL LIBRARY: 56bl/br, 57b, 58ca, 59tc/bl/br/ 60cb; TEXTILE ART SOCIETY: Benoy K Behl 33tc; THEATRE AND TELEVISION ASSOCIATES: Gopi Gajwani 29br; TULSI: Hemant Mehta 269tl; COURTESY OF THE BOARD OF TRUSTEES OF THE V & A MUSEUM: 52cl/ca/cb.

Works of art have been reproduced with the permission of the following copyright holders: © National Gallery of Modern Art, New Delhi: 30 & 31 (all pictures except 30cl).

SPECIAL ASSISTANCE IN PHOTOGRAPHY
Ajai Shankar, Director-General, Archaeological Survey of India, New Delhi; Aman Nath; Anjali Sen, Director, National Gallery of Modern Art, New Delhi; Aruna Dhir, The Oberoi Hotel, New Delhi; Dr Daljeet Kaur, National Museum, New Delhi; JC Grover, National Museum, New Delhi; Jyotindra Jain, Crafts Museum, New Delhi; OP Jain, Sanskriti Museum; Dr RD Chowdhouri, Director-General, National Museum, New Delhi.

Front endpaper: All special photography except SHALINI SARAN: tr.

JACKET
Front - DK PICTURE LIBRARY: Aditya Patankar bc, cb; GETTY IMAGES: Suzanne & Nick Geary main image; NATIONAL MUSEUM, NEW DELHI: J.C. Arora cbl. Back - DK PICTURE LIBRARY: Aditya Patankar t, b. Spine - GETTY IMAGES: Suzanne & Nick Geary.

Every effort has been made to trace the copyright holders, and we apologize for any unintentional omissions. We would be pleased to insert the appropriate acknowledgments in all subsequent editions of this publication.

Further Reading

ARCHITECTURE

Delhi and its Neighbourhood Sharma, Y.D., Archaeological Survey of India, Delhi 1982.

Delhi, the City of Monuments Dube, D.N. and Ramanathan, J., Timeless Books, New Delhi 1997.

Fatehpur Sikri Brand, M. and Lowry, G.D. (eds.), Marg Publications, Mumbai 1987.

Indian Architecture Brown, P., (2 vols), D.B. Taraporevala Sons & Co. Pvt. Ltd., Bombay 1964.

Mughal Architecture Koch, E., PRESTEL-Verlag, Munich 1991.

Mughal India Tillotson, G.H.R., Penguin, London 1991.

Sacred Architecture Pereira, J., Islamic Books & Books, New Delhi 1994.

Stones of Empire Morris, J., Oxford University Press, Oxford 1983.

Taj Mahal: The Illumined Tomb Begley, W.E., Aga Khan Program for Islamic Architecture, Massachussetts 1989.

The Architecture of India Grover, S., (2 vols), Vikas Publishing House Pvt. Ltd., New Delhi 1981.

The Forts of India Fass, V., Collins, London 1986.

The History of Architecture in India Tadgell, C., Phaidon, London 1990.

The Palaces of India Fass, V. and Maharaja of Baroda, Collins, London 1980.

The Penguin Guide to the Monuments of India (Vol 2) Davies, P., Viking, London 1989.

CULTURE AND CRAFTS

A Second Paradise Patnaik, N., Sidgwick and Jackson Ltd., London, 1985.

Catalogue of the Crafts Museum New Delhi 1982.

Curry and Bugles Brennan, J., Penguin, London 1992.

Dance of the Peacock Bala Krishnan, U. and Kumar, M.S., India Book House, Mumbai 1999.

The Essence of Indian Art Goswamy, B. N., Mapin International, San Francisco 1986.

Hanklyn-Janklin Hankin, N., Banyan Books, Delhi 1992.

Indian Art Dehejia, V., Phaidon, London 1997.

Indian Painting Randhawa, M.S. and Galbraith, J.K., Vakils, Feffer & Simon Limited, Bombay 1982.

Masterpieces from the National Museum Collection Gupta, S.P., National Museum, New Delhi 1985.

Paradise as a Garden Moynihan, E.B., George Braziller Inc., New York 1979.

The Arts of India Birdwood, G.C.M., Nanda Book Service, Delhi 1997.

The Golden Calm Kaye, M.M. (ed.), Webb & Bower, Exeter 1980.

The Painted Walls of Shekhawati Nath, A. and Wacziarg F., Croom & Helm, London 1982.

The Splendour of Mathura Art and Museum Sharma, R.C., DK Printworld (P) Ltd., New Delhi 1994.

FICTION

A Passage to India Forster, E. M., Penguin, London 1924.

A Suitable Boy Seth, V., Viking, New Delhi 1993.

City of Djinns Dalrymple, W., Flamingo, London 1994.

The Raj Quartet Scott, P., Heinemann, London 1976.

Train to Pakistan Singh, K., Ravi Dayal Publisher, Delhi 1988.

HISTORY

A History of India (Vol 2), Spear, P., Penguin, London 1956.

A Princess Remembers Gayatri Devi, Rupa and Co., New Delhi 1995.

Annals and Antiquities of Rajasthan Tod, J., Oxford University Press, Oxford 1920.

Delhi Between Two Empires Gupta, N., Oxford University Press, Delhi 1981.

Delhi and its Monuments Spear, P., Gupta N. and Sykes, L., Oxford University Press, New Delhi 1994.

Freedom at Midnight Lapierre, D. and Collins, L., Vikas Publishing House Pvt. Ltd., Delhi 1976.

India Britannica Moorhouse, G., Paladin Books, London 1984.

Indian Mythology Ions, V., Paul Hamlyn, London 1967.

Jaipur Nath, A., India Book House, Mumbai 1993.

Lives of the Indian Princes Allen, C. and Dwivedi, S. London 1985.

Myths and Symbols in Indian Art and Civilization Zimmer, H., Harper and Brothers, New York 1962.

Symbols in Art and Religion Werner, K. (ed.), Motilal Banarsidass Publishers Pvt. Ltd., Delhi 1991.

The History of India Dodwell, H. H. (ed.), 6 vols, Cambridge University Press, Cambridge 1934.

The Great Moghuls Gascoigne, B., Dorset Press, London 1971.

The Wonder that was India Basham, A.L., Rupa and Co., New Delhi 1966.

NATURE AND WILDLIFE

Bharatpur: Bird Paradise Ewans, M., Lustre Press, New Delhi 1992.

Book of Indian Animals Prater, W., Bombay Natural History Society, Bombay 1948.

Book of Indian Birds Ali, S., Bombay Natural History Society, Bombay 1941.

The Garden of Life Patnaik, N., Doubleday, New York 1993.

In Danger Manfredi, P., Ranthambhore Foundation, New Delhi 1997.

Indian Wildlife Israel S. and Sinclair T. (eds.), APA Publications, Singapore 1989.

Nature Watch Singh, K. and Basu, S., Lustre Press, New Delhi 1990.

Birds of India Grewal, B., Local Colour, Hong Kong 2000.

Tigers: The Secret Life Thapar, V., Elm Tree Books, London 1989.

Glossary

ARCHITECTURE

ashram: hermitage
bagh: garden
bangaldar: curved roof derived from Bengali hut (see p26)
baradari: pavilion with 12 pillars (see p196)
basti: settlement (see p81)
charbagh: quadripartite garden (see p27)
dharamshala: charitable rest house for pilgrims
ghar: house, crypt (see p114)
gali: lane
jaali: carved lattice work on stone screens (see p25)
katra: side lane (see p89)
khirkee: window
kotla: a citadel or fortified area within a city
kund: pool, tank (see p117)
mahal: palace
mardana: men's quarters in a palace
maqbara: burial-palace, mausoleum, sepulchre (see p142)
masjid: mosque
mehmankhana: guesthouse
minar: freestanding tower
minaret: tower in mosque for calling the faithful to prayer
pol: gate (see p183)
toshakhana: state treasury (see p190)
zenana: women's quarters in a palace

CRAFT AND CULTURE

bandhini: tie-and-dye (see p86)
dholak: drum (see p97)
Dhrupad: style of North Indian classical music (see p28)
ganjifa: set of playing cards (see p141)
gharana: school of classical music or dance (see p28)
ikat: tie-and-dye yarn woven in a pattern
katha: epic tale (see p29)
matka: earthenware pot
mela: fair, fête
patachitra: painted scroll with mythological tales (see p141)

phad: painted cloth scroll from Rajasthan (see p194)
pichhwai: cloth painting depicting Krishna lore
raga: melodic structure with a fixed sequence of musical notes (see p28)
rasa: mood; essence (see p29)
shahtoosh: a fine shawl, now banned, that can pass through a ring. It is woven from the down of the endangered chiru antelope.
tala: rhythmic cycle of varying beats (see p28)
thal-posh: dish cover (see p190)

DRESS

burqa: concealing cloak worn by Muslim women
chador: ceremonial pall of cloth or flowers placed over a Muslim tomb (see p82)
dhoti: unstitched garment of Hindu men which covers the lower half of the body
gota: gold or silver frill
jootis: slippers (see p186)
khadi: hand-woven, hand-spun cloth popularized by Gandhi (see pp58–59)
lehenga: flounced skirt (see p93)
mukut: crown (see p186)
zari: gold thread

RELIGION

aarti: ritual of Hindu worship
ahimsa: non-violence
amrit: sacred nectar of the gods (see p23)
Balaji: one of Hanuman's many names in North India (see p197)
bhajan: devotional song (see p28)
Chishtiyas: followers of the 12th century Sufi saint, Moinuddin Chishti (see p82)
dharma: duty, calling (see p141)
kalasha: urn (see p115)
lila: divine sport (see p163)
linga: phallic emblem of Lord Shiva (see p86)
madrasa: Islamic theological college

Mahabharata: famous Hindu epic (see p141)
namaaz: ritual prayers of Muslims
pir: Muslim saint (see p82)
puja: ritual prayer (see pp22)
Ramayana: epic on the legend of Lord Rama
samadhi: memorial platform over site of cremation (see p97)
sati: practice of self-immolation by a widow on her husband's funeral pyre
Shaivite: followers of Shiva
tirthankara: Jain prophet
Upanishads: philosophical texts regarded as sacred scripture, dating to the later Vedic age (see p20)
Vaishnavite: followers of Vishnu
Vedas: texts codifying Aryan beliefs and principles, these were orally transmitted until transcribed into Sanskrit as the Rig Veda, Sama Veda, Yajur Veda and Atharva Veda (see p20)
yagna: vedic rite

MISCELLANEOUS

badal: cloud (see p182)
bahi khatha: cloth bound account book (see p186)
charpoy: string cot
chowkidar: watchman
Doctrine of Lapse: this gave the British the right to take direct control of princely states that did not have an undisputed heir (see p56)
haat: open-air market
ikka: pony trap (see p191)
jheel: shallow lake
katar: two-sided blade
loo: hot westerly wind that blows over North India from April to June
machan: look-out post
mohur: Mughal gold coin
nawab: a Muslim prince
pachisi: a ludo-like dice game (see p171)
Raj: the period of British rule in India (see pp56–57)
Satyagraha: a form of moral protest started by Gandhi (see pp58–59)
thakur: Hindu chieftain

Phrase Book

Hindi is the national language of India and even though it is not the mother tongue of a major proportion of the population, it is spoken widely in this region. All nouns are either masculine or feminine and the adjective agrees with the noun. Most masculine nouns end with –aa (as in rather), most feminine nouns end with –i (as in thin), while all plural nouns end in –e (as in hen). Verb endings also differ if it is a man or woman speaking. In the present tense, a man ends his verbs with –a, a woman ends hers with –i.

In an Emergency

Help!	Bachao
Stop!	Roko
Call a doctor!	Doctor ko bulao
Where is the nearest telephone?	Yahan phone kahan hai?

Communication Essentials

Yes	Haan
No	Na/ naheen
Thank you	Dhanyavad/Shukria
Please	Kripaya/Meharbani se
Excuse me/sorry	Kshama karen/Maaf karen
Hello/goodbye	Namaste
Halt	Rook jao
Let's go	Chalo
Straight ahead	Seedha
Big/Small	Bara/Chhota
This/That	Yeh/Voh
Near/Far	Paas/Door
Way	Raasta
Road	Sarak
Yesterday	Beeta hua kal
Today	Aaj
Tomorrow	Aane wala kal
Here	Yahaan
There	Wahaan
What?	Kya?
Where?	Kahaan?
When?	Kab?
Why?	Kyon?
How?	Kaise?
Up	Upar
Down	Neeche
More	Aur zyada
A little	Thora
Before	Pehle
Opposite/facing	Saamne
Very	Bahut
Less	Kam
Louder/harder	Zor se
Softly/gently	Dheere se
Go	Jao
Come	Aao

Useful Phrases

How are you?	Aap kaise hain?
What is your name?	Aapka naam kya hai?
My name is …	Mera naam … hai.
Do you speak English?	Angrezi ati hai?
I understand	Samajh gaya/gayi
I don't understand	Nahin samjha/samjhi
What is the time?	Kya baja hai?
Where is …?	…Kahaan hai?
What is this?	Yeh kya hai?
Hurry up	Jaldi karo
How far is …?	… Kitni door hai?
I don't know	Pata nahin
All right	Achha/Theek hai
Now/instantly	Abhi/Isi waqt
Well done!	Shabash!
See you	Phir milenge
Go away!	Hat jao/Hato
I don't want it	Mujhe nahin chahiye
Not now	Abhi Nahin

Useful Words

Which	Kaun Sa
Who	Kaun
Hot	Garam
Cold	Thanda
Good	Achha

Bad	Kharaab
Enough	Bus/Kafi hai
Open	Khula
Closed	Bund
Left	Baayan
Right	Daayan
Straight on	Seedha
Near	Paas/Nazdeek
Quickly	Jaldi
Late	Der se
Later	Baad mein
Entrance	Pravesh
Exit	Nikas
Behind	Peechhe
Full	Bhara
Empty	Khali
Toilet	Shauchaalaya
Free/no charge	Nih shulka, muft
Direction	Disha
Book	Kitab
Magazine	Patrika
Newspaper	Akhbaar

Shopping

How much does this cost?	Iska kya daam hai?
I would like…	Mujhe … chahiye.
Do you have…?	Kya aap ke paas … hai?
I am just looking	Abhi dekh rahen hain
Does it come in other colours?	Yeh dooserey rangon main bhi aata hai kya?
This one	Yeh wala
That one	Voh wala
Black	Kaala
Blue	Neela
White	Safed
Red	Lal
Yellow	Peela
Green	Hara
Brown	Bhura
Cheap	Sasta
Expensive	Mehanga
Tailor	Darzi

Bargaining

How much is this?	Yeh kitne ka hai?
How much will you take?	Kya loge?
That's a little expensive	Yeh to mehanga hai
Could you lower the price a bit?	Daam thoda kam kariye
How about XX rupees?	XX rupeye lainge?
I'll settle for XX rupees.	XX rupeye mein dena hai to dijiye

Staying in a Hotel

Do you have any vacant rooms?	Aapke hotel mein khali kamre hain kya?
What is the charge per night?	Ek raat ka kiraya kya hai?
Can I see the room first?	Kya mein pehle kamra dekh sakta hoon?
Key	Chaabhi
Soap	Sabun
Towel	Tauliya
Hot/cold water	Garam/thanda pani

Eating Out

Breakfast	Nashta
Food	Khaana

Water	Pani
Ice	Baraf
Tea	Chai
Coffee	Kaufi
Sugar	Cheeni
Salt	Namak
Milk	Doodh
Yoghurt	Dahi
Egg	Anda
Fruit	Phal
Vegetable	Sabzi
Rice	Chaawal
Pulse (lentil, split pea etc)	Dal
Fixed priced menu	Ek daam menu
Is it spicy?	Mirch-masala tez hai kya?
Not too spicy, ok?	Mirch-masala kam, theek hai?
Knife	Chhuri
Fork	Kanta
Spoon	Chammach
Finish	Khatam

Numbers

1	Ek
2	Do
3	Teen
4	Char
5	Panch
6	Chhe
7	Saat
8	Aath
9	Nau
10	Dus
11	Gyarah
12	Barah
13	Terah
14	Chaudah
15	Pundrah
16	Solah
17	Satrah
18	Atharah
19	Unnees
20	Bees
30	Tees
40	Chalees
50	Pachaas
60	Saath
70	Sattar
80	Assi
90	Nabbe
100	Sau
1,000	Hazar
100,000	Lakh
10,000,000	Karod (crore)

Time

One minute	Ek minit
One hour	Ek ghanta
Half an hour	Aadha ghanta
Quarter hour	Pauna ghanta
Half past one	Derh
Half past two	Dhai
A day	Ek din
A week	Ek haftah
Monday	Somwar
Tuesday	Mangalwar
Wednesday	Budhwar
Thursday	Veerwar
Friday	Shukrawar
Saturday	Shaniwar
Sunday	Raviwar
Morning	Subah
Afternoon	Dopahar
Evening	Shaam
Night	Raat

Road Map of Delhi, Agra and Jaipur